By Kurt Vonnegut

A Man Without a Country
Armageddon in Retrospect
Bagombo Snuff Box
Between Time and Timbuktu
Bluebeard
Breakfast of Champions
Canary in a Cat House
Cat's Cradle
Deadeye Dick
Fates Worse Than Death
Galápagos
God Bless You, Dr. Kevorkian
God Bless You, Mr. Rosewater
Happy Birthday, Wanda June
Hocus Pocus
Jailbird
Like Shaking Hands with God (with Lee Stringer)
Look at the Birdie
Mother Night
Palm Sunday
Player Piano
The Sirens of Titan
Slapstick
Slaughterhouse-Five
Timequake
Wampeters, Foma & Granfalloons
Welcome to the Monkey House
While Mortals Sleep

KURT VONNEGUT

Letters

Delacorte Press ▤ New York

KURT VONNEGUT

Letters

EDITED AND
WITH AN INTRODUCTION BY

Dan Wakefield

Copyright © 2012 by The Kurt Vonnegut, Jr. Trust
Illustrations © Kurt Vonnegut and the Origami Express

All rights reserved.

Published in the United States by Delacorte Press, an imprint of The Random House Publishing Group, a division of Random House, Inc., New York.

DELACORTE PRESS is a registered trademark of Random House, Inc., and the colophon is a trademark of Random House, Inc.

Grateful acknowledgment is made to the following for permission to reprint previously published material:

DELL BOOKS, A DIVISION OF RANDOM HOUSE, INC.: Letter from Kurt Vonnegut, Jr., to Charles Drake dated November 16, 1973, from *Palm Sunday* by Kurt Vonnegut, copyright © 1981 by Kurt Vonnegut. Reprinted by permission of Dell Books, a division of Random House, Inc.; ALFRED A. KNOPF, A DIVISION OF RANDOM HOUSE, INC., FABER & FABER LIMITED, AND CURTIS BROWN, LTD.: Excerpt from *Markings* by Dag Hammarskjold, translated by W. H. Auden and Leif Sjöberg, translation copyright © 1964 and copyright renewed 1992 by Alfred A. Knopf, a division of Random House, Inc., and Faber & Faber Ltd. Foreword copyright © 1964 by W. H. Auden and copyright renewed 1992 by Edward Mendelson. Rights throughout Canada and the United Kingdom are controlled by Faber & Faber Limited. Electronic book rights are controlled by Curtis Brown, Ltd. Reprinted by permission of Alfred A. Knopf, a division of Random House, Inc., Faber & Faber Limited, and Curtis Brown, Ltd.; G. P. PUTNAM'S SONS, A DIVISION OF PENGUIN GROUP (USA) INC. AND JONATHAN CAPE, A MEMBER OF THE RANDOM HOUSE GROUP LIMITED: Letter from PFC Kurt Vonnegut, Jr., to his family dated May 29, 1945, from *Armageddon in Retrospect* by Kurt Vonnegut, Jr., copyright © 2008 by the Kurt Vonnegut, Jr. Trust. Used by permission of G. P. Putnam's Sons, a division of Penguin Group (USA) Inc. and Jonathan Cape, a member of the Random House Group Limited.

Photo credits for insert following page 198: Courtesy the Bowdoin College Archives, Brunswick, Maine: p. 8, top; courtesy Otis Kidwell Burger: p. 4, top and bottom, and p. 5; courtesy of Don Farber: p. 12; © Allen Ginsberg/CORBIS: p. 15; from the Gail Godwin Papers, Southern Historical Collection, Wilson Library, UNC at Chapel Hill. Reprinted by permission of John Hawkins & Associates, Inc.: p. 8, bottom; courtesy of Jerome Klinkowitz: p. 9, bottom; courtesy Loree Wilson Rackstraw: p. 9, top; Harry Ransom Center, The University of Texas at Austin: p. 7, top and bottom; copyright Buck Squibb: p. 16; Time Life Pictures/Getty Images: p. 14; Alex Vonnegut photo, Richard Vonnegut collection: p. 1; courtesy of Edie Vonnegut: pp. 2, 10, and 11; courtesy of Nanny Vonnegut: pp. 3 and 6; courtesy of Dan Wakefield/The Lilly Library: p. 13.

Library of Congress Cataloging-in-Publication Data
Vonnegut, Kurt.
Kurt Vonnegut: letters/edited by Dan Wakefield.
p. cm.
Includes index.
ISBN 978-0-385-34375-6
eBook ISBN 978-0-345-53539-9
1. Vonnegut, Kurt—Correspondence. I. Wakefield, Dan. II. Title.
PS3572.O5Z48 2012
813'.54—dc23   2012001544

Printed in the United States of America on acid-free paper

www.bantamdell.com

9 8 7 6 5 4 3 2 1

First Edition

All drawings courtesy of The Kurt Vonnegut Trust, Donald C. Farber, Trustee.

Postcard on pages 406–407 courtesy of Asa Pieratt.

Book design by Victoria Wong

To the memory of Kurt Vonnegut, a writer
for the world, a friend for life; and to Mark and
Barb Vonnegut and Don and Annie Farber,
friends who carry on the spirit of Kurt.

CONTENTS

Introduction xi

The Forties 3

The Fifties 28

The Sixties 72

The Seventies 152

The Eighties 270

The Nineties 336

The Two Thousands 393

Editor's Note and Acknowledgments 415

Index 419

INTRODUCTION

The letters by Kurt Vonnegut collected in this book tell the story of
a writer's life—a writer whose influence is still widely felt throughout the world and, by every indication, will continue to be felt for
a long time to come. They are as personal, as witty, as entertaining,
and as disarmingly profound as the work he published in novels,
stories, articles, and essays. No outside interpreter will ever be able
to express this life as truly and as deeply as these letters he wrote
to his children, his friends, his publishers, his academic advocates,
his critics, and those who sought to ban his work.

Reading these letters has allowed me to know my friend Kurt
Vonnegut better and to appreciate him even more. Nothing came
easy for him. Nothing deterred him—not the many editors and
publishers who rejected his books and stories; not the anthropology department of the University of Chicago, which rejected not
one but two of the theses he wrote for his M.A. degree (awarding
it to him only after he was famous); not the Guggenheim Foundation, which rejected his first application for a fellowship; not the
doubting relatives and friends from home like his uncle Alex, who
said he couldn't read *The Sirens of Titan,* after Kurt had dedicated
the book to him, or his aunt Ella Stewart, who would not stock his
books in the bookstore she owned in Louisville, Kentucky, because
she found them degenerate; not his Cape Cod neighbors who didn't
read his books and expressed no interest in what he did for a living; not the school boards that banned his books (and in one case
burned them in a furnace) without ever reading them; not the aca-

demic critics who spurned and dismissed him; not the backbiting reviewers who tried to drag him down after he became famous; not the bureaucrats he battled for the rights of writers throughout the world; not the right-wing Christian religious groups that condemned this man who described Jesus Christ as "the greatest and most humane of human beings." Anyone who imagines a writer's life has ever been easy—even one who eventually achieves fame and fortune—will be disabused of that fantasy after reading these letters. And they will be inspired.

. . .

I first heard the name Kurt Vonnegut in the spring of 1950, my senior year at Shortridge High School in Indianapolis, when I admitted to a teacher that I wanted to be a writer. His brows furrowed in concern, he rubbed his chin for a moment, nodded, and said, "Well, there's one boy did that—boy named Vonnegut." I learned that "the Vonnegut boy," who got his start writing for the *Shortridge Daily Echo,* had published his first short story in *Collier's* magazine earlier that year. To me, that meant he had reached Mount Olympus.

Neither that high school teacher nor anyone else in the world—with the exception of his childhood sweetheart and high school classmate, Jane Marie Cox, who became his first wife and the mother of his first three children—believed that Vonnegut would become a world-famous writer whose work would be translated into all the major languages of the world. His oldest son, Mark, wrote in his memoir, *Just Like Someone Without Mental Illness Only More So,* that during the years of Kurt's struggles, "My mother . . . knew my father was going to be famous and it was all going to be worth it. She believed more than he did that he would someday be a famous writer. . . ."

Growing up in Indianapolis in the 1930s and '40s, my friends and I and our families all knew the name Vonnegut—the Vonnegut Hardware Company had its headquarters downtown, and there were branches throughout the city. In summers during high school,

Kurt worked at the main store for his great-uncle Franklin Vonnegut, making up packages in the shipping room and for a while
running a freight elevator. He later wrote to a fan in Indianapolis
who had also worked in that store: "My idea of hell was shaped by
that experience. Hell is running an elevator throughout eternity in
a building with only six floors." But he respected the company
begun by his ancestors, commenting in *Palm Sunday:* "I liked what
we sold. It was honest and practical."

I knew as a kid what the Vonneguts had contributed to the city
in terms of business, but I was ignorant until much later of the
family's immense cultural contributions. Kurt's great-grandfather,
Clemens Vonnegut, emigrated from Germany in 1848 and settled
in Indianapolis in 1850 and not only established the Vonnegut
Hardware Company but also became a major influence in the city's
cultural affairs. He founded the Freethinker's Society of Indianapolis and the Indianapolis *Turngemeinde,* the center for German
culture and gymnastics in Indianapolis. It later became known as
the Athenaeum Turners, serving the whole community and offering theater, lectures, and music as well as gymnastics. The building
that houses it today is called the Athenaeum.

Clemens served on the school board of the city and became its
chairman; he was a strong advocate of public education, seeing to
it that classics, history, and social sciences were part of the curriculum. A believer in physical fitness, he exercised daily in all weath-
ers, carrying large rocks in each hand, dropping them to chin
himself on low-hanging tree limbs. Little wonder that Kurt found
Clemens, a skeptic who wrote his own funeral oration, "the ancestor who most beguiles me." Noting that Clemens was described as
"a cultivated eccentric," Kurt wrote in *Palm Sunday:* "That's what
I aspire to be." Both Kurt's grandfather Bernard ("who didn't like
the trade in nails") and his own father, Kurt, Sr., aspired to do
something in the arts and became prominent architects in Indianapolis. Bernard Vonnegut, the first licensed architect in Indiana,
and his partner, Arthur Bohn, designed some of the most important buildings in the city, including the John Herron Art Museum,

Shortridge High School, and the Athenaeum. The year Bernard died, his son, Kurt, Sr., graduated from M.I.T. and returned home to become an architect and join his late father's partner in the business.

• • •

In a speech at the Athenaeum in 1996, Kurt told his audience: "I bring you a piece of Indianapolis history that may astonish you. This landmark building, designed by my grandfather Bernard Vonnegut, who I never knew, wasn't always called the Athenaeum. Some people, I've heard, splashed yellow paint on its façade when it was called something else."

It was originally called *Das Deutsche Haus,* but in the anti-German sentiment that swept the country during World War I, its named was changed. (Today the popular restaurant in the building, the Rathskeller, boasts a "Vonnegut Room," with a bust of the author.) Anything German was viewed with suspicion or hostility throughout the country during the war; in Indianapolis, which owed much of its cultural heritage to its German families, the city orchestra was disbanded because the soprano soloist was German, the restaurants serving German food renamed their *kartoffel* salad "liberty cabbage," and the board of education stopped the teaching of German in the schools.

"At about the same time as the yellow-paint monkey business," Vonnegut continued, "my father, Kurt, who had been Bernard Vonnegut's partner in architecture, received an anonymous note telling him, 'Stop teaching your kids Dutch.' And he did. . . ."

So Kurt's older brother and sister, Bernard and Alice, stopped hearing German at home, and by the time Kurt was born on November 11, 1922, no German was spoken there. His parents raised him "without acquainting me with the language or the literature or the oral family histories which my ancestors had loved," he wrote in *Palm Sunday.* "They volunteered to make me ignorant and rootless as proof of their patriotism."

In his Athenaeum speech, Kurt said, "During the Second World

War, there was a saying in my family and others that the only thing wrong with Germans was that they were in Germany. I say now that everything there is to admire in German culture, the poetry, the music, the architecture, the etchings, the beers, the wines, the sentimentality about Christmas, the work ethic, came from several Germanies. Everything I loathe about it came from one." He meant, of course, Nazi Germany, which he told the American Psychiatric Association in 1988, "gave us a nightmare from which, in my opinion, there can never be an awakening."

The family fortune made from the hardware business, as well as his grandfather and father's successful architecture company, enabled Kurt's parents to enjoy a lavish lifestyle and send their children to the socially elite private schools of the city, the Orchard School for boys and Tudor Hall for girls. But when the Great Depression hit, almost all building stopped, and Kurt, Sr., was forced to close his office. Kurt was taken out of private school and sent to Public School No. 43, which his mother, Edith, who was from one of the grand and wealthy German families of the city (the Leibers), regarded as a tragedy. She assured him that when the Depression ended he would resume his proper place in society, playing tennis and golf at the Woodstock Country Club and enjoying the privileges of the elite. Young Kurt saw it another way, as he explained in *Palm Sunday*:

"We were at least as well off as most of the people I went to public school with, and I would have lost all my friends if we had started having servants again, and worn expensive clothes again, and ridden on ocean liners and visited German relatives in a real castle, and on and on. . . . [Mother] could not understand that to give up my friends at Public School No. 43 would be for me to give up everything."

Kurt always said he was lucky to have been born in Indianapolis. "That city gave me a free primary and secondary education richer and more humane than anything I would get from any of the five universities I attended [Cornell, Butler, Carnegie Tech, Tennessee, and Chicago]."

I felt the same way, which was one of many bonds I was fortunate to share with Kurt Vonnegut. Another bond—the one that originally launched our lifelong friendship—was our mutual ineptitude at sports. I had read all four novels he'd published when we met for the first time in 1963 at a friend's house in Cambridge, Massachusetts, when Vonnegut was living on Cape Cod. There were eight people at the dinner, so I was only able to exchange a few jokey comments about high school with Kurt, but I liked him at once. He was a tall, thin, tousle-haired man with a shaggy mustache and a kindly Midwestern demeanor. His offbeat sense of humor and his openness, his friendliness to everyone there, made me feel I knew and could trust him and gave me the courage to send him a book I wrote the next year, called *Between the Lines,* which combined journalistic articles with personal commentary. In the book I confessed that my dreams of athletic glory in high school were shattered by my inability to break the seven-minute mile— a time I imagined a well-conditioned grandmother might have equaled. Kurt wrote me back a warm, funny letter, confessing that he, too, had been unable to break the seven-minute mile in high school and that we had so many of the same teachers and experiences, "I almost feel that there shouldn't be two of us."

• • •

I didn't realize till years later how deeply Kurt's "nonathletic" experience in high school had affected him. When he'd finally gained fame and fortune after years of struggle and moved to New York, he was sitting up late one night by himself, drinking bourbon, and called Indianapolis information, asking if they had a listing for the man who'd been the football coach at Shortridge High when he was there. Kurt said that in his era there had been a tradition of faculty members giving "joke presents" to well-known seniors at a gathering of the class. He told me he had been "a tall, skinny, gangly kind of kid" in high school, and the coach had "awarded" him a subscription to the "Charles Atlas Bodybuilding Course." The course was famous for its ads showing how a ninety-pound "weakling" could become a muscular hero. It had hurt and embarrassed him, and it still rankled, even after all his success. He told me that when he got the coach on the phone all those years later, he said, "My name is Kurt Vonnegut—you probably don't remember me, but I wanted to tell you my body turned out just fine."

I thought no more about it until I read, in his introduction to a collection of his stories called *Bagombo Snuff Box*, a reminiscence of coming home from high school one afternoon and sitting down to read a short story in *The Saturday Evening Post*. He began: "It is raining outside, and I am unpopular." I knew from reading his high school yearbook that Kurt had been president of the Social Committee, which sponsored dances and parties, co-chairman with his best friend, Ben Hitz, of a "hilarious comedy act" in the prestigious Junior Vaudeville, a member of the Student Council, an editor of the *Daily Echo*, and, most impressively to anyone who went to Shortridge, he was one of the ten senior boys nominated for "Uglyman"—which did not mean the ugliest but the most-popular boys. Along with the ten most-popular girls, nominated for "Bluebelle," these twenty were voted on by the entire student body as the pinnacle of high school popularity.

Kurt's friend from high school Victor Jose, a fellow member of the Owls Club (one of the many social clubs that were not sponsored by the faculty but flourished at Shortridge in my time and theirs), also worked with him on the *Daily Echo*, and after their service in World War II, they worked together in the Chicago News Bureau in 1947, remaining friends and corresponding off and on throughout their lives. When I asked Vic Jose how Kurt could have felt himself "unpopular" after all his high school kudos and accomplishments, he said he felt it must have related to "Kurt's adversarial relationship with the so-called sports heroes of our time. . . ."

Kurt poked fun at the sports gods, "probably in his writing, probably in the *Echo*," Jose recalled. "Anyway, there was bad blood there, and, in retaliation, some of the jocks caught Kurt in some unobserved location, picked him up, and stuffed him in a trash can somewhere in the [school] building. I know all this only secondhand, Kurt never told me, but it was common knowledge. It was no lighthearted joke but seemed to fester with time, because it surfaced at our fiftieth reunion." Two of the "jocks" of the class opposed having Vonnegut give the main speech at one of the fiftieth-reunion events—but the rest of the organizing committee insisted on having him as the headliner. The point became moot when Kurt called two days before the event to report that he'd contracted Lyme disease and wasn't able to come. At the sixtieth reunion, Jose said, the same former "jocks" were disgruntled that the class was presenting a bronze bust of Kurt at a Saturday-night dinner at the Athenaeum and left the dinner before the presentation was made to their most famous classmate.

Kurt wrote in an introduction to *Our Time Is Now: Notes from the High School Underground* (1970) that "High school is closer to the core of the American experience than anything else I can think of." I believe from my own experience that those adolescent years shape much of our attitudes and perception of the world throughout our life and that Kurt's lifelong love of the underdog began with his antipathy to the "sports gods" of his time—and his humiliation by them in the trash-can incident. Seeing his father lose his fortune and having to close down his architecture office during the Depression, then losing what little business was left when building stopped during World War II, was surely also a significant factor in Kurt's becoming a champion of the underdog throughout his writing.

Writing about the Republican Convention for *Harper's* magazine in 1972, Kurt concluded that "The two real political parties in America are the Winners and the Losers. The people do not acknowledge this. They claim membership in two imaginary parties, the Republicans and the Democrats, instead. Both imaginary parties are bossed by Winners. When Republicans battle Democrats, this much is certain: Winners will win."

There are two sources that are quoted throughout Vonnegut's writing, or are referenced in it, that seem essential to his outlook.

One is the Sermon on the Mount. Invited to preach on Palm Sunday at St. Clement's Episcopal Church in New York in 1980, he said, "I am enchanted by the Sermon on the Mount. Being merciful, it seems to me, is the only good idea we have received so far. Perhaps we will get another good idea by and by—and then we will have two good ideas." The other is a quote from Eugene V. Debs, his fellow Hoosier, from Terre Haute, Indiana:

"While there is a lower class I am in it. While there is a criminal element I am of it. While there is a soul in prison I am not free."

He called that quote of Debs's "a moving echo of the Sermon on the Mount" in *Timequake* and used it as the epigraph to his novel *Hocus Pocus,* whose protagonist is "Eugene Debs Hartke." Hartke was named "in honor of Eugene Debs . . . a Socialist and a Pacifist and a Labor Organizer who ran several times for the Presidency of the United States of America, and got more votes than has any other candidate nominated by a third party in the history of this country."

• • •

In Vonnegut's novel *Cat's Cradle,* about a proudly false prophet named Bokonon, he introduces his concept of a "*karass.*"

"Humanity is organized into teams, teams that do God's Will without ever discovering what they are doing. Such a team is called a *karass* by Bokonon . . . 'If you find your life tangled up with somebody else's life for no very logical reasons,' writes Bokonon, 'that person may be a member of your *karass.*' "

It was one of the great good fortunes of my life to find myself in Vonnegut's *karass,* and lucky for both of us to be in the same *karass* with the publisher Seymour "Sam" Lawrence, who Kurt said years later in *Timequake* had "rescued me from certain oblivion, from *smithereens,* by publishing *Slaughterhouse-Five,* and then bringing all my previous books back into print under his umbrella."

Sam had published *Slaughterhouse* in 1969. A year later, when my agent sent my long-awaited (by only *me*) first novel to ten publishers, three made offers, but Sam was the only one who loved it. He asked if I minded him sending a copy to Vonnegut, since my novel was set in his own hometown of Indianapolis, and his endorsement would help Sam get the okay from his co-publisher and financial backer, Delacorte Press. I said it was all right with me, but at that point I had met Vonnegut only once in my life and I had no idea what he'd think of the novel. The book I had sent him in 1965 was nonfiction, and my novel was nothing at all like Kurt's novels in style or story. The next thing I heard was that Kurt had sent a telegram to Sam Lawrence, telling him he must publish my novel and "get that boy in our stable."

Kurt was like the godfather of that novel, *Going All the Way* (though his own suggested title was *Getting Laid in Indianapolis*). Sam even commissioned him to be my editor, and Kurt sent me a letter with ten suggestions to improve the book, stressing I should do only the things that "rang a bell" with me and not do anything just because he suggested it. I did seven. (Vonnegut requested and received from Sam an Eames chair as payment for his editorial work.) Kurt came up from Cape Cod to Boston, where I was living, and took me to lunch at his favorite restaurant, Jacob Wirth's, an old German alehouse with sawdust on the floor. He later came up with his wife, Jane, to celebrate the publication. As if that weren't enough, he reviewed the novel for *Life* magazine, breaking all the rules of book reviewing by confessing he was a friend of mine and he would praise the novel even if it was "putrid," but he would not give his "word of honor" it was good and proceeded to endorse it with his word of honor.

As far as I know, it was the only time a writer gave his "word of honor" in a book review or used the word "putrid." He was always coming out with words that surprised you, words like "putrid," which you hadn't heard for a long time—maybe since childhood—but seemed to perfectly suit the situation.

During the hippie days, Kurt and I were once invited to visit a Vermont commune (made famous in the era by its founder, Ray

Mungo, in his book *Total Loss Farm*). Ray told us that he and his friends wanted to learn how to survive in primitive conditions because "We would like to be the last people on earth." Kurt said, "Isn't that kind of a stuck-up thing to want to be?" I hadn't heard anyone bold and honest enough to use the term "stuck-up" since high school, but it fit the occasion perfectly.

In his conversation as well as his books and stories, Kurt was always speaking the unspeakable—articulating what other people thought but were too politically or socially correct to say. It was in his DNA to point out that the emperor had no clothes, that there was an elephant in the room that everyone else was pretending not to notice. "You know, the truth can be really powerful stuff," Kurt observed in *A Man Without a Country.* "You're not expecting it."

Vonnegut spoke at a memorial service for his old friend Richard Yates; he not only championed Yates's work, he also loaned money without question to this masterful but often struggling writer, who was never fully appreciated until after his death. In a spontaneous remark at the memorial service, Kurt said Yates was just as good a writer as another friend, Nelson Algren, but had never received the same literary acclaim. As if thinking aloud, Kurt noted that Yates, unlike Algren, had never had an affair with Simone de Beauvoir; then he paused for a moment, and added, "These things count." There was spontaneous laughter, the kind that comes when someone says something others recognize as true but none have the wit or courage to say.

Vonnegut wrote in that same spirit of naked honesty, which explains why many people (including some of those Indiana relatives) were offended by his books. He wrote the way people spoke and used the words that are used in everyday speech, which often led to his work being banned by public-school boards and attempts being made to remove them from public libraries across the country. Vonnegut's worldwide bestseller, *Slaughterhouse-Five,* was actually burned in a furnace in Drake, North Dakota, on orders from the local school committee. His searing letter to the chairman of the Drake school board, like a number of his letters protesting such attempts, supporting teachers and librarians, and defending the First Amendment, will be found in this book.

. . .

Vonnegut's writing, like his conversation, is often surprising, because it makes you laugh and makes you think by saying what was on your mind—or *in* your mind—that you hadn't dared say or think. It is disarming because it is done with such seemingly simple language and style that it sometimes seems shocking, and it is the shock of self-recognition. Robert Scholes, the first academic critic to recognize Vonnegut's work (and one of the most perceptive), explained in his book *The Fabulators* in 1967 that Vonnegut ". . . uses the rhetorical potential of the short sentence and the short paragraph better than anyone now writing, often getting a rich comic or dramatic effect by isolating a single sentence in a separate paragraph or excerpting a phrase from context for a bizarre chapter-heading. The apparent simplicity and ordinariness of his writing masks its efficient power . . ."

This very "simplicity and ordinariness" made things difficult for most reviewers and critics, who resorted to pigeonholing him in ways that misconstrued and maligned his work. When Vonnegut worked in public relations for General Electric, he was "completely surrounded by machines and ideas for machines, so I wrote a novel [*Player Piano*] about people and machines . . . And I learned from the reviewers that I was a science-fiction writer. I didn't know that. I supposed that I was writing a novel about life," he explained in the essay "Science Fiction" in *The New York Times Book Review* (later collected in *Wampeters, Foma & Granfalloons*). "I have been a sore-headed occupant of a file-drawer labeled 'science fiction' ever since, and I would like out, particularly since so many serious critics regularly mistake the drawer for a urinal."

The categorization did not prevent Vonnegut from using elements of classic science-fiction writing—imaginary planets and

life-forms, space travel to other worlds—to illuminate human di-
lemmas as down-to-earth as love and hate, fear and folly, in places
as "real" as Schenectady and Indianapolis, Dresden and Cape Cod,
the Galápagos Islands and West Virginia. By 1967, even before the
breakthrough bestseller *Slaughterhouse-Five* blew apart the conventional lines between science fiction and literature (with its hero,
Billy Pilgrim, coming "unstuck in time" and moving between decades and places as distant as Toledo, Ohio, and the planet Tralfa-
madore), Robert Scholes could see that "Just as pure romance
provides us with necessary psychic exercise, intellectual comedy
like Vonnegut's offers us moral stimulation—not fixed ethical positions which we can complacently assume, but such thoughts as
exercise our consciences and help us keep our humanity in shape,
ready to respond to the humanity of others."

Young university teachers and critics like Jerome Klinkowitz
and John Somer began to teach Vonnegut's work and write about
it, first in a collection of essays called *The Vonnegut Statement,* in
1973. They dug out of libraries and old magazines previously uncollected articles and essays and convinced him to publish them in
book form, as *Wampeters, Foma & Granfalloons,* in 1974. They
were joined by other young academics like Peter Reed, Marc Leeds,
and Asa Pieratt, who appreciated, taught, compiled, and interpreted his work to new generations.

None of this attention, or the success that followed *Slaughterhouse-Five,* made Vonnegut immune to the outburst of rancor
that came in the negative response to his 1976 novel *Slapstick.*

"What was unusual about the reviews was that they wanted
people to admit now that I had never been any good," Vonnegut
told his interviewers from *The Paris Review.* "The reviewer for the
Sunday *Times* actually asked critics who had praised me in the past
to now admit in public how wrong they had been. . . . The hidden
complaint was that I was barbarous, that I wrote without having
made a . . . study of great literature, that I was no gentleman, that
I had done hack writing so cheerfully for vulgar magazines—that I
had not paid my academic dues."

The interviewer asked if after the barrage of bad reviews he "needed comforting."

"I never felt worse in my life," Kurt answered. "All of a sudden critics wanted me squashed like a bug."

Maybe it felt like being stuffed in a trash can by the high school jocks.

• • •

Vonnegut has often—and aptly—been compared to Mark Twain, as a public speaker as well as a writer. When the critic Granville Hicks reviewed *Slaughterhouse-Five*, he wrote that he had heard Vonnegut give a speech once and that he had "a vernacular appeal" like Twain's and a "personal presence" that was captured in his novel. Kurt told Jerome Klinkowitz, "People do seem to like my work best when they've heard me speak first."

The first time I heard Kurt give a speech was at a Unitarian Universalist General Assembly in Rochester, New York, in the eighties. The Unitarians are the only religious denomination that Vonnegut could comfortably identify with, since they have no creed or dogma and "welcome people of different beliefs" including "Atheism and Agnosticism, Buddhism, Humanism, Paganism, and other religious or philosophical traditions," according to the "Beliefs and Principles" explained on their website. They even include Christians, and I was there as a member of King's Chapel in Boston, one of the few Christian churches in the Unitarian Universalist Association.

Most Unitarian churches are Humanist, and though Kurt was not a member of a church, he was honorary president of the American Humanist Society, which made him a highly appropriate speaker for this assembly. He described himself as a "Christ-loving atheist" and has said, "In order not to seem a spiritual quadriplegic, to strangers trying to get a fix on me, I sometimes say I'm a Unitarian Universalist."

Kurt started his talk with a surefire crowd-pleaser for the occasion. He was wearing a round pin on his lapel, like a political campaign button, and he said it explained his admiration for the Unitarians. "It has a picture of a frankfurter and a big 'X' through it," he said. "It means, 'No Baloney.' " That brought cheers as well as laughs. He was off and running, and, as usual, he won over his audience, which he was able to do regardless of the occasion. I heard him speak in different places for different purposes after that, and whether speaking with anger and passion against the first invasion of Iraq at All Souls Unitarian Church in New York or with humor and nostalgia on "Spirit and Place" at Butler University in Indianapolis, he was always able to do as a speaker what he did as a writer, which was follow E. M. Forster's rule: "Only connect!"

• • •

Kurt connected with friends as well as with audiences. One of the elements that run throughout these letters I chose out of more than a thousand is the sustaining friendships that ran throughout his life, from kindergarten to high school and Cornell and the Army, with relatives from home (even those who dismissed his books), his children, his students, teaching colleagues, fellow writers, scholars and critics who wrote about his work. His letters are like his books, stories, articles, and essays—they make you think, raise your spirits, evoke your anger at injustice, make you see things in new ways, question society's "accepted wisdom," and, always, entertain.

Vonnegut's heroes included the comedians Laurel and Hardy and the radio satirists Bob Elliott and Ray Goulding, whose *Bob & Ray Show* made his generation laugh. Kurt liked to laugh and make other people laugh, sometimes with silly jokes that came out of the blue. As I walked down the street with him in New York after lunch one day, he suddenly turned to me and said, "What's the opposite of an upholsterer?" After a minute or so I said, "I give up," and Kurt said, "A down-polsterer," and rasped out his coughing laugh.

He also laughed about himself and the unintentional slips he made from his Humanist views. "Humanists," he explained in *Timequake*, "try to behave decently and honorably without any expectation of rewards or punishments in an afterlife." Kurt told me after one of our New York lunches that he really messed up while giving a eulogy for his friend Isaac Asimov, the noted science-fiction writer, who'd preceded him as honorary president of the Humanist Society.

"I said I was sure that Isaac must be in heaven now," he said with a smoky cough and a laugh. "I forgot."

If it turned out there *was* an afterlife, Kurt reserved places in it for people he loved. In his last novel, *Timequake,* he said he was sure his first wife, Jane, was in heaven, and so was Sam Lawrence, the publisher who saved him from "smithereens."

. . .

Kurt never failed to show support for his writer friends. The year before he died, he came to a talk I gave at St. Bartholomew's Episcopal Church in New York about a book I had recently published, and afterward he took me to dinner. While he had a Manhattan, his customary predinner drink, and I had a glass of wine, two young men kept staring our way from another table. Finally one of them got up and came over to ask, "Are you the real Kurt Vonnegut?" Kurt said he was and immediately introduced me and told the stranger about my new book, urging him to read it, which the poor guy had no interest in at all. After Kurt politely answered some questions about himself and his work, he gave a smart hand salute of dismissal and the man thanked him, backed away, and returned to his table. It was typical Kurt, diverting attention from himself to try to promote the unknown book of a friend, responding to a stranger's well-meaning intrusion with grace, and taking leave of him with dignity, leaving both friend and fan well treated, living the commandment that he made his habit, to "Do unto others as you would have others do unto you."

He wrote in *Timequake:* "When I myself am dead, God forbid, I hope some wag will say about me, 'He's up in heaven now.' "

For the record, let me say of Kurt Vonnegut: "He's up in heaven now."

KURT
VONNEGUT
Letters

THE FORTIES

Vonnegut graduated from Shortridge High School in 1940 and enrolled in Cornell University. Due to his family's financial troubles brought on by the Depression, he was told by his father and older brother not to waste time on "frivolous courses" but to study practical subjects, such as physics, chemistry, and math. He continued the social and writing activities he had engaged in at Shortridge, joining the Delta Upsilon fraternity and writing for *The Cornell Daily Sun,* becoming a columnist and managing editor.

He was failing his courses (after a bout with pneumonia) when he enlisted in the U.S. Army in 1943 and was assigned to the ASTP (Army Specialized Training Program), which sent him to Carnegie Tech and the University of Tennessee for training in mechanical engineering, then assigned him to the 106th Infantry Division. While he was home on leave from Camp Atterbury, outside Indianapolis, before being sent overseas, his mother, Edith Leiber Vonnegut, committed suicide from an overdose of sleeping pills on May 14, the day after Mother's Day. "It is not known why my mother killed herself," Kurt wrote in a letter of "biographical stuff" he sent to Professor Klinkowitz on December 11, 1976. "She never said anything about the awfulness of fighting against the homeland or anything like that. In fact, I don't recall my parents' ever having spoken of Germany as the homeland. . . . It was war itself that wrecked my mother, and not war against Germany. Also, she was taking an awful lot of barbiturates at a time when the side-effects were thought to be negligible."

There were other factors, as recounted by Kurt's "Uncle John" Rauch in "An Account of the Ancestry of Kurt Vonnegut, Jr., by an Ancient Friend of his Family" (quoted by Kurt in *Palm Sunday*). Rauch, a Harvard graduate and Indianapolis lawyer (and not really Kurt's uncle but the husband of a first cousin), wrote that "With her other financial problems the prospect of losing her son in the impending holocaust made her cup of troubles overflow. She became despondent and morose. Wanting money desperately, she attempted to write short stories which she could sell, but it was a futile, hopeless venture; a tragic disillusion. She simply could not see daylight."

As an advance intelligence and reconnaissance scout with the 106th Infantry during the Battle of the Bulge, Vonnegut was taken prisoner by the German Army and sent to Dresden, where he survived the firebombing of the city in an underground meat locker with other prisoners. He wrote in his "biographical" letter to Klinkowitz that "practically all my fellow prisoners were stockpiled in ASTP. Our own suspicion afterwards, since we had so little ammunition and were still awaiting winter equipment, and never saw an American plane or tank, and were not warned that the Germans were massing large numbers of tanks for one last major attack, is that the 106th was bait in a trap. In chess this is called a gambit. Take the exposed pawn and you've lost the game."

Kurt's lifelong friend Victor Jose, who went to Swarthmore with Jane Cox, believes that when Kurt was home on leave in 1944 he went to see Jane, whom he had met in kindergarten and dated when they went to Shortridge High School together. Victor remembers that Kurt "appeared on the scene just in time" to persuade her to break off her relationship with a college boyfriend and wait for him till he came home from the war. Kurt later wrote a fictionalized version of such an encounter in his short story "Long Walk to Forever" (collected in *Welcome to the Monkey House*).

After being honorably discharged from the Army in July of

1945 and awarded the Purple Heart, Kurt married Jane that September in a Quaker ceremony (Jane and her family were Quakers). A voracious reader, Jane had graduated from Swarthmore College as a Phi Beta Kappa the year before and was awarded a prize for having the best personal library of any graduating student. Kurt later told a friend that the books Jane brought to their marriage were her "dowry." Kurt wrote in *Fates Worse Than Death* that, during their honeymoon, "She had me read *The Brothers Karamazov*. . . . She considered it the greatest of all novels."

Kurt and Jane were both accepted into graduate programs at the University of Chicago and moved to that city in December of 1945. (Jane dropped out of her classes in Slavic languages and literature when she became pregnant in 1946.) Like many returning veterans, Kurt used his G.I. Bill to supplement his education, studying for a master's degree in anthropology, and also worked as a reporter at the Chicago News Bureau. When his thesis was rejected—a comparative study of the Ghost Dance Society of the Plains Indians and the Cubist painters—and his first son, Mark, was born in 1947, Kurt decided to drop out and apply for jobs to support his family. (Their daughter Edith was added two years later, and their third child and second daughter, Nanette, was born in 1954.) Kurt turned down an offer from Bobbs-Merrill publishers in Indianapolis to accept a position in public relations for General Electric in Schenectady, New York, where his older brother, Bernard, worked as an atmospheric physicist. The pay was better, and both Kurt and Jane wanted a change of scene. Kurt's classmate Victor Jose told me that "If they stayed in Indianapolis, they feared that Jane would be expected by her family to join the Junior League, and she and Kurt didn't like that 'socialite' kind of life. They both were rebels even then."

Working in public relations by day, Kurt wrote short stories at night and on weekends and sent them out to the leading popular and well-paying magazines of the era. This was "the golden age of magazines," when William Faulkner published stories in *Collier's,* F. Scott Fitzgerald appeared in *The Saturday Evening Post,* John

Steinbeck in the *Woman's Home Companion,* and Ernest Hemingway in *Esquire.* Four weeklies and six monthlies published three or four stories in every issue, and "the Vonnegut boy" was able to make a (precarious) living, support his family, and begin his career as a writer, selling short stories to those magazines.

Unlike his mother's failed efforts in the same enterprise, Vonnegut succeeded. The break came when Knox Burger, a Cornell graduate who'd gone on to become fiction editor at *Collier's* magazine, recognized Kurt's name on a story submission. He asked in a scrawled note at the bottom of a rejection slip if he was the Kurt Vonnegut who'd gone to Cornell and written for *The Cornell Sun.* It turned out to be the start of a relationship that led to acceptance of his first short story and launched his career as a writer.

May 29, 1945

[Le Havre]

FROM: PFC. K. VONNEGUT, JR., 12102964 U.S. ARMY

TO KURT VONNEGUT, SR., AND FAMILY

This was the first letter that PFC Kurt Vonnegut, Jr., wrote to his family after being released as a prisoner of war.

Victor Jose, Kurt's friend from Shortridge High School in Indianapolis (and later the Chicago News Bureau), wrote in a note to me that "I believe this letter was first read publicly in 1945 at a meeting of The Portfolio Club of artists and literary people [in Indianapolis], to which my parents belonged." Jose said his parents told him the letter was read to the group by Kurt's father, who was also a member of the club.

This letter recounts the experience—the firebombing of Dresden— that would shape the theme of Kurt's later work and come to its powerful fruition with his 1969 novel Slaughterhouse-Five, *which became an international bestseller and catapulted its author to worldwide fame. There is also a foreshadowing of his future style in the understated dark irony of the grim events he reports and his own survival. "But not*

me . . . but not me" seems later to echo in the phrase that would fa-
mously be repeated in much of his published work: "So it goes . . ."

Dear people:

I'm told that you were probably never informed that I was
anything other than "missing in action." Chances are that you
also failed to receive any of the letters I wrote from Germany.
That leaves me a lot of explaining to do—in precis:

I've been a prisoner of war since December 19th, 1944, when
our division was cut to ribbons by Hitler's last desperate thrust
through Luxemburg and Belgium. Seven Fanatical Panzer Divisions hit us and cut us off from the rest of Hodges' First Army.
The other American Divisions on our flanks managed to pull out:
We were obliged to stay and fight. Bayonets aren't much good
against tanks: Our ammunition, food and medical supplies gave
out and our casualties out-numbered those who could still
fight—so we gave up. The 106th got a Presidential Citation and
some British Decoration from Montgomery for it, I'm told, but
I'll be damned if it was worth it. I was one of the few who
weren't wounded. For that much thank God.

Well, the supermen marched us, without food, water or sleep
to Limberg, a distance of about sixty miles, I think, where we
were loaded and locked up, sixty men to each small, unventilated,
unheated box car. There were no sanitary accommodations—the
floors were covered with fresh cow dung. There wasn't room for
all of us to lie down. Half slept while the other half stood. We
spent several days, including Christmas, on that Limberg siding.
On Christmas eve the Royal Air Force bombed and strafed our
unmarked train. They killed about one-hundred-and-fifty of us.
We got a little water Christmas Day and moved slowly across
Germany to a large P.O.W. Camp in Muhlburg, South of Berlin.
We were released from the box cars on New Year's Day. The Germans herded us through scalding delousing showers. Many men
died from shock in the showers after ten days of starvation, thirst
and exposure. But I didn't.

Under the Geneva Convention, Officers and Non-commissioned Officers are not obliged to work when taken prisoner. I am, as you know, a Private. One-hundred-and-fifty such minor beings were shipped to a Dresden work camp on January 10th. I was their leader by virtue of the little German I spoke. It was our misfortune to have sadistic and fanatical guards. We were refused medical attention and clothing: We were given long hours at extremely hard labor. Our food ration was two-hundred-and-fifty grams of black bread and one pint of un-seasoned potato soup each day. After desperately trying to improve our situation for two months and having been met with bland smiles I told the guards just what I was going to do to them when the Russians came. They beat me up a little. I was fired as group leader. Beatings were very small time:—one boy starved to death and the SS Troops shot two for stealing food.

On about February 14th the Americans came over, followed by the R.A.F. Their combined labors killed 250,000 people in twenty-four hours and destroyed all of Dresden—possibly the world's most beautiful city. But not me.

After that we were put to work carrying corpses from Air-Raid shelters; women, children, old men; dead from concussion, fire or suffocation. Civilians cursed us and threw rocks as we carried bodies to huge funeral pyres in the city.

When General Patton took Leipzig we were evacuated on foot to Hellexisdorf on the Saxony-Czechoslovakian border. There we remained until the war ended. Our guards deserted us. On that happy day the Russians were intent on mopping up isolated outlaw resistance in our sector. Their planes (P-39's) strafed and bombed us, killing fourteen, but not me.

Eight of us stole a team and wagon. We traveled and looted our way through Sudetenland and Saxony for eight days, living like kings. The Russians are crazy about Americans. The Russians picked us up in Dresden. We rode from there to the American lines at Halle in Lend-Lease Ford trucks. We've since been flown to Le Havre.

I'm writing from a Red Cross Club in the Le Havre P.O.W. Repatriation Camp. I'm being wonderfully well fed and entertained. The state-bound ships are jammed, naturally, so I'll have to be patient. I hope to be home in a month. Once home I'll be given twenty-one days recuperation at Atterbury, about $600 back pay and—get this—sixty (60) days furlough!

I've too damned much to say, the rest will have to wait. I can't receive mail here so don't write. May 29, 1945

Love,

Kurt-Jr.

July 4, 1945
Indianapolis

TO ELLA VONNEGUT STEWART,
FROM KURT'S UNCLE ALEX VONNEGUT

This letter from Kurt's uncle Alex, his father's brother, to Ella Stewart, a cousin, reports on picking up Kurt (known in the family then as "Kay" to distinguish him from his father, Kurt, Sr.) from Camp Atterbury, outside Indianapolis, when Vonnegut returned home from his service with the U.S. Army during WWII. Uncle Alex had taken Kurt's older sister, Alice, with him on the trip.

Dear Ella:

Kay is home. At lunch yesterday noon Kurt told me that Alice had telephoned to her. Kay had called from Camp Atterbury. Would they please call for him at about 3 o'clock; he felt certain that he would be able to get away at that time. I was pleased that Kurt asked me to go with him and Alice to get the boy. It was the first time I had been at Atterbury. What an immense place: barracks, barracks stretching over many square miles and thousands of soldiers and many German Prisoners of War. We went to the Officers' Club No. 1, where Kay had told us to meet him. It was ten minutes after three, but no Kay anywhere in sight. Juke boxes playing and soldiers and Wacs dancing. A busy ice-cream stand, with pies and Coca-Cola also available. Alice was nervous. She feared she might vomit. We got Coca-Colas and sat on the front porch. A dozen soldiers sitting around passing the time away. The general atmosphere was boredom.

In the distance we saw a tall lad approaching, carrying a big heavy bag. Could it be Kay? Those long legs. It might be; it was! We let Alice go to meet him. A hug and a kiss. "Now, no emotions, please!" Kay pleaded. They both wiped their eyes. A hug from his father. A formal handshake from me. The big bag was picked up and carried to Kurt's Dodge car. Kay opened the back of the car and threw the heavy bag in. He is tall as ever, the same long eyelashes but, oh, that face! Well browned from the recuperation center at Le Havre and the fifteen-day trip across the Atlantic.

"I want to drive the car!" He drove us home. I wish I could have taken down in shorthand or, better yet, I wish I could have had a dictaphone to record what that lad of twenty-two years (he'll be 23 in November—November 11th) told us. He speaks well. He is articulate. And he spoke continuously from Atterbury to Indianapolis. But what did he say? What didn't he say! What hasn't he seen? What hasn't he endured and suffered.

Nothing that I can write here will give an adequate impression of what we heard. Mind you, he was driving and talking, and it's only some forty-odd miles from Atterbury to Louise Adams' house where Jimbo had been parked for the afternoon. As a result of his experiences after being taken prisoner on that ghastly day when the 106th Division was suddenly and quite unexpectedly overwhelmed, he lost forty-five pounds. "I had never been really hungry before. I did not know what it means to be thirsty. To be really hungry is a strange sensation. You go nuts! But you mustn't give up. If you give up—if you don't care, if you lie down and don't care, your kidneys go bad and you piss blood, and then you can't get up again and you just wilt away."

"What do they say over here about the bombing of Dresden?" Yes, we told him that we knew that Dresden had been bombed.

He saw Dresden before it all happened—in 24 hours! He was in
the midst of it—confined with 150 Prisoners in the Municipal
Slaughter House, which was not bombed. "As one guy said,
'Well, there were one hundred and fifty pigs here, and now 150
Infantry Prisoners.' Now you lie down in any part of Dresden
and see all over the area that once was that beautiful, beautiful
city. Hardly fifty houses standing in the vast area. And don't think
it was not an outrage to destroy that city! You can't imagine what
it means. And who was killed? Two hundred fifty thousand
men—mostly older men, of course—and all the women and all
the children. You cannot describe what it means to be bombed.
And think of it! The people of Saxony never had any use for Hitler and that whole gang of S.O.B.s! Hitler came to Dresden only
twice. He never got a welcome. And Dresden had practically no
air raid shelters. It was assumed that Dresden would not be
bombed. Everything is gone. All the Art Galleries—everything!"

"What's that scar behind your ear?" Alice asked. "That's
where the SS beat me." "With what?" "With a scrub-brush!"

And then the tale about their fellow prisoner who stole a can
of beans and was tried and had to sign a document acknowledg-
ing that he had committed some heinous crime—he didn't even
know what he was signing. And he didn't know that on the next
morning when four of us were taken out with shovels (and we
didn't know) that we would have to dig his grave. And in front of
it, he was shot—with his back to the firing squad! (And then the
driver of the Dodge car burst into tears.) "The sons of bitches!
The sons of bitches!"

The Russians? "Believe it or not, I was kissed by a Russian
Major! He asked me how we were treated by the Russians. I told
him just fine! He said they were having quite a bit of trouble with
some of their own men who were not aware of the fact that the
Americans were fighting on our side."

"You ought to see the hordes of Russians that are now
swarming in to Saxony. When the advance troops first came, all
the Germans were scared pink and hid in cellars. But they came

in fine order, and they threw loaves of bread to the people, and they drove in fine American Lend-Lease cars, and they were spic and span. But then after a few days came the hordes of Russians. Talk about your Southern American negroes! Jesus! Those Russian masses are terrifying. They looted everything in sight. There was not a herd of cattle left in all Saxony. And do you really know what Vodka is like? Jesus! It's just straight alcohol, and they drink it by the tumbler full. Really, some scientists should investigate how it is possible for man to drink such stuff in such huge quantities. They are men! Oh, Christ, it was terrible—the rapings and everything that went on."

"Believe me! I know what's going to happen in Europe. Now the trouble really starts. The French hate the Americans; the Poles and Russians hate the Germans; the Poles hate the Russians; everybody hates the Germans—except the Americans, who are giving the Germans five eggs every week in the territory occupied by American troops. And I am here to say that I've got it in for the British. They aren't good sports. You ought to see the negro troops in France. Are they going big! But don't tell me that the American negro isn't a good fighter. They are just as brave and good soldiers as any of 'em—American, German or Russian. It's fun to see the negroes gamble with their money: 'Yeah! Shoot another ten sport. I got lots and beaucoup of money—beaucoup of money!' And they shoot it away—all of their beaucoup of money. And what they are doing to the French girls! It's no wonder the French feel so bitter against the Americans."

When we arrived at Louise Adams' house we picked up the baby, which Kay had not seen since October, 1944. It was in that month that he left home. "Kay," I said, "you'll have to be patient with us civilians. We'll probably say things that are mightily offensive to you because we haven't enough imagination to understand what you have gone through." Kay's response was: "Oh, hell! I want to be a civilian myself. I'm sick and tired of being in the infantry. I want to get out of the army. Look at me. My arm and leg muscles have all atrophied. But I'll have 76 days of furlough here at home, and then I'm off to Florida where I'll be housed in one of the finest hotels in Miami. I've got my pullman reservations right here. And then . . . well—then what? Damned if I know. But I want to get out of the army, I tell you. I want to get out. I've had enough of it. And I'm goddamned sick and tired of the whole damnfool bloody mess. I'm sick of it!"

January 26, 1947

To Jane Vonnegut

As the wife of a writer of the era, Jane Vonnegut took on not only the customary household duties but a whole set of other jobs that were expected of wives by their writer–husbands, including editing and copyediting, mailing of manuscripts, acting as intermediary between husbands and their agents, editors, and publishers, serving as in-house publicists and marketing assistants, and in most cases typing up manuscripts. Kurt was always proud of the fact that, unlike most writer-husbands, he never asked Jane to do any of his typing, which in itself made him a vanguard of liberation in that era.

CONTRACT between KURT VONNEGUT, JR. and JANE C. VONNEGUT, effective as of Sunday, January 26, 1947

I, Kurt Vonnegut, Jr., that is, do hereby swear that I will be faithful to the commitments hereunder listed:

I. With the agreement that my wife will not nag, heckle, and otherwise disturb me, on the subject, I promise to scrub the bathroom and kitchen floors once a week, on a day and hour of my own choosing. Not only that, but I will do a good and thorough job, and by that she means that I will get *under* the bathtub, *behind* the toilet, *under* the sink, *under* the icebox, *into* the corners; and I will pick up and put in some other location whatever moveable objects happen to be on said floors at the time so as to get under them too, and not just around them. Furthermore, while I am undertaking these tasks I will refrain from indulging in such remarks as "Shit," "Goddamn sonofabitch," and similar vulgarities, as such language is nervewracking to have around the house when nothing more drastic is taking place than the facing of Necessity. *If I do not live up to this agreement,* my wife is to feel free to nag, heckle and otherwise disturb me until I am driven to scrub the floors anyway—*no matter how busy I am.*

II. I furthermore swear that I will observe the following minor amenities:

a. I will hang up my clothes and put my shoes in the closet when I am not wearing them;

b. I will not track dirt into the house needlessly, by such means as not wiping my feet on the mat outside, and by wearing my bedroom slippers to take out the garbage, and other things;

c. I will throw such things as used up match folders, empty cigarette packages, the piece of cardboard that comes in shirt collars, etc, into a wastebasket instead of leaving them around on chairs and the floor;

d. After shaving I will put my shaving equipment back in the medicine closet;

e. In case I should be the direct cause of a ring around the bathtub after taking a bath, I will, with the aid of Swift's Cleanser and a brush, *not* my washcloth, remove said ring;

f. With the agreement that my wife collects the laundry, places it in a laundry bag, and leaves the laundry bag in plain sight in the hall, I will take said laundry to the Laundry not more than three days after said laundry has made its appearance in the hall; I will furthermore bring the *clean* laundry back from the Laundry within two weeks after I have taken it, dirty that is;

g. When smoking I will make every effort to keep the ashtray which I am using at the time upon a surface that does not slant, sag, slope, dip, wrinkle, or give way upon the slightest provocation; such surfaces may be understood to include stacks of books precariously mounted on the edge of a chair, the arms of the chair that has arms, and my own knees;

h. I will not put out cigarettes upon the sides of, or throw ashes into either the red leather waste-basket, or the stamp waste-basket which my loving wife made me for Christmas, 1945, as such practise noticeably impairs the beauty, and the ultimate practicability of said waste-baskets;

i. In the event that my wife makes a request of me, and that request cannot be regarded as other than reasonable and wholly within the province of a man's work (when his wife is pregnant, that is), I will comply with said request within three days after my wife has presented it: It is understood that my wife will make no reference to the subject, other than saying thank you, of course, *within these three days;* if, however, I fail to comply with said request after a more substantial length of time has elapsed, my wife shall be completely justified in nagging heckling and otherwise disturbing me, until I am driven to do that which I should have done;

j. An exception to the above three-day time limit is the taking out of the garbage, which, as any fool knows, had better not wait that long; I will take out the garbage within three *hours* after the need for disposal has been pointed out to me by my wife. It would be nice, however, if, upon observing the need for disposal with my own two eyes, I should perform this particular task upon my own initiative, and thus not make it necessary for my wife to bring up a subject which is moderately distasteful to her;

k. It is understood that, should I find these commitments in any way unreasonable or too binding upon my freedom, I will take steps to amend them by counter-proposals, constitutionally presented and politely discussed, instead of unlawfully terminating my obligations with a simple burst of obscenity, or something like that, and the subsequent persistent neglect of said obligations;

l. The terms of this contract are understood to be binding up until that time after the arrival of our child, (to be specified by the doctor,) when my wife will once again be in full possession of all her faculties, and able to undertake more arduous pursuits than are now advisable.

April 26, 1947
[Chicago]

To Personnel Office, General Motors

This was the standard letter Vonnegut sent out to a number of potential employers, stating his qualifications and references.

Personnel Office
General Motors Corporation
Detroit, Michigan

Dear sirs:

By October of this year I expect to have a Master's Degree in Anthropology from the University of Chicago. I am twenty-four, married, and the father of a very young child. I will be in need of a job at that time. Would General Motors be interested in hiring a person with my qualifications?

I was not an Anthropology student prior to the war. I took it up as part of a personal readjustment following some bewildering experiences as an infantryman and later as a prisoner of war in Dresden, Germany. The study of the Science of Man has been extremely satisfactory from that personal standpoint. It should also make me valuable to an organization such as yours, for I have considerable insight—through training in cultural anthropology and social psychology—into human relations, and would, with some instruction, make an able personnel or labor relations man [. . .]

I have had experience in other fields as a student. For three years before the war I was preparing to be a biochemist at Cornell University, with my time divided equally between chemistry and biology. For one of my three Army years I was sent to Carnegie Tech and then to the University of Tennessee for a course in Mechanical Engineering. I have no degree in Biochemistry, neither do I have one in Mechanical Engineering as the Army saw fit to terminate both courses before they were finished.

As to extra-curricular interests: most of my spare time at Cornell was spent in working for the Cornell Daily Sun, a corporation independent of the University, run wholly by students; an Associated Press member, an excellent daily tabloid. This was no mean job, consuming about thirty hours each week. I was made Managing Editor shortly before I was called to active duty.

I have been offered two jobs with advertising agencies as a copy writer, two as a newspaper reporter, one as a teacher in a private school, one as a trainee in a publishing house. Have you anything to offer? [. . .]

April 27, 1947
Chicago

To Don Matchan

Though the second page of this letter is missing, it reveals political views that Vonnegut would espouse throughout his life.

Don Matchan
Valley City Times-Record
Valley City, N.D.

Dear Mr. Matchan:

This morning's *Chicago Sun* carried a UP dispatch, telling of
your "inflammatory" editorial policy, and of the ultimatum with
which you have been presented for your failure to "reflect the
thinking of the people in the community."

I gather that you intend to reject the ultimatum and give local
reaction a first-rate fight. Like thousands of others who have seen
the same story, I find your vigorous struggle exciting, inspiring,
and absolutely crucial. Through your front page ballots you dem-
onstrated that you are endorsed by an overwhelming majority of
your readers; your opposition seeks to demonstrate that a
wealthy minority can coerce the press whenever it wishes to do
so, without regard to the community's will. Your predicament is
one of a thousand faced by progressive editors all over America.
Such editors usually lose. To speak in terms of humanity, in terms
of *change* engendered by compassion and yearning for a better
life on earth for the human species, is to incur the fury of those
fortunate few who are wonderfully well off in Valley Cities over
the face of creation under *the system as it now stands*.

That is not to say that those who plan to put the *Times-Record*
out of business are evil. Presumably among those citizens of Valley
City who now favor pro-labor attitudes, who back cooperatives
and other institutions which give low income individuals a measure of security in a basically insecure dog-eat-dog economy, there
will be a few who will come to be rich. They will then find such
collective movements detrimental to their incomes, and will strive
to thwart them. What must be realized is that the main trouble
with free enterprise, with rugged individualism which gives every
man the right to make as wide a margin of profit as he has the wit
to wheedle, is that there is simply not enough wealth to go
around. If there is to be no ceiling on the amount of money a man

can take out of our economy, then concomitantly there can be no firm foundation below which a human being cannot sink. What capitalists must realize is that you are fighting to make capitalism survive, not to destroy it; you are fighting to eliminate the seeds of destruction inherent in the status quo. Thank heaven for your struggle to give succor to that proportion of our society which must remain in moderate circumstances . . .

September 1, 1947

[Chicago]

To Helen and Walter A. Vonnegut, Jr.,
and their son, Christopher Robin "Kit" Vonnegut

"Colonel" was the family nickname of Walter A. Vonnegut, Jr., Kurt's cousin and, like Kurt, a great-grandson of Clemens Vonnegut, who came to the United States in 1848.

DEAR COLONEL & HELEN & KIT:

God bless you three. By now you must have set up temporary housekeeping in the cabin, and we are eager to hear of your progress to date and of your grandiose plans for the future. You have our love and our envy—the two items, as nearly as we can tell, one person most wants from another. You three have taken exceptionally shrewd advantage of your constitutional right to pursue happiness.

Our footsteps are in no wise so certain. The overall impression we gave when we last saw each other hasn't changed much: things are in one helluva state of flux. Last night we had our anniversary celebration at Jacques, a magnificent clip joint at 900 N. Michigan where one may live beyond his means under the stars in a flagstone courtyard. We toasted a merry future for you, for us, for George Seldes, Harry Truman, the Indonesian Republican Government, and the U.N. Atomic Control Commission. Through a mellow martini mist we tried to see what might be in

store for us. Our vague prospectus is this: we may move to Indianapolis and take a job offered by public Bobbs Merrill; we may
move to Schenectady and take a job offered by the public relations department of General Electric; we may move to Dayton,
Ohio, and take a job offered by the *Dayton Daily News*. A repre-
sentative from G.E. is going to interview me this evening: the
Secretary-Treasurer of Bobbs Merrill is coming to Chicago to talk
with me sometime during this next week. We'll let you know how
these interviews turn out.

At the present time, I am working for the Chicago City News
Bureau, a press association which gathers news in Cook County
for all (yes, dammit, the *Herald-American* and *Tribune* too) of
the Chicago papers. Victor Jose is going to work for the same organization next week. The News Bureau is part of a gruelling ap-
prentice system: in order to land a job on any of the Chicago
papers, one must begin as I have now begun. The job pays next
to nothing. However, there are an immense number of applicants
for jobs because the experience is highly respected and valuable. I
am a police reporter. I covered a case last week wherein a woman
of 54 (Mrs. Sosnowski) sawed her husband (Anthony) into two
foot lengths, and carried his segmented mortal remains a distance
of nine blocks and threw them into the river. She had to make
several trips. "He died like a dog; now I'll die like a dog," she
said. "I'm glad he's dead, the dog."

I have been admitted to candidacy for the master's degree. I've
had to cook up a new thesis topic: "The mythologies of North
American Nativistic Movements." We have run out of money, so
it may be some time before I can complete the thesis. It seems ex-
pedient that I make some sort of economic adjustment as soon as
possible.

Incidentally, three of my pictures were on view in Goodspeed
Hall in the No Jury Student Art Exhibit there. No one bought
any of them, though I thought my prices were extremely reasonable. Good taste has yet to come to the corn belt.

And now, here is Jane:

Hello, dearhearts—as we look dazedly (too many martinis last night) into the third year of marriage, which all of a sudden loometh ahead, we wish like everything that you were going to be around to share this gay life with us. . . . We miss you very much, dear friends. . . . It is a dismal feeling to start out on a walk of a Sunday afternoon knowing that we won't end up at 4310 Lake Park Ave. . . . I had better not dwell on this subject or I shall become maudlin. . . .

I was interrupted in the middle of a paragraph by the calling up and coming of this nice man from G.E. He was on a trip recruiting men for his public relations dept. and right now it looks very much as though K. will be one of his recruits. The job sounds very good, and as though it has a future, and certainly pays better than a newspaper would. Through it may be K. could get to be a Science Editor on a paper eventually, but without going through the long gruelling experience of reporting. . . . This is all still very much in the IF stage, since we still have to make contact with Bobbs-Merrill, and decide between them. . . . Not half as exciting as Pioneering, but anyhow, it is a form of progress. Something is bound to happen soon. My husband and your cousin is working himself to a frazzle at the job he has now—days off are rare, and we haven't had a Sunday together for weeks. For awhile he was on the 4pm to midnight shift, but that's over now. It was Wild. But it is wonderful experience, we keep telling ourselves.

Bernie called a few nights ago unexpectedly, and he and Bow and Petie are in Indy for a week. He's coming here tomorrow (I think) and then we are all going to Indy and have a big reunion. We just this minute made this plan, since also just this minute we got a letter from Col. Moorhead (the man from Bobbs-Merrill) saying he'll pay K's expenses if K will come there to talk to him! Is not this all exciting—and killing birds with stones, too. I have never met Bow, and K. has never met Petie, and none of them have ever met Mark . . . Wheeeeeeeeeeee!

Speaking of MARK—he is progressing but handsomely. He is

getting Huge—15 lbs, 12 oz. already, and he does the most wonderful things, like laughing out loud. He only eats three times a
day, just like us, which astonishes me, but is all he wants, and
eats all sorts of things like meat and vegetables, and cereal, and
fruit. . . . He is an eternal joy, as you three know so well. . . . And
how is KIT???? Please now, reciprocate in kind by bragging back
at us about our wonderful god-child. . . . Does he walk yet? How
did he take the trip? How did you all take the trip, for that matter? Kiss your beautiful child for us, and give him a happy drool
from his cousin Mark. I think Kit would be more interested in
Mark now that he makes noises. . . . Would that they could grow
up together. . . .

The enclosed picture is the only moderately good one we've
taken yet. Have you ever seen such a tummy? This was taken
over a month ago, so he's changed still more. . . . I hope you are
busily taking pictures of Kit and yourselves and the beautiful
scenery, of course, and will send them to us. . . .

And now I must go marketing, or we will go hungry. . . . We
are anxiously awaiting word from you. I hope all is going well,
and cabins are beginning to sprout all over the landscape, and
you are all well and happy.

Goodbye for now, and lots love, XXX
      K and J and M

                                                  October 15, 1947
                                                  Alplaus, NY

To Kurt Vonnegut, Sr.

*Vonnegut had moved with his family to Alplaus, New York, outside
Schenectady, after accepting the job at General Electric.*

Dear Pop:
    Your eldest son has treated your youngest like a prince. God
bless him for that. I own a home now. Albeit humble, it's ours,

and we'll love it I'm sure. And it's not so humble as the $7000
I'm paying for it. I'm selling 2½% bonds to get the money. I want
no debt. This is the cheapest way for me to finance our home,
and no recession can take it from us. It's a good little house, well
built, and pleasant to see. Please come soon to examine it at your
leisure.

Our furniture is in Bernard's barn, and moving it by his trailer
will give us one helluvan appetite and double hernias this next
week-end. Our new G.E. refrigerator came today. Our stove
should be here in a week or so. Bernard and I are examining automatic washers with more than casual interest. The Bendix will
probably do more to lower the maternal death rate than did twi-
light sleep. If an automatic washer were to displace the commercial laundry and diaper service, Jane and I would have the gadget
paid for in less than a year [. . .]

I have received a cordial letter from the Anthropology Department at Chicago, saying that I may take my Master's finals at
whatever Eastern university I choose. I shall probably have the
examinations, ten hours of them, proctored by Bernard's tenant,
Bob Finholt of Union. That will be in December, I think. The thesis is another matter. It will take a while longer. I'm hoping to be
sent to New York on business so I can do work in the Columbia
Library.

Perhaps you saw the news accounts that mentioned Bernard
as being aboard the hurricane-busting B-17. This was a news-
man's mistake. Bernard got into the farewell picture but not into
the plane.

I left the Middle West for Schenectady because the General
Electric Company offered me a more congenial, better paying job
than did anyone else. And, as Allie and Jim were quick to per-
ceive, people like us cannot afford to live in Indianapolis. Maybe
we'll come back some day—but not now. I think we'll do a more
honest job of living away from what will always be home.

I like my job. I'm not sorry that I took it, for it's better than I
expected. It has an agreeable dignity to it, and demands of me a

certain craftsmanship in which I can take pride. That, you'll agree, is important. Moreover, I'm earning, for the first time, enough to support my wife and child. And I'll have the will and time and energy to write what I please when my work is done. . . .

                                                  November 28, 1947
                                                  Schenectady, NY
To Alex Vonnegut

Kurt later wrote this explanation to the literary critic Jerome Klinkowitz and others who were writing about his work and had questioned him about the background of the letter to his uncle Alex and its aftermath:

"I had just come to work from Chicago as a flack for General Electric, where Bernard was a celebrity, thanks to his discovery that particles of silver iodine can sometimes precipitate super-cooled clouds as snow and rain.

"Uncle Alex had somehow seen a syndicated photograph of Bernard, credited to the Schenectady Gazette, *and had written that paper, enclosing a dollar for the print. The* Gazette *had gotten the picture from my new employer, the News Bureau of General Electric. The* Gazette *sent the request to my new employer, and my new boss handed it to me.*

"I supposed mistakenly that Uncle Alex knew of my situation, and would recognize the infamous name Guy Fawkes as a pseudonym, and would understand that the letter was a delightful family joke. He in fact blew his stack, took the letter to a lawyer, asking what legal steps he might take to regain his self-respect, and promised to write a letter to the President of GE, telling him he had an employee who did not know the value of a dollar. Before he could take such steps, somebody else told him who Guy Fawkes was, and where I was, and that I was surely the author."

GENERAL ELECTRIC COMPANY

GENERAL OFFICE SCHENECTADY, N. Y.

1 River Road

Schenectady 5, N. Y.

Dear Mr. Vonnegut:

Mr. Edward Themak, city editor for the *Schenectady Gazette,* has referred your letter of November 26th to me.

The photograph of General Electric's Dr. Bernard Vonnegut originated from our office. However, we have no more prints in our files, and the negative is in the hands of the United States Signal Corps. Moreover, we have a lot more to do than piddle with penny-ante requests like yours.

We do have some other photographs of the poor man's Steinmetz, and I may send them to you in my own sweet time. But do not rush me. "Wee bit proud," indeed! Ha! Vonnegut! Ha! This office made your nephew, and we can break him in a minute—like an egg shell. So don't get in an uproar if you don't get the pictures in a week or two.

Also—one dollar to the General Electric Company is as the proverbial fart in a wind storm. Here it is back. Don't blow it all in one place.

Very truly yours,

Press Section

Guy Fawkes: GENERAL NEWS BUREAU

June 24, 1949

Alplaus, NY

To Knox Burger

Knox Burger was fiction editor of Collier's, *and he not only published Vonnegut's first short story but also became a significant mentor and friend. In his* Paris Review *interview decades later, Kurt wrote that Knox "got me a couple of agents who were as shrewd about storytell-*

ing as he was." The agents were Kenneth Littauer, who had preceded
Knox as fiction editor of Collier's, *and Max Wilkinson, who had been*
a story editor for MGM.

In the same interview, Vonnegut said, "And let it be put on record
here that Knox Burger, who is about my age, discovered and encour-
aged more good young writers than any other editor of his time."
Vonnegut dedicated his 1968 short-story collection, Welcome to the
Monkey House: *"For Knox Burger. Ten days older than I am. He has*
been a very good father to me."

Dear Knox:

George Burns, who, never having read anything of mine, takes
a casual interest in my writing career, allowed as how he had a
friend on *Collier's* fiction staff who might be able to give me some
help. The friend turned out to be you.

This information cleared up a mystery of several months'
standing—a not wholly unjust pencil message on the bottom of a
rejection slip: "This is a little sententious for us. You're not the
Kurt Vonnegut who worked on the *Cornell Sun* in 1942, are
you?" It was signed by Owen Buyer, Orme Bruyes, or Dunk
Briges, all persons unknown to me.

In reply to your question: yes, I am the Kurt Vonnegut. I am
glad to know that you are the Knox Burger, and that you are
doing so well for yourself.

Sorry you didn't care for the story. I got a typewritten letter
back on it from the *Post. Story* has now had it for a month.
You're right. It was a dog.

I have since finished a 20,000-word novelette, and begun another, which will probably wind up at about 12,000 words. Has
the new *Collier's* any use for pieces of such lengths?

I plan to be in New York Tuesday and Wednesday of next
week. What are the chances of having lunch with you?

Yours truly,

Kurt Vonnegut

October 28, 1949

[Alplaus, NY]

To Kurt Vonnegut, Sr.

*The first short story Vonnegut sold was "Report on the Barnhouse
Effect," which appeared in* Collier's *on February 11, 1950.*

Decades later, Vonnegut recounted (in Fates Worse Than Death:
An Autobiographical Collage) *that while this story "is no milestone in
literature . . . it looms like Stonehenge beside my own little footpath
from birth to death." He wrote that his father glued cheerful messages
to pieces of Masonite and protected them with varnish; he did that
with this letter from Kurt, and on the back of that piece of Masonite
he glued a message, "in his own lovely hand," a quotation from* The
Merchant of Venice:

> An oath, an oath, I have an oath in Heaven:
> Shall I lay perjury on my soul?

*Kurt added: "The letter is signed with my first initial, which he often
called me."*

Dear Pop:

   I sold my first story to *Collier's*. Received my check ($750
minus a 10% agent's commission [from the Littauer and Wilkinson agency]) yesterday noon. It now appears that two more of my
works have a good chance of being sold in the near future.

   I think I'm on my way. I've deposited my first check in a savings account and, as and if I sell more, will continue to do so
until I have the equivalent of one year's pay at GE. Four more
stories will do it nicely, with cash to spare (something we never
had before). I will then quit this goddamn nightmare job, and
never take another one so long as I live, so help me God.

   I'm happier than I've been for a good many years.

   Love.

   K

THE FIFTIES

His job in public relations for General Electric not only provided Kurt with a salary to support himself and his family, it also gave him ideas for short stories as well as his first novel, *Player Piano*.

As Vonnegut later explained in his *Paris Review* interview, the payment of $750 for his story "was six weeks' pay at G.E. I wrote another, and he [Knox Burger] paid me nine hundred and fifty dollars, and suggested that it was perhaps time for me to quit GE." Kurt took the advice and moved to Osterville on Cape Cod. His price for a story eventually "got up to twenty-nine hundred a crack," he told his interviewers. "Think of that."

No matter what Vonnegut was paid for his stories, it wasn't regular, much less guaranteed. When I met Kurt for the first time in 1963, he looked back fondly on what seemed like "a magical year" in those early days, when all the stories that he sent out were sold, but there was also a year when none of them sold. "My cash cows the slick magazines were put out of business by TV," he later explained. *Player Piano* was published in 1952, selected by the Doubleday Fiction Book Club in 1953, and reprinted the following year under the title *Utopia 14*. Knox Burger, who had left *Collier's* to become an editor of paperback originals at Dell, published *The Sirens of Titan* in 1959. Despite these publications, Vonnegut had to take an assortment of jobs to keep afloat during the decade.

One of Kurt's ill-fated efforts to earn money in this period was a tryout to write for *Sports Illustrated,* a new magazine of Time

Inc. He was assigned to write an article about a racehorse that had bolted when the starting gun went off at Aqueduct and jumped over the railing of the infield. After thinking about it for an hour or so, Vonnegut wrote, "The horse jumped over the fucking fence," walked out of the office, and went home.

At one point he tried inventing a board game, but it didn't sell. Perhaps the oddest and most challenging of his odd jobs was becoming the owner and manager of SAAB Cape Cod, an automobile dealership in West Barnstable, where he had bought a house. He wrote in the introduction to the 1999 collection of stories *Bagombo Snuff Box* that "If you left a Saab parked for more than a day, the oil settled like maple syrup to the bottom of the gas tank. When you started it up, the exhaust would black out a whole neighborhood. One time I blacked out Woods Hole that day. I was coughing like everybody else. I couldn't imagine where all the smoke had come from."

His son, Mark, recalled in his memoir, *Just Like Someone Without Mental Illness Only More So,* "When Kurt tried to sell Saabs, he usually did the test drive with the prospective customer in the passenger seat. I tried to tell him not to go around corners so fast, especially if the customers were middle-aged or older, but he thought it was the best way to explain front-wheel drive. Some of them were shaken and green. He didn't sell a lot of cars. 'Maybe you should just let them drive,' I suggested. . . . I'll always remember my father as the world's worst car salesman who couldn't get a job teaching English at Cape Cod Community College." He did get a job teaching at a school for disturbed teenagers and writing copy at a Boston ad agency. He was turned down for a Guggenheim Fellowship in 1954.

Kurt and Jane conducted a Great Books course on Cape Cod, and from reading *The Odyssey* he got an idea for a play, which he called *Penelope.* He hoped it would be such a big hit that it would "free me to write plays for the rest of my life." The play ran for one week at the Orleans Arena Theatre on the Cape.

In 1957 the family's net income from writing—including a loan from Kurt's agents—came to $3,909.86, which was an improvement over the previous year. The difference between that and what the family needed to live on was made up from an inheritance from Kurt's father and his working at the Boston ad agency for seven months—as recounted by Jane in her 1987 book, *Angels Without Wings: A Courageous Family's Triumph over Tragedy* (published under her newly married name, Jane Vonnegut Yarmolinsky). "We didn't let ourselves think about the economics of what had to be done," she wrote. "We just did it. What we were really living on was hope."

In the midst of this already precarious picture, in 1958 Kurt and Jane took in the four suddenly orphaned children of his older sister, Alice, and her husband, James Adams. Within twenty-four hours of each other, Alice had died of cancer at age forty-one, and her husband was killed when his commuter train crashed off an open drawbridge in New Jersey. Kurt went to Rumson, New Jersey, and brought the four children and two dogs back to live with him, Jane, and their three children on Cape Cod. They raised the oldest three boys, and the baby was taken in a year later by an Alabama relative of James Adams.

Though the three Adams boys became part of the family, they were never legally adopted, as is often assumed and written. "That would have taken a lot of time and money, which we didn't have," Mark Vonnegut explained to me. Kurt, Jane, and the rest of the family often used the term "adopted" as the easiest way to explain it to the outside world.

The Adams boys they took in became known—in what was an affectionate term within the family—as "the orphans."

"In the ten years prior to the orphans," Mark wrote in his memoir, "he [Kurt] had published one novel and a bunch of short stories without coming close to making a living at it. The roughly ten years disrupted by orphans produced *The Sirens of Titan, Mother Night, Cat's Cradle, God Bless You, Mr. Rosewater, Welcome to the Monkey House,* and *Slaughterhouse-Five.* Not so bad."

February 16, 1950

Alplaus, NY

To Miller Harris

S. Miller Harris had written for The Cornell Sun *during the time that Kurt also wrote for the paper and in WWII served in the infantry in Europe. After the war he began writing short stories and sending them to magazines while working at the Eagle Shirtmakers, founded by his great-grandfather Jacob Miller in 1867. He published a short story in* Harper's *magazine in 1948 and a humorous golf story in* Collier's *in 1952. Harris told me in 2011 (while on his way to a menswear conference in Las Vegas) that he had "tried to write nights and weekends in the early years. Lonely mission soon aborted. Shirt business consumed my days. All seven of them." He served as CEO of Eagle Shirtmakers from 1946 until 1985, and at ninety was "still designing and marketing upscale shirts. Fun. Easy. Keeps me young." Harris and Kurt remained friends and corresponded intermittently throughout Kurt's life.*

Fred Simon Rosenau was a friend of Jane Cox's at Swarthmore and served with the Office of War Information in the Far East during WWII. He met Kurt at the University of Chicago and then worked in publishing for Doubleday in New York City.

Dear Miller:

Yours of February 8th gratefully received and pleasantly at hand.

I have been keeping sort of vague track of you through one Fred Rosenau, a small acquaintance I made at the University of Chicago. He says you run a shirt factory. Then again, he's paranoid. He thinks he runs Doubleday & Co., Inc.

There is also Knox: he says you wrote a very funny story about golf (go ahead and piddle while the world's stockpiling H-bombs), which he bought. Since my admittedly flashy beginning with "Report on the Barnhouse Effect", I have been banging out reams of tripe in a lunatic get-rich-quick scheme. It hasn't panned out. I think Knox figured he had a discovery for a minute there, but now he's beginning to look to Yaddo again. Shit on him, boy.

Since my father is a poor but honest architect, I don't have a shirt factory. I do have a wife and two kids, though. So I work for General Electric, writing publicity for them:

SCHENECTADY, N.Y., Feb. 16—General Electric engineers have developed a stupefying new electrical device which will make the second coming of Christ a matter of mere academic interest, it was announced here today. . . . etc.

Cynical, cynical little hack,

I will knife you in the back.

It is a terrible job, so writing stories for a living is a very attractive notion. It's possible that I'll be able to make the grade in the next year. God, I sure hope so. In which case, I will, of course, write a novel about G-E. It'd be about 20th Century Man, proving that he is happy—and that the glum people, like us, are a pathetic and noisy minority who write.

I am not a communist. My squad sergeant was. Philadelphia boy in fact. [. . .] You mustn't tell. He's the poor man's Alger Hiss. Worked for the Power and Light Company there. [. . .]

Since seeing you last, I have been an A.S.T.P. engineer, an infantryman, a P.O.W. in Germany, a graduate student of anthropology (sea shells) at Chicago, a police reporter in Chicago, and now a public relations man (How the hell are you, you old sonofagun. Cigarette? Martini?) . . .

February 28, 1950

Alplaus, NY

To Miller Harris

The "Harper's piece" Kurt refers to is the short story Miller Harris wrote called "Brassard, Mourning, Official," which was published in Harper's.

Dear Miller:

O.K., so people who want to write for a living are doomed to failure. I have other angles, about which this letter is.

This letter is to Harris the shirtmaker. I have a proposition for a man who can manufacture and market bowties. Can you? I know nothing about the garment trade, so perhaps the whole thing is preposterous.

Anyway, I have an idea for a bowtie. If you heard this idea, I think you would agree that it would be a sensational teen-ager fad for a few wild, lucrative weeks.

Does this sort of thing interest you? The tie would cost virtually nothing to make—no mechanical gadgets, no wires, no electronic tubes. It's just a plain, ordinary bowtie (no, it doesn't glow in the dark, dammit), put together like any other bowtie. But there is one thing about it that would make it a natural for promotion.

Are you interested? If you are, and if the idea is any good, how will you reward me?

* * *

You don't discourage me about writing. I have a pitch, which I think will pay off. I have no scruples about selling to slicks. I would be very content if I could do it consistently. I hope to build a reputation as a science-fiction writer. That's the pitch. We'll see.

* * *

This tie item is a very hot one. If you're a man of any enterprise and bowtie manufacturing facilities, you'll be wise to write at once for details, samples, etc.

* * *

What kind of shirts do you make? Can you give me a factory price on some blue, oxford cloth, button-down, 15–35's?

* * *

Doubleday wants me to expand "Barnhouse" into a full novel.
That way, I could make another $750.

* * *

Missed your *Harper's* piece. Heard it was fine. Will look it up.
Kurt

Undated, 1950

[Alplaus, NY]

To Miller Harris

*This letter to Miller Harris concerns Kurt's idea for manufacturing
bow ties and would seem to have been written between the letter to
Harris of February 28, 1950, and his letter to Harris of May 19, 1950.*

Dear Miller:
   Like I said, I don't know anything about the garment industry,
so maybe this is ridiculous.
   I don't think so, though, teen-agers being what they are. Also,
As neckties go (however the hell it is neckties go), this one ought
to be about as cheap to manufacture as possible. It's nothing but
a piece of ribbon. No lining, no stitching, no nothing special.
   I made this one myself. It could doubtless be improved upon
by professionals.
   It is rather flashy in color, don't you think? That is the only
color you would manufacture.
   What will sell this bowtie (I keep telling myself) for a couple
of fast weeks is this, old friend:
   This here bowtie is made out of the ribbon the Atomic Energy
Commission uses as its official marker for dangerously-
radioactive areas.
   Atomic, see?
   Marks off "hot areas", get it?
   So we make up a batch; get them out to the wholesalers, then

cut loose with the promotion. One way or the other, it will all be over in a hurry.

Will invest.

Hell, you ought to be able to make one of these things for a dime, easy. Not only would you (we) be selling a tie with special merchandising features, you'd be undercutting the competition on bowties in general. With the Atomic gimmick, you can make them as lousy as you damn please. At a retail price of $ .50, they'd go like hotcakes. We would do a landoffice business. We would be making money hand-over-fist. Etc.

I just equipped this tie with a clip for the hell of it. Probably cheaper with an elastic, eh?

A quick lick.

I am now kicking myself for letting you in on this.

Regards

Kurt

May 19, 1950
Alplaus, NY

To MILLER HARRIS

The story Kurt sold to Collier's *was "All the King's Horses," pub-lished February 10, 1951, and included in Kurt's first book of stories,* Canary in a Cat House, *published in 1961. It was later included in the short-story collection* Welcome to the Monkey House *in 1968. "Der Arme Dolmetscher," an uncollected nonfiction piece, was published in* The Atlantic *in July 1955.*

Dear Miller:

[. . .] Vonnegut sold another story to *Collier's* and still another to the *Atlantic*. [. . .] The *Atlantic* piece is the funniest thing I ever read. Actually, the thing has been a kind of curse. In the evenings, when I should be writing, I'm generally howling over my carbon copy. You'll die. And you said writing doesn't pay. All I have to do is write ten stories a year for the *Atlantic,* and I'll have $1250 coming out of my ears.

I, too, have a serial, 18,000 words, finished, being typed, and murder. I can never get women into my stories. Let's agree right off that I'm not a fruit (or just ever so little incipient like the best and worst of us), and then try to explain *that* one. [. . .]

Kurt

October, 1950

Alplaus, NY

To Miller Harris

Vonnegut's story "Thanasphere" was published in Collier's, *September 2, 1950.*

Dear Miller:

[. . .] That was nice of you to read "Thanasphere." I don't think it was too hot. What went before and what will be appearing shortly are a good bit better to my way of thinking. Burger is charming to my face, but is giving my offerings pretty shabby treatment. With my manuscripts (a good, substantial mediocre output), he plays like he's choosing the O. Henry collection for next year. The mortality is awful.

God knows you should be depressed, watching the Phillies. Otherwise things (today) don't sound so terrible to me. You'll start writing again, and it'll be first rate. You'll be a bigtime writer *and* a bigtime shirt manufacturer, and won't that be nice?

Bring your beautiful wife up here sometime. It isn't much of a trip, we'd love to see you, and you could check over the Arrow operation in Troy. I offer this suggestion with high hopes that you'll take it seriously. I haven't had friends since the start of World War II, and would like to develop one or two for appearance's sake. [. . .]

Kurt

October 31, 1950
Alplaus, NY

To Knox Burger

It appears from the letter that someone at Collier's *had objected to the ethnic identity of the villainous guerrilla leader, named "Pi Ying," in the story "White King" that was published as "All the King's Horses."*

The joke signing of the name "George Sokolsky" over his own name was a reference to the Hearst newspaper columnist of the time who was a fervent anti-Communist of the far right and supporter of Senator Joe McCarthy.

Dear Knox:

Enclosed find a revision of "White King." If you have Mr. Anthony's memo at hand, you'll see that I have made an effort (successful in each case, I think) to do something about every one of his explicit comments.

The business I discussed on the phone with you tonight can best be amplified over a couple of drinks sometime. I am a brilliant rationalizer over a couple of drinks.

First off, leave me point out that nobody in the village or anywhere else would wince if the villain of my story were Baron Wolfgang von Steinhaus Kriegswald, scourge of the infamous S.S., ca. 1942.

Second off, I am a registered Democrat, pro-Fair and New Deal, distressed by the new anti-subversive laws, hate McCarthy, enflamed by Communist smears on liberals—etc., etc. But, dammit, Knox, I don't like Communist Russia any more than I did Nazi Germany. There are some 3,000 Americans dead in Korea, killed in a chess game with Russia looking on. That is a lot of dead people and a plenty sickening situation. I have sixteen on my chessboard, which is peanuts. Them as may say I am insensitive to put an inflammatory thing like "White King" on the market are, perhaps, too insensitive to a casualty list as long as King Kong's arm.

In Christ,
    George Sokolsky
    Kurt Vonnegut, Jr.

February 11, 1951
Alplaus, NY

To MILLER HARRIS

Dear Miller:

Thought, rather fuzzily, about something I want to add to my recent letter to you. It's this business about the school: school of painting, school of poetry, school of music, school of writing. For a couple of years after the war I was a graduate student in the Anthropology Department at the University of Chicago. At the instigation of a bright and neurotic instructor named Slotkin, I got interested in the notion of the school (I'm going to explain what I mean in a minute), and decided to do a thesis on the subject. I did about 40 pages of the thing, based on the Cubist School in Paris, and then got told by the faculty that I'd better pick something more strictly anthropological. They suggested rather firmly (with Slotkin abstaining) that I interest myself in the Indian Ghost Dance of 1894. Shortly thereafter I ran out of money and signed on with G-E, and I never did get past the note-taking stage on the Ghost Dance business (albeit damn interesting).

But Slotkin's notion of the importance of the school stuck with me, and it now seems pertinent to you, me, Knox, McQuade, and anybody else whose literary fortunes we take a personal interest in. What Slotkin said was this: no man who achieved greatness in the arts operated by himself; he was top man in a group of like-minded individuals. This works out fine for the cubists, and Slotkin had plenty of good evidence for its applying to Goethe, Thoreau, Hemingway, and just about any-body you care to name.

If it isn't 100% true, it's true enough to be interesting—and maybe helpful.

The school gives a man, Slotkin said, the fantastic amount of guts it takes to add to culture. It gives him morale, esprit de corps, the resources of many brains, and—maybe most important—one-sidedness with assurance. (My reporting what Slotkin said four years ago is pretty subjective—so let's say Von-negut, a Slotkin derivative, is saying this.) About this one-sidedness: I'm convinced that no one can amount to a damn in the arts if he becomes sweetly reasonable, seeing all sides of a picture, forgiving all sins.

Slotkin also said a person in the arts can't help but belong to some school—good or bad. I don't know what school you belong to. My school is presently comprised of Littauer & Wilkinson (my agents), and Burger, and nobody else. For want of support from any other quarter, I write for them—high grade, slick bombast.

I've been on my own for five weeks now. I've rewritten a nov-elette, and turned out a short-short and a couple of 5000-worders. Some of them will sell, probably. This is Sunday, and the question arises, what'll I start tomorrow? I already know what the answer is. I also know it's the wrong answer. I'll start some-thing to please L&W, Inc., and Burger, and, please, God, MGM.

The obvious alternative is, of course, something to please the *Atlantic, Harper's,* or the *New Yorker.* To do this would be to turn out something after the fashion of somebody-or-other, and I might be able to do it. I say might. It amounts to signing on with any of a dozen schools born ten, twenty, thirty years ago. The kicks are based largely on having passed off a creditable counter-feit. And, of course, if you appear in the *Atlantic* or *Harper's* or the *New Yorker,* by God you *must* be a writer, because everybody says so. This is poor competition for the fat checks from the slicks. For want of anything more tempting, I'll stick with money.

So, having said that much, where am I? In Alplaus, New York, I guess, wishing I could pick up some fire and confidence and originality and fresh prejudices from somewhere. As Slotkin said, these things are group products. It isn't a question of finding a Messiah, but of a group's creating one—and it's hard work, and takes a while.

If this sort of thing is going on somewhere (not in Paris, says Tennessee Williams), I'd love to get in on it. I'd give my right arm to be enthusiastic. God knows there's plenty to write about— more now than ever before, certainly. You're defaulting, I'm defaulting—everybody's defaulting, seems to me.

If Slotkin's right, maybe the death of the institution of friendship is the death of innovation in the arts.

This letter is sententious crap, shot full of self-pity. But it's the kind of letter writers seem to write; and since I quit G-E, if I'm not a writer then I'm nothing.

Yours truly,

Kurt

February 26, 1951

[Alplaus, NY]

To Miller Harris

The "things bound into scratch pads" were standard rejection slips from The New Yorker, *one of which was enclosed with this letter.*

Dear Miller:

I've had several hundred of these things bound into scratch pads.

My wife and I will be in New York City from March 29 through March 31. Is it possible that you will be there, too? We could probably engineer Burger's picking up a check that would knock down Crowell–Collier another half point.

I took the liberty of recommending FOR THE LAST TIME (or something that sounded a whole lot like that) to Knox. I expect you'll be getting pretty quick action now.*

Kurt

*Sold two to him myself on Friday.

> Undated, marked Winter, 1951
> [Osterville, MA]

To Knox Burger

The play Penelope *was performed for one week at the Orleans Arena Theatre on Cape Cod.*

Dear Knox:

I received a telepathic message last Saturday at 10 a.m. that you were being operated on. Anything to it? The 7th, that is.

[. . .] My play is all finished. About 100 copies have been mailed out to famous actors. Apparently I did O.K. on the revision. Now I'm back on short stories. They are cruel little bastards. I hate them. I will hear about the Guggenheim in early March. If I get it, I will finish up another play that's fairly close to being done right now.

I sure do like plays. If *Penelope* goes over, I will have taken the giant step that will free me to write plays for the rest of my life. If not, I won't have taken the giant step. If not, so what? I am a nihilist.

Regards to the gang at Sardi's—

Kurt

April 12, 1952
Osterville, MA

To Knox Burger

Dear Knox:

Thanks for your letter of April 10. I will go on writing short stories, and Littauer will go on showing them to you, and perhaps you'll go on finding some that fill your current needs.

I don't think you got stung on "Tomorrow and Tomorrow and Tomorrow." I think it is funny and not far from an important truth. The Schwartzes are hopeless and helpless the way Sad Sack was hopeless and helpless, the way Charlie Chaplin's little tramp was hopeless and helpless. Sad Sack and the little tramp are the really beloved American folk heroes (for America here and now), not Paul Bunyan and Colonel Flip Corkin and Andrew Carnegie.

This country is being managed to death, being public related to death. You say, "I don't want you to be alarmed at all this." Well, taken along with everything else, it is terribly alarming and depressing.

If, in trying to be a weighty thinker, I have been a crashing bore, then that is a professional matter, and I should be ashamed, and should humbly promise to try to do better. And I will try. But the Commandant's Desk was buried because it was critical of the Army (mildly, oh so mildly), "Tomorrow and Tomorrow and Tomorrow" because it did not seem to conform to accepted mores; the first version of the cave story because it was pessimistic . . . How can humor be written without pathos? How can problems be pointed out without criticism? How can new ideas be introduced without contrasting with old ones? Who are the good editorialists that I should study in order to become a good editorialist myself?

Wild as my stories may be, I would never make World War III seem little more hazardous than and as interesting as an automobile trip from New York to Los Angeles in a Stutz Bearcat.

"Don't touch any of the atom-bombed buildings, Angel—you'll get your lily-white hands dirty on the charcoal."

"Don't kiss me now—here comes somebody."

"Why, who's that scrambling over the rubble toward us but Jacob Malik, wearing a zoot-suit, chewing gum, playing with a yo-yo, and rooting for the Dodgers. Have some of mom's apple pie, Jake."

Well, Knox, I can't think of a letter more mis-addressed than this one. I don't know why I should be writing you all this (coals to Newcastle), except that yours of April 10 compels an answer, and I wouldn't be such a damn fool as to say anything but "Yessir, you're so right, sir," to Mr. Anthony. I want more *Collier's* money, need more *Collier's* money, and will do my best to get it.

It doesn't appear that I can go on much longer making a living as a short story writer. After the novel comes out, picking its way through beds of tender mores and folkways with the grace of a ballet dancer, I hope to get a job in Hollywood. I've got a wife and two kids, and have to do something that will bring in money steadily.

K.L. [Kenneth Littauer] has a new short story critical of American big business practices, and will have another in a similar vein in about two weeks. After that he'll get one maybe you'll like. About two guys battling to the death over a woman, and doing it on present day Cape Cod, wearing mediaeval armor and in the shadow of a reproduction of a castle about two miles from here. I dunno—maybe you'll buy it. I'll make the bad guy a Fabian socialist.

Just finished up page proofs on the book. It'll be out in July, I hear.

Jane and I will probably be in New York for a few days in May—at which time we'll come to see you.

I should own a shirt factory.

Where's the *New Yorker* for our generation?

I'd like to develop as a writer, but who's got the bar-bells and the gymnasium?

Supreme irony, Luce calling ours the silent generation.

Yours truly,

Kurt Vonnegut, Jr.

May 29, 1952
Osterville, MA

TO KNOX BURGER

White Collar *was a study of the American middle class by the well-known Columbia University sociologist C. Wright Mills.*

Dear Knox:

[. . .] *Collier's,* in taking its stand in favor of big business, has sided with one of two forms of socialism being forced on the people of this country. Only question is who's going to administer the enervating paternalism, the humiliating paternalism. As is shrewdly pointed out in *White Collar,* bureaucracy is nothing more than modern business practice applied to government. I think big business is a terrible thing for the spirit of the country, as our spirit is the best thing about us. Making us a nation of ass kissers. Only way, or virtually the only way, to get ahead these days. Deadly. Change the title of manager of sales to the Duke of Schenectady, and you start wondering if maybe the Revolutionary War was subversive.

Yours truly,

Kurt Vonnegut, Jr.

July 21, 1952
Osterville, MA

TO KNOX BURGER

The book that Kurt thanks Knox Burger for reading and taking an interest in is Player Piano, *Vonnegut's first novel, published that year by Scribner. "Max" is Max Wilkinson, one of Kurt's original agents along with his partner Kenneth Littauer. Knox has left* Collier's *to become a book editor for Dell, a paperback publisher. "Otis" is Knox Burger's first wife.*

Dear Knox:

It's good of you to read the book and take an interest in it. I'm sorry about its roughnesses and slow passages. So help me God, I didn't know they were there. They wouldn't have been there (in profusion, I guess) if the book had passed through the hands of an editor, but it went from me to the typesetters, [. . .] What roughnesses and slow passages are you talking about? [. . .]

Some enterprising advertising salesman sold Scribner's on advertising the book in S-F magazines, or they wouldn't have thought of it. I took Rosenau to Scribner's so he could give their advertising & publicity set-up the double-0, and he was favorably impressed. Young and enthusiastic and optimistic and energetic, said Rosenau, though inexperienced (in terms of Rosenau). $1500 has been appropriated for them to spread around on ads for the book, and it's going to go to some S-F magazines, *The New Yorker,* the *Saturday Review,* and the *N.Y. Times Book Review.* And there's a fair chance, I hear, of our getting a couple of $35,000 pages from Life for nothing. Nothing sure about that, of course. I saw a G-E career broken once, because a guy went around telling all the vice presidents that he'd placed a big G-E story with Life. It's been about five years since Life accepted it, and any day now . . .

I guess the jacket is pretty dead. I was on it originally, but was taken off because the green made me look like death warmed over. That's what they said.

I'd love to make Max sweat, Knox, but I've never got it straight what it is he's supposed to do for me. I hope to become a more difficult client as time goes on, but right now I don't know what to ask for.

Exciting new things happening to *Collier's.* A fiction folio. What alarms me is the ease with which the folio may be detached from the rest of the book. And so many surgeons looking for a quick and easy reputation. Fictionectomy. Dakin's incision. Literary jim-crowism (step to the back of the bus).

Maybe it's a fine thing. The fiction folio in the 7/26 issue looked more substantial and interesting than the article folio. As long as fiction is going to be set apart, the point of separation in the book should be more dramatic than it is. I didn't find the little red box on page 42 until the third trip through. If the articles get any worse, the fiction folio should secede.

For $20,000, I will put the article side back on its feet during the next year. I was editor of the General Electric Monogram, which never lost a subscriber. This is a firm offer. Love to Otis.

Kurt

February 9, 1953

[Osterville, MA]

To Knox Burger

Sport:

Things are getting somewhat sticky with me mentally, and I would appreciate any words you might have picked up down there in the city with respect to treatment.

The nut of the matter is that I can't write anymore, and I'm not very nice to my family anymore either.

This I would have taken up with you during my last visit, if the opportunity had come up—which it didn't.

You and Littauer & Wilkinson, Inc., and F.R. Rosenau have small patience, I gather, with head doctors. But here I am, anyway, seemingly in need of one.

I don't imagine things, understand, and I don't do strange things, and I don't write incoherently. It's just that I don't seem to be very nice or useful or enthusiastic anymore.

So, be a good chap, will you, and tell me if you ever knew anybody who got any good out of psychotherapy. Case histories of writers would be most to the point.

Kurt

February, 1953
[Osterville, MA]

To Knox Burger

Vivien Kellems was a manufacturer who gained fame for fighting the U.S. government over paying withholding taxes and was a heroine to tax protesters. In 1952 she published Toil, Taxes and Trouble.

Dear Knox:

I had my eighty-foot driveway shoveled out by two ten-year-olds so I could go have my head examined by a psychiatrist in S. Dennis. Are people supposed to keep stuff like that a secret? Is telling about that like George Burns saying, "We don't have any kids yet, but, brother, you should see us try?" Well—shit, I say. It's o.k. to be in bad taste as long as it's interesting.

I go see the guy tomorrow. That's the first time—tomorrow. [. . .]

Thanks for the clipping about the Soviet youth. You sent me another one about that Cornell prick who was so far right he had to forge Vivien Kellems' signature on his campaign literature. I never told you, but I was in the Cornell Club bar for about an hour, eating peanuts by myself, while he talked at the top of his lungs to a guy I took to be his lawyer. Nobody else was there, and he didn't seem to care what the hell I heard. He sounded crazy to me. He was talking about how he had some youth organizations crying about the spot he was in. He seemed to think the whole thing was pretty damn funny—incredibly funny. That's it: he couldn't believe it, it was so funny. Nuts as a fruitcake. Talk about insignias, too. Couldn't get the details.

Cripes—I sure hope this guy can unblock me. All this farting and stomping and running in place is driving me nuts. I know in my heart I am ready to be a perfectly peachy writer.

A winner of two Peabody Awards, 42, staggered into Barnstable to take up permanent residence. Got fired from an ad agency for telling a nightschool class you had to be a big meathead to get along in advertising. He said his boss was boss because he was the biggest meathead of all. The talk was taken down on tape, and somebody thought it was so refreshing, he sent it off to a trade journal. The journal ran it in full. The guy's boss said he was firing the guy not because he was offended, but because some of the clients might misunderstand. This guy says he'll kill himself before he'll go back to Madison Avenue. My guess is he'll kill himself anyway. He wanted to know didn't anybody in Barnstable play chess, and I said I did, so he came over and killed a quart of Bellow's Partner's Choice and beat me. Beat me by a hair, I'm proud to say.

Kurt

February 20, 1953
Osterville, MA

To KNOX BURGER

Dear Knox:

Prolific son of a bitch that I am, I finished a short story yesterday, and so am in a position today to answer my mail. I have alread disposed of Lt. Charles A. Rogers ("I'd like to mention in particular the fine emotional effect you produced in the short chapter on Hacketts, the soldier.") and Ruth May of the English MacMillan Co. ("I am sending along the Macmillan Spring Catalogue with the blurb of your book on page 7.").

And now, old friend, I come to your wise and helpful letter of Friday, the 13th. It's a lovely letter in many ways, Knox. It's a wonderfully generous letter.

I'm O.K. again, I think—and, all things considered, I don't suppose I was very sick minded. ("Them was his exact words, calm as a cucumber, just two days afore he run hog wild with the meat cleaver.") [. . .]

Jane and I are running a Great Books Course in Osterville,

and the reading last week was Plato's *Republic,* Books I & II. In Book I., Socrates talks to an old duffer about what old age is like. The old duffer says in effect (I can't put my hands on the book just now) that he feels as though he'd been freed from a cruel and unreasonable master. [. . .]

Spring is coming, and I'm finding that I love this village very much. It's probably home.

Sitting here in the studio, right now, writing a good friend, and writing at my ease, I'm reminded of an uncle (Alex V.), who, after sauerbraten and several schooners of dark beer and quarter cigars, said, "If this isn't good, what is?" He says it often. It's a fine line.

I'll return the books soon.

Burn this letter.

Yours truly,

Kurt

March 6, 1953
Osterville, MA

To Harry Brague

Harry Brague was Kurt's editor at Scribner's, which published Player Piano *the year before. Bennett Cerf was cofounder of Random House and won the landmark court case against government censorship* United States v. One Book Called Ulysses; *Cerf published the unabridged version of the James Joyce classic in the U.S. for the first time. He also published famous writers including William Faulkner, Eugene O'Neill, Truman Capote, and Ayn Rand and gained further fame as a weekly panelist on the TV quiz show* What's My Line?

Dear Harry:

Your letter of March 6 is a warming one, and full of good news, too.

The last time I saw you, I was in New York with the notion of having my head examined. Somehow, the subject never came up.

If I could write another pretty good book, Harry, I would. The trouble seems to be that I'm a compulsive, irrational writer, rarely on top of the creative process, but that my id, or whatever it is that Hemingway and Faulkner get in touch with way down deep, down among the dead men, isn't a very interesting one—not even to me.

I'm going to stay away from New York from now on. That saloon around the corner from Scribner's always makes me feel like the dullest bastard on earth, without even dilettante status in the arts. I'll come back when Bennett Cerf taps me, and not before.

I've started several books since the last one, and they've all poohed out. If I got a grip on myself, made myself be a little soldier about them, I suppose I could finish them all. But that's fetishism, I think, writing books to write books.

Right now I'm working on a novella that pleases me and will be finished in about a week. But it's a little thing, too little for a book. Finishing it is about as far ahead as I can see.

Thanks for your encouragement and interest. I appreciate Scribner's investment in me, and hope with the enthusiasm of a vested interest that there will be a handsome payoff. However, 1953 looks like the year of the crashing apathy.

Anyway, I keep trying, and if I get something past page 100, you'll be the first to know. [. . .]

Kurt

August 15, 1953
Osterville, MA

To Harry Brague

The book Kurt is working on is Cat's Cradle, *which Scribner eventually lost interest in and was finally published by Holt, Rinehart and*

Winston in hardcover in 1963 and as a Dell paperback two years later.

Dear Harry:

It's good of you to get me the $500. I'll try to pay it back, and I don't plan to ask for the second $500.

The money will keep me in business here for a few more weeks, and the dream is that something extraordinarily nice will happen in that time. If something nice doesn't happen, then something terrible will happen. I'll have to get a job.

The trouble is that the short stories aren't selling. Until I sell one or two, I can't work on the book, eager as I am to finish it. When you get it, it'll be the whole thing, not half. Maybe around Christmas. Wouldn't that be fine.

Yours truly,

December 11, 1953

To MILLER HARRIS

Dear Miller:

[. . .] I'm happy with Cape Cod. The place is loaded with romantics who've fled the big cities, and they're all wise in interesting and special ways. Me too.

I haven't been in New York for damn near a year. No sense in a man with writer's block going to New York. I've been bathing in hot water and Epsom salts, and finally sold two stories in two weeks to the *Saturday Evening Post,* so maybe I'll show my face down there again after the holidays. Any chance of your being there? New York, I mean. *The Post* is in New York, isn't it? If it isn't New York, it's Dayton, and I'm damned if I'll go to Dayton. Jane and I did a dizzy thing a couple of days ago, and it turned out to be the best lark in years. We went to Harvard for two days. We just walked in and sat down in different classrooms, and nobody came around collecting tickets. Heard Sirokin on

Spengler, A. Schlesinger, Sr. on the Hudson River school of painting, A. Schlesinger, Jr. on Hawthorne and Melville, Handlin on
colonial America's attitude toward European intellectual movements, McClusky on the Supreme Court Decisions relative to Je-
hovah's Witnesses, and so on. More fun than a barrel of
monkeys, till reeled the mind. Best thunderclap came from Spengler, to the effect that science is either true or false, art is either
shallow or deep. Second best came from some Supreme Court
Justice, Jackson, I think, to the effect that one man's right to
swing his fists stops where another man's nose begins.

You'll write someday, Miller. It's in the cards. Be of good
heart.

Kurt

February 7, 1954
Osterville, MA

To Harry Brague

*The book Kurt reports to his editor that he is working on that is
"going to be a good book" is* Cat's Cradle.

Dear Harry:

It's good to hear from you. And welcome to Lewis Benjamin
Brague [Brague's new baby boy].

I've squandered all my time on short stories and scripts that
haven't sold, for the most part. It was a gamble worth
taking—but, like most gambles, it didn't pay off. So I haven't got
a book and I haven't got any money.

Well, neither bitch is quite justified. I've got a little money left,
and I've got a book going. It's going to be a good book, Harry.
We're just all going to have to be patient.

He who travels fastest travels alone, and my wife is pregnant
for the third time.

There's a good chance I'll finish this book this year. I want to finish it very much, and I'm busting to get at it and keep at it all day, every day. But I've got to earn that freedom with short stories.

That's what I'm trying to do now, and I think I'll make it. I've got an office in downtown Osterville now, shared with a C.P.A. I've had it for a week now, and I find my spirits are going up and up and up.

Ha!

Yours truly,

Kurt

March 11, 1954
Osterville, MA

To Harry Brague

Booth Tarkington (1869–1946) was a writer who, like Kurt, lived in Indianapolis and attended Shortridge High School. He was Vonnegut's first literary hero. Tarkington went to Princeton, where he founded the Triangle Club, and after he graduated returned to live in Indianapolis. He won the Pulitzer Prize in 1919 for his novel The Magnificent Ambersons, *which was later made as a movie by Orson Welles. His novel* Penrod and Sam *was compared with Mark Twain's* Tom Sawyer.

Dear Harry:

Just finished reading your pleasant letter of March 9. I was going to write you this morning anyway, to thank you for sending me money far ahead of the contract schedule. A generous and helpful thing to do, believe me.

I seem to be out of the slick short story business completely. I can't do the trick anymore, and wasted 1953 grubbing around the inside of my silk hat for rabbits—in vain.

So, as Ken told you, I've become something much more important—a playwright. Ken has one play now, and will have another in two weeks or so, and I can see two more past that. I'm on a jag, after two dead years, and nothing nicer could possibly happen to a writer. A play jag. The philosophical restrictions of slick short stories finally whipped me. The formal restrictions of plays are delightful and stimulating.

Sure, Harry, I'd love to have you look at the play Ken has now. I didn't know you were interested in plays. It's called *Celeste,* and I think maybe it's pretty funny. I grew up one block away from Booth Tarkington, and sang carols to the old man on Christmas Eve, 1945, a couple of months before he died. *Celeste* is Penrod and Sam brought up to date, in a way—not like Mickey Rooney, and not like the Dead End Kids either.

I haven't lost sight of the novel. I'm pecking at it. I want to do it. It's more important to me than the plays—but the plays offer me the last long shot I've got at becoming solvent enough to become an honest literary man.

I'm pretending I'm Eugene O'Neill, down with T.B. for a year, with nothing to do but write plays. The T.B. fiction isn't far from the truth. My wife is down for nine months with the dry heaves that characterize her pregnancies. I will say my kids are nicer than O'Neill's. As for my play—I'm enclosing a carbon, the only copy I've got, which is pretty rocky in spots, but which will give you an idea of how the play goes.

Kurt

May 7, 1954
Osterville, MA

To KNOX BURGER

Gabriel Heatter was a radio commentator who gained fame during the WWII era for the introduction to his broadcasts: "There's good news tonight." Though he was known for his positive spin on events, Heatter's broadcast about the Army–McCarthy hearings that Kurt heard did not find any such silver lining.

Those hearings of charges and countercharges between the red-baiting Senator Joseph McCarthy and the U.S. Army lasted from March until June of 1954 and were widely broadcast and televised. The hearings were believed to accelerate the downfall of McCarthy, who was condemned by the U.S. Senate on December 2 of that year.

The fall of Dien Bien Phu that May marked the end of French colonial power, when their army was defeated by the Viet Minh communist guerrillas and the stage was set for America's entry into the Vietnam War.

Leah Salisbury was a successful theatrical agent.

Dear Knox:

My tickler file reminds me that I haven't written you for a while, and that I'd better drop you a note so as to keep on the right side of you in case you ever become commercially useful to me again.

Last year, I remember your writing about going to a class reunion. And I cried on your shoulder about my not belonging to any class, like Karl Marx. Well, I was wrong. I belong to the Class of '44, and I've been asked to come back.

Even though Cornell, in 1942, refused to give me a certificate stating that I had left the place under no cloud to go to war. It was their contention that I had left under a cloud.

And guess who's turned out to be such a wonderful writer that he's been tapped to write a book about Cornell?

I haven't decided yet whether I'm going to be nice about it or not. No matter what I do, there'll be plenty going on inside their heads, you can bet. What I represent is a challenge to the ivory tower, to the whole system of academic testing and evaluation—and I don't see how any of them can miss that.

I'm not going to the reunion, in the costume and levy-paying sense. I may be in the neighborhood, and I may drop in. But I refuse to be a member of '44.

Incidentally, did you know that Chrysler has in fact been

badly hurt? Only 16% of the market remains to them, and their used cars are drugs on the market. There's something you're supposed to do to make money out of a stock when you know it's going *down,* but I forget what it is. Miller told me once. Put and call, I think. But it's pretty special, and there's a good chance somebody besides Chrysler will get badly hurt.

As Gabriel Heatter said last night, in considering the McCarthy–Army hearings, "It's out of hand. Somebody's going to get hurt." I think he's dead right—and nothing's ever made the validity of tragedy clearer to me. Nobody can extricate himself. Nobody can stop being himself. And it all adds up to a great, grinding, merciless engine.

Lovely. The mechanics are lovely, that is. It doesn't hit me *here,* in the heart. And neither does the 3:59.4 mile.

But the fall of Dien Bien Phu does. That just about broke my heart, and filled me full of all kinds of primitive feelings—one being that that's the way to go; another being that I wouldn't mind too much getting into a rifle and grenade fight in some clean, dry, sunny place near a first-class hospital.

It looked for a while like I might qualify for a position with Time, Inc. But, in the final analysis, apparently, something was lacking—fiber, skill, wisdom? God knows.

So, in this personal tragedy of my own, I've sent Scribner's six chapters of a revision of a revision of a revision of what you condemned out of hand; I've accepted a challenge to write a book about Cornell during the summer; and I've set out earnestly to become a playwright. I'm doing this last thing by writing plays and listening to Leah Salisbury's reasons for wanting nothing to do with them.

How much are you making these days? A lot more?

When do you move to the Berkshires so we can visit you?

I'm taking Jane to Shelter Island, at Max's invitation, on Memorial Day weekend. I think we'll have a good time.

What news?

P.S. I believe in mental telepathy, and now sense strongly that you are writing me a letter that will cross with this one.

Kurt

May 11, 1954

To Knox Burger

The quote Kurt mistakenly attributes to James Whitcomb Riley, the "Hoosier Poet," is a slight misquotation of a locally popular poem of the period called "Ain't God Good to Indiana?" by William Herschell. The refrain was: "Ain't God good to Indiana?/Ain't He, fellers? Ain't He though?" Riley wrote a number of poems with similar style and sentiments that every Hoosier schoolkid of the era knew, like "Little Orphant Annie" and "When the Frost Is on the Punkin."

Arthur Godfrey's neighborly chatter and ukulele-strumming humor transformed him from a radio star into one of the first TV variety-show hosts and a household name in the 1950s.

May 11, 1954
Mark's 7th Birthday

Dear Knox:

Find enclosed a package of Jack-and-the-Beanstalk-type seeds that got me through a very bad summer—last summer. Every day I went out to see how much the things had grown, and every day I was flabbergasted. I would quote the late James Whitcomb Riley: "Ain't God good, fellers—Ain't he, though?"

When you get right down to it, wit isn't any help anywhere—and you and Otis having it out must have been brilliantly witty, if nothing else. Too bad.

I bought a television set day before yesterday. Best sample of American enterprise I've seen since a young man sold me a subscription to all the Crowell–Collier publications five years ago. A guy came into my office (over the Osterville Package Store), and said, "It's about time you got television. You're going to have it by four this afternoon." He was a man in a genial mood to dicker, and he damn well wasn't going to leave without having made an offer I was bound to admit was reasonable. Hey presto!

At four, I began watching a parade of sad young men and women I thought had died with F. Scott Fitzgerald. Pretty damn good plays, most of them, gutsy, real, and beautifully produced. And almost all of them about New York. Unsettling business for an artist, where everything that happens in New York has universality, and everything that happens outside is ethnography.

I wish you wouldn't tell me about people who are good writers and hold good jobs and inherit a lot of money besides.

My brother, on his tornado theory, has run into the same thing Louis Pasteur ran into. He's been turned down by a professional journal. They won't print his theory. Even I can see (I really can, and so could you) that he is right and the reactionary (and not very bright, actually) meteorologists* are wrong. Plain and simple. [. . .]

*My brother is a physicist.

I have a friend who recently survived an emotional ordeal far worse than yours, and came through with flying colors. He was fired by Arthur Godfrey.

So—stiff upper lip.

I don't think Jane and I will make it to New York during the Shelter Island expedition. I hope to see you, however, on my way to Ithaca—around the eighteenth of this month. Will you be in town?

Kurt

P.S. Have you read Aristotle's *Poetics*? I just did, and found in there everything any editor or writer ever told me about putting a story together. I couldn't think of a single amendment based on discoveries since 322 B.C. It's clear, and it isn't very long—and you might well recommend it to promising youngsters. Like me.

October 26, 1954
Osterville, MA

To Knox Burger

The baby was Nanette "Nanny" Vonnegut, the second daughter and third child of Kurt and Jane.

Bernard Baruch was a successful financier and statesman who became an adviser to Presidents Wilson, Roosevelt, and Truman.

Dear Knox:

There's been big catharsis around here, with the baby out of Jane's belly, with a new play mailed off to L&W, Inc., today—
[. . .]
We bought a big house in Barnstable. Two-hundred years old. View of the Barnstable dunes, and on a fresh water pond with some fish in it. Six fireplaces. This is probably the financial manipulation that will finish me. If I pull it off, I'm another elder statesman, like Baruch.

We won't move in until next spring. It's a better house than the one we were so hot about, and ten-thousand dollars cheaper. Six fireplaces. Plenty of guest rooms. A guest apartment, in fact.

Six fireplaces.

Kurt

November 30, 1954
Osterville, MA

To Harry Brague

Thomas Wolfe wrote You Can't Go Home Again.

Dear Harry:

I just got back from a visit with my father. Thomas Wolfe was dead right.

Thank you for your good wishes and *The Ramayana* and the *New Leader*. That was a delightful reference to my book—first rate snobbism. If the reader hasn't read Vonnegut's *Player Piano*, God help him.

Look, old friend, as a psychological device, let's pretend there isn't ever going to be another book written by me. Then, one bright day, into your office will come a manuscript, and we'll all be proud as Punch.

Honest to God—I don't think there's ever going to be another book, I can't imagine where the time is going, and I get sick if I think about it too much.

Hokay?

In Christ,

Kurt

February 1, 1955
Osterville, MA

To Knox Burger

The "big old twelve-room house in Barnstable" is the house that Vonnegut would live in with his family till he went to New York in 1970. He left the house to Jane and the children and it has remained in the family ever since, occupied now by their daughter Edie, who lives there with her husband and two sons.

Dear Knox:

[. . .] We passed papers yesterday on the big old twelve-room house in Barnstable, five miles due north of here. Now we own two houses. By God, I sure wish we didn't. Expensive.

When we move into the big one, in a month or so, come on up. We've got a guest wing. With a fireplace.

Jesus—wouldn't it be nice to write just one play a year, or just one anything?

I've pretty well pooped out as a hack. The old Moxie is gone.
[. . .]

Everything's going to be just grand, though. Jane says so. She
says she knows it in her bones. And I no kidding believe her. I'd
better, with two houses and $20,000 in mortgages.

Kurt

October 25, 1955
West Barnstable, MA

To Knox Burger

*Robert Alan Aurthur was a screenwriter, director, and TV producer
who worked for some of the distinguished live television programs of
the 1950s, such as* Studio One, Playhouse 90, *and* Producers' Showcase. *These programs featured highly regarded writers and playwrights such as Gore Vidal, Horton Foote, and Paddy Chayefsky, top
directors like Sidney Lumet and George Roy Hill (who later directed
the movie of* Slaughterhouse-Five*), and famous actors—Robert Redford got his first leading role on* Playhouse 90. *These hour or ninety-
minute programs contributed to the reputation of the 1950s as the
"Golden Age of Television."*

Dear Knox:

Tell me: have things improved or deteriorated?

About a month back I worked up a theory to the effect that
women don't like screwing as a rhapsody of see, feel, hear, touch,
and taste—but they do like the power their attractiveness as targets for screwing gives them. A couple of years ago I worked up
another theory, about compassion and bad conscience, I think it
was. And a close friend remarked that the theory had everything
but originality. And so it is with this one. I've also come to think
that this one also lacks validity, and that women are damn moody
things. A bundle of contradictory theories is called for. God

knows *that* lacks originality, which is one of the very tough things about being in the writing game, eh?

Anyway—I worked a little at this one, and actually got around to juxtaposing two very fancy things. One was Freud's statement that, damn near on his deathbed, he still didn't know what women wanted, and his statement about Joyce's *Ulysses,* in effect: "I should know women so good." The other was the Molly Bloom part of *Ulysses.*

I now need a key. The key is what *women* think of the Molly Bloom part of *Ulysses.* I can't even get my own wife to read it. And it's no more a subject for mixed conversation than the Hottentot apron. Still I'd like to know—and it's just the kind of thing Leopold Bloom went around in his carpet slippers wanting to know.

And isn't that the balls of a book? Greatest one, I think, but then I've never read *War and Peace,* and I don't expect I ever will.

Right now I'm faced with a typically New York problem, which is how to bring my mediocrity before the public. I've written a play which some people [. . .] think is screamingly funny, and which some people [. . .] say stinks. My life (at 33 years of age) hangs by a thread. That damn play has just got to be produced. Yet, it looks like it won't be.

My sister is poverty-stricken, and I mean poverty stricken, at age 38, and she says she is damn well fed-up with the character-building aspects of disappointment. Me too.

A power play is called for. I was all set to run a series of brilliantly brutal plays through Robert Alan Aurthur, when NBC benched him. How to mousetrap the $64,000 question?

What next?

You intimated in your last letter that your job was getting on your nerves. You never talk about it, so I suppose it's none of my business. But, in a mood of friendly curiosity, let me ask, what's the big trouble with it?

I read a couple of Maxim Gorky short stories last night, and both of them had as their theme that wicked peasants were forced to be wicked by social injustice. In one story, a mean, thieving, lying, greedy peasant actually makes this case in heaven before God and Jesus Christ, and brings *tears* to Their eyes!

Well—I would never tolerate such theories of irresponsibility in stories of mine, but I will suggest them in letters. Jesus, Knox—isn't this a paltry generation? Depression, wars, atomic weapons, and the old buggers living forever, building bigger and bigger institutes for the painless gelding of the young.

I get letters like this (I take my pen in hand, and—) from a guy who has the Anchor Fence franchise in Key West. He wants to be a writer, too.

About your not putting me up in your house, Knox: that's O.K. If you had asked of me, I would of refused. I don't have a very good time in New York when I stay in somebody's house, so I stay in hotels now.

Yours truly,
Kurt

November 14, 1956
West Barnstable, MA

To Henry Saalfield

This letter to an Ohio game company proposing a children's board game called "HQ" was one of Vonnegut's variety of attempts to make money. The proposal was turned down.

Mr. Henry Saalfield
Saalfield Game Company
Akron, Ohio

Dear Mr. Saalfield:

I am writing to you at the suggestion of your cousin and my neighbor, Mike Handy.

I have invented a board game, which Mike has seen and seems

to like. I have played the game about a thousand times, and it works like a dollar watch. The bugs are out of the rules.

It is similar in mood to chess, and is played on a standard checkerboard. It has enough dignity and interest, I think, to become the third popular checkerboard game.

The counters represent artillery, infantry, armored, and airborne units, and textbook tactical situations develop on the board. Because of unique features of these rules, these situations and their solutions are amazingly realistic. The game would, I'm quite sure, satisfy the faculty of West Point as a tactical demonstrator.

The counters are pretty as they can be. Plenty of sales appeal there—particularly for veterans itching to show how much they know about tactics.

A nine-year-old can learn it. All the neighborhood kids can play it and love to play it.

I am hoping, of course, to interest you and your company in producing and marketing the game. If, on the basis of the enclosed set of rules, you are at all interested in seeing more, I will, upon hearing from you, send you a pilot-model set of the colorful playing pieces. Patent is now being applied for, so you would be adequately protected if you were to take it on.

Very truly yours,

Kurt Vonnegut, Jr.

October 26, 1957

West Barnstable, MA

To Harry Brague

The book Vonnegut refers to is an early, unfinished version of his second novel, The Sirens of Titan.

Dear Harry:

Since the interest of Scribner's in my book is mild, would you return what you have of it, and let me see if I can't arouse some

interest in it elsewhere? It is my sorry position to be in need of
moral, editorial, and financial help; and Scribner's feeling, obviously, is that they cannot afford to risk any of these in my case.
However much I may sympathize with Scribner's view (and I do
sympathize sincerely), the fact remains that I am stuck with the
risk of being me. I am compelled, therefore, to spread the risk
around a little, if I can.

    Yours truly,

      Kurt Vonnegut, Jr.

                                      April 15, 1959

                               West Barnstable, MA

To CHARLES SCRIBNER'S SONS

The novel referred to here as "Cat's Call" eventually became Cat's
Cradle. *Sam Stewart, a colleague of Knox Burger's at Dell, signed up*
Cat's Cradle *as a paperback original in 1962. The following year
Stewart moved to Holt, Rinehart and Winston and arranged with Dell
to publish and keep the novel in hardcover for two years before Dell's
paperback edition.*

Gentlemen:

    You have been in possession of a portion of a novel of mine,
"Cat's Call," for more than two years now. This surely consti-
tutes a rejection. Would you kindly return the manuscript to me
at the earliest possible convenience.

    I realize that you are in the position of trying to protect an in-
vestment of several hundred dollars. However, the best chance for
you to recover that money, it seems to me, is to let me submit the
novel elsewhere. You would share in the advance, if any. I think I
could talk a paperback house into an advance that would make
us both happy.

    Yours truly,

      Kurt Vonnegut, Jr.

To Knox Burger

Knox had suggested in 1957 that Kurt write a science-fiction novel for his new line of mass-market paperback originals, and Kurt revived the idea for The Sirens of Titan; *it was published in 1959. Dell published 177,500 in its first printing, though the few reviews dismissed it as science fiction. It later became popular with college students during the sixties. (In 1961 it was issued in hardcover by Houghton Mifflin.) After* Slaughterhouse-Five *made Vonnegut famous,* Sirens *reached an even wider audience.*

Dear Knox:

We always have a nice time when you and your family come up here, so please come whenever you can. In the future I think we should plan to do some work when you come—four hours a day, say. Among the things we should try to catch is a four-character one-set Broadway smash. It's about time for us to catch one. [. . .]

As for *The Sirens of Titan*: I have made all the revisions suggested by Jane, and this morning the messy manuscript goes to a typist. In ten days she promises a flawless original and one carbon. I will send the original to you and the carbon to Ken & Max. And that will be that, I think. You must know how grateful I am for your having given me the chance to do the book, and for your having showed it around to hard-cover people, and for all the rest of it.

Last night we had cocktails with a woman who is an intimate friend of the man who holds the world's record on East Coast Tuna. The record is somewhere between 900 and 1000 pounds. The fish was landed off *The Chantey* out of Provincetown—Captain Charley Mayo. Mayo was out the day we were out. Remember? *The Chantey* was the only boat that took a fish the day we were out. Mayo costs $100 a day, and he damn near never misses. He's an ex-Madison Avenue type, incidentally—a Dartmouth. The world's record fish took eleven hours to land. And the guy who landed it slept for thirty-six hours straight when they got him to bed. Christ—I keep thinking of Mark in the fighting chair, tweaking the line between his thumb and forefinger, and saying, "I think maybe I've got one on."

Kurt

Summer, 1959
[West Barnstable, MA]

To Knox Burger

Ray Bradbury was a well-known and successful writer of "science fiction," one of the few whose literary merit was recognized outside (or in spite of) the genre. His novel The Martian Chronicles *had been published in 1950.*

Dear Knox:

[. . .] I remember the trimming you gave me at ping pong, and anybody who can trim me at ping pong is a marvelously coordinated person. With a decent hip, you may well become another Jim Thorpe.

I wrote Ray Bradbury a letter, telling him I was moving to the West Coast to get closer to Disney Land. I think I may really move out there. This winter was damn near the end of me. I can't stand another winter cooped up with all these kids, knowing that stepping out of the front door is like falling overboard on the Murmansk run.

As long as you're moving, why don't you move all the way, too?

Yours truly,

Kurt

Undated, marked 1959
[West Barnstable, MA]

To Knox Burger

Knox had left Dell to move to Gold Medal Books, another paperback
house, but Sirens *was still published by Dell.*

Dear Knox:

Christ—I sure wish I could go to Florida with you, and maybe
I will, if you're serious. I've got to get away for a little while, God
knows.

The Guggenheims turned me down. It seems that Professor
Orman Sweetbreads needs still another year to complete his mon-
umental work which hopes to prove that King Tut and Herman
Melville influenced each other hardly at all.

Tell me, old man—does that fact that you have left Dell mean
that my book will not be published? Was my book one of the several chief things that led to your resignation?

And tell me—when one is being frog-marched by life, does
one giggle or does one try to maintain as much dignity as possible
under the circumstances?

I got an extremely friendly letter back from Ray Bradbury. I
called him Mr. Bradbury and he called me Kurt. I told him I was
thinking of moving to California, and he said sure, come ahead.
He said he would introduce me to some people, and he said it
was warm all the time out there. Can you imagine someplace
where it's warm all the time?

Kurt

December 7, 1959

[West Barnstable, MA]

To Knox Burger

Dear Knoxo:

I look at the Sunday book review sections, and I say to myself, Jesus, why should anybody ever write another book. There are so many books, and I bet a lot of them are good, too. One book for every good reader.

I am glad Otis has an exciting thing going for her—the new ceramic technique. She should be able to hang a few of those things on posh saloon walls, at $500 a crack or so. I will speak to my friend, who is a decorator.

He is a decorator for motels—which isn't to insult Otis. It is to insult him.

As I told you before, I am making an 18-foot piece of sculpture for him. It is not on spec. I have a contract, and I have to deliver on December 15. The price is a grand. So far I am in for $65.00, and I am about three-quarters through. The thing will hang on the wall of the restaurant of Logan International Motel, Logan International Airport, Boston. Welded steel, brazed copper and bronze, and a ball of Quincy granite. Jane and I had a charming afternoon, incidentally, chasing around Quincy, looking for granite balls. Turns out the damn things haven't been made since before the second World War—a lost art. What I was after was a ball ten-inches in diameter, and one guy offered to try and get me one for $150.00! Wow. For the sake of anti-climax, let me say that I finally found an old one for $17.00.

Is it too soon to wish you a merry Christmas?

Thanks for the money. I mean to get back to that book damn soon.

A couple of years ago, Max told me that the worst thing that could happen to a young playwright was to have a play produced in a Cape Cod summer theater. Two days ago, he wrote to ask the name of the theater here on the Cape that produces the works of young playwrights. It seems he has a client who is a young play-wright.

I am no longer a young playwright. I am a middle-aged sculp-tor.

Very gracious of you to show my book to movie people—and to promote my cause generally. What can I do for you?

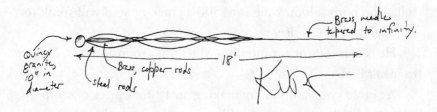

December 29, 1959
West Barnstable, MA

To NORMAN MAILER

Norman Mailer, like Kurt, had served as a PFC in the infantry in World War II. His novel The Naked and the Dead, *based on his expe-rience of combat in the Pacific, had become a bestseller. He had re-cently written* Advertisements for Myself.

Mr. Norman Mailer
G.P. Putnam's Sons
New York, N.Y.

Dear Mr. Mailer:

I have just finished reading your ad for yourself—a lot of it twice, at your suggestion. Since my reputation is worthless, my comments on the book would be worthless, so fuck them.

Listen: I have an anecdote about you which you should use in your next book about you.

One time I entertained you and Si and Billy in my house at the head of Commercial Street in Provincetown—call it the summer of 1950. Anyway, I was a writer, too—not red hot, but self-supporting. And my mother-in-law from Indianapolis was in the house, too. She got very drunk. You left after a while, and you stood out on my front porch wondering where to go next. My mother-in-law was about two feet away from you, indoors, separated from you by a windowshade drawn over an open window. She said to me in a loud, indignant squawk, "Well—I think you're cuter than he is." And I put my hand over her mouth.

Later on, we decided that Norman Mailer had not heard.

We sure hoped not.

Did you hear?

It's a fact, incidentally—I *am* cuter than you are.

Respectfully

Somebody named Kurt Vonnegut, Jr.

THE SIXTIES

The sixties were a turning point for the whole country and for Kurt Vonnegut as a writer. His work would have special resonance for the dynamic new youth culture and its values, especially in questioning the status quo and challenging the accepted wisdom (though Kurt did it through storytelling rather than the usual political or cultural manifestos). The two most specific and significant events of importance to Vonnegut, though, were his being invited to teach at the highly regarded Iowa Writers' Workshop at the University of Iowa and his offer of a three-book contract from publisher Seymour Lawrence, which gave him financial freedom to devote himself full time to his writing.

Vonnegut was interviewed in October of 1966 by the noted academic critic Robert Scholes, while Scholes was teaching in the English department of the University of Iowa and Vonnegut was teaching at the Writers' Workshop. Scholes was the first and most perceptive academic critic to write about Vonnegut's work. In *The Fabulators,* a 1967 study considering Vonnegut along with critically acclaimed novelists like Lawrence Durrell and Iris Murdoch, Scholes explained that Vonnegut "uses the rhetorical potential of the short sentence and short paragraph better than anyone now writing, often getting a rich comic or dramatic effect by isolating a single sentence in a separate paragraph or excerpting a phrase from context for a bizarre chapter-heading. The apparent simplicity and ordinariness of his writing mask its efficient power . . ."

During their interview, when Scholes asked Kurt if he expected a turn in his fortunes as a writer, Vonnegut said, "I never expect anything good to happen. I never expected the university to hire me. I thought I was going to starve to death."

He was "offered the job [at Iowa] at the last minute when Robert Lowell decided not to appear," Kurt told Steve Wilbers, who was writing a history of the Iowa Writers' Workshop for a dissertation in 1976. "I needed the money. I needed the stimulation. I needed the change in scene . . . It turned out to be a very bright thing for me to do. Suddenly writing seemed very important again. My neighbors on Cape Cod didn't read me, didn't read anything, so I had felt like a pointless citizen there. In Iowa City I was central and spectacular. This was better than a transplant of monkey glands for a man my age."

"I was also elated by belonging to a huge and extended family of artists. As for my students: They were so able and interesting, most of them, that I thought of them, almost from the first, as colleagues. I remain in touch with many of them to this day, and colleagues are what they have truly become." His students included Gail Godwin, John Irving, and others who went on to become writers, editors, and college professors. His fellow teachers, the writers Richard Yates, Nelson Algren, Vance Bourjaily, Paul Engle, and José Donoso, a leading Chilean novelist, also became friends for life.

In an autobiographical opening to *Slaughterhouse-Five,* Vonnegut wrote cryptically: "I taught creative writing in the famous Writers Workshop at the University of Iowa for a couple of years . . . I got into some perfectly beautiful trouble, got out of it again."

His reference was to a brief affair and lifetime friendship with one of his students who was "a single mom, with two kids," in her second year of graduate work at the Writers' Workshop: Loree Wilson Rackstraw. Kurt later gave her permission to use any of the letters and other writing he sent her, which she quoted from in her book about their friendship (*Love As Always, Kurt: Vonnegut As I Knew Him*). She wrote that their friendship "was sustained mostly by the U.S. Postal Service over the years."

Kurt received the lowest salary of any of the Iowa faculty because he did not hold an advanced academic degree—in fact, he did not have a college degree at all. Since he had finished his course work for the master's degree in anthropology at the University of Chicago, Vonnegut needed only to write a thesis the anthropology department would accept to get his M.A.—and, with it, a much-needed raise in salary. So he tried again.

This time he wrote a thesis comparing stories of primitive societies to contemporary short stories. This, too, was rejected—he was told that it wasn't valid to compare primitive and civilized societies. In 1971 (after he was rich and famous and did not need a twenty percent raise anymore) he was awarded a master's degree in anthropology from the University of Chicago, on the grounds that his novel *Cat's Cradle* (published in 1963, before Vonnegut went to Iowa) made "a contribution to the field of cultural anthropology." So it goes. Kurt spelled out his reaction in *Palm Sunday,* "The University of Chicago . . . can take a flying fuck at the moooooooooooooooooooon."

• • •

While teaching at Iowa in 1966, Vonnegut wrote a review of a new Random House dictionary for *The New York Times Book Review* and got a fan letter that would change his life. The letter was from Seymour Lawrence, a former editor of the Atlantic Monthly Press, who had opened his own publishing company the year before in a one-room office at 90 Beacon Street in Boston. He admired the style and humor of Vonnegut's review and told him to stop by his office if he ever needed a new publisher. Lawrence had also begun to hear murmurings of an underground following for Vonnegut's novels, especially *Cat's Cradle,* which was being passed around in well-thumbed paperback copies by admiring college students.

Kurt left Iowa when he got a Guggenheim Fellowship in 1967 (on his second try) and went back to Dresden to see if it would help him with the novel he'd been trying to write about his experience there in WWII. He then returned to Cape Cod to finish the book.

Knowing he would soon be running out of money again, and unable to interest his previous publishers in his unfinished novel, he went up to Boston and rang the bell at 90 Beacon Street, introducing himself to Sam Lawrence and offering him the unfinished manuscript. Sam read it and offered Vonnegut a three-book contract for both hardcover and paperback rights. It was a publishing windfall for an author in those days, and Kurt warned Sam Lawrence his books "didn't make money." He said his last one had sold only 1,500 copies.

"You write the books," Sam said, "and I'll worry about the money."

Neither of them had to worry about money again. Lawrence bought the rights to all Kurt's previous books, first published *Welcome to the Monkey House* in 1968, and the next year brought out *Slaughterhouse-Five,* which became a worldwide bestseller.

Had *Slaughterhouse-Five* been written and published in the 1950s, it would not have made the same impact. The timing of the novel's publication was eerily right, for by 1969 many Americans had become critical of the war in Vietnam, not only because the Tet Offensive of 1968 illustrated how badly we were faring in the conflict but also because of the revelation of atrocities like the My Lai Massacre, the use of napalm against civilian populations, and the saturation bombing of Cambodia and Laos that began in March of 1969—the same month *Slaughterhouse-Five* was published. A novel based on the firebombing of Dresden during WWII would not have seemed as relevant in the preceding decade as it did now; it would not have struck such a nerve.

The events in Vietnam and the protests against the draft, led by college students, increased the growing influence of the youth culture, who made Vonnegut their literary hero in questioning the accepted wisdom of the status quo. Kurt was as surprised as anyone and had never wanted to be a "spokesman" of the young. He was very leery of the hippie phenomenon and wrote a searing account of one of their heroes, Maharishi Mahesh Yogi, guru to the Beatles and assorted movie stars ("Yes, We Have No Nirvanas," published in *Esquire* and collected in his book *Wampeters, Foma & Granfalloons*). He satirized the stylish popularity of Eastern meditation, saying we had the same thing in the West—reading short stories, which also lowered your heart rate and freed your mind from other concerns. He said short stories were "Buddhist catnaps." He thought the Maharishi was a phony but he loved the music of the Beatles, spoke up for Abbie Hoffman, and admired Allen Ginsberg.

When the hippie leader Ray Mungo (founder of the Liberation News Service) and my friends from his commune told me they wanted to meet Vonnegut, I said they would have to do it on their own. After *Slaughterhouse-Five,* Kurt was swamped with letters and requests for meetings, asked for advice, invited to speak and be interviewed, and I didn't want to add more intrusions into his privacy. When the commune delegation showed up at his doorstep on Cape Cod, he didn't invite them inside but asked, "What can I do for you people?" He took them for a walk and talked and listened to his young admirers and it all ended with laughter and mutual appreciation.

Vonnegut never changed his style of dress, eating, or smoking during that decade (or any other), sticking to Pall Malls over pot, whiskey over cocaine and LSD, meat and potatoes over vegetarianism, and was skeptical of all new fads.

"I did smoke a joint of marijuana once with Jerry Garcia and the Grateful Dead, just to be sociable," he confessed in *A Man Without a Country.* "It didn't seem to do anything to me one way or the other, so I never did it again."

January 23, 1960
West Barnstable, MA

To Knox Burger

Stephen Potter was the British author of popular books of mocking self-help, most famously Gamesmanship *and* One-Upmanship.

The book referred to here as "Nation of Two" would be published as Mother Night.

Hakenkreuz *is the German word for "crooked cross," the Swastika, symbol of the Nazis.*

Dear Knox:

Thanks for the blind carbon—something like those fish in Mammoth Cave who've lost their eyes. An old man I worked with at General Electric never kept carbons. When somebody asked to see a carbon of such and such a letter, the old man would sit down and write the carbon he thought the somebody would most like to see. The old man's name was Clyde Waggoner. He was hired away from the *N.Y. World* by G.E. in the year of my birth, 1922. Let's see—that was a year before you were born, wasn't it? I make Mary Otis for vintage 1927. How close am I?

One of the great things in *The Iceman Cometh* is where the male lead tells about his married life and how his wife thanked him sincerely for whatever he did and would have thanked him for murdering her if she had had the opportunity. Why do I bring that up? Well, it turns out not to be particularly relevant—in fact not relevant at all except that I find myself thanking you often. I don't expect this to drive you to murder.

I thank a lot of people often—but mostly for nothing. Most people aren't very good at their jobs. You are superlative at yours, which is editing, and, since I am a writer, my gratitude is extravagant.

Like symbiosis—which, as Stephen Potter pointed out, was removed from the list of O.K. words in 1951. And wasn't 1959 a fine year for viable? And my children all know that you and I were present at what must have been the birth of perjorative. (I just tried to look it up, can't find it anywhere. I must have misspelled it badly.)

So how is the house? Beautiful, I'll bet. There was a simple formula in *Better Homes and Gardens* once about how much a person should spend on furniture. For a ten thousand dollar house you should have ten thousand dollars' worth of furniture. You can extrapolate from there to cover your own situation. The only person who ever really did it, I suppose, was William Randolph Hearst.

Another very long chapter of "Nation of Two" goes to the typist this weekend. In about two weeks I hope to have maybe 100 more pages, which will take us to about page 150, which should entitle me to another good whack of money, eh? Process this thing quickly, and we will hit the Nazi revival right on the nose. Big black Hakenkreuz on the cover.

Kurt

February 3, 1960
West Barnstable, MA

To Norman Mailer

Dear Norman:

That was gracious of you to reply to my rude and silly note. And you are right in saying that what I write is slick. My mood with respect to my writing is wry. Eliza Doolittle's father was one of the undeserving poor and I am one of the undeserving artists.

I wish you much luck, since you are the writer in my generation who could do the most with some real good luck. I would love to see somebody in my generation do something marvellous.

The ten-year-book will be important, without question. You are going to be disappointed in one respect, however: no matter what you say or how you say it, it will be published and widely read. When society found out it was honoring works of art by censoring them, it stopped doing it.

On your way to or from Provincetown, please do us the honor of stopping by. We're on 6A. We have no horse or Mary Jane, but plenty of gin, God knows. Since part of your big novel takes place on Cape Cod, and, since we've lived on the Cape for ten years now, we could tell you some true and useful things that you might not know.

Yours truly,

Kurt Vonnegut, Jr.

February 24, 1960

West Barnstable, MA

To NORMAN MAILER

Dear Norman:

Delightful news in yours of February 18.

Honored.

Please don't let us down.

Like we will kill a lobster.

As a Marxist, you should know about the Socialist Labor Party, if you don't already. I went to an SLP fund raising party at Waltham a while back, and it was like a Sunday school picnic—rosy-cheeked kiddies and buxom housewives all over the place, nice cars in the parking lot, lower middle class Swedes and Germans at the speakers' table, and all the ham you could eat.

Only everybody was a Marxist.

So what's the joke? Turns out it's a free country after all.

As long as you're ineffectual, which bodes well for me if not for you.

Yours truly,

Kurt

March 10, 1960

[West Barnstable, MA]

To KNOX BURGER

The "Gold Medal book" is the novel that would become Mother Night. *The Sirens of Titan had been published in paperback by Dell the year before and would be brought out in hardcover the following year by Houghton Mifflin, though the projected one-volume edition of three novels did not materialize.*

The last sentence of the letter, offering "a few bills" to help out Knox, who was presumably in a temporary financial bind, is typical of Vonnegut's lifelong generosity to friends and fellow writers, even at this time of his own continuing money pressures.

William Zeckendorf, Sr., was a well-known real estate developer.

Dear Knox:

[. . .] Now that I've got a little money from *McCall's,* I'm back to work on the Gold Medal book again. Houghton-Mifflin, incidentally, is quite serious about doing the *Sirens* in hardback, maybe bringing out it, *Player Piano,* and *Cat's Cradle* (which I am capable of doing now) in one volume.

I was very sorry to find you so depressed by your property problems. The fact remains, however, that you do have valuable property, easily worth what you've put into it. You have absolutely not been hosed in that respect, have in fact increased the value of the property (beyond your investment) like a young Zeckendorf. The presently alarming period will soon be behind you, I'm sure. And if, during this period, a few bills would help, I think I could find them.

Yours truly,

Kurt

May 12, 1960

[West Barnstable, MA]

To Knox Burger

Richard Gehman was a prolific writer of magazine articles, nonfiction books, and novels, including Driven, *referred to here. He was also prolific in his personal life, marrying five times and fathering forty children.*

"Shell Scott" was the popular detective hero of more than three dozen private-eye novels by Richard S. Prather, published by Fawcett/ Gold Medal Books; these paperback originals eventually sold over forty million copies and spawned their own Shell Scott Mystery Magazine.

Dear Knox:

Thanks so much for your long letter of April 29. I am glad to hear you in such boisterous spirits.

Not only did I read the whole letter—I read the books, too. $5,267.49 to Gehman! Yummy! That is certainly a grand advance. *Driven,* incidentally, is regarded as a damn fine book in these parts, and is the main reason Jane likes Gehman.

I will review all the books if you want me to, but I gather that what you're after is a book by me. Well sir, just before taking off for Blighty on Sunday I will put into the hands of my typist some more pages. She will mail them directly to you whenever she gets them done.

How do these sons of bitches write thirteen books, or thirty-three, for Christ's sakes—or sell serials to the Post and then to the movies? Twenty million copies of the Shell Scott books in print. That was a pretty damn demoralizing letter you wrote, now that I think of it.

I will tell you a true story. There is a little old nothing old lady in Indianapolis who kept telling Jane's mother that we should call on some relative of hers while we were in England. We told Jane's mother we wouldn't have time for dull calling, but Jane's mother forgot to tell the little old lady, so she put the plan into operation, and we are expected to come calling on the relative. [. . .] The relative is having a cocktail party to which we are invited, and he is eager to do all he can to make our visit to London interesting. You know who he turns out to be? The cultural attache of the American Embassy, and the cocktail party is a big blast for all the top London theatrical people. [. . .]

Love to everybody,
Kurt

June, 1960

[West Barnstable, MA]

To Knox Burger

Dear Knox:

Thanks for the very funny clipping about Boston advertising. It was waiting for me when I got back. I enclose a school paper of Edith's—suitable for framing.

The trip was a smashing success. Some people came over last night to hear all about the trip, supposedly, but they spent the evening drinking up our tax-free Scotch and talking about their own exploits in the Old World. I bought you a necktie (Kenya Rifles), but somebody got it last night.

I continue to work on the book. I presume you got a few more pages from the typist last week.

Macmillan of England is quite interested in *The Sirens*. They haven't made a firm decision about it yet.

Boy—did I ever see some pretty whores!

Yours buoyantly,

Kurt

June, 1961

[West Barnstable, MA]

To Knox Burger

UNTITLED POEM

Two little good girls,
Watchful and wise—
Clever little hands
And big kind eyes—
Look for signs that the world is good,
Comport themselves as good folk should.

They wonder at a father
Who is sad and funny strong,
And they wonder at a mother
Like a childhood song.
And what, and what
Do the two think of?
Of the sun
And the moon
And the earth
And love.

July, 1961
West Barnstable, MA

To Knox Burger

Kurt's reference to "this teaching job" that he hopes "will fill me with a little more zowie" was a school on Cape Cod for boys with behavior problems.

Gordon Forbes was considered one of the best "doubles" tennis players in the world.

Bill Stern was a famous sportscaster of the thirties and forties. He had his own radio show that featured stories of famous athletes who overcame great odds.

Dear Knox:

August would be fine. That's not a bad guess as to when the fish will be back in force. During June, even the village idiot was taking ten and twenty a day, dangling an unbaited bent pin in the cesspool of the county jail. Now even Brooks, with live sea worms, is getting skunked.

As I told you, I've doubled the range of my boat by doubling the fuel supply, so maybe we can venture up the coast to Wellfleet, which has a reputation for bigger fish. Also—if the money falls in on me between now and then (I will never let go of that dream), we can hire Charley Mayo in Provincetown, and no kidding catch a tuna.

I am glad you find life stimulating. I do, too, kind of—but not nearly enough. I am hoping that this teaching job will fill me with a little more zowie. What I'd really like to do, I think, is make a movie. A commercial artist friend of mine up here nearly flipped his wig, and he did the very bright thing of going out to a working ranch in Colorado, ditching his twanging wife and kids, and riding and fishing and stepping in fresh bear dung and things like that. Did it for six weeks. What is called for is violent physical movement. The Brahmins up here have the violence thing beautifully worked out with tennis and sailing. I'm not good enough at either one to frisk with them, which makes me sulky and soreheaded, and explains, I'm sure, my yen for class warfare. I would be on the side of the volunteer firemen. I still can't believe Gordon Forbes learned to be a tennis champ in such a short time. Even Bill Stern would have some trouble swallowing that tale. Some body.

I used to ride a horse pretty good, and I used to swim better than good. I suppose I had better take up those things again, or maybe painting, or maybe woodcarving, or maybe studding up those parts of the fucking house that are falling down.

What in hell are you doing that's stimulating? Taking heroin? Tell me.

Yours truly,
Kurt

September 16, 1961
West Barnstable, MA

To Knox Burger

Canary in a Cat House *was a collection of twelve stories published as a Fawcett paperback; eleven of the stories were later included in* Welcome to the Monkey House, *published in 1968 in hardcover by Dela-corte/Seymour Lawrence. Axel's Castle: A Study of the Imaginative Literature of 1870–1930 was a heavyweight book of literary criticism by Edmund Wilson, the leading critic of the time, on the works of the great writers of the era, including T. S. Eliot, William Butler Yeats, Marcel Proust, James Joyce, and Gertrude Stein. Kurt opened his Saab automobile dealership on Cape Cod in the spring of 1957, and closed it that December. He continued to occasionally use his stationery with the SAAB CAPE COD letterhead.*

SAAB CAPE COD

E. 6A, W. Barnstable, Mass.

FOrest 2-6161, 2-3072

Kurt Vonnegut, Manager

September 16, 1961

Dear Knox:

As you promised, *Canary in a Cathouse* is a damn good look-ing book. My thanks to the artists. Husband and wife, are they? I'd like to own the original art for the back cover when Gold Medal is through with it. Would that be possible?

I've put the completely edited copy of *Mother Night* into the mail for you. All I've done to it is add one page to the introduc-tion. I think I must have sent you such a page earlier, along with a letter, and it was never spliced in. For cover art, what about a skeleton dressed and posed as a kittenish whore?

I've been reading *Axel's Castle*—have learned that I am a classicist, now moving (by using the first person) into romanti-cism. Marvellous. Good for me. The trouble is that the radio is on all the time, with news every hour and bulletins any time, and the facts of life bop me at random between militarism, da-daism and onanism. It is hard to know whether to shit or go blind. [. . .]

I'm doing a play on the side. That goes easy, God bless it. It isn't arch. It is both comic and tragic, in the modern manner. I'm really very fond of the modern manner. When it's done, I hope you'll help me in getting it into the hands of some modern people.

Yours truly,

Kurt

SALES, PARTS, SERVICE FOR THE SWEDISH SAAB AUTOMOBILE

October 18, 1961

West Barnstable, MA

To Knox Burger

Harvey Kurtzman was the cartoonist who founded MAD *magazine and at the time of this letter was also editing a humor magazine called* Help! The New York Times *later described him as "one of the most important figures in postwar America" because of his impact on pop culture.*

Dear Knox:

Thank you for the advance copy of Harvey Kurtzman's fast-acting *Help*. I admire it. I think I understand some of it.

As a test of my understanding, let's see if I can now sell an idea for money to *Help*. I offer the idea in the form of a letter which I would appreciate your forwarding. It goes as follows:

Dear Mr. Kurtzman:

I have been a queasy fan of yours for a good while now. I would be enormously pleased if something of mine got into Help. Would the idea of shelter-hopping kits interest you? Families too big or too lazy or too poor to build adequate fall-out shelters could buy from our company quite cheap kits guaranteed to open any shelter yet recommended by Civil Defense.

The cheapest kit, selling for $14.95, say, would consist of a World War Two surplus cylinder of Cyklon B, guaranteed by I.G. Farben, and a shaped charge for blowing the lock on any shelter door. More luxurious kits might include C.D. uniforms, all-clear signals; tape recordings of beloved family pets scratching to be let in, tape recordings of old A.B.C. speeches on the harmlessness of fallout; grenades, bazookas, flamethrowers, etc.

We recommend that no informed person go anywhere without the basic kit, since the necessity of getting into a shelter is likely to arise at any time. We therefore package the kits to look like attache cases, lunchpails, hatboxes, shopping bags, copies of *Dr. Zhivago,* etc.

As a rule of thumb, we recommend that, for minimum safety during nuclear war, each person be equipped to take over three shelters. We say this, because there are bound to be disappointments—meagerly equipped shelters, shelters furnished in bad taste, septic tanks mistaken for shelters, etc.

One town figured the appalling cost of building community shelters, decided instead to buy enough kits to take over the shelters of an adjoining town, thereby saving enough money to send the high school band to the next Orange Bowl game.

With every order goes a subscription to our news letter, which tells who is building shelters where, what they are putting into them, and how the owners intend to defend them. Etc. More details on request.

Kurt

Spring, 1962
West Barnstable, MA

To Knox Burger

Kurt's reference to the book that "took me ten years to do" was Cat's Cradle.

Dear Knox:

[. . .] People in Cotuit and Indianapolis tell me that the book is getting a big display. They had trouble locating copies of *Canary in a Cathouse.* Not so with *Mother Night.*

I felt unusually peculiar during my last visit to New York, since two books were hanging fire simultaneously—*Mother Night* and the thing I did for Dell. I have reality for myself, apparently, only to extent that people approve or disapprove of what I write.

Also: the thing I did for Dell took me ten years to do, though it wasn't worth anything like ten years—and I now have a sense of an era's having ended. I never used to wonder what to do next. Now I wonder what in hell to do next. [. . .]

I'll let you know when the fish arrive. About the middle of May, I expect.

Kurt

January, 1963

[West Barnstable, MA]

To Knox Burger

The teaching job was the one for the school for boys with behavior problems that he had hoped—mistakenly, as it turned out—would give him more "zowie." He taught there from September 1962 until January 1963.

Dear Knox:

[. . .] I quit the teaching job, after doggedly finishing out a full semester. It was killing work—and I don't mind work all that much, but it was a racket, too. I'll tell you how the racket works sometime. I'm writing a play about it. [. . .]

Yours truly,

Kurt

July, 1963
[West Barnstable, MA]

To Knox Burger

Frederick Wiseman produced The Cool World *in 1963, a feature film based on the novel by Warren Miller. He later gained renown as a documentary filmmaker, winning many awards for his work.*

Dear Knox:

Thanks for the books.

An interesting young guy named Fred Wiseman is optioning *Cat's Cradle* for a movie, on a limited partnership deal. The advance isn't much, but I'll own an actual 8% of the production. His other films—*The Connection* and *The Cool World*. As Jane points out, he has a fondness for C's. Do you know him? He's a lawyer who got hooked on films.

This property you talk about—is that your mother's land on Lake George? How much will you sell me five acres for?

It is miserably hot up here, and the shrubs and trees are turning brown. No damn rain at all. [. . .]

Yours truly,

Kurt

Summer, 1963
[West Barnstable, MA]

To Knox Burger

A.J.P. Taylor was a British historian whose controversial book The Origins of the Second World War *argued that the outbreak of the war in 1939 was due to accidents of history rather than an intentional plan on the part of Hitler.*

Dear Knox:

Take this cheerful thing of A.J.P. Taylor's, and make some other people happy with it. I remember a girl I met once in

Stow-on-the-Wold, and she said to me, "Don't you try to sell England to me." I still sell it every chance I get. Funniest people in the world. Ben Hitz, my best man, went to a wedding of a British cousin a while back, was charmed by the insulting speech the British best man traditionally delivers on the faults of the groom. The groom beamed and bowed throughout. You and Miller have done good work in bringing the creative insult into currency, but I can't think of another American in the field. Your pal, Lenny Bruce, incidentally, turns out to be about as good a writer as any around. [. . .]

Yours truly,

Kurt

September 25, 1963

West Barnstable, MA

To Knox Burger

The SRL referred to was the Saturday Review of Literature, *a popular and influential weekly of the era.*

Dear Knox:

Would you be at all interested in a collection of my non-fantastic stories, if they were called:

CLEAN STORIES FOR CLEAN PEOPLE
IN DRUGSTORES AND BUS DEPOTS.

Yours truly,

Kurt

P.S. Did you happen to see the letter in the SRL, where a professor at Hunter named his ten favorite novels during the past ten years—and *Mother Night* was one of them?

October, 1963
[West Barnstable, MA]

To Knox Burger

Dear Knox:

My boat is out of the water now, so why don't you invite me to come to your Connecticut spread in order to shoot some upland game? About this bass thing: they are still around, and I went out the other day and got three very easily, and could have killed every fish in the harbor, if I'd had the time. I found out that they can take or leave a needlefish, but that they have to bite every popper they see. The needlefish is a class bait. The slobs use poppers.

You ask what I am doing for you as compared with all you are doing for me, and all I can answer is that I put you in a favorable light whenever the opportunity presents itself. If I had a lot of money, I would give you some.

I wrote you about a week ago, and asked you what you maybe thought was a snide question, but I was serious. I ask you again: is there a chance that a collection of my non-SF stories would sell under the title:

CLEAN STORIES FOR CLEAN PEOPLE
IN DRUGSTORES AND BUS DEPOTS.

Yours truly,
Kurt

November 12, 1963
West Barnstable, MA

To Mr. Cordell

Walter Vonnegut, Sr., was an actor who was married to the actress Marjorie Potts. She played opposite George M. Cohan in the original

Broadway production of Eugene O'Neill's Ah, Wilderness! *As a child, Walter, Jr., was also in the cast (he is Kurt's cousin and the lifelong friend who is known in the family as "the Colonel"). Marjorie divorced Walter, Sr., who was an alcoholic, and married Don Marquis, an author and playwright who gained fame as the creator of* Archy and Mehitabel. *Archy was a talking cockroach who hopped from key to key on Marquis's typewriter at night, writing poems and stories about Mehitabel the cat. The characters were reproduced in popular columns that Marquis wrote for leading newspapers of the 1920s and '30s, including the* New-York Tribune *(renamed the* New York Herald Tribune *in 1924) and the* New York Sun. *Three books of poems by Archy were published.*

Dear Mr. Cordell:

Your pleasant letter of November 4 only got here today. How nice to know that someone has read my book.

I don't think we've met, which is too bad. I can't think now which Vonnegut it was that went to Purdue. I'm glad I wasn't the one who got pushed into the Candida part anyway. I would have been rotten.

Walter Vonnegut was my favorite relative. He was the most talented member of his generation (within the family, of course). Booth Tarkington spotted him, got him onto Broadway. His cousins and siblings looked upon him as a frightful failure, because he died of booze in his early fifties. But he'd had a lot of wonderful parts and brilliant friends, far, far from Indianapolis. Essentially, what he'd done was use himself up, which is what people are supposed to do. Not that I recommend booze.

Yours truly,

Kurt Vonnegut

November 23, 1963
West Barnstable, MA

To Knox Burger

This was the day after President John F. Kennedy was assassinated in Dallas, Texas, by Lee Harvey Oswald.

Norman Mailer wrote an essay on "Hip" in Dissent *magazine; it was later collected in his nonfiction book* Advertisements for Myself.

Dear Knox:

After yesterday's demonstration in Dallas, I think I finally understand Norman Mailer's Philosophy of Hip.

What books do you think influenced Oswald most—after *The Manchurian Candidate?*

I'm writing to tell you that *Canary in a Cathouse* is apparently starting to pay off for me. I hope Fawcett got something out of it, too. I had a call from NBC Hollywood day before yesterday. Rod Serling wants to do a script of "The Euphio Question". That indicates to me that somebody is keeping the book around, and is going to comb it from time to time. So thanks. [. . .]

Kurt

January 21, 1964
West Barnstable, MA

To Mark Vonnegut

Mark was sixteen at this time.

Percy Leen and her husband, Dexter, were good friends of Kurt and Jane.

Dear Mark:

Well, you keep announcing boisterously and proudly new ways you've discovered of being a bum. You might give the next

guy who wants to buy a painting from you a lesson in art appreciation that goes like this: A small tube of paint costs a dollar, a
canvas costs two dollars, and the minimum legal wage in this
country is now a dollar and a quarter an hour. Percy Leen did me
the big favor of admiring my paintings and actually hanging them
on her walls. I figure this honor cost me about forty bucks or
more every time she awarded it to me. Americans have yet to
catch on to the fact that painters actually have to pay for their
materials, just as though they were in business or something. Jack
Teagarden, the guy everybody agrees was the greatest living trombone player by far, died broke about a week ago. He didn't take
dope. He wasn't a drunk. He just didn't get paid much for being
the greatest living trombone player. [. . .]

    We'll see you soon. We're going to bust our asses on the
slopes again the day before we pick you up. We must be nuts. We
have no talent that way at all.

    Love,
    K

April 9, 1964
West Barnstable, MA

To Knox Burger

The book he had just finished was God Bless You, Mr. Rosewater. *It
was published the following year in hardcover by Holt, Rinehart and
Winston and was the first of Vonnegut's books to be widely reviewed.*

Dear old Knox:
    Hey listen—I just finished a book about twenty minutes ago,
and do I ever feel loony and great. Happy as a bird. Tweet, tweet,
tweet, tweet. [. . .]
    Boy am I happy.
    Kurt

May 25, 1964

West Barnstable, MA

To Rust Hills

Rust Hills was fiction editor of The Saturday Evening Post.
John Barth and Alan Harrington were contemporary novelists.

Dear Mr. Hills:

How pleasant to hear from you. I'm honored that you should like *Cat's Cradle*. As for the next book, which is called *God Bless You, Mr. Rosewater,* I know that Holt plans to give you first look. They should have the final revision within ten days.

I was a client of Littauer & Wilkinson for about fourteen years, quit them a year and a half ago, sold *God Bless You, Mr. Rosewater* on my own, appointing Holt its agent. And then, because Max Wilkinson is probably my closest friend, things got patched up again in a half-assed, non-contractual way. All my short stories go through Max. When I get the book out of the way, I hope to do some short stories again. I sold a lot of stories to the Post in the bad old days, but you mustn't hold that against me.

I've got the Barth and Harrington books on order. I've avoided them because I've suspected they were good.

I look forward to having lunch with you. I expect to be in New York in the middle of June. I'll give you plenty of advance notice.

The book to follow *Rosewater,* incidentally, will be a novel about a small group of American P.W.'s caught in the bombing of Dresden. I was in such a group. I don't know if such a tale would interest the *Post,* but the twentieth anniversary of the raid will fall on February 13, 1965.

Yours truly,

Kurt Vonnegut

June 4, 1965

West Barnstable, MA

To Knox Burger

Kurt refers here to his daughter Edith, his son, Mark, and Steve
Adams, one of the three Adams boys he and Jane raised.

Friedrich Dürrenmatt was a Swiss playwright who gained fame
with his play The Visit *in 1956; his most recent play at this time had*
been The Physicists. *The Tom Wolfe collection was* The Kandy-Kolored
Tangerine-Flake Streamline Baby.

Dear Knox:

Those are good and tempting directions you sent me, and I
hope to use them in a month or so. I assume you know how to
get here, in case you want to come here. We'd love to see you.
Edith, who says we are always cutting up her friends, started cutting up our friends one night, but she had nothing but good
things to say about you. [. . .]

I suppose I've already crowed to you about this: Mark got
into Swarthmore, and Steve got into Dartmouth, both first
choices, in the toughest college entrance year in history. No schol-
arships.

So here I am at the male menopause, to all practical purposes
complete. We filled out a very complicated scholarship application form for Swarthmore, had to account for every cent we had
or might get, and Swarthmore wrote back that no scholarship
was necessary. Mark was flabbergasted, and started investigating
on his own to find out what I had hidden around, and Jane has
stopped making poor mouths, though she will carry the lines
made by them to the grave. I am rich.

Jane's father died at about 74 a couple of weeks back—stroke,
stroke, stroke, and then the old people's friend, pneumonia. He
looked just like Gary Cooper, talked less. During our nearly 20
years of marriage, he sent us one postcard. When Jane took on all
the Adams kids he said not a word. He had been half-way

through Marine basic when the first World War ended, so the V.A. sent a flag over to the mortuary, and the Mr. Joyboys spread it on the casket. My mother-in-law made them take it off because that sort of thing was only for men who had given their lives for their country. She was right. There was a huge gangster floral piece at the head of the casket. Jane looked at the card afterwards, and learned that it had been sent by the Wabash Valley Quarter-Midget Racing Association. Wrong corpse.

As you may have noticed, the *Times* gave me two damn unfriendly reviews. They have since asked me to review in quick succession a new book by Duerrenmatt and the Tom Wolfe collection. Doing the Tom Wolfe thing *properly* (for the *Times*, the *Times*, for Chrissake!) is a ball-buster. If they are too chicken to have a staffer do it, then they should pay me a grand.

I have started writing short stories again, in brand new ways. I'm changing fast. The new ways are probably terrible. I can't judge.

Kurt

June 25, 1965
West Barnstable, MA

To MILLER HARRIS

Miller Harris had written to the Cornell Alumni News *for the Class of '43 a report on Vonnegut's accomplishments and publications, closing with Graham Greene's quote calling Kurt "one of the best living American writers." In 1963, Greene had called* Cat's Cradle *one of his three favorite novels of the year, in the London* Spectator.

Dear Miller:

I am most deeply touched—particularly since you came right out and said the lies about my career which I have only dared to hint at. I am not kidding: that little piece in the *Alumni News* will do more to firm up my reputation than anything that has been printed about me so far.

I am extremely dense, and so continue to be startled whenever I realize that you aren't a cynical bastard at all. Since I now have it in my head momentarily that you are a sentimentalist, I will tell you that I have a son entering Swarthmore next fall, and that he is the age I was when you and I first met. I will give him your name and address, and tell him to call you in the expectation of making a powerful new friend. He is a tough little bastard, a 145-pound line-backer from Mount Hermon, who is blind as a bat without his glasses. His name is Mark, and I like him, and he's very good at math and radical chess.

Since you advised me so well at the start of my career, I'll ask you to do it again at the end of it: Should I become a resident writer at the University of Iowa? I got offered the job yesterday. They would pay me a grand a month, have me teach about five hours a week, and write the rest of the time. I guess maybe it's a good idea, because I'd do just as much writing as I do now, and get $8,500 I wouldn't get otherwise. How's that for using the old head?

Listen: I think you can safely become Salinger now. The competition is through.

Come see us.

Love,

Kurt

July 11, 1965

West Barnstable, MA

To John C. Gerber

John Gerber was chairman of the English department of the University of Iowa and issued the official invitation to Kurt to teach at the Writers' Workshop.

Dear Dr. Gerber:

I'm very pleased to be invited out there. What writer wouldn't be? I have a novel about the Great Depression in progress, and will finish it there. My wife and children will stay here. There are too many of them to move.

I presume that the University has some sort of housing bureau. I'm too busy to come house-hunting, so would you ask them to reserve something for a Lecturer who hopes to do a lot of writing in the place, who will be visited occasionally by his wife?

Yours truly,

Kurt

August 7, 1965

West Barnstable, MA

To Knox Burger

Dear Knox:

You've always been such a graceful and easy guest that you're welcome to come fishing any time you like. I have a hide-a-bed in my study, and that's for you.

I don't put my boat out on a mooring any more, because kids were always taking it out without my permission (kids not my own), and the weather was bashing the engine night and day. So it sits on a trailer in my yard, and I don't have to bother with going down to the yacht club and rowing out to a mooring any more. I just go down Scudder's Lane and stick her in. With this particular rig, we can cross the Cape and kill blues for a change, if that would interest you. I haven't tried that yet. I killed my first and last blue in 1952. They're big this year.

I suppose I'll take off for Iowa City about September 10. I don't want to go, but everybody says it will be good for me. Jane will be left here with just two little girls. Think of it, all the people who used to live here. It will be a strangely good winter for Jane. She has taken up the piano, and, with me gone, she'll take up reading and writing again. She used to be excellent at both. [. . .]

Did I understand you correctly—that you are thinking of becoming an agent? Whenever you start talking about something like that, you become cryptic and evasive, not to say hunted-looking.

After a performance of *Treasure Island* at the Cape Playhouse last week, the cast went out on the lawn to mingle with the audience of children. The children, as has always been the custom, collected autographs of the American Theater Wing actors. Edith Vonnegut, as a gypsy, gave her autograph to Caroline Kennedy, a wide-eyed little kid. [. . .]

Kurt

September 17, 1965
Iowa City

TO JANE VONNEGUT

Paul Engle was director of the Iowa Writers' Workshop.

Dear Woofy:

My first act as Writer in Residence was to steal about eight pounds of this stationery while waiting in Paul Engle's unguarded office for the great man to show up. When he appeared at last, he proved to be a lean, gray-haired, slightly crooked Supreme Court Justice dressed like Harry Belafonte. His only advice was to buy a season ticket to the football games at a 50% faculty discount, which I did immediately. It cost $15.00. If you would cause the check to bounce, you would be a heroine to Writers in Residence everywhere. Tomorrow we play Washington State. I hope we win.

To those, like yourself, who think universities are beautiful, with their chapels and botany buildings and schools of dentistry and all that, this must surely seem a lovely place—and even I am moved. Seriously, folks, I am glad to be back in the Corn Belt again. Word of honor: I like it. Word of honor: it's good looking as anything. These people are boobs about a lot of things, but they're just like the Jews when it comes to EDUCATION.

But you should see the apartment I have. I don't recommend that you see it. I opened the door for the first time, and I thought, "My God, Otis Burger has been here before me!" It has a vileness, a George Price uninhabitability that no amateur could achieve. I must sleep in the very first Hide-a-bed ever created, which was created from the rusty wreckage of the first Stutz Bearcat. Jesus, is it ever a cruel and ugly old bed! I have a bath with a stall shower, a full kitchen, less ice-cube trays, no curtains or windowshades, and this livingroom–bedroom with the hide-a-bed. You wonder what creates beatniks? Landlords! "Live like a pig for $80.00 a month," say my surroundings. Very well. Very well.

So I will write to the Del Prado, and say that we want the same room we had on our honeymoon four years ago. Better there than here, if you want to talk about love somewhere during the proceedings.

Well—I'm the guy who said that marvelous thing about queer travel suggestions being dancing lessons from God, and here I am, and there you all are. And I love you. What do I have from home? One picture that must stand for you all—my darling Edith's picture of herself. That's it.

K

September 17, 1965

[Iowa City]

To Jane Vonnegut

Nelson Algren and Vance Bourjaily were both on the faculty of the Workshop. Algren had gained fame with his novel The Man with the Golden Arm, *which won the National Book Award in 1950 and was produced as a major motion picture starring Frank Sinatra. Bourjaily gained literary acclaim for his first novel,* The End of My Life, *in 1947 and published many other novels.*

Dear Wife:

Some technical poop: We in Iowa City are on Central Standard Time, whereas most of the people around us are on Central Daylight Time. This means that, until you go back on standard time, you will be three hours later than me. I will explain: When it is three o'clock here, it will be six o'clock there. If you call me at ten p.m., it will only be seven here. After you go back on standard time, if you call me at ten p.m., it will be eight here. I can't be any clearer than that. Tell Nanny, and then, when you need to know, ask her what the hell is going on with all this time business. Anyway, my phone isn't hooked up yet. When it is, I'll call you up and tell you what the number is. Ideally, you should call me most of the time. That way, you can take advantage of cheap calling rates that won't be available to me until three hours later. Just wait until it's six o'clock there, and we screw 'em good.

I stopped off to see your mother in Fort Wayne. She's in a smashing new hospital with a woman who was struck by a tornado while asleep. Your mother is her same sparky self. She will be the sole survivor of World War Three. You should be thinking seriously of rigging an apartment for her. I've got a hunch, and I think she does, too, that maybe she had better live with us during a good part of what remains of her old age, which I would suppose to be plenty. The lawyer she sold Harve's firm to is going to sue the hotel for a blue million. He is very burned up about that step down from the bathroom. Riah's problem right now is to get somebody to take her from Fort Wayne to Indianapolis after her discharge, which will be within the next five days. No Cox has volunteered, and she's damned if she'll ask. I told her to try a Vonnegut, and she said she might. Bob has told her to go to Europe before she's dead, and she has agreed to this. Maybe next summer.

Algren hasn't appeared yet. I haven't yet met Bourjaily.

Things will get social tomorrow, I think—after the GAME.
Engle has invited me to a big cocktail party. They don't know
how great I am yet. It will take them about six weeks to understand. A couple of letters were waiting for me: a nutty thing
from Angela Jones, and an interesting thing from Warren
Miller, who is editor of the *Nation* now. He wants me to review
for him. All of a sudden, everybody is yelling for ignorant
reviewers.

I didn't put the slightest scratch in Mark's automobile.
It ran like a dollar watch all the way. I did blow a tire,
though—ten miles outside of Iowa City. I'll buy him a new
one, and a radio, too. I love him. I will try to buy his love in
return.

Explain to Mr. Jordan that I am not home just now, but that I
will beat the shit out of him at Christmas. I am no kidding going
to the gym every day. We have a swimming pool the size of
Rhode Island, and punching bags galore.

Love,
K

September 21, 1965

[Iowa City]

To Jane Vonnegut

Dearest Jane:

Your charming package of messages arrived this morning,
made my love and loneliness acute. Such pangs. I'm a homesick
little boy. I'm on the second floor of the sort of frame house
Penrod lived in. It's crazy—all the land these people have,
and they build their houses chockablock on teeny weeny
lots. Maybe they're sick of land. There are alleys everywhere.
I had forgotten how romantic alleys are. My apartment is like
this:

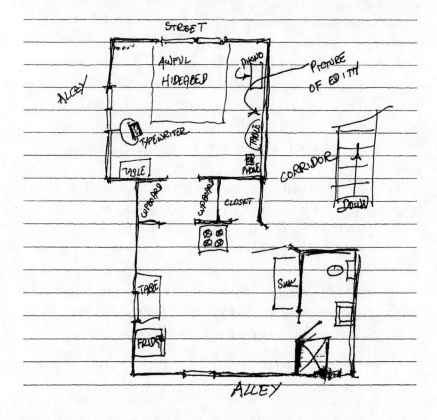

I like the apartment better each day. It's friendlier than I thought—a nice, soft old shoe. I work well in it. I've already managed to send off a big part of the *Rosewater* treatment to Harrison. That whole package, which is more a complete scenario than a treatment, should be finished in ten more days. It should be worth some money to us. It's full of brand new *Rosewater* lines and situations—had to be, since a book is a book and a film is a film. It's kind of a sequel.

I will tell you what I really like: the looks and the feel of this town. The university is right in the middle of it, and the town exists only because of the university. The idea is medieval and exciting and beautiful. Dexter [Leon] would faint for joy. Give him my love, by the way. I can and do walk to all the stores and to work. The Unitarian church is a block away, and I went last Sunday. It's a great club.

I don't make my professorial debut until tomorrow afternoon. All that's going on now is registration. I have yet to make new friends. I'm a laggard that way. Things will start bubbling tomorrow maybe.

Love you

    K (over)

P.S. About your coming here: The stunt is to fly to Chicago, then Cedar Rapids, and I'll pick you up there. Chicago is about 350 miles away. We can have a very nice time here. You say when.

September 24, 1965

[Iowa City]

To Jane Vonnegut

Gertrude Buckman worked at Collier's *and did typing for Knox and Kurt.*

    Marguerite Young was a writer from Indianapolis who later gained a literary cult following for her novel Miss MacIntosh, My Darling.

    Their dire warnings were unfounded, as Kurt became friends with Engle and Bourjaily, as well as his other distinguished colleagues on the writing faculty.

Dearest Jane:

    I enclose letters from Mark and Steve. They guessed correctly that I was in far worse shape than you. Mark just might bust his ass this year. That's a brutal schedule. Then again, he's got a terrific case of the smarts, and he's beautifully prepared. With such a challenging schedule, he may be one prep school kid who doesn't lose his forward motion because college is such a pipe. Steve has a beautiful understanding of himself. A very good boy.

    Things around here are starting to get amusing. As I've already said, at a minimum the town is a Utopia. I can walk to everything, and everything's cheerful and clean. Three blocks from here is an enormous new indoor swimming pool. No one is ever there during school hours, and a dip costs me a dime. And there's that neat church, and my laundry, and my dry cleaner, and all that crap. I am used to my vile pad now. I work pretty well here now, which is the main thing—and any minute now my telephone will be installed.

Nelson Algren arrived with his very pretty and young wife at the very last minute. He is most friendly to me, and knows my work well. Gertrude told me that Paul Engle was her least favorite person in this world, and Marguerite Young warned me that Bourjaily would cut my throat if I went over big with the students, so I am watchful. Bourjaily and Engle both treat me rather oddly. [. . .] They never heard of me before, and I still act as though I were somebody. Algren is their prize. Algren is here, by the way, because he's broke. He worked a deal where he wouldn't come unless they gave his wife a job, too. She's an actress, and they found her something to do in the Speech Department.

Queer as it seems, I still haven't met my students. Registration and speeches by the president and faculty meetings and all that have used up this first week. I will finally hold my first class at 3:30 this afternoon. There is a curious thing about this obviously first-rate English Department: only ten per cent of its 600 undergraduates are men; and only 25 per cent of its graduate students are women. The graduate men all come from the East or West Coasts. Nelson and I have no futures in the field, since we have no degrees. Bourjaily is loaded with them, and is a university career man. We all have offices, by the way—but no telephones.

Along with your music appreciation course, I think you should also take some simple piano lessons, so you can follow the music better. Promise to do that?

This is a good idea—no matter how lousy it may feel to both of us from time to time. It's like that crazy dieting we did. It will make us love life and each other and the children even more than we do.

K

September 28, 1965

[Iowa City]

To Jane Vonnegut

Dearest Jane:

In an unmoored life like mine, sleep and hunger and work arrange themselves to suit themselves, without consulting me. I'm just as glad they haven't consulted me about the tiresome details. What they have worked out is this: I awake at 5:30, work until 8:00, eat breakfast at home, work until 10:00, walk a few blocks into town, do errands, go to the nearby municipal swimming pool, which I have all to myself, and swim for half an hour, return home at 11:45, read the mail, eat lunch at noon. In the afternoon I do schoolwork, either teach or prepare. When I get home from school at about 5:30, I numb my twanging intellect with several belts of Scotch and water ($5.00/fifth at the State Liquor store, the only liquor store in town. There are loads of bars, though.), cook supper, read and listen to jazz (lots of good music on the radio here), slip off to sleep at ten. I do pushups and sit-ups all the time, and feel as though I am getting lean and sinewy, but maybe not. Last night, time and my body decided to take me to the movies. I saw *The Umbrellas of Cherbourg,* which I took very hard. To an unmoored, middle-aged man like myself, it was heart-breaking. That's all right. I like to have my heart broken.

My enormous Form of Fiction class, which has grown to about 80 students, and which is still growing, thanks to late registrants, is being broken up into two sections ("A" and "B"—what else?), each meeting for two hours once a week. "A" meets from 3:30 until 5:30 on Tuesday, and "B" meets at the same time on Wednesday. So, from Wednesday at 5:30 until Monday at 4:30, when my workshop meets, I have nothing to teach. This may seem like a remarkably soft schedule, tailored to the airy needs of a writer in residence, but it is actually a little heavier than the schedules of most of the regular English staff. Allan Vestal, an old

Shortridge friend who is a full professor in the Law School, teaches only four hours a week, and his classes are much smaller than mine.

I have incidentally changed the name of my course, since I am the only one teaching it, to Form and *Texture* of Fiction. Hi ho. It's going pretty well. At our first meeting, the students were bitter about the hugeness of the class. They're somewhat mollified by its being divided up, and I'm starting to get some friendly playback. They're starting to catch on that Mr. Vonnegut can be funny. That's the only thing I know how to be, and of course never got a chance to be funny in Barnstable. You've got to take the goods with the bads.

Anyway, as you can see: when you come out here for your first visit, we can go to Chicago (six hours by car), or do anything we damn please after class on Wednesday. If you are as interested in sex as you say you are, there is a really lovely book about it in my study—on a top shelf. It's red, and it's called *The ABZ of Love*.

Love from A to Z—
        K

P.S. Nelson Algren has disappeared.

                                        September 29, 1965
                                        Iowa City
To Rust Hills

After his departure from The Saturday Evening Post, *Rust Hills became fiction editor of* Esquire.

Dear Rust:
        [. . .] Having had one kid turn twenty, and having sent two others off to college, I am undergoing changes of heart and soul, so I'm trying to find new ways of writing that suit the changed

organs. So there are bound to be clinkers—maybe nothing but clinkers for the rest of my days. But I am hopeful.

The news of your impending departure from the *Post* is going to break plenty of hearts in the writing profession. I just gave the news to Vance Bourjaily, and he cursed and moaned some. That you unselfishly busted your ass on behalf of good writing is widely known, and I will make it even more widely known this afternoon, when I meet with a class of sixty-five. I am trying to give my course strong undertones of sociological realism, making my students think hard about not only what stories and authors are, but what audiences are, too.

I have sniffed around a little, and there is every indication that you would be most welcome here. I think the presence of a first-rate editor would round out the staff handsomely. I gather that all the money has been spent for the coming academic year, so the possibility of your being taken on before next September is slim—but not invisible. I suggest that you write Paul Engle at 724 Bayard Street, if you're at all serious. He is the man who can find extra money right now, if he really wants to, or make a spot next September absolutely firm. You had better write him immediately, though, because he's leaving for nine months in Europe a couple of weeks from now.

You'd like it here. Really. It's cozy.

Kurt

September 30, 1965

[Iowa City]

To Nanette Vonnegut

Nanette "Nanny" Vonnegut is the second daughter and third child of Kurt and Jane. Mark Vonnegut explains that "I called Jane 'Aunt Jane' so as not to call attention to 'the orphans' [the Adams boys] not having a living mother or mom, which I didn't stop until I was thirty. I called Kurt mostly 'Dad,' as I believe my sisters did as well. Most of Barnstable referred to Jane as 'Aunt Jane.' Kurt was 'Unky K' or 'K' to the orphans. 'Aunt Mother' and 'Uncle Father' must have been in jest or sarcasm. . . ."

Dearest Nanny:

I have sent you a very stupid birthday present today by air mail, and I hope it gets there in time. Just because it is stupid and didn't cost much doesn't mean I don't love you. I hope you understand that. Because I am so far away (and so very lonesome), I have to let Aunt Mother get you something really good. Please tell me what the really good thing was.

I did you a big favor. I fixed things so that Aunt Mother and Edith can't get mad at you because you got something from me and they didn't. I sent presents to them, too. But their presents didn't cost half as much as yours did.

I am getting a lot of good work done here, which is why I came here. I write a lot, and teach a lot. The students say they like me, and they have gone out and bought books I have written, and they say they like those, too. Most of my students have already graduated from college, but they keep on going to college anyway. I guess they are comfortable in college. Tell Aunt Mother that they are practically all men, older than Jim, and that the few girls are very nervous and unattractive, the way girls get if they go to college too long.

Tell Aunt Mother, too, that I signed and mailed the Harper's contract today, and that Uncle Max will be coming to see her soon with the money.

I want you and Aunt Mother and Edith to come out here and live with me after Christmas vacation, or whenever your first semester ends. We couldn't fit into this terrible little place I have now, but I am starting to look for something better. You will like this pretty little town. It is fun to walk around, and there are lots of movie houses and good stores, and practically everybody is either a kid or a teacher. There is also a beautiful indoor swimming pool, a huge one, that costs only a dime.

Love from your Uncle Father,
    K

P.S. The last time I saw you, you were certainly one of the nicest people I had ever seen. Now I hear that you are learning to dance. That makes you just about perfect.

October 2, 1965
[Iowa City]

To Jane Vonnegut

Dearest Jane:

Things are a lot better. I went riding at the Bourjailys' farm yesterday afternoon with Mrs. Bourjaily (Tina), found that I loved it, still rode damn well. I had forgotten that I ever did anything physical damn well, but, by God, even I must admit that I ride damn well. Vance doesn't care for the sport. He is a great hunter, a blood sport man. Max, of course, despises all blood sport men, and I kind of think he is right. Only Vance has turned out to be a most generous, wise, and friendly man. I stayed for supper, and the Algrens came. They're fine, too. Nelson gave me a big red sticker for my little automobile. It said, "STOP THE WAR IN VIET NAM!" I stuck it on my car, but the car was wet, and the sticker blew off before I was half way home, and I'm just as glad. My gladness doesn't have anything to do with how I feel about Viet Nam. It has to do with how I feel about stickers.

I haven't moved into my new quarters yet, will probably do so in about five days. Two very clean Chinamen are living there now, for very temporary shelter. They'll be leaving soon. The apartment is the entire first floor of a Victorian mansion. It is on seven acres, has an orchard, a grape arbor, a barn. It's on a hill. This is a hilly place, which surprised me, and the river is lovely. You can just about imagine what the first floor of such a house is like: an entrance hall, a parlor to the right of it, a dining room back of that, and a kitchen as modern as ours back of that, and a porch back of that. And then, to one side of the dining room, and back of the entrance hall, a luxury bedroom and bath. The

furnishings are gorgeous—pieces belonging to the same astonishing period as the house. There is a washing machine in the
basement. The Chinamen have been sleeping in separate areas,
one (they all look alike to me) in the bedroom, and one on a bed
set up in the entrance hall. It will be fun spotting two beds for
Edith and Nanny. If Edith wanted to come out right away, she
could have the bed in the front hall, which isn't nearly as exposed as it sounds. Everybody comes and goes by the back
porch.

Paul Engle, who is about to leave for a nine-month tour of
Europe, has been conscience-stricken about my bad living quarters and the hugeness of my classes. I am carrying as heavy a load
as anybody in the English Department, which isn't the way things
are supposed to be at all with a Writer in Residence. Anyway, he
has gotten me this great house, and has just begged the head of
the English Department, Dr. Gerber, to give me a raise from
$8,500 to $12,500—a raise instead of the cash bonus he originally suggested to help me afford the better house. He thinks
what will happen is that I will get maybe a $1,000 raise, at least.
If I got only that much, it would mean that suddenly my rent was
all taken care of. Not bad. And I might get more.

Your adoring husband,

K

P.S. You write beautifully. I wish just one of my students had as
much talent & charm & wisdom as you.

October 7, 1965
Iowa City

TO EDITH VONNEGUT

*Kurt's daughter Edith would come to Iowa City and attend University
High School, which she would soon "find a paradise."*

Dearest Edith:

Mom tells me that you are planning to come out here and live with me around November 12. That is fine with me. I have plenty of room for you, and I could sure use some company.

There are two high schools in Iowa City, and everybody on the English faculty tells me that they are both first-rate. They have to be good, because all the parents in town are college professors. Kids in this town, incidentally, seem to have one hell of a good time, as you will soon see.

The school closest to me—about six blocks from my house and two blocks from my office—is the University High School. It isn't run by the city. It is run by the University's College of Education. They are supposed to have a long waiting list, but I talked to the principal today, and he said you would be most welcome. I had a look at the art department, and it's huge, and they're doing all kinds of marvelous stuff. Art is big in the city. The University has a very famous art school, which has studies all around my office. Tell Mom that the principal of your new school and several of the teachers have doctor's degrees. That shouldn't worry you. That just means that you'll get better teaching than you're used to.

I had better warn you about a couple of things: I can be pretty boring company sometimes, and winters out here are unbelievably cold. But we'll have a nice time anyway. This is a crazy Victorian house, with funny, elaborate furniture. You'll have all the privacy you want. I'll give you the two front rooms, and close the huge doors that can separate them from the rest of the house. That way you'll have a bedroom and sitting room all your own, and a very flashy connecting bath we'll have to share. Our kitchen is also flashy. You'll be amazed by your sitting room. It has two nice couches, several easy chairs, a piano, and a chandelier. You'll have to share it, of course, when Mom and Nanny come.

Love,
Dad

October 20, 1965

Iowa City

To Jane Vonnegut

Dear Jane:

Be sure to bring your bathing suit when you come. We can have an olympic pool almost all to ourselves on weekday mornings. It's nice and warm.

I got you a sensational birthday present, so you really must come soon. There are a couple of parties over the weekend of the 29th, so you'll get to meet my colleagues and their wives under cheerful and easy circumstances, Algren, Starbuck, Bourjaily, Donoso. Donoso is particularly neat. He is probably the greatest living Chilean novelist. Algren told him: "I always thought it would be fun to belong to a country that skinny." [. . .]

I gave my thesis to a thesis-typer around here named Mrs. Meek. She is, according to the schedule, four days away from having her second baby. I can believe it. She said I would get my thesis back either right before or right after the baby. She says that having babies makes her feel marvelous, makes her work even harder right before and right after. She's a lot like you in that respect.

This place is full of the dumbest, sweetest mice. I haven't the heart to harm them—and neither will Edith, and neither will you. They don't do anything bad. They keep me company and make me laugh.

Sometimes the classes go good, sometimes they go lousy. That's show business.

Harrison will be sending you another grand in about thirty days. Lawsy, how dem grands do pile up.

Love,

K

P.S. Remember: I can just as easily pick you up in Cedar Rapids as here (almost), so go there, if that's any more convenient for you. Haven't got a damn thing on all day Friday. [. . .]

I wish my students could write [. . .] simply and clearly, and keep a story moving as well. They are damned if they will tell a story simply and directly, and I have discovered the reason for this. It is not the fault of their previous teachers. It is their own fault: they have no stories to tell. I am going to take them on walks, and make them look at people. I have just ordered them to buy a book, which is to be the core text for my workshop. No workshop has ever had a text before. The book? That Steichen collection of photographs *The Family of Man*.

November 1, 1965
Iowa City

To Knox Burger

"Tina" is the wife of Vance Bourjaily.

Dear Knox:

I received a report recently to the effect that you have been exceptionally blue—and it makes me so God damned sad. Please, buddy—won't you do things about it? Life could be so great for you.

I am teaching very hard, since I am so hopelessly square. My kids can write, unfortunately. Algren's kids can probably write, too, but he is doing himself and them a favor by telling them to get out of town. Jane is out here for a week. She has to go back to nurse her mother, who has a busted hip. And I gave her a polaroid for her 43rd birthday, and she took the greatest picture of Algren that the world has ever seen. We will get copies made. He is a most pleasant fellow, with a pixie wife about Mark's age. He insisted that his wife be given a job, too, and she is busting her ass in the Speech Department, working about twelve hours to his one.

Bourjaily has very quickly turned into a friend. We had him and his wife over for drinks a couple of nights ago, and everybody said it was amazing that they came. It was the first time they had been out since the accident, evidently. I ride horseback with Tina from time to time. It's crazy. I used to be a real good rider, and then I forgot all about it. I keep thinking I can't do anything, which is dead wrong. I also swim every couple of days, and do pushups and situps, and smoke worse than ever, and write not at all.

During my first two weeks, I wrote a master's thesis in anthropology, which I've owed Chicago for 18 years. I called them up when it was done, and they said I could still have the degree if it was any good. It might be good. I am waiting for the typist to return it to me so I can find out. It's about how a story-teller, any good story-teller anywhere, works.

I'm glad I came, to the extent that I can be glad about anything. You want to come out here? Why not? There are four movie houses within a block of each other, and they change bills every three days. Scotch is $4.90 a quart.

Cheer up,

Kurt

November 12, 1965

Iowa City

To Paul Engle

Paul Engle was in Stockholm at this time.

Daniel Boorstin was a lawyer and university professor at the University of Chicago. His 1961 book The Image: A Guide to Pseudo-Events in America *popularized the term "pseudo-event"—an event whose main purpose was to serve the goals of advertising and public relations.*

Murray Krieger was a literary critic whose 1960 book The Tragic Vision: Variations on a Theme in Literary Interpretation *helped establish him as a leading literary critic and theorist.*

Wayne Booth was another influential literary critic on the basis of his 1961 book The Rhetoric of Fiction. *He was also dean of the un-dergraduate school of the University of Chicago and a professor at the university.*

Harper & Row reprinted Mother Night *in hardcover in 1966.*

Dear Paul:

I was pleased to have the nice clipping from England. I hadn't seen it. It reached me yesterday, which was incidentally my 43rd birthday. Yesterday was also the day on which Vance asked me if I would like to come back for a second year. I said yes. Yesterday was also the day on which I played host to my editor at Harper & Row, Roger Klein. Roger made courtesy visits to Starbuck, Justice, Algren, and Bourjaily, and was very taken by my best student, Ian MacMillan. He promised to do his best to get *Harper's Magazine* to publish something of Ian's. You ask me to tell you of any good students in my care. Well, speaking conservatively, Ian is one of the three best writers I ever met. I'm going to see if I can't make money start coming out of his ears within the next six months.

And I have two others who are somewhat shallow and deriva-tive, but funny and shrewd—Berman and Lehrman. They could probably both make it in Hollywood.

My son Mark telephoned me (yesterday, again) from Swarth-more College to tell me that the Quakers aren't inclined to do much for the living, swinging arts. He wants to come out here to live with me and study film. I'm going to make him stay there at least two years, to get the square academic foundation the school is justly proud of providing. My daughter Edith is already out here, finding the University High School a paradise. My wife was out here last week, but had to go back to nurse her dotty mother, who is recovering from a broken hip in our house on the Cape. She will be out here with me for the whole of the second semester.

What ideas have I had for improving the workshop? I've only had two ideas, and both are very likely lousy. The first would be to require workshop people to study some other art form, music, painting, or whatever. The second would be to create a seminar for a tiny core of students who, like MacMillan, can already write like crazy. If we had such an elite, the workshop could maintain its fancy reputation no matter how many poor students got in.

My wife and I had dinner with Dan Boorstin and Murray Krieger's brother a week ago—in Chicago. You were mentioned favorably. Dan rigged things so that I got to see Dean Wayne Booth, and Booth is going to rig things so that I can speak at Chicago soon. He knew my work. I'm always amazed when somebody knows my work.

Say hello to all those yellow-haired sex maniacs for me.

Kurt

November 30, 1965

Suzanne McConnell, one of Kurt's students in his "Form of Fiction" course, saved and passed on to me this assignment, explaining that Kurt "wrote his course assignments in the form of letters, as a way of speaking personally to each member of the class." Ms. McConnell took to heart his advice to pretend to be a "useful editor on a good literary magazine," and later became fiction editor of the Bellevue Literary Review *as well as publishing stories, essays, and reviews for a number of literary magazines.*

FORM OF FICTION TERM PAPER ASSIGNMENT   November 30, 1965

Beloved:

This course began as Form and Theory of Fiction, became Form of Fiction, then Form and Texture of Fiction, then Surface Criticism, or How to Talk out of the Corner of Your Mouth Like a Real Tough Pro. It will probably be Animal Husbandry 108 by the time Black February rolls around. As was said to me years ago by a dear, dear friend, "Keep your hat on. We may end up miles from here."

As for your term papers, I should like them to be both cynical and religious. I want you to adore the Universe, to be easily delighted, but to be prompt as well with impatience with those artists who offend your own deep notions of what the Universe is or should be. "This above all . . . "

I invite you to read the fifteen tales in *Masters of the Modern Short Story* (W. Havighurst, editor, 1955, Harcourt, Brace, $14.95 in paperback). Read them for pleasure and satisfaction, beginning each as though, only seven minutes before, you had swallowed two ounces of very good booze. "Except ye be as little children . . . "

Then reproduce on a single sheet of clean, white paper the table of contents of the book, omitting the page numbers, and substituting for each number a grade from A to F. The grades should be childishly selfish and impudent measures of your own joy or lack of it. I don't care what grades you give. I do insist that you like some stories better than others.

Proceed next to the hallucination that you are a minor but useful editor on a good literary magazine not connected with a university. Take three stories that please you most and three that please you least, six in all, and pretend that they have been offered for publication. Write a report on each to be submitted to a wise, respected, witty and world-weary superior.

Do not do so as an academic critic, nor as a person drunk on art, nor as a barbarian in the literary market place. Do so as a sensitive person who has a few practical hunches about how stories can succeed or fail. Praise or damn as you please, but do so rather flatly, pragmatically, with cunning attention to annoying or gratifying details. Be yourself. Be unique. Be a good editor. The Universe needs more good editors, God knows.

Since there are eighty of you, and since I do not wish to go blind or kill somebody, about twenty pages from each of you should do neatly. Do not bubble. Do not spin your wheels. Use words I know.

POLONIØUS

December 3, 1965

Iowa City

To Paul Engle

Paul Engle broke his ankle while on a trip to New York and was there at the time Kurt wrote this letter to him.

Dear Paul:

[. . .] I guess I'm doing fairly well here, but I've had a couple of classes die on me recently. That makes me feel lousy—a show that fails. I'm crazy about the workshops and the consultations. The academic classes are something else again, since I don't really know anything. Up to now, my ignorance has made me strong. Now I don't feel so hot about it. A lucky crapshooter is what I've been.

Anyway, muggy distress is good for me. My writing goes well. My daughter is living with me now, going to the University High School. My wife and another daughter will be out here after Christmas, and they'll all contrive to keep me sane. This is a good little house, but there are surveyors all over the grounds, marking them up into what appear to be cemetery lots with room for two. [. . .]

Cheer up. Your workshop here is an amazingly beautiful gift to the world. I wish you were here to talk to sometimes.

Kurt

January 20, 1966

[Iowa City]

To Knox Burger

Dear Knox:

So how goes it? I've been careful not to tell people you're not living with Otis any more. At least four other people have told *me* about it, though, a couple who don't know you at all. You're famous, and people notice what you do. [. . .]

Speaking of wives—good old Jane will be out here in a week or two with Nanny, will stay till summer. Something telepathic has busted between us, and I don't know how to fix it. I'd like to fix it. Sometimes when I talk to her I feel like the Ambassador from New Zealand presenting his credentials to the Foreign Minister of Uruguay. It's formal and strange, and not at all sexy. I can't get it up for her any more. Anybody else, simply anybody else, I can get it up for—but not for her, and she's a darling, loyal girl. I'm punishing her for mothering all those kids, I suppose. I dunno. We'll fix it up some way.

At Christmas I had the damnedest revulsion to Cape Cod, loved my family but hated the house—don't want to live there any more. I've been invited to teach here for two more years, which will take care of this tired gypsy for 1966, 1967, and 1968 anyway. I've accepted. Mark is leaving Swarthmore in June, honorably, and is going to enroll out here. He wants to go someplace big, with a film department and a drama department and an art school and a music department and all that. We've got it. He got off a great crack about Swarthmore: "Swarthmore is a hot little incubator that spits out dead babies." That's my boy.

To NELSON ALGREN

This was written on the bound proof of the Harper & Row hardcover edition of Mother Night.

Dear Nelson:

There's a little stiffness when we talk—which is my fault. The thing is: I'm awed. You're one of the few important artists of our time, and the only one I know. What a peculiar interlude this Iowa City thing has been, eh? I wonder if there's any sadism in Paul's bringing writers out here, knowing damn well that they'll cease to write.

Affectionately—
Kurt Vonnegut

March 5, 1966
Iowa City

To KNOX BURGER

David Markson was a novelist who had just received a big advance for a western spoof called The Ballad of Dingus Magee, *which was made as a movie starring Frank Sinatra. Markson later turned to writing experimental novels, including* Wittgenstein's Mistress, *that were highly regarded by many critics and writers, including Kurt.*

Madame Nhu, known as "the dragon lady" because of her glamour and political intrigue, was the wife of the South Vietnamese president's brother and chief adviser; she later blamed the U.S. for her country's loss of the war.

Dear Knox:

[. . .] Jane and Nannie are out here now, and everything seems roughly O.K. I had psychosomatic angina for about a week in advance. It's gone now.

I'm sorry that conversation with you in Chicago was so flat. When I heard about Markson getting $75,000, everything went white. People shouldn't talk to me about money.

It isn't any of my business how things are with you, but I still hanker to know. Is the break to be formalized and so on?

Nelson Algren is fucking up monumentally out here, as an old Wobbly would and should. He's not only bopping the Workshop in newspaper interviews—he's also down several thousand bucks in a pot-limit poker game run by racketeers from the Graduate School.

Madame Nhu's father was out here a couple of nights back, explaining why we should bomb North Vietnamese population centers. The audience wanted to kill him.

Kurt

April 3, 1966
Iowa City

To Knox Burger

Dear Knox:

[. . .] I got a big (for me) raise from the university, and they've made it clear that they want me to stay and stay and stay. I suppose I will. I don't feel much like writing any more, and I don't feel sad about it, either. Within the next few months I'll finish the Dresden book, which will be about the size of the Bobbsey Twins, and that'll be the end for a while. It reads like a telegram, and it's the one I always thought it was my duty to write. A Message to Garcia.

So what happened on your expedition to the Bahamas?

Kurt

October 14, 1966
Iowa City

To William Price Fox

Richard Yates, author of Revolutionary Road, *became a fellow faculty member and a lifelong friend of Kurt's. William Price Fox was a humorist whose novels include* Southern Fried *and* Ruby Red. *Both Vonnegut and Yates liked his writing and successfully campaigned for him to be hired to teach at the Iowa Writers' Workshop.*

Dear Bill:

Yates and I would like to get you on the faculty here, so we could have a clear majority in the Writers' Workshop of people with no fucking degrees whatsoever. I'm one, Yates is two—you'd make three. And the fiction staff is five. But your manuscript arrived in the same mail with your friendly letter, and I've weighed it in my hands (the manuscript), and I've remembered all that's gone before, and you're going to be a blooming culture hero and millionaire. I'll be frank with you, though: you'll be short as long as you live. Some people are tall, and other people are medium or short, and that's the way God wants it. So don't come crying to me. Some people are both tall and talented, and there you have God again. Take life as it comes. That's what I do. [. . .]

Kurt Vonnegut, Jr.

P.S. Yates isn't funny like we are. That's a horse on *him.*

October 28, 1966
Iowa City

To Knox Burger

Bill and Sarah were William Price Fox and his wife.

Evarts Ziegler was a highly respected Hollywood agent whom Knox introduced to Kurt.

Paul Horgan was a novelist and historian who won two Pulitzer Prizes for his history books on the American Southwest, where he had attended the New Mexico Military Institute. He had won a Guggenheim Fellowship and taught at Wesleyan University in Middletown, Connecticut, where he became a professor of English.

Harry Mark Petrakis was a Greek American writer of short stories and novels and an autobiography, A Dream of Kings, *which became a* New York Times *bestseller.*

Dear Knox:

I'm terribly excited. I think we're going to win our first Big Ten game in three years tomorrow. The Hawks against the Hoosiers.

I was out on the Coast a week ago, had topless pizza with Bill and Sarah after drinks with Ziegler. Ziegler sure has class. I liked him a lot. We have entered into a shapeless sort of business relationship. He will keep me in mind, but he won't think about me so often that Max will be offended. He told me that the way to write for the movies was to create a strong central character that a famous actor would demand to play. So I came home and wrote Kirk Douglas into my war book: But then I crossed him out again, because the war I saw wasn't really that way. I am stuck with the fine arts, I guess. Maybe I'll get the Nobel Peace Prize, which is 60 G's. Donald Kaul, a very good columnist for the *Des Moines Register,* suggested the other day that maybe the standard for the Peace Prize should be lowered, since nobody could be found to meet the present standards. He said maybe it should be awarded to somebody who was a really lousy shot.

That would be very nice if you would mention me favorably to Horgan and any other academic writers with power in the East. I think I have something very good going with the Rhode Island School of Design, but won't know for sure until December. I hear hints out here that I'll be offered an associate professorship and a big raise, but that isn't sure, either. The academic year coming up looks like a big one—third down, six yards to go, ball on the opponents' forty-five. Amazingly, I'll have four kids in college next year—and one in the Peace Corps and one in junior high. I feel like a charwoman in an old Adolphe Menjou movie.

The Guggenheim Foundation wrote, saying that I had been mentioned to them as a guy who might make a good Guggenheimer. So I applied. Since I am now in my forty-fifth year, this is the last year in which I am eligible.

Harry Mark Petrakis used my Cape Cod house last week, was invaded by Dartmouth football players after the Harvard game. My boy Steve, by the way, the sophomore offensive end, has played in every game so far. He is slow, but tall and good at dancing. He made the All-Cape basketball team—and football team, and baseball team. He and Dartmouth were made for each other.

Mark will probably get out of Swarthmore and get into architecture at Penn. That will make me happy. He will be the third architect named Vonnegut. I wish he were the fourth.

Love to Kitty—

Kurt

November 5, 1966
Iowa City

To Seymour Lawrence

The "Holt book" became Slaughterhouse-Five, *which Holt would turn down.*

Seymour "Sam" Lawrence had recently started his own publishing firm, with his imprint at Delacorte Press (Delacorte/Seymour Lawrence), an arrangement in which Lawrence, working from Boston, would choose his own line of authors and Delacorte (in hardcover) and Dell (in paperback) would finance, print, and distribute the books. Lawrence had been editor of the literary magazine Wake *at Harvard, worked for a year as a book salesman to learn the business, became director of The Atlantic Monthly Press at age twenty-nine and*

an editor of the Atlantic Press, where he brought in Katherine Anne
Porter's Ship of Fools *for Atlantic/Little Brown; disgruntled that he*
didn't get a share of that bestseller's earnings for his efforts, he left the
company. He briefly became a vice president of Knopf but was dis-
satisfied with working more with contracts than with authors, so he
started his own company in a one-room office on Beacon Street in
Boston in 1966.

He wrote to Vonnegut out of admiration for his New York Times
review of the Random House dictionary.

Dear Mr. Lawrence:

How pleasant to hear from you. [. . .]

My publishing plans are these: (1) to deliver a book I owe to
Holt for a small advance, and (2) look around.

The Holt book is going slowly, since I have a heavy teaching
load out here and am vaguely screwed up. Maybe it will be done
in about six months. I sure hope so.

A good movie deal is just now pending. I have also put in for
a Guggenheim. If either one pans out, I will become a full-time
writer again.

If you have a proposition, you might tell my agent about it.
He is Max Wilkinson, 500 Fifth Avenue.

Cheers,

Kurt Vonnegut, Jr.

November 17, 1966
Iowa City

To Carolyn Blakemore

Kurt had met Carolyn Blakemore when she was a secretary at Lit-
tauer and Wilkinson, his first literary agents. She had spent a weekend
with him and Jane at their house on Cape Cod, and Kurt remained
friends with her as she later became an editor at Lippincott.

Dear Carolyn:

Since I was snowed with student stuff when the Fox book arrived, I gave it to Yates. I've played hell getting it back. [. . .]

The Iowa experience is wearing thin. Two years will be plenty, I think, unless a really whopping offer is made to make me stay. It is spiritually pooping to care desperately about student work that probably isn't worth caring about. As I've told you, I do have a couple of humdingers, and I hope you get them. MacMillan especially.

Vance Bourjaily is the only writer really at home out here. He has a great big farm with woods and a lake, and his paycheck is big, and he has tenure, and he finds teaching easy as pie. His roots are down. Others stay one or two years, then flee, tearing their hair. They tear their hair because they haven't done any of their own writing while here.

I love you.

Kurt

November 18, 1966

Iowa City

To WILLIAM PRICE FOX

Kurt and Richard Yates were advocating that Fox be hired to teach in the Writers' Workshop.

Alan Pakula had produced the film To Kill a Mockingbird, *based on the Harper Lee novel, and went on to become a successful director. "The guy who had the option for peanuts" (on* God Bless You, Mr. Rosewater) *and "wouldn't sell out" was Hilly Elkins.*

Dear Bill:

[. . .] Yates and I are both making $11,000, with three months off in the summer and more than a month off in the winter. Be warned, though, that the students are so damned good that they will wear you out. I'm half way through my second year, and I'm beginning to think I've had enough. The vacancy you fill may well be mine. Or Yates'.

I had a big movie deal with Alan Pakula fall through last week. He wanted to buy *Rosewater*, but the guy who had the option for peanuts wouldn't sell out, wouldn't let go for anything, and I don't think he'll ever make the picture. The contract is a very bad one, drawn up by my publishers, God love them. [. . .]

If you ever get really broke again, drop me a note. I might have something I could spare. But honest to God, Bill, you're on your way up.

Hello to Sarah.

Kurt

February 4, 1967
Iowa City

To Seymour Lawrence

At a meeting with Sam Lawrence at his office in Boston, Kurt was offered the three-book contract for both hardcover and paperback rights. Delacorte/Dell was one of the few publishers at this time that were able to offer contracts for both hard and soft cover editions, which meant they were able to put up bigger advances than were customary in that era. This enabled Sam Lawrence, publishing through Delacorte/Dell, to build an impressive list of American fiction writers, eventually including Richard Yates, Tim O'Brien, Jayne Ann Phillips, Tom McGuane, Frank O'Connor, and others. Sam's advances put many novelists, like Kurt, "on their feet as writers." His faith that writers he believed in who had not yet become big moneymakers would eventually earn back their advances and make his company a profit was borne out—most dramatically of all by Kurt Vonnegut.

Dear Sam:

I'm glad you're glad. I can't imagine that you are as happy as I am. You're putting me on my feet as a writer. I've been living off-balance ever since I started freelancing in 1950. We'll do some good books together.

In building your list, you should definitely take a look at the works of Jose Donoso, whose agent is Carl Brandt. Jose has been teaching out here with me for the past two years. He is a world citizen, nominally a Chilean. He speaks English beautifully, and why wouldn't he? He's a product of Princeton.

I'm reading his latest novel, *This Sunday,* in manuscript. It is smashing. Fuentes is terribly excited about it, and so is everybody else who has seen it. And Donoso is full of books to come.

Ask Brandt for his form sheet. Knopf is publishing Donoso now. The marriage is weak.

Cheers,

Kurt

April 24, 1967

Iowa City

To Robie Macauley

The story Robie Macauley, fiction editor at Playboy, *bought became the title story of the collection* Welcome to the Monkey House.

The short story called "Captured" was part of an early draft of what later became Slaughterhouse-Five.

Mr. Robie Macauley
Fiction Editor, PLAYBOY
Chicago, Illinois

Dear Mr. Macauley:

Thanks so much for buying my story, and for paying me so extraordinarily well for it.

You have asked for more, so please find enclosed a short story called "Captured," which is actually the first episode in a war book I'm working on.

If it's of interest to you, let Max Wilkinson know at 500 Fifth
Avenue, New York. If not, return it to me here.

I'm about to leave this joint, as I know you did years ago.
Two years is enough, I've found. We're being absorbed by the
English Department, and, on that account, we swing very little
these days.

After June 24, I'll be freelancing again—probably forever,
with my base, in case you should want to reach me, in Barnstable, Cape Cod, Massachusetts.

Cheers,

Kurt Vonnegut, Jr.

August 10, 1967

[West Barnstable, MA]

To Dick Gehman

Kurt gives his advice to Gehman on coming to teach at Iowa.

Dear Dick:

That's great. You'll be an excellent teacher. Your ego will demand it, and so will your students. You'll have an appalling number of real writers entrusted to your care. The classes don't matter
much. The real business, head-to-head, is done during office
hours in the afternoons. Mornings are for writing—and so are
most of the afternoons. The Workshop has always been staffed by
professionals, so staffers have almost always been self-educated
and worse-educated than you. Forget your lack of credentials.
The University is perfectly used to barbarians in the Workshop,
thinks nothing of it. I have no degree. Yates has no degree. Algren
had one, but tried to hush it up (Journalism B.A., U. of Illinois).
And so on. You will be as glorious as any full professor because
you know REAL WRITERS and REAL EDITORS in BOSTON
and NEW YORK.

There are plenty of quite pleasant bars with pool tables in

back. I was fond of Donnelly's. Restaurants are poor generally. You go to Cedar Rapids for seafood. Go to the Lark for steak. There are four movie houses which change their bills about every three days, and Iowa City is a college town and nothing else, so the bills are good. You'll keep up easily with the movie thing.

Every so often you will go nuts. All of a sudden the cornfields get you. Fly to Chicago or New York. Cancel classes whenever you damn please. Nobody will be checking up on you. And use the Cedar Rapids Airport instead of the Iowa City Airport. Fly United instead of Ozarks.

The new head of the Workshop, George Starbuck, is a close friend and a great man. Trust him entirely. The former head, Paul Engle, is still around, is a hayseed clown, a foxy grandpa, a terrific promoter who, if you listen closely, talks like a man with a paper asshole. He has a Taiwanese mistress, Leslie Nieh, who will have an office near yours. He is mad for gooks. Forget him. Graduate assistants write his books for him. Burn this letter.

Vance is a poor teacher, spends most of his time on his farm, wants to be a full professor. He is very powerful politically, and, as we know, a fine friend and writer—but, like I say, he is lazy as hell around the Workshop. My feeling about this is mainly—so what? He will want you to hunt with him. Do it. He's a master. Like you, he's a great cook.

Don't ball undergraduates. Their parents are still watching.

Run with the painters. I did. The best guy in Iowa City is painter Byron Burford. There isn't anybody to watch out for. Nobody pays any attention to anybody else, so there isn't any jealousy or competition or any of that crap. Lecture as Gehman, not as a college professor. Gehman is who they hired. Be very commercial.

Go to all the football games. They are great. Iowa should be a .500 club this year.

Cheers,

Kurt

September 11, 1967

West Barnstable, MA

To Robert Scholes

Robert Scholes was a literary critic on the faculty at the School of Letters at the University of Iowa, where he met Vonnegut. This letter is in response to Scholes sending Vonnegut a copy of his book The Fabulators, *which discussed the work of John Barth, John Hawkes, Iris Murdoch, and Lawrence Durrell as well as Vonnegut. It was the first recognition and praise that Kurt had received from a recognized literary critic.*

Scholes wrote that "Vonnegut, in his fiction, is doing what the most serious writers always do. He is helping, in Joyce's phrase, 'to create the conscience of the race.' What race? Human certainly, not American or German or any other abstraction from humanity. Just as pure romance provides us with necessary psychic exercise, intellectual comedy like Vonnegut's offers us moral stimulation—not fixed ethical positions which we can complacently assume, but such thoughts as exercise our consciences and help us keep our humanity in shape, ready to respond to the humanity of others."

When Kurt jokingly said he was "burned up that Barth won," he was not referring to an award but to Scholes ranking Barth "at the top of the fabulators in the book," Scholes told me.

The critic whom Kurt referred to as "David" was David Hayman, one of Scholes's colleagues at Iowa at the time and a Joyce scholar.

Dear Bob:

I am groping now for the word that means a person who has traveled widely and speaks several languages. I think the word I want is cunnilinguist. How does it feel to be one?

I assume you guys are home and cataloguing the lantern slides. Your perfectly neat book about me and the others arrived yesterday. If you hadn't supplied an index which pinpointed every mention of me, I wouldn't have been able to put it down until I'd read it all. I'm a little burned up that Barth won, but tomorrow is another day. My first book was more promising than his first book, which is something a careful critic wouldn't forget.

Seriously: I have read the whole book, and you've amused me, and you've taught me many things that are comforting or stimulating, or which can be turned into money in the bank. You write handsomely. At several points you wrote so well that I was moved to protest: Let's leave the writing to the writers, Scholes. If you don't know how a critic is supposed to write, I commend to your attention *The Tragic Vision*.

Where you really get racking along like a happy Dixieland band is on page 97. You had to call it a pretty feeble fable, I suppose, but I give you my word of honor that it's totally marvelous. It's even true.

You may or may not have noticed that I said some unkind things about academic critics in the *Times Book Review* a few weeks ago. It wasn't an attack. It was kind of a kidding thing. But I didn't mean you and I didn't mean David. What you guys write is too open and amiable to be academic criticism. It's just writing. There's a difference, believe me. Some real dumb bastard could read you guys and understand a good deal of it and be glad.

All goes well here. One of my sons is going to be a Unitarian minister. I'm pleased. What does that indicate—that that should please me? I haven't been to Dresden yet—mainly because the writing has been going fairly well and I hate to interrupt it. Jane and I will get our passports renewed today, and then maybe we'll hop over real quick.

Love to the little woman, and cheers.

Kurt

September 12, 1967
West Barnstable, MA

To Sam Lawrence

Vonnegut was going to "get to work" on the short-story collection that became Welcome to the Monkey House.

Alain Robbe-Grillet was part of the avant garde movement of French nouvelle roman *writers and a leading French intellectual.*

Dear Sam:

Please send me all the short stories you have. Max is sending me some stuff from his archives. And I'll go to work.

Sure—I'll write an introduction, a position paper that will put me right up there with Robbe-Grillet.

Harper & Row is having a lot of writers write prefaces to books which have been around for a while. I'm going to do one on *The Sirens of Titan.* The prefaces will be brought out in one volume. Saul Bellow has argued that the writer should not think of himself as a shaman. I'm arguing that that's what a writer should be. Isn't that exciting? [. . .]

Cheers,

Kurt

P.S. Oxford has just brought out a book by Robert Scholes, *The Fabulators,* which has a very friendly section about me in it.

September 18, 1967
West Barnstable, MA

To Sam Lawrence

Kurt's first application for a Guggenheim Fellowship had been turned down in 1959. He was awarded a Guggenheim in 1967 to go to Dresden and do research on the novel he had been working on that would become Slaughterhouse-Five.

Dear Sam:

[. . .] I am going to Europe to research the war book with Guggenheim money for about a month—starting October 16.

I hope to get everything you need for the collection [*Welcome to the Monkey House*] to you within the next five days. I've written to Playboy for proofs of the title story, since I somehow lost my copy between Iowa and here.

Yours truly,

Kurt Vonnegut, Jr.

October 7, 1967

West Barnstable, MA

To Knox Burger

John Ciardi was director of the Bread Loaf Writers' Conference, as well as poetry editor of the Saturday Review of Literature. *Ciardi wrote an angry response to Vonnegut's satire of a writers' conference where Ciardi had taught the past summer (the West-Central Writers' Conference, sponsored by Western Illinois University in Macomb, Illinois). Vonnegut's piece, called "Teaching the Unteachable," appeared in* The New York Times Magazine *and is collected in* Wampeters, Foma & Granfalloons.

The "war buddy" is Bernard V. O'Hare, who was a P.O.W. with Kurt during the firebombing of Dresden, and became a lifelong friend.

Kitty Sprague is the second wife of Knox Burger.

Dear Knox:

A while back you urged me to do something with German and Germany and all that, so I have been brushing up on my fifty-word vocabulary, and I am off to Berlin next Tuesday. I'll have an old war buddy with me. He is now a D.A. in Pennsylvania. We must want the syph pretty bad. Anyway—we're going to East Berlin and Dresden and Prague and Vienna and Budapest and Warsaw and Leningrad, and it'll take maybe a month. *Play-*

boy is going to pick up part of the tab. I'm going to do a piece on post-war architecture behind the Iron Curtain. Seriously. Jane and Edith are meanwhile going to Madrid to visit Jose Donoso, my Chilean pal. And we will all meet after I am sprung from the Lublinka. Edith, incidentally, went to two life-drawing classes in art school, and was promoted from Freshman to Senior. She draws better than the teachers do.

My boy Steve, a junior at Dartmouth, was all set to be a first-string offensive end this year, but then two sophomore super-stars got ahead of him, so he's mainly on the bench. He ran all summer and lifted weights, but so did they. Part of the trouble, I think, is his having been a super-star as a kid. He topped out last year. In about a year he'll be boozing and smoking with his Uncle, and getting fat.

A student of mine has a story in this month's *Atlantic*—and there's a sweet little credit line which tells whose student she was.

Ciardi certainly shit all over me in the *Saturday Review*. What a nasty old poet he must be. My only response has been to cancel my subscription by telegraph. I don't subscribe. If I can remember to do it, I will send him roses for the opening festivities at Bread Loaf next summer.

A guy told me Kitty fell off a bike this summer. She is so beautiful. I hope she is not scarred.

Cheers,

Kurt

October 7, 1967
West Barnstable, MA

To Sam Lawrence

Dear Sam:

I'm flying to Berlin with an old war buddy on Tuesday next. We're going to do East Berlin and Dresden and Prague and Vienna and Budapest and Warsaw and Leningrad. *Playboy* is picking up part of the tab. They've commissioned me to do a piece about post-war architecture behind the Iron Curtain. How's that for raw sex? We'll be gone about a month.

I think I'm leaving you in good shape with respect to the short story collection. All that's missing is the "Dictionary" piece. I don't have a copy, but the *Times* is sending me one. Put "EPICAC" [a short story used in *Welcome to the Monkey House*] wherever you like. The name of the machine is all in caps.

Peace,

Kurt

October 29, 1967

West Barnstable, MA

To Sam Lawrence

Dear Sam:

I am home again, and I will tell you about Berlin and Dresden and Vienna and Salzburg and Hamburg and Helsinki and Leningrad, if you really want to hear about them. But you would be out of your head to ask. Anyway, I saw a lot of stuff I can use.

The main point of this letter is to extort another favor from you. As you know, I have a very fancy agent who easily gets sore or hurt. He has recommended, pointlessly, I am persuaded, that I switch publishers yet again in England. I am now with Tom Maschler at Cape, and that is where I want to stay very much. Would you please tell Max gravely that you think I should stay with Cape, too?

I sent you the dictionary piece yesterday. That makes us square. Right? The trip has simplified the war book for me. *Slaughterhouse-5*, since I have now seen with my own eyes what I was trying to remember. Dresden, "The Florence of the Elbe," is now like Cedar Rapids in 1936—the music, the clothes, the buildings, everything.

As I understand our contract, I can start drawing monthly money any time after September 1. Could I have my first check December 1?

Cheers,

Kurt Vonnegut, Jr.

To Gail Godwin

Godwin was a student of Kurt's at Iowa and went on to become a distinguished novelist.

Dear Gail:

I miss all you guys—but my work is going a whole lot better.

You were smart to quit the Workshop. I don't think it is a very useful enterprise. Vance appears to have handled you foolishly, boorishly, maybe, but he has a point. Are you willing to pander to popular tastes in order to be published? If so, write about a love affair. It isn't so terrible to write for the women's magazines. That is how I supported myself more or less for about twelve years. I do not feel dishonored. What the hell. You'd be surprised what you can say in a woman's magazine these days.

And I've taken jobs a damned sight worse than writing for Hallmark. Most people have. But you really want to make it as big as Muhammad Ali, don't you—to be that popular and wise in a magically simple way? I'd like to help. And you want to be a satirist, too—or to write really strong stuff, anyway. Women don't customarily handle oil paints well, you know—or black and white. I don't know if you have it in you to be crude. I write with a big black crayon, you know, grasped in a grubby, kindergarten fist. You're more of an impressionist. If you want to kind of try what I do, take life seriously but none of the people in it. The

people are fools, and I say so the instant they're onstage. I don't
let them prove it slowly. The author is very much around, and he
is opinionated. Women are usually much too subtle and polite to
intrude like that.

Again: write a love story, and it will be a good love story, and
it will sell. That's life. [. . .]

Cheers,

Kurt

                                          November 28, 1967

To Draft Board #1, Selective Service,
Hyannis, Mass.

Gentlemen:

My son Mark Vonnegut is registered with you. He is now in
the process of requesting classification as a conscientious objector.
I thoroughly approve of what he is doing. It is in keeping with the
way I have raised him. All his life he has learned hatred for killing
from me.

I was a volunteer in the Second World War. I was an infantry
scout, saw plenty of action, was finally captured and served about
six months as a prisoner of war in Germany. I have a Purple
Heart. I was honorably discharged. I am entitled, it seems to me,
to pass on to my son my opinion of killing. I don't even hunt or
fish any more. I have some guns which I inherited, but they are
covered with rust.

This attitude toward killing is a matter between my God and
me. I do not participate much in organized religion. I have read
the Bible a lot. I preach, after a fashion. I write books which express my disgust for people who find it easy and reasonable to
kill.

We say grace at meals, taking turns. Every member of my
large family has been called upon often to thank God for bless-

ings which have been ours. What Mark is doing now is in the service of God, Whose Son was exceedingly un-warlike.

There isn't a grain of cowardice in this. Mark is a strong, courageous young man. What he is doing requires more guts than I ever had—and more decency.

My family has been in this country for five generations now. My ancestors came here to escape the militaristic madness and tyranny of Europe, and to gain the freedom to answer the dictates of their own consciences. They and their descendents have been good citizens and proud to be Americans. Mark is proud to be an American, and, in his father's opinion, he is being an absolutely first-rate citizen now.

He will not hate.

He will not kill.

There's hope in that. There's no hope in war.

Yours truly,

 Kurt Vonnegut, Jr.

March 26, 1968

West Barnstable, MA

To José Donoso

Maharishi Mahesh Yogi taught Transcendental Meditation and popularized his "TM" in the 1960s, when he gained fame as the guru of the Beatles, actress Mia Farrow, and many other movie stars and celebrities. Kurt was not a fan and wrote an article about him for Esquire *("Yes, We Have No Nirvanas") that is collected in* Wampeters, Foma & Granfalloons.

Dear Pepe:

I think about you and your lovely wife and your nice new baby all the time. And we miss you like crazy. I don't write because the letters never seem any good. That's silly.

I recommended you highly for a Guggenheim today. I think you're sure to get it. You certainly deserve it, and your credentials are brilliant these days. Your money will start about the time mine stops. Enjoy it in good health.

Jane is at loose-ends these days—but sweet and cheerful, as always. Our neighbors are awfully dumb, and the nights are awfully still. She has a guru—Maharishi Mahesh Yogi. He has taught her to do a thing called *transcendental meditation,* which is sort of skin-diving in one's own mind. It means a lot to her. There is obviously rapture in the depths.

I work on my barn in the afternoons, turning part of it into a comfortable, very private apartment for you. Please come soon. Scrabble?

Peace,

Kurt

April 22, 1968

West Barnstable, MA

To Robert Scholes

Matthew J. Bruccoli was a scholar who wrote or edited more than fifty books on writers of the 1920s and 1930s, including Hemingway, Fitzgerald, John O'Hara, and Thomas Wolfe.

Dear Bob:

I keep meeting guys who knew you at Virginia. Matt Bruccoli, for instance. He likes you fairly much, and is *really* bughouse about your wife. I guess I can understand that. I met him when I spoke at Ohio State on the occasion of their adding the two-millionth volume to their library. The book was *Don Quixote.* I told them that should have been one of the first books they got.

Bruccoli was obviously highly regarded at Ohio, but the place so enrages him that he has submitted his resignation. He's looking for work. Could Iowa use him?

Bruccoli incidentally offered me mountains of money for all my manuscripts. Since I don't need money right now, I'll just leave the stuff to my kids. At which time the stuff will probably be worthless. What the hell.

I am about a week from finishing the new novel. It sure has been hard. It isn't very long. From now on I am going to follow familiar models and make a lot of dough.

My warm greetings to David [Hayman].

Gehman was here a couple of weekends ago, cooked all the meals.

Cheers,

Kurt

May 28, 1968

[West Barnstable, MA]

To Mark Vonnegut

Dear Mark:

I ask a favor for your mother's sake: please look awfully nice at your graduation. She is a dear, romantic girl, and I want her to be as happy as she can possibly be at the graduation of her only son.

I am talking about hair, of course. The beard is fine, and characteristic and, hence, beloved by one and all. What I am suggesting is that the hair on top of your head be styled somewhat—that you look like nobody else on this earth, perhaps, but, in a movie star way, look handsome as hell all the same. So she'll nearly swoon. You have achieved this before. You can achieve it again.

Edith promises to be home in time for your graduation. Promises, promises.

Love,

K

June 11, 1968

West Barnstable, MA

To Sam Lawrence

Granville Hicks was a book critic and author.

Dear Sam:

How was the trip? The manuscript of *Slaughterhouse-Five* should be waiting for you there. I mailed it off to you yesterday. Max has a copy, too.

About the promotional tour of colleges which the publicity lady at Dell has proposed:

The economics of such a tour would be confusing, Sam, since I am not only in the writing business but the speaking business, too. Without any manager or promotion, I now get $500 and all expenses for speaking, and am offered more engagements than I care to fill. Over the years, I have worked up a quite funny act that seems to be worth that much. Granville Hicks saw it, wrote about it in the SRL a few weeks back.

Dell now suggest that I do this for nothing, in order to sell books. It seems to me that this would be unbuilding my speaking business, and that the number of books my appearances would sell would be small. If there is a dollars and cents argument to the contrary, I would like to hear it. I want to be cooperative.

I will be the keynote speaker, incidentally, at a convention of about 400 college and university newspaper editors, members of the United States Student Press Association, at Valparaiso University, Valparaiso, Indiana, on August 17. I will also be Writer in Residence at the University of Michigan during next January.

Yours truly,

Kurt

July 18, 1968

[West Barnstable, MA]

To Knox Burger

Kurt had dedicated Welcome to the Monkey House:

> *"For*
> *Knox Burger*
> *Ten days older than I am.*
> *He has been a very good*
> *father to me."*

The "war book" was Slaughterhouse-Five.

VISTA is the national service program designed to fight poverty, founded in 1965 as the Volunteers in Service to America.

The late Senator Eugene J. McCarthy was the first candidate to challenge incumbent president Lyndon Johnson for the Democratic nomination in 1968.

Dear Knox:

I am glad that my dedication tickled you. I thought you would be jaded by now. How many books have been dedicated to you so far? Twenty, I'll bet. [. . .]

I have turned my old barn into a studio, as I may have told you. Your father's splendid bat is up on the wall. My son Mark, incidentally, is having a one-man show of oils in a place called Newfoundland in the Poconos. I am amazed. Last Christmas Jane and I gave Mark and Edith huge canvases—nine feet long and six feet high. Mark filled his up in two hours flat. Edith is into her third month with hers. The trouble with Edie is that she can draw like Albrecht Dürer. She wastes hour after hour getting everything exactly right. Too bad.

I guess I told you that I finally finished my war book. And that turned me off. I sure don't want to write any more. I try to think up new things to do—like Vista, maybe. Really. I sit around here with my thumb up my ass while my wife works her guts out at McCarthy headquarters.

Love to Kitty. Come up in the fall, and we can watch the ducks and geese come through. There'll be no need to shoot. I've got a little house up in the marsh, by the way, and a little blue rowboat named "Bob" comes with it. I am the only guy who ever goes out on the marsh. Really: I never see another soul. Maybe I should learn the names of the plants and birds.

About smoking: it takes two weeks to quit. Unless you have two free weeks, forget it. Expect to act crazy. I sure did.

Cheers,

Kurt

September 14, 1968
West Barnstable, MA

To Bernard V. O'Hare

Slaughterhouse-Five is dedicated to Mary O'Hare, the wife of Bernard. The other dedicatee is Gerhard Müller, the taxi driver who took Vonnegut and O'Hare to the real-life slaughterhouse where, as fellow prisoners of war, they survived the firebombing of Dresden.

Dear Bernard:

Would you please look over the enclosed pages and let me know if they would offend you or Mary in any way. God knows I wish you no harm.

It's a crazy book. *Ramparts* is talking of running the whole thing in installments.

Cheers,

Kurt

February 9, 1969

West Barnstable, MA

TO SAM LAWRENCE

Calder Willingham's novel published that year was Providence Island.

Dear Sam:

Well—we're off practically. We're leaving on February 11 for three days in San Francisco, which we've never seen. And then a week or more in Hawaii after that. It's a tough life.

I'm speaking at the University of Washington on February 25, in case your salesmen want to try to get Seattle to overstock me. Then home.

I guess it was Calder Willingham who beat me out of being a Literary Guild Selection, eh? So it goes. Experimenters lose every time. I'll bet you this, though: I'll bet I stay in print longer than he does.

What are the chances of *The Sirens* coming out in an attractive edition? My mail continues to indicate that people like that book best of all—and they all make jokes about the ghastly cover.

IBM's magazine is going to print my speech to the physicists. I hope the *New Yorker* and *Newsweek* see fit to say something nice about it.

Peace,

Kurt

April 4, 1969

Hyannis, MA

TO ROBERT SCHOLES, BY WESTERN UNION TELEGRAM

Kurt was responding to Robert Scholes's front page review of Slaughterhouse-Five *in* The New York Times. *He proclaimed Vonnegut* "a true artist" *who was* "among the best writers of his generation."

SPY IN NEW YORK READ TIMES REVIEW TO ME ON TELEPHONE.

WOW. NEXT TIME YOUR KID COMES FOR HANDOUT HE GETS CAV-
IAR AND HUMMINGBIRD'S TONGUES. LOVE

CROESUS

May 7, 1969

West Barnstable, MA

To Mark Vonnegut

Dear Mark, old chess and ping-pong pal:

I'm glad we never hunted together. Happy birthday.

We have a saying here: "Mark knows what he's doing." We
believe it. We love you. We respect you. We think you will have a
wonderful life. Your close friend Bob Boles suggests that you are
perhaps the kindest person he ever knew.

You also paint like nobody's business.

I suppose you are heading into a shit storm with Draft Board
One, but maybe not. There is a good chance that they will accept
your C.O. plea peacefully. I hope so. With a little luck, your two
years of alternate service could be almost lovely.

The New York Times Magazine has asked me to do a piece
about the coming landing on the moon. What should I say?

Advice *my* father gave me: Never take liquor into the bedroom.
Don't stick anything in your ears. Be anything but an architect.

Your good mother is putting a present in the mail for you.

Cheers,

K

May 9, 1969

West Barnstable, MA

To Dan Wakefield

Slaughterhouse-Five *was a national bestseller, and eager fans lined up
for Kurt's autograph at bookstores throughout the country—except in*

his hometown of Indianapolis, which he found ironic. (The city later canonized him by proclaiming 2007 "The Year of Vonnegut"—which, again ironically, would prove to be the year he died.) L. S. Ayres was a leading department store in Indianapolis and had its own book section.

Dear Dan:

[. . .] At the request of Ayres, I went to Indianapolis last week, appeared on a TV show and a radio show, then signed books in the bookstore. I sold thirteen books in two hours, every one of them to a relative. Word of honor.

The next book is about Indianapolis. Yours, too, I bet. I stopped by Shortridge, which is still unbelievably great. [. . .]

Peace,

Kurt

June 16, 1969
West Barnstable, MA

To Sam Lawrence

Herman Wouk was the bestselling author of The Caine Mutiny, *which became a movie starring Humphrey Bogart. He wrote many other successful novels.*

Dear Sam:

[. . .] Was pleased and startled to receive a letter from Herman Wouk, a stranger. He said this among other things: "Your book came through singing clear, a tragic tale masked in ferocious grotesque humor, to me flawlessly achieved." How do you like them apples?

Peace,

Kurt

July 3, 1969
West Barnstable, MA

To Sam Lawrence

"The Swede" referred to was a Swedish publisher.

Dear Sam:

Thanks for the salt water taffy. The box was only one-third full when it got here. I suppose the stuff shrivels if it is taken away from the salubrious air of the Boardwalk.

The Swede and his wife will be here tomorrow. We will put them up in our barn. We expect to have an awfully nice time—really. I used to have a dealership for SAAB automobiles, you know. The same company made Messerschmitts during WWII.

I enclose my letters from Herman Wouk. He is a very commercial guy, of course, so I don't see how he can fault us for bad taste if you ask permission to quote him.

Jane and I are planning to spend three months in Greece next winter, starting right after Christmas. You know any colonels over there?

Cheers,
Kurt

July 11, 1969
West Barnstable, MA

To Knox Burger

Knox's "future plans" were to start his own literary agency.

Dear Knox:

[. . .] I have kept my mouth shut about your future plans. For my own sake, I hope with all my heart that they work out. One sort of interesting thing to think about: Elkins' option on *Cat's*

Cradle finally dies on August 29th, with no chance for renewal. The cult continues to grow, if my mail is any indication.

We had dinner last night at the home of Charles Dickens' great granddaughter, Monica Dickens Stratton. Her husband, a retired U.S. Navy man, does all her typing for her—on mimeo stencils. Then he runs them off. They live near Otis Air Force Base because he has PX and Commissary privileges. They have stables and a jumping paddock and a training paddock and all that, and the main house and guest house are being greatly expanded. I didn't ask, but I'm sure all the money is coming from *Oliver!* They are the sweetest, happiest people I know. They have a wonderful breed of dog all their own—poodles crossed with golden retrievers.

Cheers,

Kurt

October 17, 1969

West Barnstable, MA

To Sam Lawrence

Breakfast of Champions, the novel that followed Slaughterhouse-Five, *would be published in 1973.*

Dear Sam:

This is to tell you that you had better cancel all plans for the new book, *Breakfast of Champions*. I've stopped work on it for reasons of health.

I've got to quit smoking. When I do that, I quit writing. So there we are. I know. I've been through it before.

Sorry—but I don't want to suffocate.

Cheers,

Kurt

THE SEVENTIES

At the beginning of the seventies, Vonnegut's life turned upside down. His son, Mark, wrote in his memoir that in 1969 Kurt "went from being poor to being famous and rich in the blink of an eye." He continued the transformation in 1970 when he moved from the small bucolic town of West Barnstable on Cape Cod, where he had lived, worked, and raised his family, to New York City, smash in the middle of Manhattan. His children were all grown and had left home, and he left the marriage of nearly a quarter century that he had expressed problems about in a letter to Knox Burger when he was teaching in Iowa ("Something telepathic has busted between us"). In the same letter he said, "At Christmas I had the damnedest revulsion to Cape Cod, loved my family but hated the house—don't want to live there anymore."

"It was a time of change, of good-bye and good-bye and good-bye," Vonnegut wrote in an introduction to the book publication of his play *Happy Birthday, Wanda June,* speaking of the time he left the Cape and moved to New York. It was a time "when my six children were no more [living at home in the family house on Cape Cod]. . . . I was drinking more and arguing a lot and I had to get out of that house. . . ." In writing *Wanda June* (based on his play *Penelope,* which was performed fifteen years before on Cape Cod), "I was writing myself a new family and a new early manhood." He regarded the actors as his "new family," though after the last performance in 1971, "My new family dissolved into the late afternoon."

During his work on the play, the photographer Jill Krementz came to "chronicle" him photographically, and he began a relationship with her that led to their living together in a townhouse he bought on East 48th Street in Manhattan in 1973. Together they bought a house in Sagaponack on Long Island in 1977 and were married in 1979. Many famous writers were Long Island neighbors in summer, such as James Jones, Irwin Shaw, Nelson Algren, and Truman Capote.

Vonnegut found and became part of other extended families, which he felt were so important—the family of American writers (symbolized by his induction into the National Institute of Arts and Letters) and the family of writers throughout the world. He became an officer of PEN, fighting for the causes of writers who had been jailed in totalitarian countries and working tirelessly to champion his Russian translator, Rita Rait, whom he would finally bring on a visit to the U.S. in 1984.

He used to say that when history later looked back on America, it might well regard Alcoholics Anonymous as this country's greatest contribution to the world—because it provided people with an extended family, one whose members would greet them and give them a place to go in every city in the country and around the world. He was proud of the fact that his uncle Alex had founded the first Alcoholics Anonymous chapter in Indianapolis.

Though never a member of a church, Kurt often advised people who had just gotten out of prison, or were for any reason lonely or new in a community, to join a church because it provided an instant extended family.

• • •

The public awareness of Vonnegut and his books continued to spread in 1972 when an excellent movie was made of *Slaughterhouse-Five* by the highly regarded director George Roy Hill. Kurt was delighted with the film; he told me later: "They did the movie just like they did *Gone with the Wind*—they simply 'put the novel on the screen.' "

As he and his books became famous, there were more and more attempts to censor them, and he passionately defended the teachers and librarians who fought for their right to use them in schools and libraries. After the burning of copies of *Slaughterhouse-Five* in a furnace in Drake, North Dakota, on orders of its school board, and the banning of it by the school board in Levittown, New York, Vonnegut wrote in an op-ed piece for *The New York Times* on March 24, 1976, that "Whenever ideas are squashed in this country, literate lovers of the American experiment write careful and intricate explanations of why all ideas must be allowed to live. It is time for them to realize that they are attempting to explain America at its bravest and most optimistic to orangutans.

"From now on, I intend to limit my discourse with dimwitted Savonarolas to this advice: 'Have somebody read the First Amendment to the United States Constitution out loud to you, you God damned fool!' "

• • •

Vonnegut's first novel after *Slaughterhouse-Five* was *Breakfast of Champions,* published in 1973. In the same year, "Two nice young college professors," Jerome Klinkowitz and John Somer, published *The Vonnegut Statement,* a collection of essays on the author and his work. They also dug out all his articles and essays from the past twenty years and persuaded him to select among them for a collection called *Wampeters, Foma & Granfalloons* (three words he'd made up in *Cat's Cradle*), which came out in 1974 and hit the bestseller lists.

Following all this attention and success—which made him a popular figure on the lecture circuit and the subject of magazine and TV interviews and articles—his novel *Slapstick* in 1976 was battered by bad reviews. Responding to his *Paris Review* interviewer's question of whether that novel had received "some bad reviews," Vonnegut said, "Only in *The New York Times, Time, Newsweek, The New York Review of Books,* the *Village Voice,* and *Rolling Stone.* They loved me in Medicine Hat."

The reviews of *Slapstick* hurt but did not deter him, and three years later he followed it with a well-received novel based on the Watergate scandal, *Jailbird*. He used the technique of entering the novel with his own personal memories and experience, as he first had done in *Slaughterhouse-Five*.

One of the biggest changes in his life and career had come in 1970 with a break in his friendship and professional relationship with Knox Burger. Knox told me he started his literary agency with the belief that Kurt would be his star client and was shocked when it didn't work out. Knox said he wrote Kurt a long letter advising him on his career and that Kurt had not liked it and told him he "didn't want an uncle." Kurt's loyalty to his first agent, Max Wilkinson, and Wilkinson's reluctance to let him go was part of the tangle of misunderstandings. Bad blood developed between Knox and Kurt, which continued for a number of years, but finally the friendship, if not the business relationship, was restored.

Later the same year Kurt formed what was to become a life-long professional alliance with the theatrical attorney Don Farber, whom he had met at a dinner party on Long Island. Farber served as Kurt's agent, negotiator, and adviser in personal as well as professional matters—in every part of life imaginable, from dealings with wives and children to publishers and producers. Don and his wife, Annie, became Kurt's closest friends and advisers, cornerstones and bulwarks of his life in all its aspects from the time they met.

In the midst of all the crises and changes in his life and the tremendous amount of work he did in this decade, Vonnegut found time for fun and good-humored enterprises. Taking time out from all his personal and professional concerns and pressures, Kurt wrote to Don Farber that "This is to let you know that I have gone completely bonkers, and am sponsoring a softball team in Lafayette, Indiana." He asked Farber to send a check, "certain that this is a tax-deductible item. If Joe's Diner and the local funeral home can deduct their teams, so can I."

February 28, 1970

West Barnstable, MA

To Knox Burger

Knox had opened his literary agency.

Dear Knox:

I got back from Tortola last night—read your exciting news today. I am all for you, old friend. You are going to be refreshed. We will of course do business sooner or later. About my TV show: we have money now from Canada and Mercury records, and we are going to make a pilot in Toronto in a month or so. If the pilot works, it will be time to draw up really fancy contracts.

You are going to be red hot, old buddy. I am delighted.

Love,

Kurt

April 11, 1970

West Barnstable, MA

To Dan Wakefield

Jim Goode was another Shortridge High School graduate, who had worked for Life *magazine and then for* Playboy. *When I told him that Kurt was going to review my novel for* Life, *he said it was an example of the power of "The Shortridge Mafia."*

Ray Mungo was a founder of one of the first communes and wrote a book about it called Total Loss Farm, *and founded the Liberation News Service. He and some of his commune buddies had paid an un-announced visit to Kurt, and they invited Kurt, Sam Lawrence, and me to come to their first "May Day Celebration" as "honorary uncles of the commune."*

Dear Dan:

Tell Jim that it would be stupid for the Shortridge Mafia to surface like that. It is working like a dream, and nobody suspects anything so far. We could lose millions, and what could we gain? We're all on Easy Street. Forget it.

One time in the lobby of the Century Club I heard a couple of guys exclaiming along these lines: "It's a high school, but everybody who went there talks about it like it was a fraternity or something." They were talking about Shortridge.

To be serious for a moment: I don't want any more publicity for quite a while. I'd love to see you, though. I'm crazy about your buddy Mungo.

Cheers,

Kurt

April 13, 1970
West Barnstable, MA

To Mrs. Josephine Harris

Dear Mrs. Harris

[. . .] I went to a high school (Shortridge, Indianapolis) which had a daily paper, so everybody was crazy about writing. Many good writers have come from Shortridge—because of the paper. The student writers get an immediate response from an audience rather than from one tired teacher. This makes writing seem exciting and relevant.

It takes about two years for a student to show important changes in his ability to write. Creative writing programs lasting only a semester or a year simply don't allow enough time for growth. Ideally, the student should have the same teacher for two years.

The teacher should think of assisting the student to *become* a writer, rather than think of teaching the student how to write. The teacher should watch for clues as to what the student is attempting to become, then help the student to become that. It is cruel and destructive to make the student try to become something he was not meant to become. He can become only what he was meant to be.

Good luck,

Kurt Vonnegut, Jr.

April 14, 1970
West Barnstable, MA

To Knox Burger

The "old friend" Kurt refers to is his original agent, Max Wilkinson.

Dear Knox—

[. . .] As for my own situation: There is this old friend (literally old), who I don't want to hurt. Why should I hurt him? Also: he's doing a good job. I think he should retire—not for my sake but for his. He will retire soon—or maybe even knock himself off. I wish somebody would buy him out. I understood somebody was going to buy him out. At any rate: I will come with you when he closes down or when my departure can be an affectionate farewell rather than a kick in the balls.

Kurt

April 24, 1970
West Barnstable, MA

To Knox Burger

Dear Mr. Burger—

I have written my agent, Mr. Max Wilkinson, thanking him for all he has done for me. I have reminded him of the many times he has expressed disgust for the agency business in recent months.

I have told him that I wish you to represent me from now on. Will you?

Yours truly,

Kurt Vonnegut, Jr.

P.S. It was right that a few weeks should pass. I deny that I kicked you in the balls. Peace.

May 12, 1970

West Barnstable, MA

To Donald C. Farber

Vonnegut had submitted a television script to Max Wilkinson, and the agent introduced him to Don Farber, a theatrical lawyer. Farber became Kurt's lawyer, agent, adviser, and friend throughout his life.

Dear Don—

It was so pleasant having supper with you and Anne two nights in a row. You wear very well.

I have put in the same mail with this letter two versions of *Penelope*. These are rare manuscripts, so don't let them get away. They represent the condition the play was in when it was given its last production, a preview intended to attract investors, in the Village in about 1963. It went over pretty well, and it was a smash in summer theater up here, at the Orleans Arena Theatre. Anyway—I will have to rewrite it again, to bring in the current fucking war and all that. Maybe the time is ripe at last, now that we have our own Peloponnesian Wars. We can do the Aristophanes thing.

Clear all deals with Max. Knox represents me only on stuff still not written. O.K.? Max is still my closest business associate. I've tried to help Knox by lending my name.

Cheers,

Kurt

June 26, 1970

West Barnstable, MA

To Bernard Malamud

Bernard Malamud's novel The Fixer *won both the National Book Award and the Pulitzer Prize in 1967. His other novels included* The Natural, *which was made as a movie starring Robert Redford.*

Kurt had been invited to teach a course at Harvard in the fall se-mester of 1970.

Dear Malamud—

Thanks for your friendly note. I hoped to see you the next morning. I wanted to learn more about doing the thing at Harvard. I'm grateful for your tip about not making them read too much—that they already read too much. Good.

Since I didn't glimpse you at the graduation ceremony, I assume you missed seeing, among other things, two campus mongrels fucking inside a circle of girls waiting for their diplomas.

Cheers,

Kurt

July 15, 1970

West Barnstable, MA

To Richard Thomas Condon

Condon was the author of the bestselling novel The Manchurian Can-didate, *which became a movie starring Frank Sinatra.* Any God Will Do *was his novel about a madman's search for identity.*

Dear Mr. Condon—

That's friendly—your note about *Slaughterhouse-Five.*

You've been on my conscience for several years, since I did a very stupid review of *Any God Will Do* for the *Times.* I lacked the brains and bounce at the time to see that it was excellent, and I was pleased when the *New Yorker* later praised it to the skies.

I hear the Swiss want to throw out all the foreigners. Does that mean you, too?

Cheers,

Kurt Vonnegut

July 16, 1970

West Barnstable, MA

To Knox Burger

Colette Collage *was a musical performed off Broadway, written by Tom Jones and Harvey Schmidt, authors of* The Fantasticks.

Dear Knox—

[. . .] *Mother Night* is owned by an outfit named Film Sense, which has spent a lot of money for what I hear is an exciting script. They renew their options enthusiastically. We are now at the point where each renewal is money in addition to the original deal. Fred Zinnemann is said to be on the hook.

I am presently scared stiff because my moldy old play *Penelope,* renamed *Happy Birthday, Wanda June,* is supposed to open at the de Lys on or around October 1. We have a lease on the theater from August 14 on, and will do our casting when the lease begins. I have spent the last six weeks rewriting it. It was in dreadful shape when I dug it out of mothballs, and may be in worse shape now. I am waiting for the opinion of our director, Gerry Freedman, who recently did *Colette.* The producer is Les Goldsmith, who impulsively optioned it over dinner at Don Farber's house. Don worked out the deal. Goldsmith remembered it vaguely from the days when he was story editor at Paramount.

Cat's Cradle ceases to be the property of Hilly sometime in

August. A lot of people seem to want it, including Peter Fonda. Alan Arkin is coming up here in a week to say that he and the guy who produced Little Murders want to do *Cat's Cradle* next—with Arkin writing and directing. Max and Ziegler will represent me on this, since Max has been watching out for the property from the beginning, since he went through so much shit negotiating and negotiating with Hilly. [. . .]

    Kurt

September 11, 1970

[West Barnstable, MA]

TO KNOX BURGER

This marked the end of the on-and-off, back-and-forth discussions between Kurt and Knox about his representation.

Dear Knox—

    I'm sad and embarrassed about what business considerations and other muggy matters have done to our friendship. You're right—there *is* a lack of comfortableness there. As for your backing off: continue to name me as a client, if that is at all useful. I'll continue to recommend you to others gladly, and to say that you are one of two agents I have—if that is at all useful. The reality is that Max is so deeply woven into my past that he has sold or is entitled to sell virtually everything I'll write for the next dozen years. Also: I am going more deeply into the theater business with partners—and lawyers will necessarily do most of my negotiating from now on.

    Yours truly,

    Kurt

September 14, 1970

West Barnstable, MA

To Gail Godwin

Robert Coover was highly regarded as a postmodern novelist and short-story writer, at that time noted for his 1969 collection, Pricksongs & Descants.

Dear Gail—

I have a play opening in New York on October 7, and one of the lines in it goes, "What a pity. Educating a beautiful woman is like pouring honey into a fine Swiss watch. Everything stops." I hope this won't be the case with you. I liked your book, and I know for a fact that Harper & Row is extremely proud of it. When I wrote a puff for it, I added the bit about kinky eroticism as a joke, as a way of saying hello. The book really is kinkily erotic, but it would take me a while to explain why. Anyway, Harper & Row thought it might sell books, so they used it.

It's tough finding teaching jobs these days, I hear, but you deserve a good job. I'll mention you to English faculties whenever I get the chance. As for the play you're doing with Coover: I think plays are really it these days. They're so sociable. And a theatrical lawyer and a West Coast producer and I have formed a producing outfit called "Sourdough, Limited." We have a red hot director and ways of getting money. We'd like a look at the play.

Cheers,

Kurt

November 23, 1970

West Barnstable, MA

To Anne Sexton

Anne Sexton was a Pulitzer Prize–winning poet. I introduced her to Kurt at a party I hosted for her book Transformations, *a personal retelling of seventeen Grimm's fairy tales.*

Dear Anne—

I've read all of *Transformations.* I'd be honored to do a short preface. My fee: two bottles of gin.

Drop me a note, if you want me to go ahead. Meanwhile, I will read the poems again, so I can be truly wise about them. Also, dear, would you let me have a collection of your earlier stuff? I've admired it here and there, but I'm sure I've missed a lot.

Cheers—

Kurt

December 2, 1970

West Barnstable, MA

To José Donoso

Vonnegut's play Happy Birthday, Wanda June *ran off Broadway at the Theatre de Lys in Greenwich Village from October 1970 to March 1971. The reviews were mixed, from* Newsweek's *". . . Vonnegut's dialogue is not only fast and funny, with a palpable taste and crackle, but it also means something" to* The New Republic's *". . . a disaster, full of callow wit, rheumatic invention, and dormitory profundity." It was produced as a movie in 1971 starring Rod Steiger. Kurt wanted to have his name removed from the movie credits but wrote in* Palm Sunday: *"This proved impossible, however. I alone had done the thing the credits said I had done. I had really written the thing."*

Dear Spic—

[. . .] The adventure of having a play produced was harrowing. The reviews ranged from adoration to hatred. My own feeling is that the play is clumsy and sophomoric. But I had to begin my theatrical career with something—and now I have in fact begun. I've written six novels. Now I want to write six plays. The play was produced off-Broadway, which means, mainly, in Greenwich Village. Unions have had easier, cheaper rules for off-Broadway productions—on the theory that the shabby little theaters were good schools for persons who would later hit the big theaters up-town. Well, the unions have now closed down off-Broadway, demanding enormous raises. So we are moving our show onto Broadway, from a 300-seat slum to a 500-seat palace. We will reopen on December 22nd, and I suppose I'll go crazy again. If I had your stomach problem, Pepe, I would be dead. It's bad enough, simply being as paranoid as you are.

My children think I am foolish to lead the life I do, and I think they're correct. But I can't think of another life that would comfort and calm me. Mark has a small farm in British Columbia now, five hours north of Vancouver. Jim Adams, my oldest boy, is also a farmer—in Jamaica, B.W.I. Edith is with him, painting some, I guess. I would hate to be a farmer.

I am teaching at Harvard two days a week. The students are mediocre, except for a chemistry major from South Korea. I agreed to teach for only one semester. I'll be glad when it's over. [. . .]

Love—
    K

December 5, 1970

West Barnstable, MA

To John Rauch

"Uncle John Rauch (1890–1976) . . . was not in fact my uncle, but the husband of a first cousin of my father, Gertrude Schnull Rauch," Kurt wrote in Palm Sunday, *in explaining and quoting at length from Rauch's manuscript entitled "An Account of the Ancestry of Kurt Vonnegut, Jr., by an Ancient Friend of His Family." Rauch was "a Harvard graduate and a distinguished Indianapolis lawyer," Kurt continued. "Toward the end of his life he made himself an historian, a* griot *of his wife's family—in part my family too. Although he was not related to it by blood, but only by marriage."*

Dear Uncle John—

I thank you for *An Account of the Ancestry of Kurt Vonnegut, Jr.,* surely one of the most valuable and cunningly made presents ever to change hands within our family.

In your amusing covering letter, you say that somebody told you that I was a great literary figure. I don't think so. A lot of people have heard of me. That is something else again. I am an American fad—of a slightly higher order than the hula hoop. An eighty-year-old man has every reason to expect to see the day when another tin god has replaced me.

Your own work may prove to be more durable. It is responsible and wise. I asked if I owned it in a legal sense, since I want to make copies for my children—so they can know who half their recent ancestors were. I'm sure that's O.K. with you, but I may want to publish it on a much larger scale. I may want to use your work as the opening of a book about my parents. Would that offend you?

My brief term as a teacher at Harvard is nearly over. It is a great university, in desperate need of the help you and Alex have told me you are withholding. The radicals are a microscopic fraction of the student population.

Thank your good wife for her contribution to the history. I will write Alex and Irma and Erna and Richard separately.

Love—

K

December 30, 1970

West Barnstable, MA

To Knox Burger

Vonnegut had borrowed "a tiny penthouse" from a friend near the Theatre de Lys in Greenwich Village to come down and watch rehearsals of Happy Birthday, Wanda June. *After the play opened in October, he rented a one-bedroom apartment on East 51st Street, commuting two days a week to teach his class at Harvard. He never returned to live in the house on Cape Cod.*

Dear Knox—

Here's the check for the books.

I hope you and Kitty will go see my play again as my guest. It's so much better than it was on opening night.

There's a jailbird in the Barnstable House of Correction who has written a crime novel. You'll be hearing from him, I think. I told him you'd had good luck with jailbirds.

Strange year just ending. Wish I knew where I was—or maybe that's exactly what I don't want to find out: Anyway—I've got an apartment now on 51st Street, between First and Second. I spend a lot of time there.

Cheers,

Kurt

February 26, 1971

New York City

To Sam Lawrence

Dear Sam:

If I had spurs, I think I would want to keep them. I probably have romantic ideas of what they are. [. . .]

It is true that I have started working on *Breakfast of Champions* again, slowly and painfully, from the very beginning. It takes me so long to find out what my books are about, so I can write them. If I had pressed onward with the book before, and finished it willy nilly, it would have been an enormous fake. It probably would have made us a fortune. [. . .]

Come see me soon. [. . .] I've stopped horsing around so much. I have now met George Plimpton, so I've reached the peak of my career as a social butterfly. Back to work.

Cheers,

Kurt Vonnegut, Jr.

March 2, 1971

New York City

To José Donoso

Dear Pepe:

[. . .] My writing is going badly. I had a play which ran for about 150 performances in New York. It was a shabby piece of work, I have decided. I wish like hell I could do something good.

I've rented a small apartment in New York at the above address, hoping that might help. It is too early to tell.

With all possible friendliness,

Kurt

March 7, 1971

[New York City]

To Jane Vonnegut

Dear Jane—

Well—I don't like being surrounded by bastards, and am not in fact surrounded by them. My saying that was romance—or bullshit, if you like. I do like being alone a lot just now, and taking care of myself. We hurt each other back and forth so much, almost absent-mindedly, that it was common sense for us to separate, if only to break the rhythm. And it has accidentally been good for Edie, having me here. I went with her to a literary bash thrown by George Plimpton last night, at a restaurant called Elaine's. She was the most attractive woman there. Larry Rivers, the painter, spent his whole time with her. She was like Liza Doolittle at the ball. Everybody wanted to know who she was. She is so cool through it all. She is very at home in the world.

Any word from Mark? None here.

Margaret Meade says that any couple which has had children has an irreversible and undissolvable relationship, which is what you say obliquely in your good letter today. I agree. It is deep and permanent.

I will have to come up there in the next couple of weeks to put the finishing touches on the mother-fucking income taxes. Amazing amounts of cash will wing their way from us to the Pentagon. Too bad. [. . .]

K

March 23, 1971
New York City

To José Donoso

Kurt's son, Mark, would describe this experience in his memoir The
Eden Express *(1975) and later in* Just Like Someone Without Mental
Illness Only More So.

Dear Pepe:

[. . .] My son, Mark, has had a nervous breakdown, and has
been diagnosed as a schizophrenic. He is in a hospital in British
Columbia. I have visited him. Jane is out there now. This isn't
the frightful news it would have been a few years ago. Amazingly, most schizophrenics respond beautifully to enormous
doses of vitamins. Mark will have to take these doses for the rest
of his life, just as a diabetic has to take insulin. The vitamins
somehow prevent his brain from releasing a substance very much
like LSD.

Please keep in touch.

I was at a banquet at Harvard three nights ago. Allen Ginsberg and I were the chief speakers. We held hands most of the
time. What a lovely man.

Cheers,

Kurt Vonnegut, Jr.

June 1, 1971
New York City

To Nanny Vonnegut

Dear old Nanny—

You certainly deserve a letter from me. A hundred letters
would be more like it, I love you so.

I will be home from time to time to see you. But I will not stay
for long. I still love your mother, but we can't be together much

without fighting. We have tried to do things about this, but nothing helps, and each fight hurts more than the last one.

I wasn't stolen away by another woman. I don't think people can steal other people. I simply went away because the fighting was making everybody so unhappy. I've done that several times before. Going to Iowa was an example. Every time I went away I simply went to aloneness. There was never any other woman beckoning me to come.

This time, for instance, I couldn't make myself come home after the play opened, and I was alone. I hardly knew Jill at all, and I didn't like her much, and whatever happened between us happened long after I'd decided home was too uncomfortable for me.

And, as you know perfectly well, people need people. And Jill is who I have now. She's awfully nice to me. I was the one who sent you the picture of you and me in Greenwich Village. I wanted you to have it.

I don't know what will happen to me next. I'll keep in touch. I think I will try to buy or rent a house in the country somewhere, and then you can come to see me, and bring Jerry. I won't necessarily be with Jill, nice as she is. That remains to be decided. It will take me a long time to make up my mind. It may be that I would get to fighting with her all the time, too. So it might be wise of me just to hire a housekeeper and live pretty much alone except for visits from you and the rest of the gang.

Love—

K

P.S.: Edith is at *Vogue* magazine at this very moment. They are testing her for a modeling job. This New York mess has been a glorious adventure for her, anyway, and the adventure never would have happened without the mess.

July 15, 1971
New York City

To Knox Burger

The Glencannon stories were a series of short stories by Guy Gilpatric, featuring a Scottish ship engineer named Colin Glencannon. They originally appeared in the Saturday Evening Post.

Dear Knox—

That's so beautiful that you sold a piece for Mark. The transaction means so much all at once. I am reminded of a Glencannon story in the *Post*, wherein Glencannon agrees to repair a pipe organ in Italy. He takes the organ apart, and he says, "This thing has more parts than a Chinese submarine."

Yours truly,
Kurt

October 2, 1971
New York City

To Nanny Vonnegut

The project he was working on for National Educational Television was aired the following year and was titled Between Time and Timbuktu.

Happy birthday, Nanny darling—

I love you so much. You're so beautiful. I was scared stiff about our long date in London, but now I have nothing but charming memories of it—mainly the gibbon apes and the panda. That was a good idea of yours: going to the zoo.

Mark is here. Edie was here all day yesterday, making hundreds of separate drawings for a one-minute animated cartoon. She is studying animation and really imaginative commercial art. She is studying commercial art under Milton Glaser, who is the number one commercial artist around town. He is crazy about her and she is crazy about him—after Geraldo, of course.

There was a very good writer named Ring Lardner who was about my father's age, and all his children and all his grandchildren became writers or artists of one kind or another. I have fantasies that my descendents will be like his. So I am having a typewriter exactly like mine delivered to you at Sea Pines—ideally on your birthday. Anyway—the gift *obligates* you to be a writer now.

I am having a lot of fun just now—writing a 90 minute script for a National Educational Television Network show which is going to be put on in March, right before the next shot at the moon. It is about the first poet to be fired into space. He is played by Bill Hickey, who was Looseleaf Harper in *Happy Birthday, Wanda June*. We have already shot some film—on the edge of a reservoir west of Boston. We pretend it's a tropical island, and we've made it look like one. There were child-like natives in sarongs, and they were attacked by terrible soldiers in helicopters and on mini-bikes. You want to be in it somewhere? We're going to be shooting for the next couple of months.

I am writing a sestina for the script. Look up "sestina" in the dictionary and try writing one yourself. It's tough, but what isn't?

Love you—

K

October 24, 1971
New York City

To José Donoso

Dear Pepe—

I had dinner in Frankfurt, Germany, a week ago, and I managed to have a primitive and charming conversation in French with Senor Grijalbo, my Spanish publisher. He had no English or German. I had no Spanish. A Frenchman wouldn't have understood a word we said, but we used it as though it were Morse code, and the messages came through slowly but clearly. I learned that he knew and admired you, and I told him to give you my love. He said you were not easily seen these days. Your good letter of October 9 confirms this.

I myself am living alone in two rooms and a garden in New York, attempting to draw useful electricity from the millions of milling strangers around me. I am no longer living with Jane for this reason, as nearly as I can tell: We are no longer capable of conducting amiable conversations. When we try to talk, to amuse each other and pass the time, our words are wooden, stilted, queer, distant, and—finally—quietly bitter. That is too bad, and many people regard me as heartless for leaving her. But the hours and days and years dragged so. I am happier now, though far from hilarious and proud. I have achieved a sort of Limbo, which is a distinct improvement over what I had before. I am beginning to write again. That had stopped for a while. I do not wish to marry again. I'm not in love with anybody else. [. . .]

I hope that Jane will fall in love and marry again. She's still beautiful.

I have become something of a public man. People recognize me sometimes, and I get a lot of invitations to speak. I turn most of them down. One I didn't turn down came from the American National Academy of the Arts, of which I am not a member. I got to deliver the main address at their annual meeting a couple of months ago. I was petrified.

You promised good news, Pepe. Here's some from me: I am working on a project for which I am being paid almost nothing, but which amuses me for days on end. The National Educational Television Network, which is America's non-commercial TV operation, has hired me to write a 90-minute show about a space shot, which will be shown three days before America has a real space shot next March. We think our space shot will be infinitely cheaper than the real thing, and a lot more interesting.

Love to Maria Pilar—

Kurt

November 13, 1971
New York City

To NANNY VONNEGUT

Dear old Nan—

Well—it could go two ways with us: you could figure you had
been ditched by your father, and you could mourn about that. Or
we could keep in touch and come to love each other even more
than we have before.

The second possibility is the attractive one for me. It's the absolutely necessary one for me. And the trouble with it is that you
will have to write me a lot, or some, anyway, and call up sometimes, and so on. We've got to wish each other happy birthdays,
and ask how work is going, and tell each other jokes, and all
that. And you've got to visit me often, and I've got to pay more
attention to what sorts of things are really good times instead of
chores for you.

Jane and I get along very well these days. Our letters to each
other are friendly—and the telephone calls, too. We feel friendlier
and more open with each other than we have for years: no more
fighting while wearing masks. Things would have gotten much
worse if we had kept going the way we were going—and life
would have looked much uglier to you.

Your mother and father like each other a lot, something you
must have doubted sometimes in the past. And we both want you
to go to Austria next semester. The drawback to that trip is that
you will be expected to write us a lot of letters. But do it anyway.
If I were younger, I think I might try to become a European. It's
friendlier and cheaper and tastier over there, but you will make at
least one really unpleasant discovery: they are wrecking their air
and water, too. The Mediterranean is turning into an open sewer,
too, just like Lake Erie. I hope that during your lifetime it will be
cleaned up again.

I love you as much as I love anybody in the world.

K

November 20, 1971

New York City

To Nanny Vonnegut

Dear Old Nanno—

That was a keen letter—and you don't have to write too many of those. It's just nice to know that there will be more than just black velvet silence out there, that a pleasant and interesting letter will drift in from time to time.

You're learning now that you do not inhabit a solid, reliable social structure—that the older people around you are worried, moody, goofy human beings who themselves were little kids only a few days ago. So home can fall apart and schools can fall apart, usually for childish reasons—and what have you got? A space wanderer named Nan.

And that's O.K. I'm a space wanderer named Kurt, and Jane's a space wanderer named Jane, and so on. When things go well for days on end, it is an hilarious accident.

You are dismayed at having lost a year, maybe, because the school fell apart. Well—I feel as though I've lost the years since *Slaughterhouse-Five* was published, but that's malarky. Those years weren't lost. They simply weren't the way I'd planned them. Neither was the year in which Jim had to stay motionless in bed while he got over TB. Neither was the year in which Mark went crazy, then put himself together again. Those years were adventures. Planned years are not.

I look back on my own life, and I wouldn't change anything, not even the times when I was raging drunk. I don't drink much any more, by the way. And a screwy thing is happening, without any encouragement from anywhere—I am eating less and less meat.

Other ideas which seem good to me appear uninvited—when I'm alone, and I'm alone a lot. I love being alone sometimes. And one of those ideas is that you are a European, were probably born one. Europe, maybe Austria, is in your DNA. I see you going to the art school where young Ted Rowley is now this coming summer. You will become fluent in German and then French. And maybe you'll get me over there. Maybe that's where I belong, too. We'd live in separate houses, of course. Probably separate countries, even. I wouldn't barge in on you and stay.

I think it's important to live in a nice country rather than a powerful one. Power makes everybody crazy.

Learn German during your last semester at Sea Pines, and you'll learn more than I ever learned in high school. I doubt that they can get you in shape to cool the college boards, so the hell with the college boards. Educate yourself instead. In the final analysis, that's what I had to do, what Uncle Beaver had to do, what we all have to do.

I am going to order you to do something new, if you haven't done it already. Get a collection of the short stories of Chekhov and read every one. Then read "Youth" by Joseph Conrad. I'm not suggesting that you do these things. I am ordering you to do them.

Any time you want to come here, do it. I have no schedule to upset, no secrets to hide, no privacy to guard from you.

Love—

    K

PS: Years ago, somebody said this about Austria: The situation there is hopeless, but not serious.

December 5, 1971

New York City

To Gail Godwin

John Casey was a student of Kurt's at Iowa. Geraldo Rivera was a TV correspondent in New York who went on to become a controversial national television personality. Edie Vonnegut was the second of Geraldo Rivera's five wives; they were divorced after four years. She married John Squibb in 1985 and lives with him and their two sons in the barn behind the house on Cape Cod where she was raised.

Dear Gail—

Whoever told you that I was a fan did not deceive you. When last we met in Iowa City, we said hello and then goodbye, microseconds apart, and you were startled by the briefness of the encounter, and so was I, and you said something approximating, "Just like *that*?" There should have been more, and I honestly thought there would be more, but then my hosts rigged things so there couldn't be more. Alas!

You and John Casey get me all excited about life and work again, and make me think about new stuff, and I try to respond intelligently. The other young writers I knew at Iowa seem to be reproductions of charming mechanical toys from another era. You're dynamite, as the young people say—and it's so amusing that you're happy, too. Go.

A queer thing has happened to me: I have completed a self, which turns out to be exactly like completing a game of solitaire. The deck has resolved itself into four suits—face up. It is time to shuffle and deal again.

Which I am doing. I am home now for the wedding tomorrow of Edith Vonnegut to Geraldo Rivera. I am luminously pleased by the match. Geraldo is half-Jewish, half Puerto Rican—a lawyer for minority types, and a popular newscaster on Eyewitness News, the ABC news show from 6 to 7 every night in New York. He has been on TV for only a year, and has won all sorts of prizes. This is a stunning love affair. They can't keep their hands off each other.

I am living most of my life alone in New York now, and trying to keep my hands off people. I have been into films and plays and TV, and now understand that other people can't help me much with what I do. So it's back to books and stories.

I can't come out there and speak. I've stopped doing that. Thank those who invited me.

Cheers—

Kurt

January 7, 1972

[New York City]

To Don Farber

Dear Don—

Thanks for all you've done and continue to do for me. I get hysterical from time to time. You remain calm. [. . .]

One cause for my frenzy is financial: I've sent gobs of savings to IRS, and soon even my savings will be gone. I am being totally ruined by prosperity, and I want Jane to see how it works. I wanted to get a small house in the country and a small car, and give up this apartment, but I don't see how I can afford even that. When you called me your two-hundred-thousand-a-year messenger (when I got the theater tickets), it was a crushing thought, because I somehow have tax liabilities in that amount, and resources approaching zero.

In order to take care of the children and Jane, I can think of only a couple of things to do: one is to wipe myself out, which I don't plan to do. The other is to stage a sort of bankruptcy, in which I turn over everything to Jane and you and Dan—copyrights, stocks, all of it, and have you guys do whatever needs to be done with whatever there is to do it with. I have to give up, because I'm obviously not bright about money at all. Otherwise, how could I be in such an impossible mess without even speculating or living especially high? Anyway—you and Jane and Dan hold a meeting. I know it is the place of the man to do brilliant things with money, but this manhood thing has me completely worn out. I just want to be a writer.

If my next book is as good as I think it is, I should be in potter's field in no time. How do all these other freaks get to Easy Street?

Yours truly,

Kurt

P.S.: I enclose an owl. I also wish to report that Vance Bourjaily's play is a perfect beauty. I've seen it. It will break your heart.

March 20, 1972
New York City

To Mark Vonnegut

Martha Friedman was a psychiatrist in New York City whom Kurt sometimes saw in therapy.

Dear Mark—

Thanks for your good letter. I am certainly more dependent on you—and on Nanny, too—than you will ever be on me.

There is a screening of *Slaughterhouse* late this afternoon—for college people. I will be there to run a discussion afterwards. There will be no big premiere. The thing simply starts running at a theater three blocks from here on Wednesday, at noon.

I was going to let my lease here run out in a month. But I'll renew it now, since I can't think of anyplace else to go. The landlord, who is an architect, is going to bust through a new front door, so people don't come in through the kitchen any more, and he's going to cut a door through from the bedroom to the bathroom. That will close up two doors in the kitchen, making room for lots more counter space. It will be a really classy kitchen when he gets through, and I'm getting deeper into the cooking thing, so I'll appreciate that.

My old war buddy, BV O'Hare, will be coming to New York to see the movie on Thursday. That will be a great adventure for me—watching him get his mind blown by a nearly perfect recreation of the past.

I am at last finishing up another book. That's what I do all the time now. Sure is a slow process, as you know. If I can ever help you with opinions on your book, I hope you'll use me. As a teacher, I was usually pretty good at helping people become what they wanted to become. I didn't try to make them resemble me.

Martha Friedman would be most affectionately pleased if you were ever to ask her for advice or information on the profession you propose to enter. She was speculating, for instance, about who would probably interview you for NYU—about how you could enchant him.

Much love—

K

April 5, 1972
New York City

TO MARY BANCROFT

Mary Bancroft was author of Autobiography of a Spy *and a number of novels and magazine articles. She had worked for the U.S. Office of Strategic Services (O.S.S.) from 1941 through 1945, translating German dispatches while living and working in Zurich, Switzerland, and acting as an intermediary between the German resistance and U.S. intelligence.*

My Lai was a village in Vietnam where, in 1968, a unit of the U.S. Army carried out a mass murder of unarmed civilians, including women and children. The My Lai Massacre was made public in 1969 and prompted outrage around the world, building opposition in the U.S. and abroad to the war in Vietnam.

Dear Ms. Bancroft—

Thanks for the amusing, generous letter.

You must know how unusual you and your friends were in the 1920's, how unusual you would be if you were young people right now. You had a good gang. Most people don't have good gangs, so they are doomed to cowardice.

The Utopian dreaming I do now has to do with encouraging cheerfulness and bravery for everyone by the formation of good gangs.

What was new about My Lai was the willingness of ordinary infantry to kill civilians at such close range. Even German infan-

trymen often refused to slaughter civilians during the Second
World War—and specialized squads of pathological personalities
had to be trucked in to do the job.

Cheers,

Kurt Vonnegut, Jr.

August 29, 1972

New York City

To Mark Vonnegut

Dear Mark—

Thanks for your good letter.

I have mixed feelings about advances on first books. They
are hard to get, for one thing, and are usually so small that
they tie you up without appreciably improving your financial
situation.

Also: I have seen a lot of writers stop writing or at least slow
down after getting an advance. They have a feeling of *completion*
after making a deal. That's bad news creatively. If you are within
a few months of having a finished, edited manuscript, I advise
you to carry on without an advance, without that false feeling of
completion, without that bit of good news to announce to a lot of
people before the job is really done.

I don't advise this strongly. It's just my advice. If you get an
advance, I'll cheer with all my heart.

As for how advances work out financially: they are risks taken
by publishers. If you get an advance of $1000, for example, you
will get no more money until your book has earned $1000 in roy-
alties for you. The publisher pays himself back out of your royalties. You haven't lost anything. He hasn't lost anything. It's a
loan, see?

If your book doesn't earn $1000 in royalties for you, then that
is tough shit for the publisher. You don't owe him anything. The

same goes for an advance of a million dollars, which is what James Jones got a couple of years ago—for *three* books.

If you get even a small advance on your book, the publisher will want to tie you up for several books, not just one. He will want to cross-collateralize those books, too. That is: if one book is a flop and another one is a best-seller, the best-seller will pay for the losses of the flop. You may not want to gamble that way. You may want all the gravy from the best-seller, and want the publisher to take the shellacking from the flop. You see?

In the house of my Father there are many options.

Thinking about money games now will simply fuck you up. Concentrate on creative games. That's your job. If your book makes a lot of money, which really good books usually don't, you will get that money as it is earned—in straight royalties.

And the really big whacks of money, of course, come from paperback sales. If you make a small fortune, it will come from paperbacks.

Sam Lawrence is eager to see your book. If you sign on with him, you will have committed yourself, as have I, to having your paperback done by Dell. So you will not get a spectacular advance for the paperback rights. But you will get spectacular checks over the years—as royalties are earned.

If you got a spectacular advance, then your royalties would be used to pay it off. You see? Same thing all over again.

And the hell with it. Write a book.

And, word of honor: I am enchanted by your having such a romantic boat. Buying it was a wise and daring thing to do. So was buying the land in Powell River.

I hope everybody understands this, however: I have been giving myself away, and will continue to do so, if I can, in order to see the money enjoyed while I am alive, and in order to escape inheritance taxes. When I die, ideally, there will be very little to tax and very little to inherit. You are inheriting now.

I am wheeling and dealing in securities and literary properties and all that, and maybe that will all pay off. Maybe not. I find it uncongenial, and wish I could retire soon—after Nanny is educated, say. That would be in the year of the two-hundredth anniversary of the Republic—1976. By then, I hope that everybody will be on his or her own feet, that I will have a pleasant house somewhere, which you will all visit often, and that you will all have pleasant homes which I can visit.

Such is my dream for the bi-centennial.

Love and admiration—

K

September 5, 1972
New York City

To Sam Lawrence

Vonnegut's article on the 1972 Republican convention, "In a Manner that Must Shame God Himself," was published in Harper's *magazine and later collected in* Wampeters, Foma & Granfalloons.

Dear Sam—

Here is my *Harper's* piece on the Republican National Convention. This should just about complete the journalism collection, or whatever we ought to call it. So put this with the other stuff.

This project slowed me down ever so slightly on the final editing of *Breakfast of Champions*. Don's secretary has done about 240 pages of the final draft, and is now on vacation. Don is sending the 240 pages over to Dell for reproduction and copy-editing. When the typist gets back, she will find the remainder waiting for her, fully edited by me.

I will then take off to see my boy in Jamaica.

Cheers—

Kurt

September 15, 1972

New York City

To Gail Godwin

Gail Godwin's book was the novel Glass People.

  The novelist John Irving had also been a student of Kurt's at Iowa.

Dear Gail—

I finished your book two minutes ago. Wow. I was sure lucky to have my life coincide briefly with your life and John Irving's life, so I can say that I must have had something to do with the way you two turned out. What a lark for a sweet old man like me.

Before I took the job at Iowa, George Starbuck told me with all possible delicacy that I should probably read a book before facing a class. I asked him to name a good one, and he suggested *Madame Bovary.* I have since suspected that, if I had asked him to name *two* good novels, he would have been stuck for the name of a second one. At any rate, I read *Madame Bovary,* so I am able to ask this: "Why must some women be Emma Bovary, and why do all intelligent women understand that some women must be Emma Bovary, and what is the big or little trick which allows some women to escape from being Emma Bovary?"

I ask this question not as your thesis advisor but as a fellow human being. And I tell you that I find a simple answer which satisfies me in your book: "Some women have to be Emma because they can't get interesting jobs."

Well—that part of me which asks such plonking questions is that part of me which did so well in Problems in Contemporary Western Civilization in Junior High School in Indianapolis a good many years ago.

My finer self acknowledges you as an absolutely first-rate artist who would respond to life with the right words and feelings

no matter what, mechanically, life happened to be. It makes me
so happy that you have a good job. [. . .]

I'll risk one more word, which is this one:

Cheers—

Kurt

September 17, 1972

New York City

To Vance Bourjaily

Dear Vance—

I'm running fifty-three days behind you, and I see mellow and
satisfying years ahead for us both.

I have done a screwy but useful thing in my newest book,
which is to give all my old characters their freedom. Really. I am
doing for them what Tolstoy did for his serfs, what Jefferson did
for his slaves. From now on, they can do as they please.

If Hemingway had done the same thing when he was fifty, he
might be alive and happy today.

I have no right to advise you, since I am a younger man, but
I'll pray for you as follows: "Lord, please make it possible for my
good friend Vance to come to New York frequently, to jazz himself with the bright lights, to make him want to write plays and
plays and plays."

Really: American theater is coming to life again, and it's so
pleasant for old poops like us to write plays. We don't have to describe anything, and there's so much white space on every page.

Früliche Geburtstag, Kinder!

Kurt

September 20, 1972
New York City

To Nanny Vonnegut

Dear Nanno—

You should know that I as a college student didn't write my parents much. You said all that really matters in your first letter from out there (unless you get in a jam)—that you love me a lot. Mark wrote me the same thing recently. That helps, and it lasts for years. I think I withheld that message from my parents. Either that, or I said it so often that it became meaningless. Same thing, either way.

I promise to take your advice, to try painting again. I quit when the slightly talented ghost who had borrowed my hands decided to take his business elsewhere. Everything was coming together before my eyes for a little while. After that came Kindergarten smears.

Most letters from a parent contain a parent's own lost dreams disguised as good advice. My good advice to you is to pay somebody to teach you to speak some foreign language, to meet with you two or three times a week and talk. Also: get somebody to teach you to play a musical instrument. What makes this advice especially hollow and pious is that I am not dead yet. If it were any good, I could easily take it myself.

One of the most startling things that ever happened to me when I was your age had to do with a woman who was my age now. She didn't know what to do with her life, and I told her that the least she could do was to learn to play the piano. By God, she did!

I plan to buy a piano. But my apartment isn't big enough for a piano, and I'm too lazy to move. Edith has the right idea for lazy people: marry somebody with energy to burn.

I'm going to England for a week next month—to go to college-town openings there of [the movie of] *Slaughterhouse-Five*. I will think of you, and I will remember with pleasure how shy we were, how sort of gummed-up we were. That was appro-

priate. It would have been hateful if we had been hilarious, like a
father and daughter in a TV show.

Don't answer this letter for years.

Remember me fondly.

Love—

K

September 30, 1972

New York City

To Peter Reed

The book was Writers for the 70s: Kurt Vonnegut. *This marked the beginning of Reed's longtime relationship with Kurt as a friend and a literary critic. Reed is professor of English at the University of Minnesota.*

Dear Mr. Reed—

I thank you for the fair and friendly and clear book about my
work. It is something new, I think, to have the work of living authors
reviewed so extensively and responsibly. It is fun for me. You have
said about me exactly what I would have wanted said if I were dead.

I have sent your book to my eighteen-year-old daughter, so
she can be absolutely certain that she has a keen old man.

My newest book, incidentally, is the work of an eager but not
particularly talented seventeen-year-old.

Cheers—

Kurt Vonnegut, Jr.

October 11, 1972

New York City

To Jerome Klinkowitz

*The work that Professors Klinkowitz and John Somer "exhumed"
and presented to Sam Lawrence, along with "an appallingly complete*

bibliography," was compiled in Vonnegut's collection Wampeters,
Foma & Granfalloons.

Dear Mr. Klinkowitz—

[. . .] You have been most useful to me in caring about what I
do. I mean that seriously. You have cheered me up. You have also
exhumed work of mine I had forgotten all about. In gratitude, I
will send you various versions of my new book, *Breakfast of
Champions,* which will be published next April or so. They will
be your property. You can do as you please with them, such as
they are.

   Cheers,

   Kurt Vonnegut, Jr.

                                                October 19, 1972
                                                   New York City

To JANE VONNEGUT

Dear Jane—

   I wish you a happy birthday in confidence that, American politics aside, it really will be a happy birthday for you. At the cost
of unbelievable amounts of pain, you have bought a new life and
a new Jane for yourself. You have always paid your dues, and
you have paid them again. We've both always paid our dues.
That's honorable. I still believe in honor, although I would play
hell defining it.

   Now that we are through the worst of our present adventure in
a world we never made, in bodies we never asked for, with heads
we only dimly understand, it seems safe to say that we hung on to
more than most broken couples do. In a crazy way, it seems to me
that we hung onto practically *everything.* We are not diminished.

   I look forward to seeing you in November.

   Much love—

   K

November 2, 1972
New York City

To Nanny Vonnegut

Dear Nanny—

Good letter from you waiting for me when I got back last night from England. You have caught onto something I only learned in the past month or so—that terrific depressions are going to crunch me down at regular intervals, and that they have nothing to do with what is going on around me.

Only now do I know what the problem is. So—only now can I begin to think about a partial solution. You're right—a change of place makes little difference. Those awful dips still come. We inherited those regular dips. I scarcely know which ancestor to thank. People who live with us are likely to find us unpleasant and terribly self-centered when we're down. There isn't much sympathy for us when we're on an automatic down. There shouldn't be much sympathy, probably. Still—

This is not to encourage you to have regular depressions, to be proud of the family disease. Get rid of it, if you can. I intend to try. I can at least know it for what it is, something I couldn't do before. Again—I don't want you to really dig the disease, so I shouldn't tell you too much about my experiences with it. I have found, though, that I handle it best in solitude. People often find this insulting, the way we retreat. It's a way of hanging onto dignity, though. There are better ways, maybe. I'll ask a doctor what they are.

Another thing which is inherited in our family: an ability to draw, and it is inherited only by females. Amazing. There is a line of women who were practically born drawing—going back and back and back.

Please send me a drawing.

Love—

   K

November 2, 1972
New York City

To José and Maria Donoso

Dear Pepe & Maria Pilar—

[. . .] As for my happiness: I live from day to day and hour
to hour. I know elation. I know despair. A doctor has pre-
scribed pills for depression, which I take from time to time, as
instructed. I still have life in me as an artist. I have finished another book. It contains one-hundred and twenty drawings by
me, as well as prose. My understanding is that I am so odd emotionally and socially that I had better live alone for the rest of
my days. During my last years with Jane, there was a formless
anger in me which I could deal with only in solitude. Jane did
not like it. There is no reason why she should. Nobody likes it.
What is it? Well—if I had to guess, I would say that it was
caused by a combination of bad chemicals in my bloodstream
and the fact that my mother committed suicide. I have finally
dealt with that suicide, by the way, in the book I just finished.
My mother appears in it briefly at the end, but keeps her
distance—because she is embarrassed by the suicide. And so she
should be.

Love—
Kurt

November 26, 1972
New York City

To Jane Vonnegut

Markings *was a memoir/book of reflections by Dag Hammarskjöld, a
Swedish diplomat who was an early secretary-general of the United
Nations, from 1953 until he died in a plane crash in 1961. He was
awarded the Nobel Peace Prize posthumously.*

Dear Jane—

I thank you for *Markings*. I open it at random, and I find a
lot about dying meaningfully, and about sacrifice and pain and
mysterious destinies. "The pulley of time drags us inexorably
forward towards this last day," he says. "A relief to think of
this, to consider that there is a moment without a beyond."
Are you really tuned in to this sort of stuff? Should I be?
Well—I'll try, but it's not my style. I, for one, am glad I didn't
die in Africa, although that opportunity was mine. I still believe
that a dog is going to kill me, and it scares me—and it pisses me
off.

He has one poem which must be about St. Sebastian, which
goes:

> Standing naked
> Where they have placed me,
> Nailed to the target
> By their first arrows.
> Again a bow is drawn,
> Again an arrow flies . . .

And so on. I know something about St. Sebastian which I'll
bet he didn't know, and which most people don't know: St. Sebastian was shot full of arrows for being a secret Christian, but
he *survived*. Seriously. He was mended, and he walked around
Rome for years, bad-mouthing the Emperor for having had him
shot full of arrows.

I understand that the book is a loving gift, and I receive it as
such, and I treasure it as such. [. . .] neither was Hammarskjöld
alive or Christian in any way which charms or enlightens me. I
think he was crazy as a bedbug—about his friend and my enemy,
death.

Love—

K

December 14, 1972
New York City

To Sam Lawrence

Dear Sam—

Loved the dinner with Updike [. . .] Did you realize that Updike had never met Mailer before, that he introduced himself to him on the street corner that night?

Love,
Kurt

January 8, 1973
New York City

To Knox Burger

William Kotzwinkle's novel The Fan Man *was published the following year and became a cult classic of hippie life.*

Dear Knox—

I will do whatever you want me to do for Bill Kotzwinkle. He deserves all the support he can get. I have already told a lot of people how good he is. If I have already said something good about him in a letter, please quote me. If I haven't done that, I will compose something. I really admire him.

As for the critical and financial vacuum I used to inhabit: the thing that burned me up about it the most was that I had to pretend to be a primitive all the time, whereas I think I was an alert and well educated professional. Nobody would say so, that was all. So I was a shit-kicker, and said gosh and shucks and so on, and asked dumb questions about the Big Apple.

Let Kotzwinkle find out what I found out about the Big Apple. Let him pretend to be a primitive, too. Let him correct his mistakes. Let him learn his lessons as I did. Let him fucking well fix his stuff so it sells, or let him go hungry. Let him Uncle Tom for somebody who knows somebody who knows somebody who actually owns a Linotype. I learned Darwinism. Let him learn it, too.

Let him talk to Darwinists, hat in hand. It's educational, and pays off in the end. As Colonel Littauer said to me one time, when I was bitter about being broke: "Who asked you to be a writer in the first place?"

Cheers,

Kurt

January 10, 1973

New York City

To Nanny Vonnegut

Dear old Nan—

It's good to know where you are. Things have settled down here. We had only been here a week or so when we saw you. It's cozy and calm now. Workmen don't ring the doorbell every ten minutes any more, don't come to wreck what previous workmen have done.

Steve & Edith are both in Jamaica—went down on the same plane about a week ago. Steve came to New York with everything he owned in an automobile, which he parked for two hours. Everything was stolen, of course. But then the damnedest thing in the history of crime happened: the police actually caught the thieves, and everything was returned to Steve only four hours after the theft. Did you ever hear of such a thing? God sure must love him.

I love him, too—but it seems to me that he is leading a dismayingly goofy life for a person his age. He claims to be a musician, but he does absolutely nothing to hustle his wares in the cities, where all the business is done. He is permanently on vacation, which is a spooky way to be. His friend Bob Sturgis was with him here. Sturgis is a very solid citizen these days, portly and grave, and a clerk to a New Jersey Supreme Court justice. Sturgis was raising hell with Steve, too, for remaining so dreamily child-like as the years roll by.

A note from Jim says: "The last few months have been very bad goat-wise—lots of sickness and death among the young kids. I think we will have it under control soon, but we have lost a lot." Too bad. At least he has inherited a new wad of cash, which should allow him to hang in there for another five years. I approve of that. It's somehow a very meaningful life he has.

And you must know that I approve of your life, too. That heavy schedule will teach you a lot of skills you'll be glad to know. Skills are magical, or I always think so anyway, whenever I see people who have them. You say you are having an identity crisis. Well, the people who seem to have the strongest senses of identity are persons who have real skills and do respectable work. It may be, though, that you would like to be comforted and enlightened by a psycho-therapist as well. That is O.K. with me. Almost everything depends on who the therapist is, though. This is a matter of luck. Martha helped me tremendously, and at very low cost, mainly by putting me in a group. Somebody else might have wrecked me. If you do go to somebody, the therapist, no matter who it is, is going to want you to talk a lot about your feelings about all the members of your family—how we all seemed to you when you were little. We probably seem that way to you now. The super shock to our family, and one of the best things that happened to it, too, was the arrival of the Adams. Your importance in the family was vastly increased, since there were suddenly so many new people for Jane and me to pay attention to. So you and I are not as close as we might have been. Or, we're just as close, I guess, but we don't know each other as well. Well, what the hell—we know the Adams better than we would have otherwise, and that's a gain which may compensate for the loss. At any rate, we have all had more pleasant and interesting and affectionate lives than most people have. Nobody has anything much to regret or apologize for.

You and I know each other in our bones, at any rate. And you can get to know me some through my books, too. It is only natural that you should feel reserved and insecure when you're with me, since I've caused two huge disruptions in the continuity of the family, and since you saw so much of me when I worked at home, when I had to raise such hell in order to gain privacy in which to write. Also, I was worried sick about money all the time, and I had no friends on Cape Cod who had any idea what my sort of work entailed. Just to clarify the two disruptions I'm talking about, I mean the adoption of the Adams and my leaving the Cape for New York.

So there we are.

I don't welcome at all the news that you won't be coming east again for a long time. That is going to be hard to take for all of us who love you so much, even if some of us don't know you as well as we should. Again, it's natural for someone your age to announce that she is cutting ties with the past, but don't really do that.

I am taking the liberty of writing a young man in Oakland about you. He was a student of mine at Harvard, a pleasant and brilliant boy from good old Indiana. His name is Jerry Hiatt. I hope you hear from him. He could be a keen friend.

Love—

K

February 4, 1973

[New York City]

To Gail Godwin

John Leonard was one of the two regular daily book reviewers for The New York Times.

Dear Gail—

That really was clumsy of you to be in New York all that time and to never call me up. It makes me wonder what other serious, easily avoidable mistakes you make every day. It must be hell for all concerned. Do you pay your bills?

I had a psychiatrist tell me that shyness is a form of hostility. They tell everybody that, you know. That was a couple of years ago, so I have had a long time to think about it. I have persuaded myself that it isn't true. It's fear and laziness and realism. It's an embarrassed apology which says in effect: "Hey—I'm sorry, I probably don't like life as much as you do."

John Leonard knows perfectly well who you are, and how well you write. All I had to do was mention your name. He'll give you work. We'll have him to a small dinner for you when you're next in town.

The past four years have been mean buggers for me. I'm sure you care, so I am pleased to say that I'm much better now. Jill has been a help.

Love—

Kurt

                                                            March 10, 1973
                                                            New York City

To Paul Engle

This letter was part of Vonnegut's continuing effort to get his Russian translator, Rita Rait, permission to travel to the United States.

Gennady Fedosov was cultural attaché at the U.S.S.R. embassy in Washington, D.C.

Dear Paul—

That's a strong and attractive letter you wrote to Fedosov. I'm glad you're on the job. Harvard, Yale and UCLA have so far expressed interest in having Rita visit them. In order not to wear her out, we should probably keep her in the eastern half of the country, unless she begs to see the rest of it. She is no spring chicken. She is sprightly and healthy, though. It would be good if the community she got to know best, to feel cozy about, were Iowa City. New York would drive her crazy.

You say some people have doubts about your foreign program. I did—mainly because I didn't think I had much to teach foreigners. Everything I knew was idiosyncratically American—not for export.

I am moved now by your stubborn determination to do solid things for international understanding. There is no question about it: you have been good for the planet.

Congratulations to Hualing on her many publications. One way or another, we will see each other soon.

Cheers—

Kurt Vonnegut

March 20, 1973
New York City

To Daniel Glossbrenner

Daniel Glossbrenner, a cousin of Kurt's, had been a captain in the famous Rainbow Division of World War I.

Dear Uncle Dan—

I only learned today, from my brother Bernard, that Aunt Edna died. It breaks my heart. You and I can both remember how much her love and generosity meant to me when I was a boy and young man.

I remember, too, that you and she were as close to each other as any couple I ever knew. So your loss is an especially crushing one.

And I remember that your love and generosity to me were the equals of hers. There is no way I can be generous in turn, since I have nothing that could be of use to you at this awful time. It is easy and natural, though, for me to love you a lot. I send that love.

Sincerely—

Kurt Vonnegut, Jr.

Kurt, age fifteen (*front and center*), at a reunion of the Vonnegut family, whose distinguished nineteenth-century ancestors brought German culture and traditions of "freethinking" to landlocked Indianapolis.

Kurt with a fellow soldier after his enlistment in 1943. The army sent Kurt to school to study calculus and thermodynamics before sending him overseas as a rifleman in the infantry.

Kurt and his former high school sweetheart Jane Cox, as newlyweds in Chicago in 1946. A Phi Beta Kappa graduate of Swarthmore, Jane had Kurt read *The Brothers Karamazov* on their honeymoon.

"We always have a nice time when you and your family come up here, so please come whenever you can," Kurt wrote to Knox Burger in 1959, the year this picture of the Burger and Vonnegut families was taken. Jane is standing under the ladder to the left of Kurt, and Otis Burger is seated on the far right. The woman looking up at Kurt is Gertrude Buckman, who worked with Knox at *Collier's*.

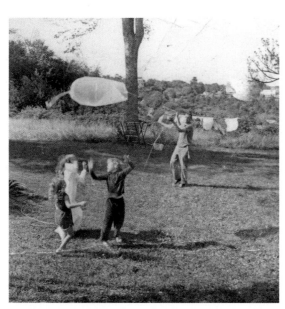

Kurt flying a homemade kite made from a garment bag with his daughter Edie (in nightgown) and Knox and Otis Burger's daughters Neall and Katherine on the same 1959 trip.

Knox Burger in 1959 at a cabin on Mount Riga in Connecticut. Kurt wrote that Knox "discovered and encouraged more good young writers than any other editor of his time."

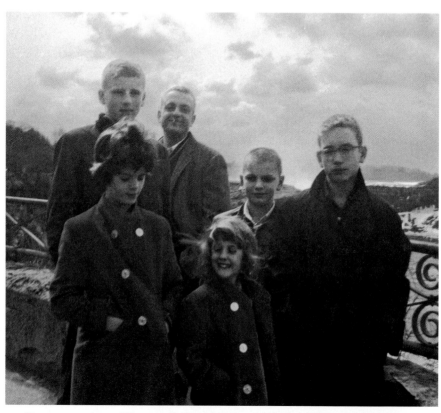

Kurt on a trip to Niagara Falls in 1963 with his children, including "the orphans"—sons of Kurt's older sister Alice and her husband—who were raised by the Vonneguts when both their parents died within twenty-four hours of each other. Left to right are Steve (Adams), Edie, Kurt, Nanny, Tiger (Adams), and Mark. The oldest Adams boy, Jim, was away at the University of Vermont.

Kurt met Norman Mailer in the early 1950s ("call it the summer of 1950") in Provincetown, and in 1960 invited him to pay a visit "on your way to or from Provincetown . . . we have no horse or Mary Jane, but plenty of gin, God knows."

Anne Sexton, the Pulitzer Prize–winning poet who was enthralled when Kurt drew her his graph of the plot of "Cinderella" at a publication party for her book *Transformations*, poems she based on *Grimm's Fairy Tales*.

Vance Bourjaily, the novelist and colleague at Iowa who, Kurt wrote to his wife, Jane, "has turned out to be a most generous, wise and friendly man."

This photo of Gail Godwin, a student of Kurt's who went on to become a successful novelist, was taken in Kurt's workshop at Iowa. He wrote her in 1971 that she was one of his former students who "get me all excited about life and work again, and make me think about new stuff . . ."

Kurt in Iowa at a Writers Workshop picnic in 1965 with Patricia Dubus, wife of Andre Dubus, a student of Kurt's at Iowa who went on to win many awards for his short stories. His son, Andre Dubus III, is a novelist whose books include *House of Sand and Fog*. Andre III's younger brother Jeb is the boy in the photo. The man in the photo is another student of Kurt's at Iowa named Ian McMillan.

Jerome Klinkowitz was one of the first academic fans of Kurt's work, and, along with John Somer, published a book of essays on his life and work, *The Vonnegut Statement*. He credits Kurt with giving him the most important advice of his life: to stay teaching in the Midwest rather than taking a job on the East Coast.

Kurt in 1969 in the garden of his home in Barnstable, and (*opposite*) on a contemplative walk at
Barnstable harbor.

The theatrical lawyer Don Farber and his wife, Annie, who were Kurt's most trusted friends, celebrating after the opening of a play in Philadelphia. In 1970 Farber became Kurt's agent, negotiator, and advisor in personal as well as professional matters. Kurt wrote to Don in 1972: "Thanks for all you've done and continue to do for me. I get hysterical from time to time. You remain calm."

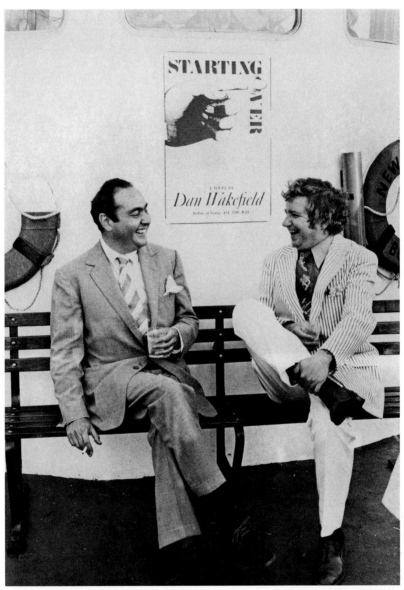

Kurt's longtime publisher Sam Lawrence on a boat party in Boston Harbor in 1973 for the publication of Dan Wakefield's novel *Starting Over*. Kurt had recently told Wakefield, "That's quite a head of hair you've got."

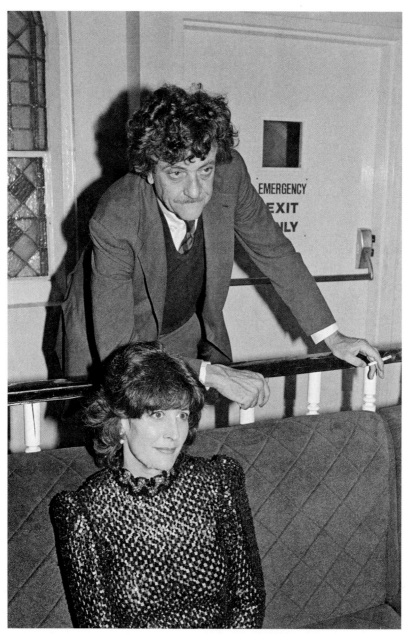
Kurt and his second wife, the photographer Jill Krementz, at a party in 1984.

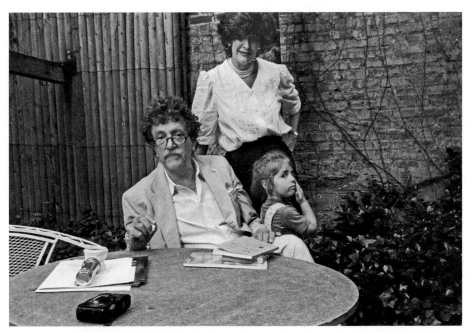

Kurt with Jill and daughter Lily in 1987.

Kurt in 2005. The quote is from William Blake's *Songs of Experience:*
"Go love without the help of anything on earth."

March 22, 1973

[New York City]

To Gail Godwin

Robert Gottlieb was editor in chief at Knopf.

Dear Gail—

Like a character in a John O'Hara novel, I called Les Beaux
Arts on Tuesday, and, like a character in a John O'Hara novel, I
was told, "She done checked out yesterday." I felt deprived, so I
must have had good times with you.

It's good to know you'll be back. Your chances of surviving as
a writer are numerous. You will become one of the three-hundred
Americans who make their livings that way. I don't even have to
see a piece of your new book to understand Gottlieb's enthusiasm
and feelings of your having made a quantum leap. It was coded in
you to make that leap. It was an easy leap, right?

Cheers—

Kurt

May 26, 1973

New York City

To José Donoso

Dear Pepe—

[. . .] You would think that people would be so obsessed by
Watergate that they wouldn't be buying books, but that's not the
case. Book sales are booming. People are suffocated by the scandal, which grinds on week after week, and they are using books,
apparently, as ways of coming up for air. Nobody is *entertained*
or enlightened by Watergate. It's torture, not show business.

You want my honest reaction to your book. I don't think it is
better than the others. It is simply bigger and flashier than the others, and so will attract more attention and perhaps lead to greater

financial success. You were a master when I first met you, and masters do not grow. They simply work. So you will never get any news of your having grown from me. Growth is for apprentices. I welcome anything you do. Just now, I would especially welcome your poetry. Personally, I prefer your smaller works, just as I prefer smaller Vermeers. But that way lies destitution, I fear.

I'm sorry that you are tired of living such a lonely life, but I will bet you that you can't do a damn thing about it without changing your profession. I have met a lot of writers by now, and they all carry twenty acres of Sahara Desert with them wherever they go. I have no idea what the explanation for this is, other than the necessary smallness of their organizations.

Maybe I will come to Chile, but not before I learn to speak Spanish. There *is* a Chile, Indiana, incidentally, not far from my birthplace. The locals pronounce it Shy-lie, and have no idea why some people smile at that.

Much love, old buddy—

Kurt

June 21, 1973

New York City

To Donald Fiene

Donald M. Fiene retired as professor of Slavic languages at the University of Tennessee. He wrote extensively on Russian language and culture and compiled bibliographies of the works of Alexander Solzhenitsyn and many other writers, including J. D. Salinger. He worked with Vonnegut in the effort to bring Kurt's Russian translator, Rita Rait, to the U.S.

Dear Don—

What can we do? We raised the money. We mobilized the academic community to welcome Rita. An invitation was sent to her more than six weeks ago. It was either lost or intercepted, most likely intercepted. When I found out she had never received it, I had Paul Engle send her another one (in the name of the University of Iowa again) about a week ago. She won't get that one either, I'll bet. Engle told me on the phone that the cultural attaché in Washington had told him that there weren't going to be *any* exchanges of writers and translators during the coming year. So there we are, and fuck all.

 Best—
  Kurt

August 1, 1973

New York City

To Emily Glossbrenner

Emily Glossbrenner was the daughter of Daniel and Edna Glossbrenner, and a cousin of Kurt's. Alex is Kurt's uncle, his father's brother. Aunt Irma is Kurt's father's sister. Raye is a cousin. Kurt "Tiger" Adams is the third son of Kurt's sister Alice and her husband, Jim.

Dearest Emmie—

 I thank you for your warm letter. You are nice to worry about me. I owe it to you to explain how I am and what I have been doing. The main thing, Emmie, is that I see my children all the time. I live in the same city with Edith, and see her a couple of times a week. Steve and Mark are now in town. We had supper together last night, and they spent the night here, and I will see them on the Cape this weekend. I visited Tiger a couple of weeks ago, and go to Jamaica to see Jim, and so on. So I in fact still head up a vivid and loving family, and will become a grandfather whenever someone decides to reproduce. Jane and I are no longer good companions. I am sorry about that, and so is she. This happens sometimes. There is no hatred between us. We talk often on the telephone, and she has worked out a quite satisfactory, by no means lonely, life of her own.

As for my unhappiness in the presence of Alex & Raye & Irma: you mustn't tell them this, but they are no good at keeping secrets, although they imagine themselves reserved and poker-faced. And they have made it clear without knowing it that they are in awe of what I dislike most about myself, the tin-horn part, the fame, and that they consider what I actually write or think as popular garbage for hippies. I dedicated my own favorite book to Alex, and he said he couldn't read it, but he supposed that the young people liked it. So that is O.K., really. I love those people, so I go see them as often as I can, and I call them up a lot. But it is very hard to talk to them. Emotionally we are nearly one flesh. Intellectually we are far, far away. And they are too old to be interested in my explanations of myself. So I don't explain. So my unhappiness in Indianapolis boils down to a profound uneasiness about being loved for everything except for what I really do. And about having to keep my mouth shut about politics and about the arts since 1914.

I would love to see you, and beg you to call me whenever you are near New York. You and I are both in reasonably good shape, it seems to me, considering how long we've lived. I will explain to you the nature of my profession, which is necessarily a bizarre and risky enterprise.

Much love—

K

August 16, 1973
New York City

TO ISAAC BASHEVIS SINGER

Singer was the author of more than eighteen novels and short-story collections, which he wrote in Yiddish and were translated into English, including The Magician of Lublin, Enemies: A Love Story, *and the short-story collection* A Crown of Feathers. *He was awarded the Nobel Prize for Literature in 1978.*

Dear Mr. Singer—

Jill Krementz showed me the friendly note you wrote to her. She deserves such warmth. You are right to think she is able and virtuous.

You are right, too, God knows, to feel that Céline was vile. I spoke to a Frenchman about Céline one time, and he said impatiently over and over, "He was base, he was base." I don't think I'd ever heard the word base used in conversation before in *that* sense. I was impressed. It was a word especially minted for the bizarre criminality of Céline. He was the one war criminal who did not wish to be forgiven or understood.

Had I known of his criminality when I began to read him, that information would have spoiled his books. But I read *Journey to the End of Night* and then *Death on the Installment Plan* in rapid succession, and with the innocence of a lonesome soldier reading paperbacks in a bus station. I was in fact a lonesome instructor who had left his family to go to teach at the University of Iowa. There is no anti-Semitism in either book, except for a glancing reference to Jews in the League of Nations. So there was no internal evidence to warn me that he was a maniac. So I admired the books and the man.

I mentioned him to others, and soon learned why he was detestable. I read his later books, which revealed him as base. I then read his doctoral thesis on Semmelweis, and found suggestions of greatness again.

So there we are. He was a rotten egg with some good parts. I think I had better shut up about him, because people are properly nauseated by such an egg. I do not feel censored or censured. I understand that I or anybody can make life uglier than it need be with praise of Céline.

I send you love and admiration, and hope we can have supper soon.

Yours truly,
    Kurt Vonnegut, Jr.

August 30, 1973

New York City

To Jerry Lefcourt

Jerry Lefcourt was the lawyer for Abbie Hoffman.

Abbie Hoffman was a political activist beginning with his partici-pation in the Student Nonviolent Coordinating Committee (S.N.C.C.), which was part of the Civil Rights Movement. He was one of the lead-ers of the Yippie movement of the 1960s and was arrested and tried for conspiracy and inciting to riot as a result of his part in the protests at the 1968 Democratic National Convention in Chicago. Police broke up the protests in a violent confrontation, and Hoffman was arrested, along with seven other leaders. In 1971 he published a book called Steal This Book, *which gave advice on how to live without pay-ing for anything. In 1973 he was arrested and charged with intent to sell cocaine and maintained that undercover police agents had en-trapped him by planting suitcases of cocaine in his office. In the spring of '74 he skipped bail, had cosmetic surgery, and hid from authorities for several years. He gave himself up in 1980, was sentenced to a year in prison, but was released after four months. In one of his trials he quoted Thomas Paine, one of the leaders of the American Revolution: "Every age and generation must be as free to act for itself in all cases as the age and generations which preceded it. . . . Man has no prop-erty in man; neither has any generation a property in the generations which are to follow."*

Dear Mr. Lefcourt:

I am writing about your client, Mr. Abbie Hoffman. I have just learned of his arrest, and I am especially shocked by the high bail which has been set.

I have known Mr. Hoffman for several years, and it should be brought to the attention of the Court that he is not a desperado who would endanger the community, if he were released on low-ered bail. Neither does it require monstrous bail to induce him to appear for trial.

It is easy for those who do not know him or have not made a study of his life to imagine that he is a wild man. Responsible historians are even now recognizing that he used clownishness as a perfectly legal and effective weapon against injustice, and that he had the best interests of the American people in mind when he behaved as he did. He has also had a high regard for the truth.

I know nothing about his present troubles, but I do know that he has been a friend, not an enemy, of society in the past. He deserves to have this recognized by the Court—in the form of a drastic reduction in bail.

Yours truly,
Kurt Vonnegut, Jr.

October 9, 1973
New York City

To José Donoso

The democratically elected president of Chile, Salvador Allende, was overthrown in a coup on September 11, led by a military junta whose leader, General Augusto Pinochet, took control of the country. "Adam" was Adam Yarmolinsky, a Harvard professor who served in many capacities in the Kennedy, Johnson, and Carter administrations. He met and began seeing Jane Vonnegut after Kurt left Cape Cod.

Dear Pepe—
Almost everybody I know is sad about what happened in Chile. I think about you often anyway—but now I think how much the death of democracy at home must hurt you and Maria Pilar. You must have lost friends. Our son-in-law, Geraldo Rivera, has just come back from Santiago with smuggled films. There were bodies to be seen, shot during curfew, apparently, and left lying where they fell when the sun came up. Curiously, or maybe not so curiously, he interviewed several university students, who told him that the overthrow was a very good thing. They could

scarcely say anything else, I guess. And Geraldo himself, a fierce democrat and closet Marxist, has concluded that the elected government was out of control, was a disaster in its own right. I am persuaded that it is now impossible to govern well almost anywhere, and that national tragedies come and go of their own will, like thunderstorms. This makes endurance the most useful human skill.

Vance, who stole my razor, tells me that he found you and Maria Pilar and Jane and Adam and everybody in a generally merry state. Hooray. I am naturally embarrassed by my separation from Jane, which has been interpreted as a faithless act. I think the passing years will make it apparent that she has been reborn into happiness and freedom which were inaccessible while I was with her. As for myself: after many black years, I, too, am becoming more resourceful and successful in the pursuit of happiness.

Cheers—

Kurt

October 26, 1973

New York City

To Vance and Tina Bourjaily

Kurt had taken a one-year appointment as Distinguished Professor of English Prose at City University of New York, but resigned at the end of the first semester.

Dear Vance & Tina—

Terrific letter from both of you, and from Pepe, too! I am still waiting for Adam to deliver my razor. Did he tell you that we have never met? I've met his parents, who seem very dear.

I am glad you got to know Jane some, Tina. She's a very good girl. We just ran out of companionship somehow. Pepe says she's happy. I sure hope so.

Listen, Vance—I am resigning as Distinguished Professor at City College when the semester ends in January. It's too much work, when taken together with all my other ridiculous obligations. They are looking for somebody to take over the job, if not in January then in September, 1974. I said I thought you wanted to try New York again for a little while. This excited the management.

Anyway, the job pays about $36,000, more than practically any other teaching job in the city, and you're expected to teach only two courses of your own choice or devising. The job isn't mine to offer. But, if you are interested, you might write to Professor Leo Hamalian, a fellow Arab, who is the boss of the Creative Writing Program. Other folks on his faculty are the likes of Joe Heller, Mark Mirsky, Israel Horovitz, and Joel Oppenheimer. Tell him you plan to be in New York City, if you do plan that, say you've heard good things about his operation from me, and ask him if he might have a job for you. His address is Department of English, The City College, Convent Avenue at 137th Street, New York, N.Y. 10031.

I'm buying a house in Turtle Bay, between 2nd & 3rd, on 48th Street. I won't have a restaurant next door any more, but I'll still have a garden. I'll have a guest room, too, which is new.

I went up to Boston University last night, gave a reading at the behest of good old George Starbuck. I hadn't seen Cathy for years. I'm crazy about her.

Love—

Kurt

November 16, 1973
New York City

To CHARLES MCCARTHY

Charles McCarthy was the chairman of the Drake School Board of Drake, North Dakota.

Dear Mr. McCarthy:

I am writing to you in your capacity as Chairman of the Drake School Board. I am among those American writers whose books have been destroyed in the now famous furnace of your school.

Certain members of your community have suggested that my work is evil. This is extraordinarily insulting to me. The news from Drake indicates to me that books and writers are very unreal to you people. I am writing this letter to let you know how real I am.

I want you to know, too, that my publisher and I have done absolutely nothing to exploit the disgusting news from Drake. We are not clapping each other on the back, crowing about all the books we will sell because of the news. We have declined to go on television, have written no fiery letters to editorial pages, have granted no lengthy interviews. We are angered and sickened and saddened. And no copies of this letter have been sent to anybody else. You now hold the only copy in your hands. It is a strictly private letter from me to the people of Drake, who have done so much to damage my reputation in the eyes of their children and then in the eyes of the world. Do you have the courage and ordinary decency to show this letter to the people, or will it, too, be consigned to the fires of your furnace?

I gather from what I read in the papers and hear on television that you imagine me, and some other writers, too, as being sort of rat-like people who enjoy making money from poisoning the minds of young people. I am in fact a large, strong person, fifty-one years old, who did a lot of farm work as a boy, who is good with tools. I have raised six children, three my own and three adopted. They have all turned out well. Two of them are farmers. I am a combat infantry veteran from World War Two, and hold a Purple Heart. I have earned whatever I own by hard work. I have never been arrested or sued for anything. I am so much trusted with young people and by young people that I have served on the faculties of The University of Iowa, Harvard, and the City College of New York. Every year I receive at least a dozen invitations to be commencement speaker at colleges and high schools. My books are probably more widely used in schools than those of any other living American fiction writer.

If you were to bother to read my books, to behave as educated persons would, you would learn that they are not sexy, and do not argue in favor of wildness of any kind. They beg that people be kinder and more responsible than they often are. It is true that some of the characters speak coarsely. That is because people speak coarsely in real life. Especially soldiers and hard-working men speak coarsely, and even our most sheltered children know that. And we all know, too, that those words really don't damage children much. They didn't damage us when we were young. It was evil deeds and lying that hurt us.

After I have said all this, I am sure you are still ready to respond, in effect, "Yes, yes—but it still remains our right and our responsibility to decide what books our children are going to be made to read in our community." This is surely so. But it is also true that if you exercise that right and fulfill that responsibility in an ignorant, harsh, un-American manner, then people are entitled to call you bad citizens and fools. Even your own children are entitled to call you that.

I read in the newspaper that your community is mystified by the outcry from all over the country about what you have done. Well, you have discovered that Drake is a part of American civilization, and your fellow Americans can't stand it that you have behaved in such an uncivilized way. Perhaps you will learn from this that books are sacred to free men for very good reasons, and that wars have been fought against nations which hate books and burn them. If you are an American, you must allow all ideas to circulate freely in your community, not merely your own.

If you and your board are now determined to show that you in fact have wisdom and maturity when you exercise your powers over the education of your young, then you should acknowledge that it was a rotten lesson you taught young people in a free society when you denounced and then burned books—books you hadn't even read. You should also resolve to expose your children to all sorts of opinions and information, in order that they will be better equipped to make decisions and to survive.

Again: you have insulted me, and I am a good citizen, and I am very real.

Yours truly,

Kurt Vonnegut, Jr.

> December 5, 1973
> New York City

To Jane Vonnegut

David Halberstam won the Pulitzer Prize for his reporting on the Vietnam War *for* The New York Times. *He wrote many books, including* The Powers That Be, *on the media, and* The Fifties, *on that decade in American history.*

Dear Jane—

Your letter of a few days ago is lovely. It is the first deeply personal letter to be received at this new address. You should know that this house is one more cozy family outpost—like Jamaica and Cape Cod. You are loved and welcome here.

It's an old house on a quiet street. Across the street is E.B. White's house, where David Halberstam now lives and writes. I now inhabit my major investment, as do you. I honestly think that it is a shrewd investment—the best I could make at this time. Should I die, the kids would inherit something which they could easily sell, and which will become more and more valuable, even as the stock market goes down, down, down.

I am making no fantastic changes in the house. The floor plan and facades are almost exactly what they were eighty years ago. I've had the plaster patched, and every surface has been given a new coat of paint.

The street-level floor is a three-room suite with a separate entrance. Jill rents that from me, and runs her business from there. I work on the top floor, where there is a guest room, too—and a little kitchen. The middle two floors are where we live.

There is a Great Depression beginning. As it begins, I find myself possibly the luckiest of all businessmen. Delacorte owes me a lot of money, receivable in April, and the savings banks will go bankrupt before Delacorte does. Barring a revolution, we should be in very good shape for at least two years. I don't know many people who can say that. Since Africa turned out so brilliantly, I hope you will take many more dancing lessons from God. We are in a position to thrive on adversity. For instance: the death of the motorized tourist business could be a rebirth for Cape Cod.

Our children have turned out brilliantly. We should be proud. Mark, Nanny, & Edith are delights. Tiger is coming here soon to talk about what he should do with his life during the gasoline shortage. Jim is in clover for, again, at least two more years. Steve worries me. I wish he were a touch more enterprising and worldly.

I will not be a strikingly punctual and vivid gift-giver this Christmas. With the house and all that, I'm running out of time.

Much love to you. I will write again in a couple of days—about growing up and surviving pain and all that.

Cheers—

K

February 11, 1974
New York City

To Leslie Fiedler

Leslie Fiedler was a literary critic best known for his book Love and Death in the American Novel *and was professor of English at the State University of New York at Buffalo.*

Dear Professor Fiedler—

Your letter of January 30 was received only this morning by me. I know nothing about the negotiations for my story until now. I am embarrassed that those who claim to represent me treated you so badly. That was wrong. You have been a good friend of mine.

I have been a freelance for a long time, as you know. I have found that the most unpleasant, friendship-straining negotiations always have to do with anthologies. The anthologist invites me to demonstrate whether I am a gentleman or not. My union implores me to hold out for high fees, in order that my brother writers will also be paid well for contributing to anthologies.

I am not greedy. Also, I am growing old and find myself in need of all the friends I can retain, and I am no longer up to untangling double and triple binds. So I am removing myself from the anthology business entirely. I have already told Rust Hills, for instance, that I do not want to be in an anthology of his on any terms. I am instructing my publisher in the same mail with this letter that nothing of mine is for sale to any anthologist at any price. Word of honor: I do not lust after the money or the fame.

As some old man in Plato's dialogues said about not feeling the sex urge any more: I feel as though I were at last allowed to dismount from a wild horse.

I hope I have conveyed friendliness somewhere in this business letter, since I like you a lot and admire what you do.

Yours truly,

Kurt Vonnegut, Jr.

February 21, 1974
New York City

To VANCE BOURJAILY

Dear Vance—

[. . .] I'm sorry you won't be living in New York. We'd love to have you in the neighborhood. I'm still very jazzed by the place.

All the big problems and all the big solutions are here, it seems to me. As for plays: well, this is the only place you can find an American audience, and both of us sure as hell need American audiences. A batch of playwrights all fifteen years or so younger than we are is doing splendidly.

I have this house now, facing E.B. White's former house in Turtle Bay. Halberstam is in there now. I work on the top floor, and we live on the next two floors, and Jill has her office at street level, with a separate entrance. It works out pretty good, only I can't think of anything to write about any more. I may have retired. I'll have to ask my lawyer.

We have guest rooms, so it will be swell if you can stay here when you next pass through. I don't quite understand the scheme you've worked out with Tina, probably because I wasn't supposed to understand. Anyway, it sounds exciting for the kids.

I don't blame you for not wanting to teach any more. It's a damaging, pooping thing to do. I've cut my teach load in half, but I still feel as though I'm waltzing with tarbaby all day long.

I see a fair amount of Gail Godwin and her lover these days. She came to Jill's birthday party a couple of days ago. She is highly regarded at Knopf. The biggest literary news, I guess, also to do with Knopf, is that Heller has absolutely finished his new book, and that it isn't funny at all. It's great, they say, and tragic. His editor and Gail's editor is the guy who sold me this house—Bob Gottlieb.

Cheers—

Kurt

March 17, 1974
New York City

To Nanny Vonnegut

Dear Nanny—

The worst thing about your being so far away is that we see so little of you, and we need you a lot.

The second worst thing is that you see so little of us, so that we cease to be our actual selves to you and become creatures of your imagination.

I admire fiction, am amused and excited by the over-simplification of life it represents. I don't want to become a character in fiction myself, however, and I want to get along very well with you. So you can do me an enormous favor by thinking of me as a person afloat in time, as you are, rather than as a character locked into the machinery of a fiction plot, with villains and temptresses and so on. The hell of it is that it is so easy to turn anybody's life into some kind of story we have heard before. If I have money now, which I do, it is almost inevitable for people who don't know me to project me into a cliched tale about how the rich behave. I vanish, and the story lives on. I am a rich guy who abandons his wife to go to the big city and live in a town house and ride around in a Mercedes and live with the Wicked Witch of the East.

The Mercedes is so self-indulgent and ridiculous that I myself confess to being aghast. It is sort of like Mark's sailboat, I guess. But the townhouse is after all simply a house in New York, where I live. If I die, you and Mark and Edith will inherit it, along with a large mortgage. I had the option of putting money into stocks, which continue to go down, down, down, or leaving it as cash, which also becomes more worthless every day. I guessed that real estate would probably increase in value, and that I could at any rate inhabit it, whether its value went up or down. Jill rents the bottom floor for $400 a month. She paid for the wallpaper and the bed and some other stuff, and pays her share of the groceries.

As for Jill herself: I would be startled if you did not have deep misgivings about her, and if you did not imagine that she disliked you. As one more floater in time, she is as jumpy as you are, and is in fact prepared to love you a great deal. I don't require that you like her, and perhaps you never will. It would help a lot, though, if you would understand that she has been very good to me during the most shattering years of my life, and that she was not the one who did the shattering. Jane didn't do the shattering, either, and neither did money or success. The entirety of life did the shattering. And everything began to come to pieces for me long before I met Jill or had money and fame. I went to Iowa all by myself, remember? Nobody knew who I was. I was lucky to get the job. I was also lucky to get away from the perpetual emergencies at home, and my personal loneliness there, and to talk to artists for a change, and to do something I hadn't had time to do since I was your age, which was to ponder who I was and what I might do with my life. No woman lured me there. I didn't know any woman there. No woman ever lured me anywhere. It's the arts and artists who are my tempters and temptresses. If there is to be a Judgment Day, it will come out then that I have been one of the most laggardly adulterers of my time. I am hopelessly monogamous.

Need of money has also been known to move me from here to there. I have been head of a family since I was four years younger than Mark, and I have had to scramble some. If I start to fail even now, it will be bad news for a lot of people. So my continued interest in success, which may seem unattractive, has to do with my gang, not just me. I would rather be a philosopher king with no property but a wooden bowl. Or maybe I wouldn't like that so much, after all. This is fun, too, and often satisfying. I get to talk to really good artists a lot of the time, and they nourish me.

And Jill nourishes me, and she will be less jumpy every time you come around, and you will become less jumpy. She has been very smart about helping me to put myself back together again. And, while she sometimes says she would really love to have a baby, since she is only human, we aren't really going to do that. Neither does she egg me on to hurry up with the divorce, which must now be the slowest divorce in history. Neither does she take any interest in the details of the divorce. We simply try to live pleasantly and fruitfully from day to day.

Wish me luck with my next book, which, like all the others, is refusing to be written. I hope it's a good one, so you'll be proud of me.

I am trying to be as generous and gentle with your good mother as I can. She seems to become stronger day by day. I'm glad about that.

One thing that makes all my books tough to write is that I try to tell stories without the almost essential elements of blame and villainy.

This letter would be a horrible one to answer, I think. So please don't try. Just know that I love you, and that I wish you knew me, for good or ill, better than you do.

    K

June 25, 1974

New York City

To William Styron

One of the leading writers of his generation, William Styron was the author of the novels Lie Down in Darkness, The Long March, Sophie's Choice, *and* The Confessions of Nat Turner, *as well as the memoir* Darkness Visible: A Memoir of Madness. *His novel* Sophie's Choice *became a movie starring Meryl Streep, who won the Oscar for her portrayal of Sophie.*

Dear Bill—

It is queer to have to say that something as mild and beautiful as your *Times* piece on Auschwitz is a brave enterprise. You frustrate people's lust for simple, easy-to-remember lessons from vast catastrophes. There will be complaints.

I hope Jill and I can see more of you and Rose in the years to come. We are going to Moscow in October, to see my translator, and perhaps yours, too—Rita Rait (Puma Paum). She is one of those who wants to stay there, and, with a little help from her friends, to make the Soviet Union more amusing and humane.

Fat chance, I suppose.

If you two have advice on how best to use four days in Moscow, it would be gratefully received.

Cheers—

   Kurt Vonnegut

July 29, 1974
New York City

To Aaron Spiegel

Dear Mr. Spiegel—

I thank you for your letter of July 19, received only today.

I do not hate all Russians, and would not have said what I did if I had supposed that anyone there would take it with such wooden literalness. Neither do I love to hate anyone, which is quite evident in my life and work.

Since you are so literal minded, believing, as you seem to, that people at all times should say exactly what they mean or say nothing, I have no hope of explaining to your satisfaction why I said what I said. I was using a form of humor called irony, saying one thing while clearly meaning another. Such humor is not to your taste, and seems dangerous to you. I, on the other hand, would not be able to make my living as a humorist if I could not use irony. It is not a form of lying, and it is not a form of intentional deception, either. It is a matter of saying one thing while clearly saying another.

Believe me, if I thought there were any harm in it, I would find some other way to make a living. I expect to hear from you that there is indeed great harm in it, with world tensions so high, and that I had better find some other way to make a living. You may be right. World War Three might well begin with someone's making a joke, and with a humorless person taking the joke as an intolerable threat and declaring war.

If I really hated the Russians, I would have made you feel it that night. I speak ambiguously only to people who have had little experience with humor.

I have worked hard for peace all my adult life. I am going to the Soviet Union for the second time this fall. My books have all been published there, and I have several Russian friends. I will go over there with the same attitude I tried to express in my statement about hating Russians. My exact meaning was this: I love the Russian people, but I think their leaders have often treated my fellow artists most swinishly, and it makes me mad.

O.K.?

Cheers—

   Kurt Vonnegut, Jr.

August 29, 1974
New York City

To Sam Lawrence

Vonnegut's new book that year was his first collection of essays, Wampeters, Foma & Granfalloons.

Dear Sam—

Thanks for the good news about the foreign sales on the new book.

And thanks, too, for the proposition on the Beatles' paperback. Sorry—I'm not interested in writing the introduction.

As for when I go to the Soviet Union: the tentative date is October 7. I'm really not at all eager to go. The Russians, incidentally, won't let me pay any of my hotel bills in my own roubles. They want American cash in advance. The same goes for my ticket on Aeroflot. The more I think about it, the less I want to go. It always gives me the heebee-jeebees to visit a dictatorship.

Cheers—

   Kurt

September 30, 1974
New York City

To Mary Glossbrenner

Mary Glossbrenner was a cousin of Kurt's; she was married to Roger Bachelor.

Dear Mary & Batch—

Your pleasant note of so long ago bobbed to the surface of the paper dunes in my disaster area of an office. I have no secretary. I had one for a little while last year, but we finally parted out of embarrassment. Neither one of us could figure out what we were supposed to be doing.

Anyway—I was warmed by all the affectionate nostalgia in your note in July, and here I am warmed again, a week before taking off for a few days of riotous living in the fleshpots of Moscow. I'm going over there to see my seventy-six-year-old translator, a magnificent woman who took a doctor's degree in physiology under Pavlov. She has been allowed out of the worker's paradise only four times in her entire life. We got to know her during one of those times—in Paris. Now she will probably never be allowed out again. She has made friends with too many of the wrong people. I raised money to bring her here for a visit. She is Faulkner's translator, too, and Salinger's. I got her official invitations from Harvard and the University of Iowa and so on. I wanted especially to show her Oxford, Mississippi, Faulkner's home. No soap.

It meant a lot to me to find you two still so young and amusing, and still so friendly toward me.

Love—

K

October 25, 1974
New York City

To Donald Fiene

Dear Don—

You're a splendid correspondent, and I am in a perpetual state of embarrassment about not holding up my end at all. I was deeply moved by your reading to prisoners, and I'm glad you've got a job. Your most recent good postcard was awaiting us when we came home last night from Europe—five days in Paris, five in Moscow, five in Rome.

Rita is generally fine, and I was glad to learn from the guys at the Moscow bureau of the NYTimes that they all know how important she is culturally. They were eager to meet this legendary person, and I was delighted to perform the introductions.

As for who I met: cultural hacks mostly. The only distinguished writers I shook hands with were Voznesensky and Simonov. I was able, incidentally, to open a savings account over there. Crazy. I have about two-thousand roubles on deposit, earning two per cent a year. I gather that several favored writers have been allowed to do this. As far as I know, I am the first American. Also: they were petrified by the international copyright agreement, because they thought foreign literature would cost them so much. They are now elated, because writers are charging on the average less than half of what they expected to pay. Please don't publish this fact anywhere. I am advising my brother writers only in conversations. It wasn't Rita who told me this news, but people might assume that it was and want to hurt her in some way.

I behaved politely. The theory is that my good behavior would do a lot to loosen up travel restrictions on Rita. That country sure is full of envy, by the way. Simonov drank a toast to this effect: "We all argue as to who our finest novelist is, who our finest poet is, who our finest playwright is—but nobody argues about who our finest translator is. It is undisputably Rita Rait." The

faces of other translators at the table shriveled as though
drenched with lemon juice.

I will see you in person sooner or later, and will tell you more
then.

Cheers—
Kurt

October 30, 1974
New York City

To Jane Vonnegut

Dear Jane—

A belated happy birthday to you. I sent a package up with
Mark, which is a fair guarantee that you never got it. But the hell
with the package. The thing to celebrate is your discovery and mas-
tery of your own sweet and melodious voice. The piece about traveling with Nanny cross country is a knockout. There isn't a flaw in
it anywhere. And it would be that well-written, even if you weren't
as well-educated as you are. The secret of good writing is caring.

I'm fresh back from the Worker's Paradise. The elevators still
don't work, and it's still perfect hell to be a Jew over there. Hi ho.
I don't intend to write about it. I was sweet as pie, and didn't ask
a single embarrassing question. And over here I never crack off in
public about Solzhenitsyn or any of the hundreds of writers in
jails and loony bins. There are plenty of others to do that. I am a
vice president of American P.E.N., and I ask favors from the other
side from time to time. And they may listen to me, since my public record is so uncontroversial. And maybe not. What the hell. I
am now trying to work out a scheme whereby all the rubles
earned by American writers before the new International Copyright Agreements (last May or so) can, if unclaimed, be pooled
into a scholarship fund for young American writers who want to
visit the USSR. This is totally my crazy idea. We'll see.

As I peter out creatively, I become more and more of a cultural bureaucrat. I don't consider this a tragedy, unless becoming older and doing what older people do is a tragedy. I suppose that Daphne has told you what is in store for both us Scorpios. Huge changes are in store, and they will be terribly interesting and wrenching, and all we can do is ride along. Well—hang on. We may wind up miles from here.

    Love—

    K

July 2, 1975
New York City

To Donald Fiene

The Russian censors evidently felt that Kurt's definitions and sketches of the American slang term "beaver" in Breakfast of Champions *were too racy for their readers. Kurt tried to help his Russian translator, Rita Rait, by drawing weasels to replace his sketch of a beaver (the animal, not the mons veneris, which he also had drawn in the American edition).*

Dear Don—

    Well, I think the authorities really are fucking around with Rita's mail. I have learned from two sources other than you that Rita has heard nothing from me, and that she needs my approval for renaming *Slaughterhouse-5* for the stage, and so on. I've written her about three times during the past six weeks, doing all she says. And still she hears nothing. I will write again. Hi ho.

    I knew a little about the beaver's being changed to a weasel. I didn't know the linking of the animal with the mons veneris was to be eliminated. I drew her a weasel during our visit to Moscow. In fact, she made me draw about ten of them.

    In my most recent letter to her, I enclosed David Hayman's report of a visit to Salinger which appeared in the *Village Voice*. I suppose the authorities junked that letter because of offensive materials on the back of the clipping.

About *The Brothers Karamazov*: it was the first book I read after becoming a civilian after WWII. My new wife (nee Jane Cox, a Phi Beta Kappa from Swarthmore) made me read it on our honeymoon in Culver, Indiana. Culver is on Lake Maxinkuckee. The cottage in which we stayed had belonged to my family for three generations. It had just been sold. The new owner let us honeymoon there because he was a sentimentalist. I also painted my first picture there. It was of a chair. It was really pretty good. I have no idea what became of it.

As for Knoxville: I had a good time there, supposedly studying mechanical engineering while in uniform. You can probably look up my grades. I got mastoiditis there. When I was healed, I was shipped as an infantry replacement to the 106th Division at Camp Atterbury, Indiana, although I never had any infantry training. My basic training weapon was the largest mobile piece in the Field Artillery, the 240 millimeter howitzer. When I went overseas as an infantry scout, nobody had bothered to teach me how to fire a machinegun or throw a grenade or use a bayonet or any of that shit. I should have sued. Talk about Minute Men!

I used to go drink beer at the Andrew Johnson Hotel, and square dance up at Sevierville, and drink corn liquor, which was then called *Sploe*.

Cheers—

Kurt Vonnegut, Jr.

August 19, 1975
New York City

To Nanny Vonnegut

Dear Nanny—

A while ago, writing from that freighter in the Caribbean, you dared me to be open with you, to join you in ding-dongingly frank dialogues.

I will try.

I don't like the way you treat me at all. You have totally wrecked me with your absent-minded, dumb Dora promises to come see me, and with your equally fog-bound, last minute announcements that your life has become so complicated, hi ho, that you cannot come.

I would find such indifference to my feelings painful, even if it came from a little kid. You are chronologically a grown-up now. But you are clearly unable to imagine me as a living, interesting, sensitive, vulnerable human being. God only knows what you think I am.

Much love—
    DAD

August 25, 1975
New York City

To Nanny Vonnegut

Dear Nanny—

Good—we'll both learn how people are wounded, and how they're healed. You have already done me a terrific favor with that letter of yours. You can do me another one immediately by realizing that my life is a total crock, just like everybody else's. So you can really cheer me up in a big way any time you come around. And I, of course, would enjoy more opportunities than you've given me to cheer *you* up.

I am sorry I left Cape Cod at such an important time in your life. If I could have stayed, I would have. I did not do it for frivolous reasons. Again: I did not do it for Jill. She was just someone who became my companion after I left.

I will guess, simply on the basis of what most psychologists believe about impressionable ages, that you were more screwed up by the sudden change of the shape of our family when the Adamses came than by my departure much later on. Then again, maybe not.

At any rate—things between us are much improved by this exchange of letters.

Much love—
DAD

November 3, 1975
New York City

To Donald Fiene

Andrei Amalrik was a Russian writer who was sentenced to hard labor after the 1970 publication of his book Will the Soviet Union Survive Until 1984?

Dear Don—

I'm glad to be vindicated about sploe. I try not to make stuff up.

Jill and I of course want to see you in December. [. . .] We'll both be around. I'm going to a P.E.N. meeting in Vienna in a couple of weeks. That's all the traveling for me this year. I'm surprised that you expect to see a production of *Slaughterhouse-Five* in Moscow. The most recent information I had on that was that it had been cancelled—probably because I, as an officer of P.E.N., sent a cable to the Writer's Union, asking them to do all they could to protect the rights of Amalrik.

Rita, I know, feels that such cables should not be sent, since they cripple efforts to produce good American books and plays over there. P.E.N. knows this, but has decided to keep up its complaints about the mistreatment of writers anyway. It's a tough choice to have to make. I think we've made the right one.

You might tell Rita that many writers (in Iran, Korea, Greece, Yugoslavia, and so on) have told P.E.N., after getting out of prison or whatever, that P.E.N.'s strident interest in them had a lot to do with their staying alive. We are, incidentally, supporting financially about a dozen Czech writers who are not allowed to publish at all, who can't even get jobs as janitors. Hi ho.

Tell her, too, that we have all agreed to pretend to celebrate "The Spirit of Helsinki" as though it were a wonderful new liberalization of relationships between artists and intellectuals of the East and West. We mention it glowingly in speeches and toasts and so on. This, too, may do some good.

Look forward to your book.

Love to all hands.

Cheers—

    Kurt Vonnegut, Jr.

November 24, 1975
New York City

To Sam Lawrence

Dear Sam—

Got back from Vienna last night. I'll tell you about it at lunch soon. Sure didn't get laid. Didn't even come close. Hi ho. International P.E.N. is an organization of terribly old European cultural bureaucrats who meet twice a year to discuss World War Two. It is mainly financed by Americans and West Germans, and I very much want to have Americans withdraw from it so we can talk about our hemisphere and the present and even the future from time to time. We got voted down on everything.

Anyway—I accidentally did some business. I enclose the address of a Bulgarian publisher, who wishes copies of everything I have published so far. As I understand it, the Bulgarians have so far published only *Slaughterhouse-Five*. This guy says (in French) he wants to publish all the rest.

A Mr. Rupel from Yugoslavia said my time had come in his

country, too, and that he will write to me very soon. I will buck
his letter to you.

Meanwhile, perhaps you should send the two boxed sets of
paperbacks to this gentleman in Sofia.

Cheers—

Kurt

November 30, 1975

[New York City]

To Edith Vonnegut

*The "show in Watermill" was a show of paintings. The "important
book" was* Nora's Tale.

Dear Edith—

I saw your charming show in Watermill yesterday. I went
alone, and had no other purpose in my trip than to see your
show. I didn't go the day before, because I thought you needed
the car for an enormous gang. You said more people were going
than the car could hold.

Anyway—I signed the book within twenty-four hours of
the time the show opened, and I saw it all, and I thought about
it all.

And, since you have no other older person around to tell you
what to do, I will tell you what to do. When I was a young writer,
I had all kinds of older people who told me what to do. They
were often right, and they were often wrong, but they were sure
around and caring. Knox Burger was one, even though he was
only one month older. Max Wilkinson was another, and Ken Littauer, to whom I dedicated *Slaughterhouse-5*, was yet another
one. I argued with them all, and in fact stopped talking to two
out of the three. Ken is dead. Knox is a bitter stranger. Only Max
remains a friend. Vitamin B-6 might have changed all that, but

it's too late now. And why shouldn't they be the ones to take mega-vitamins anyway? Why should I take all the pills?

As for what you should do next, in my opinion: I already note that you were the first of my children to publish an important book. You have no catching up to do. And life isn't a foot-race anyway. *Nora's Tale* is graver and far less fashionable than anything Edward Gorey, for instance, may ever care to do. But, again: You aren't racing Gorey or me or Mark or anyone.

And there is no reason why I should expect you to be clear-headed, either. You are sophisticated, and you are also in financial trouble—so, like me, when I was young, you have to try to do all sorts of financial and artistic things all at once.

And I agree that you should do all sorts of things all at once. You have to, since you want to be self-supporting. But I hope that one of the many things you do will incorporate your own deeply personal hopes and fears and joys and angers and so on. Such things are excluded from your show in Watermill, and from your conversations with me, as far as that goes. The things of yours which earn you the most money just now will no doubt be your cleanest, clearest works.

And you hang out with people who bring to market only things which are super-fashionable, untroubling, and super-clean.

But I want to know, even if I never see them, that the crazily thoughtful, most private part of you is making pictures, too. I would feel cheated, if that part of you were to be wholly suppressed. This is an indirect way of saying, I suppose, that I found your show serene.

This is not an invitation to go crazy. I will go crazier than anybody in the family, if anybody else in it goes crazy. That is a promise. All I am saying, Darling, is this: Trust your mind. Trust it *sometimes,* and draw or paint the passionate, irresponsible and super-wise things it sees.

Cheers & love—

    K

December 19, 1975
New York City

To Sam Lawrence

"The Relatives" was the working title of Vonnegut's novel Slapstick, *which was published the following year.*

E. L. Doctorow *is a prolific writer of novels, essays, and screenplays; his novels include* Ragtime, Billy Bathgate, *and* World's Fair.

Renata Adler's *works include the novel* Speedboat *and the nonfiction book* Reckless Disregard: Westmoreland vs. CBS; *she was film critic of* The New York Times *from 1968 until 1969.*

Dear Sam—

Merry Christmas, old fella. I enclose a small taste from the last draft of "The Relatives," so you can at last have some idea of how the thing is meant to go.

I have a perfect bugger of a time making all the lies I want to tell work together harmoniously. I think maybe they are doing it this time.

Ed Doctorow told me Renata Adler's definition of a writer at supper yesterday. She says a writer is somebody who hates to write. That sure includes me. And, as Max Wilkinson once said, "I never knew a blacksmith who was in love with his anvil." Hi ho.

Well, I am going to finish up this mother in short order, by God, and then retire. I will not be going to Key West until it's finished, which takes care of January, I'm afraid.

Much love—

Kurt

December 20, 1975

New York City

To Osborn Elliott

Osborn Elliott was editor of Newsweek.

Dear Mr. Elliott:

Peter S. Prescott says in his piece on science-fiction (December 22, 1975):

"Few sf writers aim higher than what a teen-age intelligence can grasp, and the smart ones, like Kurt Vonnegut, carefully satirize targets—racism, pollution, teachers—that teen-agers are conditioned to dislike."

That unsupported allegation about me will now become a part of my dossier there. I ask you to put this letter in the same folder, so that more honest reporters than Mr. Prescott may learn the following about me:

I have never written with teen-agers in mind, nor are teen-agers the chief readers of my books. I am the first sf writer to win a Guggenheim, the first to become a member of the National Institute of Arts and Letters, the first to have a book become a finalist for a National Book Award. I have been on the faculties of the University of Iowa and Harvard, and was most recently a Distinguished Professor of Literature at CCNY.

Mr. Prescott is entitled to loathe everything I have ever done, which he clearly does. But he should not be a liar. *Newsweek* should not be a liar.

Yours truly,

Kurt Vonnegut, Jr.

January 7, 1976

New York City

To Ambrosia

Ambrosia, *the first album of the band of the same name, was released in 1975 and included a song based on a verse from Vonnegut's novel* Cat's Cradle *("Nice, Nice, Very Nice"). The song became an FM hit.*

Dear Ambrosia—

I thank you for your holiday greetings. I was at my daughter's house last night, and the radio was on. By God if the DJ didn't play our song, and say it was number ten in New York, and say how good you guys are in general. You can imagine the pleasure that gave me. Luck has played an enormous part in my life. Those who know pop music keep telling me how lucky I am to be tied in with you.

And I myself am crazy about our song, of course, but what do I know and why wouldn't I be?

This much I have always known, anyway: Music is the only art that's really worth a damn. I envy you guys.

Cheers—

Kurt Vonnegut, Jr.

February 14, 1976

New York City

To William Meredith

William Meredith was a poet who taught at Connecticut College and whose New and Selected Poems *won the Pulitzer Prize in 1987. He was consultant in poetry to the Library of Congress from 1978 until 1980.*

Dear Bill—

Years ago I wrote in *Slaughterhouse-Five* that Billy Pilgrim would die on such and such a date. It seemed like a long time in the future when I wrote it. The date was yesterday, February 13, 1976. I thought I might actually die. Guess who got it instead? Sal Mineo.

Really: I would have forgotten that prediction, if sympathy cards hadn't come trickling in, consoling me about the coming death of Billy Pilgrim.

As for the unsuitability of my attending meetings: I know Robert's Rules of Order cold. Those rules were first published, incidentally, almost a century ago—on February 19, 1876. I did almost nothing in high school but attend meetings, seconding motions and so on. So I was perfectly content with the solemn tomfoolery of our Institute Meetings until the business of the National Book Awards came up. It seemed to me that this was an extremely daring enterprise, and that, if it was going to be a success, all persons concerned should be enthusiasts. When the going got tough, I suspected, I would find myself wandering absent-mindedly in a rear area like the late Private Slovik.

I am so glad to be friends with poets at last. Poetry is so clearly intended to be read by intimates, it seems to me, that strangers can't really be included in the deepest fun.

It's a terrific honor to get the holograph from you. Yours was certainly a loving letter, and I love you, too.

Cheers—

Kurt

March 12, 1976
New York City

To Helen Meyer

Helen Meyer was president and chief executive of Dell Publishing until 1976 and copublisher after the Dell merger with Doubleday.

The "George" referred to is George T. Delacorte, the founder of Dell Publishing.

Kurt was upset that his books published by Delacorte and Dell

could be "sold" to Doubleday, with whom Dell had merged. This was
one of the first big publishing mergers, which were to become com-
monplace in the coming years. In 1983 the merger would lead to the
end of Seymour Lawrence's publishing association with Dell.

Dear Helen—

I have never been sold like a baseball player before. It is something new for me to think about. I never expected to have to
think about it.

I can be a good sport about my past being sold to the highest
bidder. I bought and sold a lot of it myself, remember? It is just
dead merchandise.

My future is what remains of my life, though. It is sensitive
and personal, and easily crippled.

I don't want that sold to Doubleday or to anybody I haven't
selected with a lot of thought.

You can understand that, and so can George. And you and
George will surely agree, too, that I have been a productive and
cooperative and undemanding associate of yours for a far longer
time than most of the people now facing this trade.

So I ask you to return my future to me rather than to sell it.

George has generously offered to have a fountain built in my
back yard. I have thanked him, and I hope that you will again
convey my thanks to him. But ask him to cancel the project. I
shouldn't have let it go this far. When he asked me what I
wanted, I said, "A fountain," but I had something quite small in
mind—a birdbath, maybe. Now hydraulic engineers and architects and electricians are starting to arrive.

If George would like to give me something big, would he
please return my future to me? I don't want to owe books to
Doubleday. Have I really behaved so foolishly that I, who have
always hated the hugeness and heartlessness of Doubleday, must
now spend the rest of my life writing for Doubleday?

I know that, if we were to sit down and have a friendly little
talk about all this, you would have to explain to me that Double-

day has promised to keep everything exactly the way it is. You would still be in charge, and Sam would be my principal contact and buddy, and Ross and Bud and Carole and Lucy and so on would still be around. But I have seen plenty of other companies swallowed up, and such promises have always been made and always been broken. It isn't in the nature of Doubleday to leave things alone.

Yours truly,

Kurt Vonnegut, Jr.

cc—Sam Lawrence, Don Farber

March 15, 1976

To Don Farber

Dear Don—

I think we should tell Helen that we intend to go to the Authors Guild to protest the buying and selling of authors like professional athletes.

If a publisher can sell his authors to another publisher in a package deal, then he can surely sell his authors one-by-one, as well. Knopf, for example, might give John Updike's contract to Simon and Schuster, and receive Joan Didion's contract in return.

So we refuse to have me traded to anybody—in a package deal or any other sort of deal.

Sam and Helen have said over and over again that Doubleday wants Dell for its paperback expertise, as though this should have a calming effect on me. And it does calm me, too, in a way, since it means that Doubleday has little more interest in buying me than I have in being sold to them. My being sold to them, if the sale went through, would be a ridiculous, marginal accident happening in the midst of an enormous transfer between millionaires of all sorts of property. So, in order to avoid such an accident, and without depriving Doubleday of anything it particularly wants, we should ask Dell to separate me from the paperback expertise and the filing cabinets.

I am going to ask the Authors Guild to insist in future contracts that no author's contract can be handed over to another publisher without the author's written permission. If the author does not wish to have his future sold to somebody else, then he should be allowed to cancel his contract. Author's contracts should not be marketable to strangers.

Kurt

April 6, 1976
New York City

To JEROME KLINKOWITZ

Klinkowitz had written Vonnegut for his advice on whether to accept a professorship at the State University of New York at Albany or stay at the University of Northern Iowa. He later wrote to his friend Donald Fiene at the University of Tennessee that this letter from Kurt was "the most important thing he ever sent me, as it was life-changing. I stayed here and have been supremely happy, just as he suspected I'd be."

Dear Jerry—

I called my brother for his opinions on SUNY-Albany, and learned that you had interviewed him only half an hour before. So now you have more substantial information than I do. [. . .]

I am certain that you are highly valued and badly needed right where you are. That must be a nourishing situation. I envy it. If you move East, you may find that life becomes a lot less personal. You will become more of a floater. I myself am almost pure helium at the age of fifty-three.

You have a strong sense of style, since you own an old Mercedes and play jazz on weekends. Since you have asked my opinion, a foolish thing to do, I will tell you what I think is the most stylish and useful thing for you to do. This is it: Iowa is a better place than Albany. Stay where you are.

Give my love to Loree.

Cheers—

Kurt Vonnegut, Jr.

April 7, 1976
New York City

To CINDY ADAMS

Cindy Adams is a longtime gossip columnist for the New York Post.

Dear Ms. Adams—

I am charmed and amused that you should want me to be a judge in the 1976 Miss USA Beauty Pageant. I blush and laugh.

I decline your flattering invitation with best wishes and thanks. If your girls are as fond of my works as you indicate, then they will surely understand my feeling that judging them is somehow something I should not do.

Give them my love.

Cheers—

Kurt Vonnegut, Jr.

June 1, 1976
New York City

To MARGARET MILLS, THE NATIONAL
INSTITUTE OF ARTS AND LETTERS

Dear Maggie—

I thank you for your letter of May 28, asking me to join the Policy Committee of the National Book Awards.

I do not understand why anyone would think that I might wish to serve on that committee. I protested against the Institute's giving the awards in meetings and in a letter to you. Is my letter on file?

I thought it was so wrong, especially since the membership was not given a chance to vote on such an important undertaking, that I resigned as a vice president.

It is merely a technical triumph that the first awards under the Institute's management went so smoothly. They reflect the Institute's clerical and housekeeping efficiency. What they say spiritually about the Institute is embarrassing. The prizes are a silly, commercial invention, and cannot be transformed by new sponsorship. It is the new sponsor which is being transformed. It is now becoming a power in commerce. This is evidently thrilling to some of the members.

Worse: Some members seem to believe that they are bringing dignity and justice to a ridiculous apparatus of rewards and slights modeled after Hollywood's Academy Awards.

I am certain that several of the present committee persons mistrust the enterprise as much as I do, but imagine that they are serving some great wish expressed by the membership at large. This wish by the membership has never been expressed. A very few persons albeit acting legally, and with the best possible intentions, put us into this poisonous business.

The Institute should now get out of the business. If it does get out, all it will lose is commercial power and opportunities to express truly academic and humorless opinions on contemporary literature.

If the Institute stays in the business, it will inevitably become notorious for power-seeking, publicity-seeking, conceited old poopery.

Yours truly,
Kurt Vonnegut, Jr.

July 15, 1976

[New York City]

To Sam Lawrence

Jean Stafford was a novelist and short-story writer whose Collected
Stories of Jean Stafford *won the Pulitzer Prize in 1970. She did not
live to finish the book in question. She was the widow of A. J. Liebling, her third husband. Liebling was a writer for* The New Yorker,
whose articles were often published as books, including The Earl of
Louisiana *and* The Sweet Science. *Tim Seldes was Stafford's agent.*

Dear Sam—

A couple of things:

I saw Ms. Stafford yesterday afternoon, Wednesday, July 14.
She is in better spirits than I expected, although massively dependent on bottled oxygen. I saw none of the oxygen apparatus,
which is formidable, I've heard. It was all in her bedroom. Anyway, her head is in good condition, and she has about 300 pages
of a novel which she wants to get back to. She has been doing little shit work for years, reviews and so on, since Liebling's first
wife got all the income from Liebling's work. She is broke, puri-
tanically disinclined to ask help from anybody, and talking about
getting a second mortgage on her modest property—in order to
finish the book.

Nobody has an option on the book in progress. She has a sentimental attachment to Farrar, Straus & Giroux, a firm which in
turn has no vivid interest in her, I gather. They must doubt that
she can produce a book at this stage, and they are mistaken. You
are the most brilliant speculator in literary futures in our time,
and I give you this inside tip: She can produce at least one more
important book.

I think you should get in touch with Tim Seldes at once, and
say you want the book, no matter what it is, and offer an advance that will keep her going for a year or so—twenty thousand
or so.

You should also know that she has all of Liebling's pieces in her files. The best of these should surely be collected in a Delta edition, since there is such a booming interest in journalism these days.

Also: One of the best books I have read this year is a scholarly essay, vastly humane and moving, though, on Christopher Columbus—by Hans Koning, and published very recently by Monthly Review Press. This, too, should be in Delta.

Much love—

Kurt

October 7, 1976
New York City

To William Meredith

Dear Bill—

The visit to Connecticut College was a pure lark for me, and would have been for you, too, or for anybody. I was slathered with butter and rolled in sugar, as the Russians say.

As for your responses to Harriet Beecher Stowe and me: I, too, have been puzzled by her idea of crossing the Ohio on ice floes, which, so far as I know, has never been possible in modern times. And she *lived* on the river, too. There was no poetry in her, but only bravery and decency, so I suppose she was responding to the simple minded theater of her era. [. . .]

Cheers—

Kurt Vonnegut

November 16, 1976
New York City

To Donald Fiene

Dear Professor Fiene:

This is a formal statement of my motives and intentions with regard to the prospective visit to the University of Tennessee of the distinguished Moscow translator, Rita Rait:

This remarkable woman is a personal friend of mine, and is the translator not only of my works but of Salinger's, Faulkner's, Sinclair Lewis's, and on and on. At a dinner in my honor in Moscow, she was saluted by her colleagues as being unquestionably the finest translator in the Soviet Union.

She is approaching eighty, and I wish her to see the United States, whose literature she has served so well, before she dies.

The authorities in the Soviet Union, for reasons unknown to me, have been reluctant to let her travel outside the country. They are sending four translators here next spring, but Mrs. Rait is not among them.

So I am now attempting to put mild pressure on those authorities to let her come here. An invitation from me to her, person to person, has proved futile in the past, and would prove to be futile again. The best advice I have from our State Department and from friends in the Soviet Union is that an invitation must come from an educational institution in order to be considered seriously.

Your university has kindly and wisely, in my opinion, agreed to issue the invitation.

For my part, I have offered my services as a participant in seminars and as a companion to Mrs. Rait and whatever, free of charge.

I have, moreover, given the University a cashier's check for three thousand dollars ($3000.00), guaranteeing that the University will have none of its own funds at risk in this enterprise.

If Mrs. Rait is unable to come to America, then that check will be returned to me.

Now then: If Mrs. Rait comes, it will be an event of tremendous importance not just for me, but for the country, the University, and for literary people everywhere. [. . .]

November 20, 1976
New York City

To Donald Fiene

Dear Don—

The essay about me and the Soviet Union [by Donald Fiene] is a careful and friendly piece of work. I honestly did not know until now that I had such a reputation over there. I am moved. If the *New York Review,* which has never been kind to me, publishes the piece, my reputation and self-esteem will soar.

I once conceived of an experiment in which every piece of information received by a human being would be entered in a log—from birth to the age of twenty-one, say. We would then be able to determine whether that person had also inherited certain knowledge, or perhaps received it telepathically or clairvoyantly. If that experiment had been performed on me, it would be obvious that I am not an educated man. I haven't read nearly all I should. As a chemist, and then as an engineer, and then as an anthropologist, I was kept busy reading, all right. But what I read was not what is customarily thought of as being literature. The only period in my life when I studied literature with some concentration and continuity was when I was a discussion leader in a Great Books group on Cape Cod for about three years—when I was in my middle thirties. People have urged me to read this or that from time to time, and I have usually obeyed them and been grateful. Thus I discovered Blake and Céline and Edward Lewis Wallant, and on and on. As for the Russians: My wife had studied them intensively at Swarthmore, and she brought about twenty volumes of their work in Modern Library editions as the core of her dowry. So I read them, and in my heart I liked Gogol best. The quotation about "One sacred memory . . .", incidentally, was handed on a slip of paper to my wife at the end of her course at Swarthmore. The teacher was an adored old man, Harold Goddard, who customarily made a gift of a quotation to each student at semester's end. Jane still has the piece of paper. The author is named, but not the book it came from. Jane herself does not know.

The quote may be as hard to find as a quotation from Goethe, which was framed and hanging on my father's office wall for years, and which I incorporated into an early short story. In English it goes: "The gods, the eternal ones, give everything to their darlings, all the joys, the eternal ones, all the agonies, the eternal ones—everything." When *Collier's* asked me where this came from, I referred the question to my father. He said it was a famous quotation, and could be run down in a half an hour or less. Weeks later, he had dozens of frantic Germans ransacking the libraries of Indianapolis, and having no luck at all. It turned out to be a postscript to a letter from Goethe to an obscure friend.

As for how things go now with Rita: Three weeks ago I sent her a copy of Jill's beautiful new ballet book—airmail, first class. I enclosed a letter telling her that she was about to be invited to the University of Tennessee. Five days ago, a rather mournful letter drifted in from her, asking why Jill and I don't write to her any more.

Stanley Kunitz says they will never let her out. They are afraid she will have too much fun and start talking too much. My spook friend is having lunch with a Russian contact next week. The contact is just back from Moscow, and promises to tell how things really stand with Rita. He has been looking into it hard, he says. [. . .]

December 11, 1976

[New York City]

To Jerome Klinkowitz

Jerome Klinkowitz had been one of the first scholars to take Vonnegut's work seriously, and through his visits and interviews he became

a trusted friend throughout the author's life. One year after Kurt en-
trusted him with this information, he published the third of his books
on Vonnegut, Vonnegut in America: An Introduction to the Life and
Work of Kurt Vonnegut.

Dear Jerry—

Some second thoughts about the biographical stuff you sent
me:

In the chronology, for the sake of completeness, it should be
said that in 1971 I separated permanently from my wife and took
up residence in New York City.

Also: It is not known why my mother killed herself. She never
said anything about the awfulness of fighting against the homeland or anything like that. In fact, I don't recall my parents' ever
having spoken of Germany as the homeland. When I was captured by the Germans, and they asked me why I was fighting
against my brothers, I thought it was hilarious. I felt no more
closely related to them than I was to Bolivians.

It was war itself that wrecked my mother, and not war against
Germany. Also, she was taking an awful lot of barbiturates at a
time when the side-effects were thought to be negligible.

As for the sequence of houses we lived in: the Chamber of
Commerce magazine got the order all ass-backwards, and I guess
you got it from them. The truth is that the family moved into a
perfectly beautiful house in 1922, when I was born. It required
many servants. Father was its architect, and it is the most interesting thing he ever did. Evans Woollen, Jr., the hottest young architect in town these days, honored father by making it his own
home a few years ago. It is at Forty-fourth and North Illinois
Streets.

After we went dead broke in the thirties, Father wanted to sell
it right away, but couldn't find a buyer until 1939. His idea was
to build a wonderful but much cheaper house on a gorgeous lot
he had bought in the twenties in the posh suburb of Williams
Creek. The suburb remains posh. We moved into a sort of blue

collar house on Forty-second Street, almost on North Illinois, while he and Mother gathered resources which would allow them to build the new dream house.

It was completed shortly before Pearl Harbor. It is not large, but beautifully detailed and in an enchanting, wooded situation, above a creek. It required no servants. It was there mother died. So, ironically, she died in a dream house rather than in a dump.

You speak of a Mother's Day leave, which sounds as though such things were routine in the Army. I simply happened to get a three-day pass at the time of Mother's day. It was my sister who found mother dead. She woke me, and I had a look, and then we both woke Father, who was sleeping in another room. There were no notes, and the coroner was too much of a gentleman and politician to seek anything but natural causes for death. And my father never acknowledged to any of his children, though he did so apparently, to relatives his own age, that she had done herself in.

As for my thesis about the shapes of tales: I actually submitted that to the University of Chicago in 1966, while I was at Iowa.

Yours truly—

Kurt Vonnegut

January 16, 1977

[New York City]

To Vance Bourjaily

Dear Vance—

[. . .] I will be out there sometime in the springtime. I wouldn't consider the trip if you and Tina weren't out there. I can't name a date yet because I am trying to get Rita Rait, my Russian transla-tor, out of Moscow for a brief visit over here. I still don't know when she is coming, or even if they will let her out. She has made an awful lot of mistakes over the years—picking for friends people who turned out to be jailbirds later on. If she does come, I want to show her Oxford, Mississippi, among other things, since she is responsible for Faulkner's being published in the USSR. She is nearly eighty, and about as high as your coffee table. Maybe, if everything fell into place, I would bring her to Iowa City with me. She speaks English better than we do.

Cheers—

Kurt

February 4, 1977
New York City

To Frank M. Cruger, Indiana
Manufacturers Supply Company, Inc.

Franklin Vonnegut was a cousin of Kurt's and his boss at the Vonnegut Hardware Company, which was founded in Indianapolis by Kurt's great-grandfather Clemens Vonnegut.

Dear Mr. Cruger—

Anyone who writes as amusingly and gracefully as you do deserves star billing in *Who's Who*. You're a generous man to send me such a good letter. May I say, too, that it is a novelty to hear from a Hoosier who likes my work. My own relatives take a dim view of what I do. They suspect, I think, that my books make young people run wild sometimes.

I, too, was lucky enough to work for Franklin Vonnegut. It was during the Great Depression, and he made an old man's serious mistake. He was number one on the time clock, and he gave me number two. This was noticed by others, who commented on it with weary unpleasantness. My pay was fourteen dollars a week, I think. I was seventeen or so, and making as much as some of my colleagues, who were married men. I ran a freight elevator for a while. My idea of hell was shaped by that experience.

Hell is running an elevator throughout eternity in a building with only six floors.

It is too bad that Indianapolis has been rich enough to renew itself. Most of my father's and grandfather's work has now been obliterated. All that will be left, by and by, will be the Athenaeum. Have you noticed Lexington, Kentucky? It was too poor to renew itself for a long, long time. Now it is refurbishing all its wonderful old buildings—a cheap and sensible way to become beautiful again.

I dare to say much love to you.

Cheers—

Kurt Vonnegut, Jr.

March 27, 1977
New York City

To Chuck DeLa

Dear Mr. DeLa—

Your lovely letter reached me only this morning. It is dated February 18, but I assume you meant March. In any event, you're a warm and amusing writer, and you guessed what I never would have been able to guess myself—that now is the perfect time for me to sponsor a softball team in Lafayette. My head swims as I enclose a perfectly good check for $150, made out to you. Have I gone insane? Never before have I been so soft a touch.

There is one small detail: Please keep it a secret that I have actually bankrolled you. I don't want it thought that I am now hiring human billboards, so to speak, to spread my fame. I am in this for adventure and romance.

Play clean.

Cheers—

Kurt Vonnegut, Jr.

April 29, 1977
New York City

To Nanny Vonnegut

Dearest Nanny—

Santa Fe sounds O.K. I hope you get accepted there. I spent a couple of summers in New Mexico when I was a boy.

As for the divorce: I will always love your mother, as must have been evident on Sunday. But we could never live together again. Our conversations go so badly. Also: I want to be fair to Jill, who saved me from knocking myself off or turning into an alcoholic. I will not marry Jill, but I will stop asking that she live with a married man. And Jane, who is fond of marriage, should have the chance to marry again. I am not pursuing happiness through divorce. I am permanently damaged by the break-up of marriage. Those wounds will never heal. I am simply trying to make the best of an unpleasant situation. Let me say again, too, that Jill did not break the marriage. It was broken long before that—about the time I went to Iowa. There was no other woman beckoning me to Iowa. Later on, there was no woman beckoning me to New York City. I arrived both places in total solitude, and feeling simply awful.

There will be no acrimonious argle-bargle about divorce this time. We will not make the mistake of hiring two strangers to fight each other on our behalf. Jane and I will arrive at some sort of division of property, and some scheme for my sending her money regularly. She already owns the Cape house and some stocks and a large savings account in cash. I will add to that treasure, so she won't have much to worry about as long as I'm popular and productive. Then Don Farber will draw up a simple agreement, and that will be that. The legal steps will be brief formalities, without any arguments to be made before a judge.

It was beautiful and most helpful that you and Edie could both watch us that Sunday. Jane and I have had many nice times like that, and will no doubt have more.

Love—

DAD

May 9, 1977

New York City

To Mrs. James Jones, via Western Union Mailgram

Kurt admired the work of James Jones, author of From Here to Eternity, *and knew him as a neighbor on Long Island. Jones had died that day.*

I LOVED YOUR BRAVE AND HONORABLE HUSBAND AND HIS WORK. I CRY WITH GOOD REASON NOW. YOU WERE SUCH A FINE WIFE FOR HIM AND JILL AND I LOVE YOU TOO

June 8, 1977

New York City

To Jerome Klinkowitz

Dear Jerry—

[. . .] About the thesis proposal: I worked it up with a Dr. Sydney Slotkin, a brilliant and neurotic member of the department who was not well thought of, and who was on his way out. He was disreputable for relating primitive societies to industrialized societies, for wanting to study them in parallel. My thesis proposal was rejected for being just such a scheme. He had more influence on me than anybody else there, but remained quite cold to me. I visited him a couple of times after leaving. He did not seem to remember me, and was eager for me to leave yet again. He finally committed suicide by swallowing cyanide.

Love to Loree.

Cheers—

Kurt Vonnegut

August 29, 1977

New York City

To Max Wilkinson

Dear Max—

You are a good man, and I like you a lot. But I must bring to your attention the fact that you have left me, your client, in such a position that I am now paying half again and more for agency services than any other author in this country. If you had named a successor when you retired, as virtually every other retiring agent has done, then that successor would be available to perform all sorts of services for me, including giving a shit about what I'm doing now and what I might want to do next. The continuing commissions from past successes would help to pay for the attention of that successor and for some of his overhead.

You have rigged things, though, so that those commissions from past successes finance no services to me whatsoever. You have arranged things so that they are merely a sentimental salute to the past, and I have been obliged to hire Don Farber, for massive extra fees, to do what your successor would ordinarily have done.

As my agent, you have taken worse care of me than agents normally take care of authors, especially since I have done so much of the heavy negotiating myself—such as buying back my books one-by-one from other publishers, so I could resell them to Dell.

In my opinion, you should take steps to ensure that I, your client, need no longer pay so much more for needed and deserved services than other authors pay. I did not volunteer to pay so much more. I was forced into it. Perhaps my situation is more common than I have so far been able to discover, is utterly customary, in fact. If so, I will be pleased to hear of similar cases. If so, I can stop thinking that I, of all authors, am perhaps the most idiotic as a businessman.

    Yours truly—

    Kurt Vonnegut

August 31, 1977

[New York City]

To Max Wilkinson

Dear Max—

    That telephone call this morning was a painful but a necessary one. I enclose the letter I read to you over the phone, so the central issue of our talk will not become hopelessly lost in overly emotional memories.

    I have since spoken to several respected literary agents, without mentioning your name, and to the Authors Guild, too. In each case, I merely asked what the custom was when an agent no longer wished or was no longer able to function as an author's full-time, day-after-day representative in the marketplace.

    (Don did not put me up to this, incidentally. I was showing a balance sheet to bankers from Morgan Guaranty, and they were puzzled by how much I paid for representation, and they asked what services were performed for such fees.)

    I was told by the literary agents that it was customary for retiring agents to make deals with responsible successors, successors satisfactory to the authors involved. Thus did the commissions continue to pay for the alert and energetic and supportive services of some sort of office staff. There were a few famous instances, they said, when an agent died unexpectedly, before he could arrange for continuity in representation. Thus did the authors fall into the hands of heirs who knew nothing about the agency business or the author, but were legally entitled to commissions in perpetuity anyway.

I was told by the Authors Guild that they have published no position papers on what happens when an agent retires without setting up a successor, but that they were just starting to work up such a document. Continuing commissions were an accepted practice, they said, because continuing services were surely implied.

You say that you have not retired, but I tell you as your client that you have felt retired to me. I can't use what you are offering out there. And will I eventually be willed to someone even less active? If so, I would like to know about it.

Do you realize that I cannot now get representation by an active agent for ten per cent unless I write another book? How many authors of my maturity can have a real agency, only if one writes more books? Or pay double commissions?

The Authors Guild told me, incidentally, about the vaguely similar situation in which M.C.A. retired from the agency business. M.C.A. was still legally entitled, like you, to commissions from past deals for authors, which used to go into services to authors and, of course, profit. With no services to perform any more, M.C.A. might have enjoyed those commissions from the past as pure profit. But M.C.A. spared their authors the prospect of receiving no more services, unless, of course, the authors turned out more work, by making a deal with I.C.M. Each author got the agent he wanted at I.C.M., and services were uninterrupted. Nobody had to pay double commissions to get good help.

Let's keep emotion out of this as much as we can. I am correctly interested in what would be fair and business-like for both of us.

Yours truly,
Kurt Vonnegut

September 13, 1977

New York City

To Vance Bourjaily

Philip Roth's novel was The Professor of Desire.

Dear Vance—

Read your review of Roth's book in an advance copy of
NYTBR. It's unusually deep and instructive for an American
review—and beautifully written. I hope, as a reader, that you will
review a lot more. Has someone had the good sense to ask you to
do *Whistle,* by the late James Jones? Jill and I went to his memorial service in Bridgehampton. The place was so crowded that we
had to sit in the balcony. This turned out to be a privilege, since
the person sitting next to us was the Army's number one bugler,
who sounded *Taps* at the end.

Cheers—

Kurt Vonnegut

September 16, 1977

New York City

To Bernard Vonnegut

Dear Bernie—

Thanks for your good letter, with so much encouraging news
in it. I continue to marvel at your raising children with no help
from anybody. I could never do it. And, whenever I wonder how
it is going, I am utterly reassured by how Peter and Scott and
Terry have turned out. They are as sweet and interesting as anyone I know. You might tell Terry, incidentally, that it was Terence,
the Roman writer of comedies, who said: "Nothing human is
alien to me." Goethe often gets credit for that one.

When I give you advice on the kids, I am talking like a man
with a paper asshole, since I couldn't stand a child-dominated

household any more. I wanted to be more self-centered, and hang out with grownups for a change, and to work with fewer interruptions.

I take off on a business trip to Europe next Saturday, September 24. My publisher, Sam Lawrence, and I will be looking in on all my northern European publishers, visiting each for a couple of days—and winding up at the Frankfurt Book Fair on October 12, where Jill will join me. After that, Jill and I will go for a few days in Florence and Venice, neither of which have we seen before.

Much love to everybody—

K

September 21, 1977
New York City

To José Donoso

Broyard was a book reviewer for The New York Times.

Dear Pepé—

Anatole Broyard has no constituency, is famous for reviewing only short books, and was kicked out as a daily reviewer shortly before he did in your book in the Sunday *Times*. Things go badly for him. In effect, he has been busted from colonel to corporal. His response to the demotion has been an increase in bitterness in his reviews, and he will surely be busted again by and by. The publishers detest him.

I've met him only a couple of times, and we did not appear to like each other much. His pose has long been that he is not merely a reviewer, but one of the best writers of fiction around. And he did write some good stories years ago. And he has supposedly been working on an important novel for a long time. But his publisher, Sam Lawrence, is my publisher, too. And, about a year ago, Broyard introduced Sam to somebody as ". . . my publisher." Sam was finally sick of that introduction, and he took

Broyard aside, and demanded that Broyard return the advance on the novel—a novel that clearly was never going to exist. Broyard returned the advance.

That's all I know.

Sam and I take off for Amsterdam next Saturday, about the time you get this letter, I expect. We really don't know each other very well. We will be blood brothers or enemies by October 13, when we finally arrive at the Book Fair in Frankfurt. We will have been to every Scandinavian capital, and Leningrad as well. I will be bringing my translator an enormous magnifying glass and a dictating machine. Nearly eighty, she is going blind.

Cheers—

Kurt Vonnegut

November 11, 1977
New York City

To Donald Fiene

Dear Don—

Your birthday greetings are much appreciated. Jill is giving a small party here for me tonight, and Andrej Voznesenski has promised to drop by. He has beautiful Italian clothes and gets to fuck just about anybody he likes, I expect.

Sam Lawrence and I went into Leningrad by rail from Helsinki, got searched by border guards at three in the morning. I had all sorts of stuff that might have troubled them, but they didn't find any of it. It was spooky how they made such a careful search, and yet found nothing. I brought Rita a fancy dictating machine and a huge magnifying glass. I guess she really is in big trouble with her eyes. Her bosses, incidentally, sent contracts along with her, made her their sole negotiator, instructed her to tell us to accept their terms or go to hell, that they weren't all that interested in publishing me anyhow. Their offer was a generous one by Russian standards, but the shabbiness of making Rita close the deal was dishonorable in the extreme. We all felt as though we were coming down with influenza. One really great Leningrad experience, though: Sam and I saw a new production of *Dead Souls* at the Pushkin Theater, and it was so brilliantly done that Sam and I almost got nosebleeds from laughing. We needed no interpreter. Amazingly, as I discovered a week later, Sam had never read *Dead Souls*.

Sam and I were a good deal more troubled by Munich than by Leningrad. We had the shit scared out of us at Oktober Fest, where, about forty years before, Thomas Wolfe was brained with a beer stein. He eventually died as a result. Sam and I didn't get into any fights, but it was clear to us that the Germans still deserve their reputation of being the most warlike people on Earth. We got the feeling that the West Germans would enjoy having a go at the East Germans some day soon. Young people told us that they were getting out of the country while they still could.

Cheers—

Kurt Vonnegut

November 12, 1977
New York City

To Don and Annie Farber

Dear Don and Annie—

Don't let anybody tell you that smoking and boozing are bad for you. Here I am fifty-five years old, and I never felt better in my life.

The handsome vest arrived at noon yesterday. It fits beautifully, and it makes me feel like James Arness, except that my ass will never be as beautiful as his is.

Our friendship goes on and on. It's the best one I've got.

Much love—

Kurt

November 14, 1977

[New York City]

To Nanny Vonnegut

Dearest of all possible Nans—

Two superb presents and a funny–sad letter from you—on my fifty-fifth birthday. Much obliged. A couple of other family birthdays this month: Allie's on the 18th, Father's on the 23rd. I miss them. Father was a failed artist, but not an envious one. The beautiful work you and Edie are doing now would have given him exactly as much joy as doing it himself. Anybody's doing good things in the arts made him bubble and croon.

I was looking through the published Letters of Anne Sexton, a Boston poet, a friend of mine who knocked herself off a couple of years ago. In one of the letters she tells of a palindrome she saw written on the side of a barn in Ireland. A palindrome, as you probably know, is a sentence that reads the same backwards as forwards—like "Madam, I'm Adam," and "Able was I ere I saw Elba." Here's the one Anne saw, and it's the best one I ever heard: "Rats live on no evil star."

As always—love—

DAD

March 15, 1978

New York City

To Walter Miller

Walter James Miller was a professor of English at New York University as well as a poet, playwright, and literary critic. He interviewed Vonnegut on his WNYC radio and television shows, Book World *and* Reader's Almanac.

Dear Walter—

It is utterly inappropriate for you to imagine that you have displeased me in any way. Business is business, a mechanical, not very interesting adventure that has nothing to do with friendship. So I will not tolerate talk that suggests that business has wobbled our friendship at all. The mechanical thing that happened was this: I thought hard about the publication of my interviews with you, and decided that it would in no way be to my advantage. I am not eager to have such rambling talk made available to critics, and I would offend my own faithful publisher by offering something to someone else. [. . .]

Cheers—

Kurt Vonnegut

May 11, 1978

New York City

To Emily Glossbrenner

Dearest Emmy—

What an astonishing copy of a letter to receive three days after the 33rd anniversary of the end of World War Two in Europe! Good heavens, child—Alex is dead, and a third of a century has cantered by.

I learn from the letter that, if you will pardon a military expression, I was as full of shit then as I am now. As Alex used to say in various ways: Character does not change much.

Next June, I am going to cross the Atlantic in a 30-foot sailboat with Bernard V. O'Hare, a fellow scout and then prisoner so long ago. He is now a very rich criminal lawyer in Pennsylvania, but otherwise seems unchanged to me. His is the only lasting friendship I made in the war.

I remember what your father said when I got home: "By gosh, you look like a man now." I remember, too, and so sympathetically, his fear that those most in charge of society would learn nothing from the war, would go on exactly as before. He wanted everybody of importance to go to Europe at once to have a look at the ruins, before it could all be fixed up again.

Your visit meant so much to me and to Jill.

Much love—

K

May 18, 1978
New York City

To Nanny Vonnegut

Dearest Nanny—

Your sweet note of almost a week ago got here only this morning. It was mis-delivered to 321 East 48th Street, and the people there were kind enough to send it on. It might have vanished into their trash forever.

About fear: I heard a Hindu holy man say at a lecture a couple of years ago that it was crucial to learn how to make decisions without allowing fear to become involved—and that fear liked to hitch rides on all sorts of words and images. When fear intrudes on your thinking, it may be an old old fear, hitching a ride still, but one which need not really concern you any more. Example: If you do not perform brilliantly, your father will vanish from the lives of you and your mother again, and it will all be your fault somehow. That's not true, of course, so you should scrape that fear off all sorts of words and images when you think. For one thing: I never left you. I would have had to leave the planet to do that.

As for the high standards I will set for you, now that you are through with school: I never even graduated from college, you know, and made very mediocre grades in high school and college. When I got home from war, having been a private for three years, my plan was to survive some more, but I couldn't imagine how this might be done. I still don't know, and I think it must be even tougher to do now. I took whatever jobs I could find. Some were interesting. I was a hack—a term of opprobrium borrowed from a taxicab, a vehicle eminently for hire.

With all my heart, I want you to do this, if you can: Survive. You already have all the dignity and spiritual beauty that God Himself could ever require of anyone.

Much love—
FATHER

June 8, 1978
New York City

To Sam Lawrence

A Good School was a novel by Richard Yates.

Lois Gould was a bestselling novelist, known for her 1970 novel Such Good Friends.

The "new establishment" was a house that Kurt bought with Jill Krementz in Sagaponack, Long Island.

Dear Sam—

I read *A Good School* over the weekend, and passed it on, highly recommended, to Lois Gould. Dick continues to be an immaculate artist with words and emotions. There is never a mistake anywhere. And what a nourishing conclusion he reaches in this book: That, by God, it really was a good school. I am so tired of people who examine their pasts and find nothing but mortal woundings.

I will nominate him for membership in the Institute. Can you name three other members who know and love his work, who would be glad to second the nomination? I have to scrounge my own seconders. [. . .]

Yes—we are counting on your visiting our new establishment this summer. Early August might be a good time. You are such a knowledgeable fan of high living that we are on pins and needles about what you will have to say about this new joint. You will have a bedroom with a separate bath and staircase. I bought a canoe for the lake out front. If you try to take a dip at dawn in the lake, though, you are likely to be eaten by turtles the size of card tables, or to have your brains beat out by swans.

Cheers—
Kurt

October 21, 1978
New York City

To Nanny Vonnegut

The book Kurt refers to as "Mary Kathleen O'Looney" would be published as Jailbird.

Dearest Nanny—

It's delightful that somebody as nice as you should miss us. I have written you twice so far—in care of Jill's brother in Paris and in care of American Express in Athens. In each case I enclosed an application for an American Express card, which must be signed by you. There is a ten-dollar bill for walking-around money in the one to Athens. I will keep trying.

Jane and I read your letters to each other over the telephone. We celebrate you. We find nothing to complain of. You are doing what my father and grandfather did when they were your age, what used to be a conventional thing for middle class people aspiring to lives of cultivation to do: You are making *le grand tour.* Father and Grandfather both sketched, and, as you know, became architects. When they got home, they could lift all sorts of design details from their sketches.

I enclose yet another American Express application. All you have to do is to *sign* your name where I have placed a red X, and then return the form to me airmail. You might also tell me where I should send the card when I get it. It should be a place where you will pick up the card not just maybe, but without fail.

My book, "Mary Kathleen O'Looney," is progressing nicely

at last. It might be finished by the first of next year, which would make me as merry as a bird. Finishing at last will be like having a curse or a tumor removed. After that, I may really feel like tooling off to Rome to see you, or whatever.

Everybody in the family, so far as I know, is in booming health. I have been waiting to hear the first jokes about the Polish Pope. This evening I heard my first three. (1.) His first miracle was to make a blind man lame. (2.) His first official act was to pardon Roman Polanski. (3.) Everybody is waiting to see what wallpaper he picks out for the Sistine Chapel.

Much love—

DAD

November 16, 1978

New York City

To Annie and Don Farber

Dear Annie and Don—

You two have given me many extraordinary gifts over the years, but you have topped them all with Boris, the chess robot. Perhaps you knew that Boris would be a highly personal gift, since I once fancied myself quite a player. Mark was the only person on Cape Cod who could beat me with any consistency. You have refilled a great hole in my life. I play several games a day again—at my own convenience, and I love doing that.

I can beat Boris if I really concentrate—even when I give him a full minute to make each move. But if I make the slightest mistake, he is heartless, and I still can't believe the brilliance of his end games. Really—he is one smart, mean son of a bitch. The people who invented him must be ten times as smart as Einstein. Five years ago, people were saying that such a robot could never be built, since the variables in each game ran into the billions.

I have plenty to thank you two for already, not counting presents at all—and so does everybody in my family. Now you give

me this, too, the best present, word of honor, anybody ever gave
me.

I have one small legal question. If Boris and I have a falling
out for some reason, can he sue for alimony?

Much love—

Kurt

To Sam Lawrence

*Kurt had nominated Richard Yates for the American Institute of Arts
and Letters.*

Dear Sam—

The title of the book, and I want to stick with it, is now *Jail-bird*. [. . .]

Antigua was delightful, I'm sure. You publishers sure have
some easy deal.

Yates, I'm sorry to say, didn't get voted in this time. I will propose him again. The poets are swamping the straights with their
voting power, and this situation can only get worse.

Kurt

To Bernard Malamud

Dubin's Lives *was a novel by Malamud.*

Dear Bernie—

I want to thank you for writing *Dubin*, which I read all day
yesterday. It is a harrowing sort of truth which I myself could

never write about. It reminds me yet again that my own work is in full flight from truth, having thrown its pack and rifle away.

I have never studied literature systematically, having been a chemist and an anthropologist. I have picked the brains of friends who have read a lot more than I have, and continue to do so. Dubin's opinions on Thoreau and Lawrence are now my own. One thing Dubin fails to say, or he said it and I missed it, is that Lawrence himself liked to consider strong authors in unlikely pairs. Isn't that so?

If you have ever worried about growing weaker as you grew older, you need not have worried. You're about twice as strong as anybody else writing these days.

May I add that I, too, like Dubin, have been to Venice with a woman not my wife.

And I apologize yet again for not having come to your Christmas party so long ago now. I was paralyzed by depression.

Cheers—

Kurt Vonnegut

P.S.: Why does Venice mean so little to women?

April 10, 1979
New York City

To Irina Grivnina

Irina Grivnina was a Russian writer.

Dearest Irina—

Our friend Don Fiene delivered your handsome gift and sweet letter to me. They make me very cheerful. The cloth is in a place of honor in my library, along with gifts from Rita.

Our meeting in Leningrad meant a lot to me, too. You were such a vivacious guide in what may be the most beautiful city in the world. I will never forget how you took us right down by the water, at the base of the old beacon to give us the most stunning and mystical view of all.

It makes me happy that you want me to go on writing. The difficulty is not in writing but in writing well. Rita's blazing intelligence at her advanced age is an inspiration to me. I myself feel that I am growing more stupid with each passing year. Then again—Rita does not smoke as I do. I quit smoking for a month, but now I am back at it again. It is as though I have made a very bad bargain with the Devil. I cannot write unless I hurt myself some. This is stupid. In my latest book I include a quotation from Schiller, which perhaps you know: "Against stupidity even the gods struggle in vain."

Yes, there is another book by me, as Don may have told you. I have just corrected the printer's proofs. They did not even look like English to me. I think I have lost control of the language.

This is a perfectly heavenly spring here, at any rate. Last weekend Jill (whom you will meet some day) and I drove 200 versts north of New York City to see my new grandchild, a little girl named India, in a forest in Massachusetts. The father is one of my three adopted children, who is a carpenter. I also have three natural children. The carpenter is now the age I was when I adopted him, which is thirty-five. Time flies.

Tell Rita that proofs of my new book will be sent to her in about twenty days. [. . .]

Cheers—

KYPT

September 8, 1979
Sagaponack, NY

To Nanny Vonnegut

Dearest Nanny—

I want you to be the first person in our family to find this out: That Jill and I have decided to marry each other in November, probably a couple of days after Thanksgiving. Jill will then be three months shy of being forty, and we will have lived together about nine years. The first years of the relationship were tempestuous. Much of the tempest was my fault, surely. I was in a frenzied state of mourning and dismay over the failure of my once good marriage to Jane. Jill had nothing to do with that failure, but she was handy to blame. Be that as it may, Jill and I behave most affectionately and reasonably toward each other now, and unselfishly. We are in love. Our heads are clear. We are working and playing most cheerfully.

I do not endorse serial marriage for anyone. I myself have always wished to be as monogamous as a swan. I was monogamous with your mother until the very end, and will be so with Jill.

Marrying Jill was my idea. It seemed only fair. I told her parents last night at a restaurant on Shelter Island. Our table was by the water. Her parents almost fell in. They were the first to know. Now you are the second. Edie doesn't know yet. Mark doesn't know.

Here, in addition to love, is what made me decide to marry again: I spoke a couple of weeks ago at the funeral for the often great American writer James T. Farrell. His masterpiece was *Studs Lonigan*. The woman he had lived with for the past fifteen years, who had not only saved his life but had made him as happy as a puppy, was accorded no honors as a widow, since he had never made her officially his wife. That was so unfair.

Some people, in telling of my adventures and mis-adventures of the past ten years, have made them conform to the conventions of a Gothic romance, with plenty of wickedness and goodness and innocence and cunning and high living and simple living and money and craziness. It hasn't been quite that lurid. As for the money part, and I know that you are the last person to want to hear about the money part: It is not a case of winner take all. Jill has paid for half of this country house in which I write, for example, and essentially supports herself. If something should happen to me, she would get only one-sixth of what I had. So would you. So would Edith. So would Mark. Jane would get twice as much—one-third. Nobody needs protection from Jill, who has in fact come to love all of you a lot, including Adam. She is a loving person.

As for high living: The wedding will be a small and quiet one. We want no publicity whatsoever. Jill's parents will keep the good news pretty much a secret. Since this is Jill's first marriage, it should have a certain amount of glamour. The guest list is short, though—about fifty people, mostly her family, and only our closest mutual friends. It will be as secular as I can make it, since I am not a Christian of any kind. But it will take place in a church, because churches are so beautiful—and holy. Since the Unitarians believe in almost nothing, I am hoping for a Unitarian church. It will happen in New York City somewhere, probably around 4:30. The attendants will be little kids—Jill's nieces and nephews, with her father giving her away, of course. It will be very private. We don't want our pictures in the paper. We will probably give a small party in a private room at some restaurant afterwards.

As for the groom's side: I hope my brother will come. I will do without a Best Man. I will be solo up there, without accomplices. I sympathize fully with the mixed loyalties you and all the rest of my children would feel on such an occasion. So I of course invite you all, and hope you all will come. If the ceremony and party are going to cause you pain, you should not subject yourself to that pain. Your coming or staying away will not be a vote for or against anything.

Mostly, dear Nanny, I want you to know how happy I am just now, and that I have every reason to look forward to some very good years ahead. We have all calmed down.

And remain assured that I love you as much as anybody on this planet.

YOUR FATHER

September 14, 1979

New York City

To Gail Godwin

The musical adaptation of God Bless You, Mr. Rosewater, *developed by the WPA Theater Company, ran for twelve performances at the Entermedia Theater in the East Village.*

Dearest Gail—

I thank you for your kind remarks about *Jailbird.* We try to run a class operation here, but fail more often than not. The luckiest thing I ever did was to teach at Iowa for those two years. I picked up a very classy extended family that way. It made you and John and John and John and some others quality relatives of mine for life. I used to be in this trade all alone. Suddenly, I was a member of a really great gang. I never tire of asking you and the rest, "How goes it?" If you are ever in trouble, I will take you in.

I have stopped drinking. The only drawback seems to be that I can't dance like Fred Astaire any more. When I dance now, it feels like trying to dock somebody else's boat in a rainstorm.

A couple of talented young nobodies have turned *God Bless You, Mr. Rosewater* into a perfectly darling musical. It showcased last spring in a 99-seat theater. Now it is in rehearsal for a big-time production ($400,000!), and will open on October 14, after three weeks or so of previews. There is a chance that Robert might even find something to admire in the music. At any rate, I would love to give you two a couple of good tickets the next time you're in town, and we can all have supper afterwards. The producer is my daughter Edith, the painter, who turns out to have a whiz-bang mind for business. She hopes to make enough to buy a loft. She paints very big in a tiny room on Ninth Street these days. Did you ever see her stuff? She's a very convincing pre-Raphaelite.

How goes it?

Love—

Kurt

September 21, 1979

New York City

To Don Farber

Paddy Chayefsky was a playwright, screenwriter, and novelist. His
original drama Marty *was considered one of the high points of the*
Golden Age of Television, and as a movie his screenplay won an
Academy Award, followed by Academy Awards for his screenplays of
the movies Hospital *and* Network.

Dear Don—

[. . .] That is good news that you are about to be affiliated
with a big and stable firm. I have been worried about your present set-up, with only you knowing what was going on, and with
so many sudden changes in your supporting staff. I could not
help feeling that things were falling apart from time to time, causing you to be hideously overworked. That's all going to change.
That's great. There are so many little favors and bits of information I need, and there will be others I can bother under the new
set-up.

And now is surely an opportune time to restructure our relationship, if either of us feels it should be restructured. So much of
what you do for me now fell into your lap accidentally, as a result
of Max's petering out, as a result of my giving your address as my
own in *Who's Who,* and so on.

From now on, you should reply only to letters containing
business propositions. The pests wanting me to speak or to send
my autograph or to hear their philosophies of life or whatever
should be routinely forwarded to me by some clerk, without your
having to note their contents at all. If a business proposition slips
by, I will catch it here.

As for the handling of my book business and personal finances and family matters: Nothing could be more solid and satisfactory from my point of view. If this is somehow burdensome
to you, please say so. As for the aggressive merchandising, actual

boorish, frenzied Polo Lounge hustling of the movie and TV rights of my work: That is quite possibly something I should not ask you to do, and something you should not ask yourself to do. The madmen who put the big actors and directors and producers together for monster money deals are specialists, after all, behaving in ways that you don't have the time or foolishness to behave. You have enough to do already as an unassisted practitioner of law.

I talked about TV and movie sales some to Paddy Chayefsky at lunch yesterday. He is crazy about *Jailbird*, as you know. He gave me an outline of the book, scene by scene. He said I would have to do the script, that nobody else could maintain the tone. He also said that you and I should simply sit pat for a few weeks, while the book climbs to the top of the list, knocking off, we hope, *Sophie's Choice*, which sold to the movies for close to a million. If the rise of the book itself does not generate any big offers, he said, then we should turn over the merchandising to Arlene Donovan (my editor on *Sirens*) and Sam Cohn at full commission. Would that be acceptable to you? We would arrange some special compensation scheme for you in such a case, and you, as always, would have the final say as to the terms of the contract, if any.

Much love as always—

Kurt Vonnegut

THE EIGHTIES

There was art in the family genes—Kurt's grandfather and father were architects, and his father took up pottery in his later years. His older sister, Alice ("Allie"), was a talented artist; his daughters, Edie and Nanny, are professional artists; and his son, Mark, is a talented watercolorist as well as a writer and pediatrician. Kurt had always drawn for fun, doodled and drew cartoonish figures, but he hadn't used his art in his books until his drawings were used within the text of *Slaughterhouse-Five*. In 1973 he interspersed the text of *Breakfast of Champions* with jokey sketches, including a VW, a mechanical beetle, and a tombstone that his fictional character Kilgore Trout planned to tell people he hoped to have. The tombstone said: "SOMEBODY [Sometime to Sometime] He Tried." He would use such cartoonish sketches again in his novel *Hocus Pocus* and in his last book, the 2005 collection of essays *A Man Without a Country*.

His first "coming out" with a show of his artwork was held at the Margo Feiden Galleries in Greenwich Village in 1980. His art would find a new outlet and new nourishment in the next decade, and he would tackle a few different forms of writing, as in his 1980 children's book, *Sun Moon Star*, with illustrator Ivan Chermayeff. It was a retelling of the Nativity—the birth of Jesus—for children.

On February 25, 1985, he attended, with his wife, Jill, the world premiere of a new musical composition by Andrew Lloyd Webber. It was a Requiem Mass based on the one of 1570 promulgated by Pope Pius V. Vonnegut wrote of that event in *Fates Worse*

Than Death: An Autobiographical Collage that "Nobody seemed to know what the Latin words meant . . ." and nobody seemed to care in the chic, black-tie crowd. But Vonnegut cared. He found in the program an English translation of the Latin words of the Mass and "They were terrible!" He found them so terrible (nearly the entire Mass was "sadistic and masochistic") that when he got home he "stayed up half the night writing a better one," explaining that was not a vain statement, since "Anyone could write a better one and nobody could write a worse one."

He found a specialist in Church Latin at New York University and commissioned him to translate his English version of the Mass back into Latin, then ran into a composer while serving on jury duty and got him to set it to music. It had its world premiere in 1988 with "the best Unitarian Universalist choir in the country" at their church in Buffalo, New York. Published in the appendix of *Fates* are both the English translation of the Requiem Mass of 1570 and Vonnegut's version of 1985.

These diversions did not detract from Vonnegut's primary work. During this decade, as he turned sixty, he was as productive as ever, publishing his essay collection *Palm Sunday* (1981) and the novels *Deadeye Dick* (1982), *Galápagos* (1985), *Bluebeard* (1987), and *Hocus Pocus* (1990), tackling themes in his fiction from natural selection to modern art. He wrote movingly of his father turning from architecture to pottery after the Great Depression and WWII brought most building to a halt and his commissions dried up. The article, called "Sleeping Beauty," was published in *Architectural Digest* (June 1984) and was later incorporated into *Fates Worse Than Death*. It may have been inspired by a trip he took to Tokyo that spring to speak at an international conference of PEN; while there, he arranged for the Association of Japanese Graphic Artists to take him on a tour of potteries in the countryside, "in honor of my father," he told a friend.

Throughout this decade of high productivity as a writer, Vonnegut was incredibly active as a public speaker, was a spokesman for the rights of writers as an officer of PEN, and made it his personal mission to bring his beloved Russian translator, Rita Rait, to America, battling bureaucracies all the way and at last succeeding.

The eighties were an active and tumultuous time in his personal life also. He and his wife, Jill, adopted their daughter, Lily (Jill's first and Kurt's fourth child), at the end of 1982. As well as this delightful addition to his life (he adored the child), there were personal and professional pressures and upsets. Though his audience was faithful and growing—all his novels of the decade became bestsellers—critics were still pummeling him.

On February 13, 1984, the thirty-ninth anniversary of the fire-bombing of Dresden, Kurt was hospitalized after an overdose of sleeping pills and alcohol. This writer who described himself as a "monopolar depressive descended from monopolar depressives" (*Timequake*) was sent to what he called in a letter to his friend Walter Miller "the short-termer nut-ward at Saint Vincent's [Hospital]." His son, Mark, described it (in the introduction to *Armageddon in Retrospect*) as a "bizarre, surreal incident when he took too many pills and ended up in a psych hospital, but it never felt like he was in any danger. Within a day he was bouncing around the dayroom playing Ping-Pong and making friends. It seemed like he was doing a not very convincing imitation of someone with mental illness."

There were many personal losses for Kurt during the eighties. His writer friends who were "summer neighbors" on Long Island had died by the end of the decade, including James Jones, Nelson Algren, Truman Capote, and Irwin Shaw. Vonnegut was moved as well by the death of a writer friend from the 1950s, the popular and highly regarded mystery novelist John D. MacDonald. MacDonald was one of the group Kurt called "the Professionals," who started out as he did in the Golden Age of Magazines and who were also nurtured by his own early editor Knox Burger and agent Max Wilkinson.

The death that affected him most was that of his first wife, mother of his three children, and de facto mother to the three Adams boys: Jane Cox Vonnegut Yarmolinsky (in 1984, she married Adam Yarmolinksy, who served in many capacities in the Kennedy, Johnson, and Carter administrations). Jane died on December 19, 1986, after a five-year bout with cancer. A decade later, Kurt movingly recounted in an autobiographical section of his novel *Timequake* a lovely conversation he had with Jane two weeks before she died: "Jane could believe with all her heart anything that made being alive seem full of white magic. That was her strength. She was raised a Quaker, but stopped going to meetings of Friends after her four happy years at Swarthmore. She became an Episcopalian after marrying Adam, who remained a Jew. She died believing in the Trinity and Heaven and Hell and all the rest of it. I'm so glad. Why? Because I loved her."

January 4, 1980
New York City

To Donald Fiene

Kurt had, along with Edward Albee, William Styron, and John Updike, protested the supression of a Soviet literary magazine, Metropole.

Dear Don—

Well, shit—I received news this morning that Rita did not get elected an honorary member of the National Institute and Academy. It is my fault. I was so damned innocent. I thought her nomination (seconded by Miller and Updike) would be so appealing that she would be a shoo-in. Too late have I learned, unsurprisingly, that the making of honorary members is a highly political enterprise, with all sorts of lobbying and pressure plays required. Those who did make it are all international celebrities—Angus Wilson and the like. It is pointless to nominate anyone for any sort of honor, I have found, who is not as well known as Bianca Jagger.

I sent Rita a chatty and affectionate description of Jill's and my wedding. That was on November 30 or so. I have had no reply. She called me on my birthday, as she always does, and indicated that she had no work and expected no work. Things were hopeless, and she allowed me to suspect, I think, that my protest about the Metropole affair was partly to blame. I have heard from Americans who were in Moscow in the past few months that serious artists are exhausted at last, are giving up on doing anything much that might be deep or complicated. They talk now of getting out of the country somehow. Only if they can get out from under the dead weight of the bureaucracy, they now seem to feel, can they experiment and, with some luck, grow. The bureaucrats, for their part, I'm sure, would like to see the society do without serious artists entirely. Why not?

Happy New Year—

Kurt Vonnegut

May 5, 1980

New York City

To Don Farber

Sun Moon Star *was a children's book Vonnegut wrote to accompany drawings by the illustrator Ivan Chermayeff. It imagined the world as the baby Jesus saw it after his birth.*

Dear Don—

[. . .] Since the publication of *Wampeters, Foma and Granfalloons,* I have been sending a copy of every speech and article to Sam, on the theory that he would be publishing another non-fiction collection by and by. I have only a dim idea of how much stuff has accumulated in his files by now, and what its quality might be.

But I suspect that there is enough good stuff to make another collection, which I would like to call *Palm Sunday.* I have already roughed out a cover, which would feature a psychedelic cross.

Would you please have Ross or somebody at Dell look over what Sam has accumulated. Ask Dell to decide whether the pieces would make a book they would like to publish. [. . .]

It might be, in view of the impending economic collapse of the nation, that this might be brought out as a quality paperback, a Delta Book, without the possibly heavy losses in hardcover. As a quality paperback, it could be brought out in the fall without competing with the cheap paperback edition of *Jailbird*. Also, it might draw some energy from the nearly simultaneous release of the quasi-religious *Sun, Moon, Star* by Harper and Row.

Cheers—

    Kurt Vonnegut

September 12, 1980

[New York City]

To Harry James Cargas

Harry James Cargas was the author of Conversations with Elie Wiesel, Religious Experience and Process Theology, *and* Daniel Berrigan and Contemporary Protest Poetry. *He was professor of English at Webster University in St. Louis and taught courses on the novels of Kurt Vonnegut, Native American literature, and Latin American literature.*

Dear Harry—

I put this in a private letter, since I have a German name, and since I have said that Dresden should not have been bombed, and since there are a lot of people who on scant evidence would like to peg me for a neo-Nazi apologist.

Someone must say publicly, however, that holocaust studies, with the best possible intentions, are in danger of making reputable the quack physical anthropology and cultural anthropology of Hitler's time. Hitler had emotional reasons for wishing to make Jews easily distinguished from the general population of Europe.

No reputable scientist then or now could make such a distinction. When I studied anthropology at the University of Chicago immediately after the Second World War, I was told that there was no way a Jew could be described or identified. Jews in Europe were just more Europeans, physically and intellectually. Their skeletons and skulls were just more European skeletons and skulls. Their life stories were just more European life stories. The only way Hitler could find Jews to kill, finally, was to go looking for people who said they were Jews, or who were known to have ancestors who said they were Jews.

Hitler made a harmless admission a capital crime.

Holocaust studies may again make Jews as seemingly distinctive as Hitler cruelly imagined them to be. It should be remembered, too, that once his quack anthropologists got to work seeking distinctions, they were able to generalize loathsomely about Slavs and Blacks and Gypsies and Homosexuals and on and on.

Any responsible study of the Holocaust, it seems to me, must begin with the question: "What is a Jew?" It should be said that there is no scientific answer, can be no scientific answer. Any other reply has its roots in superstition.

Cheers—

Kurt Vonnegut

September 12, 1980

New York City

To Donald Fiene

Robert Dennis Crumb (known as R. Crumb) is an American artist and illustrator who was a founder of the underground comics movement.

Dear Don—

The book I did with Chermayeff, *Sun, Moon, Star,* has just come into being. I will send you a copy. Until the book was actually printed, there was not much of anything to see. All Ivan and I could do was to promise that, if the printer did what we told him to do, the result would be wonderful. Because all we had was that promise, we made no book club sales and few foreign sales. The hope now is that we, like Rudolph the Red-nosed Reindeer, will become a part of the nativity story as it is retold every year.

You are not mistaken to admire R. Crumb. He makes me proud to be an American. It seems to me that you should approach Playboy Press and *Rolling Stone* for some sort of help in getting your bibliography published. Strangely enough, Harvard University Press might also be beguiled—or, better still, Yale, whose new president boasts that he reads *Variety* every day. He also complains that his students waste too much time on the pap I write.

I have put together a collection of speeches and essays I've written since 1975—with a lot of connective tissue which is autobiographical. It is called *Palm Sunday*, is about 400 pages in manuscript, and will be brought out by Dell next spring. Under my contract with Dell, I still owe them two more novels. One is in progress, with the working title *Katmandu*. It is about a kid who kills a housewife in a gun accident when he is only eleven. The event shapes the rest of his life. The father is a gun-collector, as was mine.

As for your own career: your destiny reveals itself day-by-day, and there will come a time soon when you can look back and see almost all of it. Such is my case. You were evidently intended to be an absolutely first-rate teacher and scholar at a second rate university, which, in my opinion, is the highest rank anyone could hope to hold in this particular society. You can astonish ordinary persons with all they might feel and be.

Your fan—

Kurt Vonnegut

December 20, 1980
New York City

To Donald Fiene

The "art show" was a one-man show of Kurt's drawings and etchings at the Margo Feiden Galleries in Greenwich Village.

Dear Don—

[. . .] As for the art show: I think people were surprised by how good it was. They were also wary about making fools of themselves by buying anything. I enclose a page from the October *Horizon*. Almost all of the 55 pictures for sale were on 14" by 17" calligraphy bond, the same thick, 100% rag stuff used for diplomas now. The price for that size was and remains $400.00. There were a couple of much bigger ones for $1000.00, and five littler ones for $200.00. We sold twenty-one in all. Most were heads. A few were still-lifes and nudes. The gallery continues to show what's left. I'll have another show in a couple of years. I really tried to make wonderful pictures. This is no town for amateurs.

Steven Paul, who was the juvenile lead in *Happy Birthday, Wanda June* ten years ago, is going to start filming *Slapstick* in March—starring Jerry Lewis as both twins. I have done a script which simplifies the book radically, concentrating on the childhood and adolescence of the twins, and involving tiny Chinese communists in flying saucers. I can direct, if I want. I'm trying to decide whether I know shit from Shinola as far as movies are concerned. Probably not.

A lot of hell is being raised about Irina's arrest here and in Japan and Europe. This might help just a little bit. As for how to get Rita here: I don't think any scheme will work. Too many bureaucrats envy her having so many ardent friends in the outside world. They don't think it's fair.

PS: We'll be in Haiti from Dec. 23 until Jan. 1.

Cheers—

Kurt

Undated, c. 1981

[New York City]

To members of the American
Civil Liberties Union

Dear ACLU Member,

On April 21, 1970, a teacher at Jefferson Davis High School
in Montgomery distributed copies of "Welcome to the Monkey
House," one of my short stories, to her junior English class.

She was fired the next day for distributing "literary garbage."

The ACLU filed suit on behalf of the teacher, and on June 9,
1970, she was reinstated. Quoting from an earlier Supreme Court
decision, the judge ruled:

> Our nation is deeply committed to safeguarding academic
> freedom, which is of transcendent value to all of us and
> not merely to the teachers concerned. That freedom is there-
> fore a special concern of the First Amendment, which does
> not tolerate laws that cause a pall of orthodoxy over the
> classroom. . . . The classroom is peculiarly the "market-
> place of ideas."

Until very recently, there have been few attempts by school of-
ficials and others to censor library and textbooks.

Now, the book-burners are back.

Last June a group in Warsaw, Indiana publicly burned 40
textbooks the school board had found to be "objectionable."
Buoyed by public support, the school board then fired three
teachers and dropped nine literature courses. A federal judge upheld the school board. The ACLU is appealing the case.

The American Library Association reports that complaints to
public libraries have increased fivefold since the election.

Self-styled censors have undertaken a new national effort to
rid classrooms and libraries of books of which they disapprove.

** Rev. Tom Williams of the Abingdon, Virginia Emmanuel Baptist Church demanded that the local librarian show him who had checked out certain books, including Philip Roth's *Goodbye Columbus* and Sidney Sheldon's *Bloodline,* because he felt they were "strictly filth."

When refused, he obtained other clergy support and is now threatening to remove the library board members and to have a public referendum on the November ballot asking voters "if their tax dollars should be used to purchase pornography through the public library."

** Rev. George Zarris, chairman of Moral Majority in Illinois, has openly encouraged the removal and burning of "unfit" library books. Because of community pressure, State Senator Jeremiah Joyce has introduced a bill into the Illinois General Assembly that would make librarians liable for prosecution for distributing "harmful" material to minors.

** The Island Trees, N.Y. school board removed nine books from high school libraries, including my own *Slaughterhouse-Five* and Bernard Malamud's *The Fixer.* The ACLU successfully appealed a lower court's decision upholding the removal but the case will still be reviewed by the Supreme Court.

** A Vermont school district's ban on *Dog Day Afternoon* and *The Wanderers* was upheld by a federal court last October.

I am offended as a citizen, as a writer, and as an ACLU member that certain elements are trying to drag us backward to the darker days of censorship.

The freedom to choose or reject ideas, to read books of our choice, and to publish freely is the very bedrock of our free society. The First Amendment is a prohibition of governmental interference with free speech.

I support the ACLU for many reasons but none as critical and important as its never-ending vigilance for free speech.

Cases of textbook and library censorship have been reported so rapidly in the past few months that the ACLU is physically and financially unable to cope with the legal burden. This is personally distressing to me because the ACLU is the only organization effectively fighting the censors.

I have never written a letter asking anyone to help a cause. Because I feel so strongly about what is happening in our country today and because I know the tremendous financial burden being placed on the ACLU, I have decided to do what I can to fight this ugly and dangerous trend.

I ask you to join with me in giving a special gift to the ACLU at this critical time in history, when those on the other side are raising millions.

If each ACLU member gave at least $25.00, the ACLU could counter the highly financed opponents of civil liberties and have the legal resources necessary to challenge every single incident of school and library censorship.

No book placed in a public library should be forcibly removed. No textbook should be burned.

I urge you to send as large a check as possible to the ACLU today. I will do the same.

Sincerely,

Kurt Vonnegut

January 28, 1981

New York City

To José Donoso

Dearest of all possible Pepés—

I thank you for your illegible address, and would thank you for a clearer one. If you are happy to be in Chile, then I will be happy, too. I would prefer you to be on East Eleventh Street or so, but I am quite used to not having everything my own way. Really—Greenwich Village is not America. It is a strange, anarchical, polyglot League of Nations mandate left over from the First World War somehow, sort of like Togoland.

News: Jill, who is self-supporting and hard-working, felt that she deserved a baby, if her life was to be complete. I could not really argue with her, since she, clearly, was going to be the one who had to raise it. But she had a miscarriage a week ago, having carried the child for three months. We will start again. "Da capo," as you said to me one time, after we had had some falling out, and had to start the friendship over again.

Jane, who has so long sought to renew and reinvigorate herself through magic, through credulousness in the presence of religious quacks, has at last had startling success, I am told, with ordinary therapy. She has always been a wonderful writer, you know, who could write only with painful clumsiness. Now, Edith told me yesterday at lunch, she writes like the wind every day. Her subject: What it was like to already have three kids, and then to adopt three more. Why not? The book could easily be delightful and wise. I wish her nothing but success and happiness.

As for Edith: She has a decent studio at last, in what used to be manufacturing space on Twelfth Street, right off Fifth Avenue. She is painting enormous, surrealistic allegories. Yes—she has heard of Goya, and some others, too. There are women carrying men. The men are content to be carried everywhere.

When can we see another book?

Cheers—

Kurt Vonnegut

P.S. I had dinner with Nelson Algren in Sag Harbor (Long Island) last summer, and brought John Irving and his wife along. Nelson's jokes were more obscure than usual. It took us a couple of days to figure out that he thought John was *Clifford* Irving, the Howard Hughes hoaxer, the con man, the beguiling crook.

March 11, 1981

New York City

To Steven Paul

Steven Paul was producer of the movie Slapstick *based on Vonnegut's novel. It was released in 1982, starring Jerry Lewis and Madeline Kahn.*

Dear Steven—

I am not coming out there on March 22, as you suggested. I will not be coming out there at all. You are on your own with the movie. I have done all a writer is supposed to do, which is to give you a script. You can accept it or reject it or whatever. It isn't my duty to take part in promotional schemes, and to hang around in case rewriting is needed in a hurry and so on.

I know of no other writer who has been required by a producer to be the endlessly cooperative and participative and public person you expect me to be. So I am saying no more than any other professional writer would say. I have done my job, all of it.

I have other jobs I must do, and I intend to do them while you make your film. I wish you luck with it, of course. I am sorry it has to be made so quickly, and with the volatile star headed for a more glamorous enterprise immediately afterwards. I do not see how, with Scorsese waiting for him, Jerry can look upon *Slapstick* as anything but an interlude with possibly amusing amateurs, especially since they are willing to work so fast.

As I have already said, I have done all a writer is supposed to do, and largely on speculation. If you have promised more of me to your actors and investors, that was your idea, not mine. It would take ten years out of my life in the midst of making a quickie with such a potentially wild star and such a young and as yet unproven director. This is not to say that it couldn't turn out to be a wonderful movie. It is only to say that I could not stand

to hang around while it was being made. Yes, we are friends, all
right, but too much friendship right now could be damaging to
my health.

Please, let us be professional. Since I have done all a writer is
supposed to do, all further communications about my script
should be addressed to Don Farber. Work out the money with
him. I am not available for further services at any fee.

Yours truly,

Kurt Vonnegut

April 19, 1981

New York City

To Anatole Broyard

Dear Mr. Broyard—

I thank you for your comments on how slowly my literary
reputation is dying. Part of the problem, surely, is that all my
books remain in print, and people continue to give me credit for
having written them. There is also the confusion caused by *Jailbird,* which was much too good to have been written by someone
at my stage of decay, a red herring, you might say. I am presently
working on yet another novel which may mislead readers into believing I should be counted among the living for yet a little while.
How greedy of me. How tasteless. How pitiful.

As for *Palm Sunday,* it was quite openly loathed by your
paper and some others, and was elsewhere praised with no embarrassment apparent to me. A stranger speaks well of me in
The Nation, for example. Another did so in the *Los Angeles
Times.*

Still, I am sure you are right that there are many critics who
went to some trouble to say nice things about a book by me
which they did not like at all. I can't name them, but I'm sure
you can. I am sorry to have made them so uncomfortable,

and that sentimentality or whatever required them to tell little white lies.

I am not a critic, but I can imagine what it must be like for a critic to remain seemingly respectful and friendly in the presence of a writer he knows to be all through, to be hollow, to be a man with a paper asshole, so to speak. Here is how I am able to imagine it, and here is how a lot of washed-up writers are able to imagine it—by analogy. A lot of us have found ourselves behaving respectfully and sympathetically and cordially and fraternally and so on when suddenly encountering, God forbid, Anatole Broyard.

Yours truly,

Kurt Vonnegut

April 22, 1981

[New York City]

To Gary Grossman

Gary S. Grossman described himself as a "wellness coach for successful people."

Dear Gary Grossman—

That is friendly of you to be curious as to whether I stopped smoking or not. I still smoke a lot—and have no clear idea why.

SmokEnders worked for me, as I guess it works for everybody. The psychological consequences of my not smoking, however, were quite fancy—unpleasant for those around me, though not for me, and my work stopped cold. I felt fine.

I wrote the lady who founded the program—in response to a letter from her. She wanted testimonials from famous people she had helped. I wanted more help, and thought she could offer some, since she probably knew more about smoking than anybody. She declined to reply, and I do not like her for that.

I seem to be the victim of a truly profound addiction. I undergo radical personality changes when I stop. They are quite permanent and unattractive. I congratulate you on the stability of your own personality.

Cheers—
    Kurt Vonnegut

                                            December 18, 1981
                                               New York City

To Sidney Offit

Sidney Offit is the editor of the Library of America volume Vonnegut: Novels and Stories 1963–1973. *He has served on the board of the Authors Guild and PEN. He became Kurt's closest friend in New York.*

Dear Sidney—

I really miss you and all the other tennis pals. [. . .] You guys are the only friends I have. I am beginning to wonder if my arm will quit hurting and get strong again, the way the sports medicine doctor said it would. You went through the same thing, did you? [. . .]

I was the person, incidentally, who asked Salinger to sign *Catcher in the Rye,* and who was refused most angrily. Did you ever tell Kunes that? I used Salinger's neighbor, the Centurian Frank Platt, to sign the book for its wonderful Russian translator, Rita Rait. Salinger not only refused. He stopped speaking to Platt.

I must have told you during our ping-pong days so long ago: Truman Capote said that Salinger has been submitting stories regularly to the *New Yorker,* and that the stories, which Capote claims to have read, are awful. I asked Updike if he believed this, and Updike said he wouldn't be surprised if it were true—that

Salinger was certainly trending toward incomprehensibility. Updike exclaimed over the early stories, saying they were "so juicy!"
This was a way of suggesting, I think, that Salinger didn't have
much of an intellect. Finally, I guess, you can't make a career of
simply looking. Sooner or later, if you are going to go on writing,
you have to put some hard-edge ideas in your mind, and believe
in them the way you believe in Tinkerbell.

Season's greetings—

Kurt Vonnegut

June 21, 1982
New York City

To MARY JANE ("MAJIE") AND
WILLIAM ("SKIP") FAILEY

*Mary Jane "Majie" Failey is one of Kurt's oldest friends, from Short-
ridge High School and throughout his life. She is author of* We Never
Danced Cheek to Cheek: The Young Kurt Vonnegut in Indianapolis
and Beyond. *Her husband, the late William "Skip" Failey, attended
the Orchard School with Kurt.*

Dear Mary Jane & Skip—

No—I will not be there for Vonnegut Week. Any American
with common sense knows that if he was a jerk in high school he
will be a jerk in his own home town forever. It would be O.K. if I
were dead. [. . .]

How come you want to sell your cheery, cozy house? I love it
there.

Cheers—

Kurt Vonnegut

July 8, 1982
New York City

To Jack P. Wheeler

Paul Moore was Episcopal bishop of New York.

Dear Jack P. Wheeler—

I respond to your letter of June 13 to Paul Moore, about my sermon at St. John the Divine. I got a copy of that letter only this morning.

I was praising the Vietnam veterans. I have always respected and praised them. This was perfectly clear to the congregation which heard my sermon. I had nothing to do with the sermon's being picked up by the *Times,* which, on its own, ran about a third of it. But that third is not a misrepresentation of what I said. If people misread me, there is nothing I can do about that.

The *Times* fragment has since been syndicated all over the world, again without my connivance. I got paid nothing for it. Your letter has worried me a lot, as indeed it should. I am somewhat relieved, at least, that you are the only reader so far to suggest to me that I have spoken ill of Vietnam vets. Word of honor: that is something I never do.

Yours truly,

Kurt Vonnegut

July 25, 1982
[New York City]

To Knox Burger

The "anthology of testimonials" was collected for Kurt's sixtieth birthday party that year.

Dear Knox—

I thank you for your cracked and mean complaints of July 20. I know nothing about the anthology of testimonials you mention. Who am I supposed to tell not to bother you?

You played an important part in the lives of many young writers of our generation, and I said so in the *Paris Review.* That is a fact which deserves to be recorded.

When I turn sixty, maybe I'll decide what I really think about you. I've never done that, you know.

Get an unlisted phone.

Yours truly,

Kurt Vonnegut

July 27, 1982

New York City

To Robert Weide

With Vonnegut's support, Weide began filming him in 1988 and has continued to gather film for a documentary that has not yet been produced, including home movies going back to 1925. He wrote and produced the movie based on Mother Night, *starring Nick Nolte.*

Dear Robert Weide—

I've been out of town for most of this summer, and so read your friendly letter of a month ago only this morning. It turns out that I already know something of your work. I saw the Marx Brothers tribute, and liked it a lot. Who wouldn't?

I am honored by your interest in my work, and I will talk to you some, if you like, about making some sort of film based on it. But there is sure no great footage to start with. *Slaughterhouse-Five* is the only good movie having anything to do with me. Also: Harold Mantell made a documentary of me mostly talking seven years ago or so, which he rents out to schools. You might take a look at that. And a movie based on *Slapstick,* starring Jerry Lewis and Madeline Kahn as twins, has just been completed out there by Steven Paul Productions, whose number must be in the phonebook. He's on Hollywood Boulevard. I left my address book out in the country. Maybe Steven will show you some of it. It could be awful. I haven't seen any of it yet.

Anything that is any good of mine is on a printed page, not film. Maybe you have some ideas as to what to do about that. I don't. [. . .]

Cheers—

 Kurt Vonnegut

           October 29, 1982
            New York City

To José and Maria Pilar Donoso

Dear Pepé & Maria Pilar—

Since you genuinely wish for Jane and me to be happy, you should know that we will be as happy as anyone on Earth tomorrow afternoon at two—at the wedding of our daughter Nanny to a fine, photographically realistic surrealist painter named Scott Prior. Contrary to what you may wish to believe, one doesn't have to be Spanish to paint well. Prior's pictures, which are usually huge, look like color photographs of situations in dreams.

The gloomy reports of Jane's health are based on the informed pessimism of my son the doctor. The treatments with platinum have been stopped, since she responded with intolerable nausea that went on for weeks. So, as I understand it, she isn't being treated with much of anything just now, save for a sensible diet. So she is the same Jane you celebrate in your letter of nine days ago, except that she has lost all her hair. She will be merry, utterly open Jane at the wedding—in a wig. And who knows? She could outlive all of us.

Every author in the world must have been deeply satisfied

when Márquez got the Nobel, and every author in the world
would agree with you, that Borges should have got it first. My
guess is that Borges will never get it. I have no idea why not. I
only say that as a gambling man. What the hell. You can't buy a
really good house with the prize money any more anyway. [. . .]

As for your attachments to students we had at Iowa: those
came very close to being blood relationships. Everyone remembers you two with love of a sort which need not be renewed and
renewed like the paint on your house.

Kurt

November 29, 1982
New York City

To Mary Louise and Miller Harris

Dear Mary Louise and Miller—

I did not make up the guest list for my surprise party. It was
shaped by seemingly innocent questions put to me by Jill during
the past year. How much did I like this person or that one, and so
on. I must have spoken well of you two. Sometimes I make good
sense.

The party scared the pants off me, just as a similarly orches-
trated hallucination would have scared the pants off anybody, I
think. The particular danger it represented to me was that I
would become (1.) intolerably drunk, (2.) intolerably exhibitionistic, and (3.) intolerably sentimental. I fought off the booze, but I
did become the loud and mawkish birthday boy. Since then, I
have tried to be as much like Edith Piaf as possible, regretting
nothing, and one excess of sentimentality which I genuinely fail
to regret is my trying to thank you, Miller, for having been such a
good teacher of the liberal arts and the craft of writing at Cornell.
Back in the old days, you, although only a year older than myself,
were in loco parentis, as far as I was concerned. You carried off

that responsibility with utmost kindness and wisdom and flattering watchfulness.

Yes—I did receive the shirts, which are beautifully made. Really. That much is still right about this country anyway—Eagle Shirts. We also still make the finest harps in the world.

Much love to both of you. I was honored by your presence.

Kurt Vonnegut

December 20, 1982

New York City

To MILLER HARRIS

Dear Miller—

[. . .] On Saturday we went to Philadelphia, where we picked up from an outfit called "The Golden Cradle" a three-day old girl which we are adopting. Her name is Lily. Jill wanted a baby so much, and I had no right to deny her one. I shall survive or whatever. [. . .]

Again—thanks for all the birthday stuff.

Cheers—

Kurt Vonnegut

January 12, 1983

New York City

To ROBERT WEIDE

Dear Bob—

Got your letter of yesterday this afternoon. That's fast.

I will be going to England for two weeks, starting February 16, in order to hustle *Deadeye Dick*. I will also get to see the documentary about me which BBC shot last month. They did it for a show called *Arena*. It may be that you can make use of some of their footage. The director was Nigel Finch, a most pleasant young man. PBS has no plans, the last I heard, for showing it over here. When I come back in March, I will have a tape with me. Maybe we should both have a look at it, and then a long talk, to make sure that a show about me would look like much, could look like much. As I told you: I cooperated with BBC at the insistence of my British publisher. The project took only about six days out of my life.

As a business proposition for you, for me, and for your backers, the notion of making a movie based on a novel seems a lot more exciting. *Cat's Cradle* can be bought back from Hilly Elkins for about $100,000, what he has tied up in it. I own *Jailbird,* which was a number one best seller for several months. *Sirens* is still under option, which probably won't be renewed this year. There must be a slew of scripts for *Sirens* by now. *Mother Night* is available. People option it and drop it. *Player Piano* gets more timely with each passing day. It could be an up-to-date *Modern Times,* if you could find another Chaplin.

I hate to say this, but a great director can make a wonderful movie out of anything.

Happy New Year—

Kurt Vonnegut

February 10, 1983

New York City

To Charles Ray Ewick, Indiana State Library

Dear Mr. Ewick—

I am in receipt of a letter from your research librarian Linda Walton, which tells me that your institution is no longer able to buy books. She asks that I give the State of Indiana a copy of my latest novel, *Deadeye Dick.* I have complied with this request.

Since books are to libraries what asphalt is to highway departments, I assume that Indiana is also asking donations from suppliers of asphalt for her roads. Or has it been decided that asphalt is worth good money, and that books are not?

It may be that whoever told Linda Walton to write that letter supposed that I myself get all the books I want for free. I in fact must pay for them what bookstores pay. So what I have sent you represents an actual outlay of about $7.00, plus postage and the price of a bookbag, plus a fair amount of my time, which may indeed be worthless. Let us forget the time. Are all of Indiana's suppliers of goods making equivalent sacrifices? Or are they to be more respected than I am for the way they make their livings? Are they more manly, more practical, less decorative?

If you have a cost accountant, he can easily prove to you that Ms. Walton's letter to me cost far more than one copy of *Deadeye Dick*. If you reply to this letter, and you discuss its contents with others on State time, the cost to the taxpayers will soon exceed the retail price of my collected works bound in the finest leather.

Yours truly,

Kurt Vonnegut

March 12, 1983
New York City

To KATHRYN HUME

Kathryn Hume was a professor of English at Penn State University and a literary critic.

Dear Kathryn Hume—

[. . .] You have described, as I could never have done, all the popular literary schemes which were useless to me. I would only add that I have been much encouraged by painters in believing that startling beauty could be achieved by broken rules.

Really—modern painters have been my exemplars, and often my
friends. During my childhood in Indianapolis, local jazz musi-
cians also excited me and made me happy. My relatives, meanwhile, were saying that jazz wasn't music at all. It sure sounded
like music to me.

Cheers—

Kurt Vonnegut

March 16, 1983

New York City

To Mary Louise and Miller Harris

Dear Mary Louise and Miller—

We thank you for the dear stool for Lily, the new milkmaid
around here. Her health and disposition are excellent after three
months and a little bit more. We have been unbelievably lucky in
getting a nanny. She is an Anglo-Saxon college graduate from
Vermont, who has decided to make a career of child care. She is
nearly thirty, and held her last job for eight years, and looks a lot
like a young Katharine Hepburn. This is how it is with the An-
glos these days—the world turned upside down.

We were in England for ten days recently, and I spoke at Oxford. Mark Twain cried when he spoke there. I stunk up the joint.
I proved yet again that the British have no sense of humor.

Much love to you both—

Kurt and Jill

Kurt Vonnegut

August 8, 1983
New York City

To Rust Hills

Dear Rust—

I have spoken to several of the other contributors to the 50th anniversary issue [of *Esquire* magazine], without revealing what I myself was paid for my piece, and have discovered that nobody was offered as little as I was offered, and that everybody was paid about three times as much as I was paid, or more. I am not in the least paranoid or even pissed off about this, since your excitement and mine had to do with the glamour of the project rather than with amounts of money about to change hands. Our mutual absent-mindedness about money matters, our love of fun, if you will, quite accidentally resulted in my being treated financially as though I were the geek of the gang. I have not felt for a moment that you or anybody else at *Esquire* thought of me in that way.

But now that I have brought it to your attention that I have been paid like a geek, although I unglamorously handed in satisfactory work early on, I am absolutely certain that *Esquire* will mail me a check at once to bring my compensation in line with what you paid the others. Otherwise, finally, *Esquire* will have embarrassed me profoundly—something it surely does not wish to do.

Fraternally yours,
Kurt Vonnegut

August 24, 1983
[New York City]

To Rust Hills

Dear Rust—

What an incomparable mollifier you are.

Word of honor: I am utterly mollified. The best news, and the news I was really hoping against hope for, was that somebody else, anybody else, had been paid as little as I was.

So everything is positively hokay, and I am not a needy case anyway, and I look forward to seeing the whole issue. I am honored to be included. I might even have slipped you a little money to include me. Eat your heart out. It's too late now.

Fraternally, as always,

Kurt Vonnegut

September 7, 1983
New York City

To Robert Maslansky

Dr. Robert Maslansky met Kurt in 1974 when, as director of medical education for Cook County Hospital in Chicago, he invited Vonnegut to speak to his staff of young doctors, feeling they would benefit from hearing people with interesting ideas outside the field of medicine. Dr. Maslansky was pleasantly surprised when Kurt said he would be glad to do it, and when asked what his lecture fee would be, his answer was, "Lunch." That was it. Vonnegut "came and spoke and was perfectly delightful," Maslansky recalled. When Dr. Maslansky moved to New York to be medical director of addiction and rehabilitation at Bellevue Hospital, he looked up Kurt, and they became friends.

In Fates Worse Than Death, *Vonnegut wrote of his friend: "Dr. Robert Maslansky, who treats every sort of addict at Bellevue Hospital, in New York City, and in the jails, too, is a saint."*

Ignaz Semmelweis was an early pioneer of antiseptic procedures; he discovered that hand-washing by physicians reduced infant mortality in the Vienna General Hospital's obstetrics clinic in 1847, but some doctors were offended and rejected his theory.

Dear Bob—

What I hope I said about poetry was that I was unlikely to get the most out of it if I did not know the poet. I need the poet himself or herself as footnotes and appendix—usually. Poets I have known are James Tate and George Starbuck and L.E. Sissman and Marvin Bell and Robert Penn Warren and Bill Meredith and a few others. This is nothing but laziness on my part. Greatness can get the attention of even this sleepy soul, however. Example: William Blake. There is no chance that I could ever respond warmly to upper class sensibilities, no matter how brilliantly expressed. This is politics. Example: T.S. Eliot. Fuck him. Everybody knows he's from St. Louis—everybody but him.

If a friend, which you surely are, shows me a poem he or she likes a lot, which you have done, then, for me, that is just like knowing the poet. For me, poems are presents to be exchanged within an extended family.

As for Oak Ridge: the United States Army in its wisdom sent me to the University of Tennessee for a semester, to make me a mechanical engineer (Mechanics, A, Thermodynamics, F, Calculus, C)—before sending me overseas as a rifleman. I had never had infantry basic training, by the way. I was an artilleryman, and had never thrown a hand grenade or fired anything but a carbine or a .45. It didn't matter. When I was captured, I was an autodidact on the B.A.R.

Anyway: In the process of getting and consuming corn liquor in Knoxville, the local product being called "sploe", I met any number of boisterous, prosperous workers from Oak Ridge, whose lips had not been zipped. I wish now that I could remember what they told me they were doing. A public relations man at Oak Ridge, Richard Gehman, now dead of alcoholism and five wives (one of them Estelle Parsons, to whom he gave twins), later became a prolific magazine writer and a close friend of mine. His job was to misinform the workers I met as to what they were doing and why.

Your speculations about AIDS are of course fascinating to me, and I am sending them on to Mark. I tremble for you. Semmel-weis came to a bad end, as I'm sure you know. He finally caught on that nobody else really gave a shit about anything, and he slashed his palm on purpose with an infected scalpel. He was the particular hero of the monster Louis Ferdinand Céline.

I have spent the summer trying to find out if I am smart enough to write about Darwinism as the dominant religion of our time. The results are inconclusive, and could hardly be anything else, since my I.Q. is (for New York City) a lousy 135.

I will be taking Mark and his eldest son Zack and my brother Bernard and one of his grown sons, a sweet, celibate, unemployed alcoholic named Terry, blue-fishing off Block Island in a chartered boat this next weekend (September 10–11). After that, I will close up the country house and will be in town all winter. I intend to see a lot of you.

Cheers --

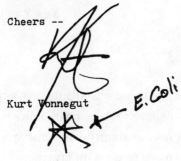

Kurt Vonnegut — E. Coli

November 16, 1983
New York City

To Robert Weide

Dear Bob—

I thank you for your Armistice Day greeting. I trust that you joined me in one minute of silence as the second hand ticked off the eleventh minute of the eleventh hour of the eleventh month.

In case you haven't seen the one-hour show BBC made of my life and work last February, I have a Betamax I can send you or show you here. I have mixed feelings about it. When all is said and done, the star was the director.

Slapstick, the dreadful movie made by Steven Paul and starring Jerry Lewis, has been shown in Europe, where it was widely scorned. It is now being recut and rescored out your way, for release in February, they say. My prayer is that it never be shown again to anybody—in any form. Lewis is supposedly the mastermind behind the changes. The double-cross was sprung when Steven Paul announced that he himself would direct the picture. Surprise!

I hack away at a new novel called *Galapagos.*

Cheers—

    Kurt Vonnegut

November 19, 1983

New York City

To Peter Reed

Dear Peter—

[. . .] It is my agnosticism which gets me into trouble with the censors, I am sure. They honestly believe that we have under law an established religion and that it is Christianity. They also believe that the Constitution has no more to do with law than a Hallmark Greeting Card.

They also believe that Anglo-Saxons really own this country, and that the rest of us shouldn't forget for a moment that we are merely guests here. The proper salutations in letters to censors and Frank Sinatra are identical: "Dear Blue Eyes—"

Cheers,

    Kurt Vonnegut

January 9, 1984
New York City

To Donald Fiene

Dear Don—

[. . .] The big news, the incredible news, is that Rita will be
here in the United States in April or May. I put her up for the
Thornton Wilder Prize for translation, inaugurated last year by
Columbia University. She won. And, by God, they are allowing
her to come over here to get it. I am also trying to rig things so
that she can be made an Honorary Member of the American
Academy and Institute of Arts and Letters at about the same
time. I tried that before, and failed—but your excellent dossier is
still on file.

I would house her here, but we have this new baby, and are
no longer able to accommodate guests overnight. We will give at
least one little dinner party for her—with no more than twelve
people. [. . .]

Happy New Year—

Kurt Vonnegut

March 22, 1984
[New York City]

To Walter Miller

Dear Walter—

[. . .] As Offit may or may not have told you, I was in the
short-termer nut-ward at Saint Vincent's, which is the third floor.
[. . .] The real sickies are on the fourth, fifth, and sixth floors. I
played a lot of pingpong and eightball with them in the rec hall
on the roof. They were so heavily sedated that they believed me
no matter what I said the score was. Now I'm an outpatient, allowed to carry matches again. Can you imagine somebody living
in Manhattan and having a psychiatrist named Ralph O'Connell?

Oh well—only a Catholic could find my atheism interesting.

As part of my therapy, I've rented a studio on MacDougal Alley, number 5, under the name of Asro. I go to work there every weekday now, just as though I had a job. Let's have lunch or something.

In Christ—

Kurt Vonnegut

April 18, 1984
New York City

To Ben Hitz

Ben Hitz was a friend of Kurt's since they were classmates at Short-ridge High School. Hitz was best man at Kurt's wedding to Jane Marie Cox.

Dear Ben—

[. . .] In two weeks I depart for my first visit to Japan, for an international conference of P.E.N. in Tokyo. I have arranged to make a tour of potteries in the boondocks—in honor of my father, who would have rather been a potter than anything. He could have given up speaking almost entirely. That was a complaint that he often made: that people talked too much.

Cheers—

K

April 29, 1984
New York City

To Peter Reed

Dear Peter—

Always good to hear from you. You are a sort of flywheel on my reputation, mentioning me often even when I myself am as

silent as a tomb. The Darwinian novel, *Galapagos,* has been a
perfect son-of-a-bitch, since I have to be responsible as a biologist as well as a story-teller. I have taken the thing apart and re-
assembled it a thousand times. I am reminded of a dream car
called the "Tucker Torpedo" which was to be produced after
the Second World War, an early DeLorean. The headlights were
supposed to turn with the front wheels and so on. It was a stock
swindle, and one of the company's engineers testified about the
prototype they built and showed around the country on a plat-
form, that the only time they started it, it went "chugga-
chugga-chug," and died. He said that, as far as he knew, it
couldn't even back up. That is the condition of most of what
I've produced in the past two years. I think maybe things are
going a little bit better now. I've rented a studio down in Greenwich Village, on MacDougal Alley, where my daughter Edith,
the painter, comes to paint for a couple of hours a day. That is
easy companionship. I take a cab to work each morning, and
then walk home every afternoon. The walk takes a lazy,
window-shopping hour.

As for Japan: I'm not going to get any prize over there. I am
to be a speaker at an international convention of P.E.N., and a
guest of the Tokyo Chapter. I told my hosts that I wanted to see
some potters and printmakers out in the countryside while I was
there, so the Association of Japanese Graphic Artists is going to
take me around for four days, in exchange for which I must give
their annual convention, coinciding with the P.E.N. conference, a
speech. Done and done. I leave here on May 8 (V-E Day), and return on the 20th, no doubt all pooped out. [. . .]

Cheers—

Kurt Vonnegut

June 24, 1984
New York City

To Jed Feuer

Jed Feuer was a musician and composer who played trumpet, founded the group Bipolar, and produced off-Broadway musicals.

Dear Jed—

I enjoyed talking to you yesterday afternoon about your hopes of turning Little Red Riding Hood into a musical, and was honored by your invitation to contribute ideas, if I could.

My ideas, for whatever they're worth, are these:

The original folktale is too simple, too well-known, and too stupidly brutal to be particularly interesting, except, maybe, as a ballet. I am thinking of adult audiences, of course. There are few opportunities in the tale for comedy or any universal truths beyond pure terror.

So I suggest this updated story line:

There is this backwoods, fundamentalist village run by a Jerry Falwell and vigilantes under his direction. The community is particularly obsessed by protecting the virtue of a great beauty, who was orphaned and raised by her grandmother. They have overdone this, since, when the show begins, she is a blowsy, song-belting twenty-eight, and ten men, all from out of town, have been killed by the vigilantes so far—for making indecent approaches, which she has virtuously reported to Falwell. Actually, the community treasures her as bait for a very cruel trap for foreigners.

So yet another foreigner shows up, the wolf, a girl-crazy but innocent sort of young Rockefeller, who has come to town to investigate his roots. His ancestors founded the town.

So everybody in town, pretending to love young lovers and so on, heads him in the direction of the trap. The not-so-young beauty does all she can to help, hoping against hope, in her genuine innocence, that he will not be another one of those monsters who wants to defile her sacred body. A fine aria for her might be "I am not meat."

That's the premise. How it all ends is subject to negotiation. As I said yesterday, in that premise are all sorts of song opportunities: the vigilantes extolling small-town life, with its hatred for outsiders and non-conformists, the wolf's singing that it is natural and good that he can't keep his hands off beautiful girls, the wolf's celebration of discovering his roots, and so on.

Yours truly,

Kurt Vonnegut

February 16, 1985

New York City

To Maria Pilar and José Donoso

Heinrich Böll was a German author who won the Nobel Prize for Literature in 1972. He had been drafted into the Wehrmacht in WWII and was a P.O.W. of the Americans, as Kurt was a P.O.W. of the Germans.

Dear Maria Pilar and Pepé—

All continues to go reasonably well here. Jill will be 45 on this coming Tuesday, and I am giving her a party at the Tavern on the Green in Central Park. I wish you two could be there, but understand that you have a rich social life where you are. We all heard about the recent dinner party. I was in London at the time, taping a conversation with Heinrich Böll for BBC. Poor, saintly Heinrich is very sick, with diabetes and circulatory problems in his legs, and without much hope for humankind. The conversation, undirected and without a third person present, was a flop, I think, because of my respect for him and his total despair. We were taped for three hours, in the hopes that one hour of good talk could be distilled from it. I haven't heard, but my guess is that they will be lucky to get a three minute show out of it.

He will surely be invited as an honored guest at the International P.E.N. Congress to be held here late in January of 1986. His feeling was that he would be too sick and weary to travel that far from Cologne. This will be the first Congress to be held in the United States for twenty years, and, since so many people are eager to come to New York, it could easily be the most extraordinary gathering of good writers in this century. American P.E.N. is of course particularly eager, Pepé, that you be among that number when, as Louis Armstrong used to say, "the saints come marching in."

I have just handed in a novel called *Galapagos,* set in Ecuador, as unlikely as that seems. That is the only South American country this provincial author has ever visited, and I doubt very much whether he understood much of what he heard and saw. The main point of the book is to complete a five-book contract with Dell Publishing. For the first time since about 1951, I don't owe anybody a book. I am not at all sure that I want to write another one. My brains aren't nearly as quick and lucky as they used to be. Also—justice doesn't seem to be the popular subject it once was, when I was young.

As you may already know: Jane is the same, good old Jane for the moment, recovering slowly, however, from an exploratory operation which did her body much violence. The exploration resulted in the discovery and removal of two small tumors which were not up to anything immediately dangerous. Her suffering makes me so damned sorrowful.

Ah me. Well—give me something to look forward to. Promise that you'll do your best to be here eleven months from now.

Love as always—

Kurt Vonnegut

May 12, 1985
New York City

To William Amos

Dear William Amos—

   I thank you for your interest in my work.

   Howard Campbell in my novel *Mother Night* was inspired by
two people, neither one of them Ezra Pound. One was the
Englishman "Lord Haw Haw," who became a funny and interesting and ultimately terrible radio propagandist for the Nazis.
His name was Joyce, and he was hanged, I think. I used to listen
to him on the radio, fascinated, and to speculate about what sort
of American might have done what he did. The other inspiration
was a seeming American who tried to recruit American prisoners
of war for the German Army, for combat on the Russian front. I
met him when I was a PW in Dresden, and my guess is that he
was a German actor. Still, I played with the idea of his being what
he claimed to be.

   So far as I know, there was no American turncoat on the
order of England's Joyce. I knew about Pound, of course, but he
wouldn't have been much use to me in *Mother Night*. I wanted
my man to be fairly ordinary. Pound was off-scale for at least two
reasons: he was cracked, and he was a world class artist. A third
reason: Pound was a passionate anti-semite. He was sincere in his
anti-semitism, as Campbell was not. This, in my opinion, made
Campbell a more alarming war criminal than Lord Haw Haw or
Pound.

   Yours truly,
   Kurt Vonnegut

August 5, 1985

New York City

TO JOSÉ AND MARIA PILAR DONOSO

Dear Pepé and Maria Pilar—

I wrote you a gloomy note, did I? Don't remember. At any
rate, I'm cheerful enough right now. The trouble was, probably,
that I couldn't finish a novel called *Galapagos*. Well, it's all
done now, and due out on October 4, coincidentally Nanny's
birthday. I also wrote a play this summer, finished it only a week
ago. The next problem is to get some theater people to read it
and tell me why it will not work. I would rather be a playwright
than anything, mainly because playwrights are allowed to smoke
backstage.

On the day I finished the play, Edith called to say that she
would be marrying on Cape Cod on September 14th. The
groom-to-be is a darling man she has been living with for about
the past three years—a John Squibb. They grew up together on
Cape Cod, and he is a Jack-of-all-trades, a housebuilder, a cabinetmaker and so on. Edith by golly actually makes a pretty good
living as an artist. Who said the Age of Miracles was past?

I see John Irving a lot, since his summer home is only a few
hundred meters from mine out on Long Island. He had me to
supper the other night with Gail Godwin. Were you and I ever
lucky, Pepé, to have such gifted students!

About the International P.E.N. Congress in January here, the
first in twenty years: P.E.N. itself doesn't have the money to bring
you and Maria Pilar here, but we are hoping that Knopf does.
They surely owe you that. There is no Government money behind
the Congress, since the political interference would be intolerable.
I imagine you Chileans have some idea what I'm talking about.

Love as always—

Kurt Vonnegut

November 15, 1985
New York City

To Donald Fiene

Saul Steinberg was a Romanian-born American artist best known for his cartoons in The New Yorker. *His work was exhibited in fine-arts museums and galleries.*

Dear Don—

Saul Steinberg said to me that the painter Ingres was hobbled by too much talent. You are hobbled by too much to write about. You help me understand why novelists are such avoiders of adventure. Real life could swamp them so easily. So not living is a sacrifice we make.

I thank you for the friendly review. I hadn't seen it. The best review so far was in *Punch*. Frivolous scientific speculation is an art form little appreciated over here. Critics who have come up through English departments don't like science mixed in with novels. They feel it should be kept in separate volumes, like *Lives of a Cell* and *The Double Helix* and so on. Victorians felt the same way about sex. It should be sequestered in manuals for specialists, they thought, it could so easily spoil a tale.

Did you notice that Rita's friend Irina Grivnina was finally sprung from the Worker's Paradise, and has now taken up residence with her family in the Netherlands? I had a little to do with that, I think, writing Dobrynin frequently about my dear friend in Moscow, and getting his embassy to O.K. my invitations, all plastered with stamps and seals, for the whole family to come visit me. When they finally got out, I sent him a copy of *Galapagos,* most respectfully and gratefully inscribed. He wrote back, thanking me for the book, and saying, as though an afterthought, that my dear friend had left his country.

Cheers—

Kurt Vonnegut

April 28, 1986
[New York City]

To Donald Fiene

Carole Baron was a longtime publisher at Dell/Delacorte who Kurt credited with helping sales of his books, and who had edited his most recent book, Galápagos. *She later returned to Dell as president and publisher.*

Dear Don—

I am especially sorry to be a lazy correspondent in your case, since you never send me anything but first rate material. You find time to be vivid in real life. Somehow I don't, and most novelists don't. Such is the territory. A novel is an enormous ball of cotton batting which sops up thousands of hours, giving almost nothing but a little lint in return. Fuck all.

As for the unbelievable scheme for the hero's getting information out of Germany in *Mother Night:* I hated it myself, but thought I had better not waste time fixing it, since the magazines had just gone out of business, and I was suddenly in the position of having to write a whole book in order to get what used to be my fee for just one story. Oh, well—people seem to find clunky flaws like that endearing. My friend John Updike, who was called "the perfect a-plus student" by James Dickey, would never make mistakes like that, and so may seem inhuman.

I am certainly trying to be more careful with the book about fictitious abstract expressionist painters I am now working on. I can afford to be. I am understandably uneasy just now about who might like the book, who I am writing it for, since my great editor at Dell, Carole Baron, left suddenly for a more congenial situation at St. Martin's. She left because Doubleday, which bought Dell and me for 35 million bucks, is in the process of liquidation, the Doubleday heirs never having cared much for books, and having let their legacy sink slowly back into the primordial ooze. I am the one name author still listed among their assets, and am presently acting in the worst possible faith in order to break my contract. [. . .]

Cheers—

Kurt Vonnegut

December 14, 1986
[New York City]

To Donald Fiene

Dear Don—

[. . .] Here is a thought I have about Salinger and Updike and Cheever and Barthelme and Perelman and O'Hara and a lot of others, which I don't intend to use in any way, but which might make a useful starting point for a critic like yourself: They were all members of the only literary extended family in history, which is *The New Yorker*. One of the things Capote said to me which rings absolutely true is that Salinger wanted to be published by *The New Yorker* or nobody. I am not a member of that unique family, nor is Mailer, nor Arthur Miller, and on and on. And yet members of that family will talk to the likes of us about who will succeed Shawn, who *should* succeed him, and so on, as though we gave a good god damn. My point is that membership in that family might skew a writer's career more significantly than his or her choice of a spouse or two. Or than his or her being a Catholic or a Jew or a homosexual or whatever. As an anthropologist much interested in the rewards and punishments applied in small groups, I feel that this is well worth looking into.

Cheers—

Kurt Vonnegut

December 28, 1986
New York City

To Helen and Walter A. Vonnegut, Jr.

Dear Colonel and Helen—

Another story has ended: that of Jane Cox (Vonnegut) Yarmolinsky, who died after a five-year-bout with cancer of the abdomen on December 19th—at about eight o'clock in the evening. This was in her home in Washington, D.C. She was comatose, and simply stopped breathing, with close friends and relatives at hand. She was cremated the next day, and had a really swell funeral on Sunday, the 21st. My brother and I were there, and all six of her children with their mates, and three of her five grandchildren. She was a devout Episcopalian at the end, but the rules of that religion were broken for her funeral, in that there were eulogies—by her saintly husband Adam, and by three of her children, Mark, Nannie and Steve Adams.

I thought you should know, since we were all so close in Chicago so many years ago.

Much love—

Kurt Vonnegut

P.S. Her ashes will be scattered over her beloved Cape Cod in the springtime. Amazingly, she wrote a book during her five years of sickness—about our adopting the Adams kids, and what our family life was like after that. I haven't seen it yet, and will have a hard time reading it for obvious reasons. Several publishers are interested in it, I hear. I am told that it looks at the sunny side of every major incident, no matter how troubling that incident may really have been at the time. She was *in character* to the end!

December 29, 1986

New York City

To Dorothy (Mrs. John D.) MacDonald

Dear Dorothy—

I am so sorry about John. I lectured at the New College down there a few months back, and asked the audience if there was anyone who knew how John was. I was told by an older man that he was much better, and I was glad to hear it.

I enclose two quite acceptable obituaries which you may not have seen. I first heard of John's death on the news late last night. The obituaries reminded me yet again of how incomplete, how *seriously* incomplete literary history must always be. How few of us know that John and I were members of an unacknowledged school of writing rooted in the Golden Age of Magazine Fiction which followed World War Two, and that, for us, "Knox Burger" and "Ken Littauer" and "Max Wilkinson" and so on were names with which to conjure.

Dear Max, who was already contemplating his own death when I met him a third of a century ago, talked even back then about "all the good people on the other side." He meant those who had died, of course. And the population of Heaven, which now includes those two great friends, John and Max, continues to grow by leaps and bounds. I don't scoff at the idea of Heaven nearly as much as I used to. My first wife Jane, whom you met, I think, and with whom I remained on friendly terms, herself crossed over about eight days before John.

John's reputation as a writer was sky high at the time of his death. The huge body of absolutely first rate work he gave the world is sure to remain popular well into the next millennium.

Think of that! I hope he knew I loved and admired him, and was grateful for the encouragement he gave me from time to time.

Very sadly yours,

Kurt Vonnegut

P.S. If our school of writing had a name, what would be a good one? I suggest this: "The Professionals."

January 8, 1987

[New York City]

To Paul Engle

Dear Paul—

Giving Paul Engle advice on writing is surely an extravagant case of coals to Newcastle. Be that as it may: the problem with writing autobiographies nowadays is that people under fifty don't know anything about the past, so you have to explain *everything*. Not only do you have to explain the Chicago Renaissance: you have to explain the Italian Renaissance, too. It really is almost that awful. And literary reputations die with authors now. Nelson Algren? Irwin Shaw? James Jones? Truman Capote? Who? Who? And you have some stories to tell us, do you, about Vachel Lindsay and Edgar Lee Masters and Theodore Dreiser? Who? Who? Who? All you can do, I guess, is be satisfied with a tiny audience. So what else is new?

[. . .] My first wife Jane died after a five year bout with cancer on December 19, with, amazingly, her very closest friend, Mrs. Donoso, by her bedside. Jane remarried, as you may know, and was Mrs. Adam Yarmolinsky. We remained good friends, and had a wonderful long talk on the telephone only three days before she died.

Cheers—

Kurt Vonnegut

January 20, 1987
[New York City]

To Peter Reed

Dear Peter—

I thank you for your friendly invitation to make a personal
appearance out that way. I'm sorry I have to say that I have
dropped out of that trade *entirely,* having gone at it hot and
heavy for many years. I came home from my tour last fall so tired
and annoyed that I canceled all future engagements, including
one at Cedar Falls next spring. You know how much I like Cedar
Falls, so this is serious.

I'm much relieved not to have to do it any more. It called for
an exhibitionistic sort of craziness which puzzled and scared me
some.

I am about a month from finishing another novel—this one
about an Abstract Expressionist painter in his seventies, looking
back on the founding of that school of radical non-representation.
It is called *Bluebeard* because he has a painting locked away
which nobody is supposed to look at until he's dead. I wish to hell
I knew what the book is *really* about. I should *know* by this time.
My God—I'm on page 305!

Bundle up out there—
    Kurt Vonnegut

March 5, 1987
New York City

To Donald Fiene

*Stephen Jay Gould, a professor of zoology and geology at Harvard and
a prolific author, was one of the leading scientists of his time. Among
his books was* Ever Since Darwin: Reflections in Natural History,
which made his opinion of Galápagos *especially relevant to Kurt.*

William Keough was professor of English at Fitchburg State College in Massachusetts and author of Punch Lines: The Violence of American Humor.

Dear Don—

[. . .] I was glad to learn of Gould's mentioning *Cat's Cradle.* We tend to like each other. We're both primitives, it seems to me, Grandma Moses of the intellect. He came to hear me lecture at M.I.T. a couple of years ago, and we had supper afterwards. I was scared shitless of what he might say about *Galapagos,* and didn't ask his opinion. But he dropped me a note, saying it was pretty good science, and that the fur-covered human mutant is fairly common.

I just finished reading a Ph.D. thesis by a guy your age named William Keough. It's about violence in American humor, and he examines Twain, Bierce, Lardner, and myself. The others wound up in despair over human nature, he says, and implies that I can scarcely do otherwise. One possible escape route is open to me, however, which was not evident to the other three. That is the extraordinarily important idea (I only now understand) which I picked up from Anthropology: culture is a gadget which can be tinkered with like a Model-T Ford. Our President supposes that his brain is producing his opinions. His brain in fact is soaked in a culture, and has never bothered to examine its ingredients. He oozes rather than thinks. [. . .]

Cheers—

Kurt Vonnegut

April 1, 1987
New York City

To José and Maria Pilar Donoso

Dear Maria Pilar & Pepé—

It doesn't feel good to have close and old friends materialize and vanish like the Cheshire cat. If you were to pick a time to do it, you could not have chosen better than the time of Jane's dying and death and the few weeks afterwards. I had important talks with both of you. At least we did not waste time talking about lightweight things.

I enclose my Requiem, Pepé, and ask you to consider it as continuous with Western Civilization. My ancestors, like yours, were Roman Catholics who for compelling reasons became free thinkers, children of the Enlightenment. So my Requiem, as clumsy as it may be, is not a symptom of AIDS, cocaine, illiteracy and Rock and Roll.

Cheers—

Kurt Vonnegut

April 26, 1987
New York City

To Jerome Klinkowitz

The reference to the "perfect fit, so our eyes must have met . . ." was in response to Klinkowitz asking Kurt if he had been welcomed by British P.O.W.s in the same camp described by the British RAF pilot Geoff Taylor in his book Piece of Cake. *Taylor wrote about an influx of American prisoners into the camp, just as Vonnegut wrote about Billy Pilgrim being welcomed by the British P.O.W.s in the German prison camp where he was sent in* Slaughterhouse-Five.

Dear Jerry—

It is a perfect fit, so our eyes must have met, and he may very briefly have tried to welcome and comfort me. But surely no friendships were formed, no names memorized. Those of us who smoked quickly became wheedling vermin who begged for tobacco along with the precious food. I think he may be off by a couple of days, although he probably kept a diary, and I did not. We spent Christmas locked in boxcars, I remember. The guards outside probably told us it was Christmas. Otherwise we would have had no idea what the date was. My woozy recollection is that we did not reach IVB until five days after that. What could be more trivial, since that war is entirely movies now. And my wife Jill spent a year as a photographer in Vietnam, and I have to laugh when she talks about it and finds that she might as well be a veteran of the Spanish–American War.

I have just read Bill Keough's thesis about violence in American humor, which deals with Twain, Bierce, Lardner and me. It's a beauty, although I am quite an anti-climax. But he says that all of us have found ourselves trapped in box canyons with our jokes, with no notions of how the human condition might be improved. And several critics of my work have said that I give the illusion of knowing how things might be revised without being able to describe such revisions. In short, I am, like many failed pieces of serious music, all gestures, all unkept promises, with no stirring resolutions to come. Conventional resolutions in humorless books, incidentally, consist of the acceptance of some option which the society has offered for quite some time: a meaningful death, the kicking of an addiction, the uncritical acceptance of some religion, becoming a hermit, returning to a person one has loved all along, and so on. Or tending the sick, or helping the poor, or shooting the person who seems most responsible for all the misery.

When I thought I was going to become a biologist of some kind, and in fact studied bacteriology, I wanted to cure diseases, and my heroes were Pasteur and the like. I was going to find out what made people sick. I had no gift for real science, however, and after the Second World War went into pseudo-science, all talk and few measurements, which is to say anthropology. And one enchantingly suggestive thing I learned (attitude I assumed), was that culture was as separate from the brain as a Model T Ford, and could be tinkered with. It was an easy jump from there to believing, as I do, that a culture can contain fatal poisons which can be identified: respect for firearms, for example, or the belief that no male is really a man until he has had a physical showdown of some kind, or that women can't possibly understand the really important things which are going on, and so on. What could be simpler, or, perhaps, more simple minded?

K

September 2, 1987

[New York City]

To Harry James Cargas

The origin of the new Requiem Kurt wrote is described in Fates Worse Than Death, *and his Requiem is published in the book's appendix. It was set to music by composer Edgar Grana and translated into Church Latin by NYU professor John F. Collins.*

Dear Harry James—

[. . .] You remind me spiritually of another Catholic, Heinrich Böll, who was carrying war guilt almost all by himself by the time he died. His neighbors scorned him for that, he said. They scarcely spoke to him. One thing I seem to be doing all by myself is pointing out in speeches that the German swastika was considered a cross, and was called one. You want to join me in making this revelation? It is wrong that people are comforted by the belief that its meaning is anti-Christian.

Sorry about your illness, but I can't help feeling that all you people who were super-jocks in childhood were simply begging for infirmities in late middle age.

Did I tell you I wrote a new Requiem, a secular humanist job which is a paraphrase of the Council of Trent monstrosity? I did it in English, and had it translated into Church Latin by an NYU professor. It took a composer I met on jury duty two years to set the Latin to music, and we may get a world premiere in a Unitarian Church in Buffalo, which has a very ambitious choral pro-

gram. Do you hate Unitarians? How can you, when you know
perfectly well the scruffy origins of the trinitarian nonsense?

Cheers—

Kurt Vonnegut

December 27, 1987
New York City

To Robert Weide

*Weide had written Kurt that he had begun work on a documentary of
Laurel and Hardy.*

*Dick Shawn was a stand-up comedian who performed in night-
clubs around the world and appeared in more than thirty movies.
Mort Sahl was a popular stand-up comedian whose attacks on the
Warren Commission Report's finding that Lee Harvey Oswald alone
was John F. Kennedy's assassin were among the political critiques that
made him controversial.*

Dear Bob—

How can I not be touched and flattered by your continued interest in my work? I now have a videotape, by the way, of the
only visible thing I've done worth watching, an onstage performance at a fund-raiser for PEN a couple of years ago. The rest is
silence.

As for Laurel and Hardy: to find yet another excuse to televise
their perfect works has to be O.K., like doing the Nutcracker yet
again at Christmastime. Nobody gets sick of perfection, if he or
she can get a few months of rest between performances. Two
other comedians who are in the first rank with Laurel and Hardy:
Jack Benny and Buster Keaton. All humanity is the audience they
were able to keep in mind. Almost nobody can do that, so I tell
writing students of mine not to try. I mock the wish to do it as
being like opening a window on a wintry night and trying to

make love to everybody on the planet. I tell them to make love to those they know.

Lenny Bruce made love to a few pals from childhood and youth, and the rest of us could listen, if we wanted. Heller still does that. I saw Sahl in his recent appearance here, and he had opened a window and was trying to make love to the world. He couldn't begin to do it right. Jackie Mason is now onstage making love in his mind to Jews in the Catskills, and I find it a privilege to hear what he says to them. I am sorry you didn't make a documentary on Dick Shawn, but nobody knew he was going to drop dead just at the moment he had got the hang, somehow, of being genuinely planetary. I caught his one-man show in Los Angeles a couple of years back, and talked to him afterwards at supper. He was dazed, just as Jonah must have been when the whale spit him up on the beach where God thought he should be, whether Jonah himself wanted him to be there or not.

Cheers—

Kurt Vonnegut

P.S.—My requiem, in Latin and set to the 48 minutes of music by Edgar Grana, will be given its premiere in Buffalo on March 13, 1988, with a huge chorus and four synthesizers provided by the Unitarians there.

August 17, 1988
New York City

To Jack Nicholson

Dear Mr. Nicholson—

A very tough and funny movie script has been written for my novel *Breakfast of Champions,* the first of my works to hit number one on the Best Seller List. That book in paperback still sells tens of thousands of copies every year.

The producers of the film, Max Youngstein and Bruce Campbell, asked me what actor should play the leading character, Dwayne Hoover, a very successful Pontiac dealer, and owner of a couple of fast food franchises, too, in an Ohio factory town of slightly under one-hundred thousand people. He is slowly going to pieces because of the success of foreign cars in the American market, because his son has grown up to be a flamboyant homosexual piano player in the local Holiday Inn cocktail lounge on the Interstate, and so on. If you know the book, then you know that he blows up spectacularly during the town's first Festival of the Arts.

I told Max and Bruce that only you could project the charismatic, absolutely beautiful, one-hundred per cent American deep-seated insanity which afflicts this man.

Thus have they sent you and nobody else the script which, again, I think is a honey.

Please do us the honor of reading it.

Very truly yours—

Kurt Vonnegut

November 16, 1988

New York City

To William G. Kennedy, Fanelon Falls
Secondary School, Fanelon Falls, Ontario

Dear Mr. Kennedy—

My publisher, Dell, has just sent me a copy of your letter of October 19 regarding the attempted censorship of my book *Welcome to the Monkey House*. You and R.A. Baxendale have my sympathy, and I am honored by your inclusion of some of my short stories in your curriculum. Your laws differ from ours in many respects, so I can offer no legal wisdom. I can only say that efforts by groups of parents to get certain works of literature withheld from an entire school community are common in this country, and have in every case been thwarted by decisions of higher courts.

Some primitive facts which may be of some slight use to you when talking about me to primitive people: I have seven children, four of them adopted. The six who are full grown are monogamous, sober members of their communities—a cabinetmaker, a television writer, a pediatrician, an airline captain, a successful painter, and a successful printmaker. They would have heard the word fuck by the time they were six, whether they had had me for a father or not. As for shit and piss: they spoke of almost nothing else when they were only three, which was surely their idea as much as mine. One man wrote me that he could learn more about sex from talking to a ten-year-old than he could from reading my collected works, which is true. Nowhere have I celebrated the use of any sort of drug, nor sexual promiscuity, nor bad citizenship.

I express dismay at violence and humorlessness in everything I write, and in my ordinary life as well. I celebrate compassion and tenderness, and parents of every persuasion should be happy to have me do that, and especially those who are enthusiastic about the Beatitudes. Speaking, as the censors do, of giving "a five year old a hand-grenade": do the censors allow lethal weapons in their homes, or tell war stories within the hearing of children, or allow children to watch TV cartoons where the mouse blows up the cat, or drops a great weight on it from on high, or digs a pit for it lined with spikes! Do they shoot animals, and then show the bullet-riddled corpses as though they were something to be proud of? I never did. As I have already said, six of my children are full grown now, and are admittedly sexy with their legal mates, and are also toilet trained, thanks to all the talk early on about shit and piss. But they surely are not violent.

Cheers,

    Kurt Vonnegut

November 30, 1988

New York City

TO LUKAS FOSS

Lukas Foss was a German-born American composer, conductor, and pianist. He had set to music texts by poets W. H. Auden and A. E. Housman, and composed the opera The Jumping Frog of Calaveras County *based on the story by Mark Twain.*

Dear Lukas—

I'm not a Christian either, but you have to admit it's one hell of a story. So:

> Angels said come to this stable rude,
> Where deep in the hay, which is cattle's food,
> Lies a baby who sleeps full of milk so sweet,
> More precious than rubies from head to feet.
> Here is my guide, sang the Angels, to Paradise.
> Am I foolish to come here, or am I wise?

> This is the place,
> He is here, He is here.
> Those who would kill Him
> Are near, are near.
> So keep Him our secret,
> So dear, so dear.
> And the Mother's name is May-ree.

> Starlight did wake me from deathlike sleep,
> So filled me with joy I did laugh and weep.
> I did follow that star to this rustic shed,
> That my starving soul might at last be fed.
> Here is my guide, said the starlight, to Paradise.
> Am I foolish to come here, or am I wise?

This is the place,
He is here, He is here.
Those who would kill Him
Are near, are near.
So keep Him our secret,
So dear, so dear.
And the Mother's name is May-ree.

Season's greetings,
    Kurt Vonnegut

                                                    January 16, 1989
                                                    New York City

To Robert Weide

*Bob Elliott and Ray Goulding were a radio comedy team known as
"Bob and Ray," who were on the air in various formats for five decades. Kurt was a fan of their satirical humor, which was full of spoofs
and parodies, and Weide had sent him tape cassettes of their show as
a Christmas gift.*

Dear Roberto—
    [. . .] The Bob and Ray stuff is one part of an adventure in
Jungian synchronicity which has enabled me at last to get going
on another book with some enthusiasm. For two years I wasn't
getting anywhere, and then those tapes gave me permission to
be, like them, intelligently ridiculous. Now I think I'm O.K. I
sure wouldn't have been O.K., though, if they and a couple of
books, one on kinship and the other about the outbreak of
World War One, hadn't arrived from nowhere in the nick of
time.
    Cheers—
        Kurt Vonnegut

March 12, 1989

New York City

To Richard Vonnegut

Richard Vonnegut was one of Kurt's cousins in Indianapolis. William H. Hudnut was mayor of Indianapolis for four terms, presiding over a time of great growth of the city's downtown area.

Dear Richard—

What a useful, meaty correspondent you are! And how *moving* on occasion. I choked up when, in a letter a few months ago, you said in effect that you would gladly give up Freethinking if you could only see your son again.

As you know, I have spent and finally wasted the past three years in trying to construct a novel around a Freethinker. Many problems with story-telling are purely mechanical, which most people don't realize. Working on a story is a lot like working on a Model-T. The son of a bitch has stopped. How can I get it to go again? In order to continue to make a living, I have given up on the Freethinker theme. As becomes more obvious every day, good citizenship is highly unpopular.

You speak of cheap paper, so I have a surprise for you. I have been part of a movement here to get publishers to print books on acid-free paper, so that they will last for three hundred years instead of thirty. We thought that this would make books cost even more, and that publishers would have to eat this cost for the good of civilization. It turns out that acid-free paper costs *not one bit more*, and that it was simply absent-mindedness, laziness and ignorance which caused publishers to accept what the paper manufacturers, for reasons unclear, were glad to stick them with. Paper was paper. Because of this period of thoughtlessness about paper, the New York Public Library now has thirty-two miles of books consuming themselves. It also has books printed in Europe three-hundred years ago which look as though they had come off the presses yesterday.

To refresh your memory: I sent copies of the Freethinker tract reprint to The New York Public Library, to the Library of Congress, to Jack Mendelson, who will surely take good care of it and show it to others, to the Episcopal Bishop of New York, Paul Moore, who is about to retire and who spent many years in Indianapolis, and to the University of Northern Iowa, in Cedar Falls. A relatively young professor there named Jerome Klinkowitz has collected a lot of my work there, and I thought he should have the tract, too, and the family tree.

What Mayor Hudnut says between the lines is that Freethinking does not satisfy because it is too lonely. Most people can't stand that much loneliness. I just barely can.

Love as always—
Kurt Vonnegut

March 28, 1989
New York City

To Peter Matthiessen

Peter Matthiessen won the National Book Award for nonfiction for The Snow Leopard *and for fiction for his novel* Shadow Country.

Dear Peter—

I thank you for having your publisher send me *On the River Styx*. The title story was the only one I'd read before, and "Travelin Man" is maybe the best story I'll ever read. You made me ponder yet again over this past Easter weekend, which we spent at the Hotel Alexander on Miami Beach, how much closer to Nature you have lived than have I. I was sitting on the balcony of our 16th floor suite at sunrise, and a big hawk flew past me, eight feet from the tip of my nose, with what was maybe a starling in its claws. Raptors love those garish hotels, of course, and nest on top of them. A cliff is a cliff, and in Florida men have to build them. But my point is that, in the Jungian nick of time, Nature came to me.

You made me marvel, too, at how easily you can climb inside black people. I already knew you could do that, but still don't know enough about your life to understand how you learned to do that. I found out something more about your life, anyway, but not that, from your dance on razor blades in "Lumumba Lives." No—I am not taking the story as autobiography. I am saying that anybody is bound to reveal a lot about himself when he dances on razor blades. I myself avoid that exercise.

This much we have in common, incidentally: I too grew up in a house with the very best books and firearms.

I once met Tennessee Williams in the steambath of a health club near here, and I broke his spirit by telling him how much I admired *A Streetcar Named Desire* and *The Glass Menagerie*. He wasn't writing that well any more. I run no risk of doing that to you by saying that a story you wrote thirty-two years ago is the best thing in this collection, which it probably isn't. You are a writer unlike Williams, of remarkable steadiness and authority no matter what age you happen to be. What a novelty! What a relief!

Cheers,

Kurt Vonnegut

April 23, 1989
New York City

To George Strong

George Strong was one of the other American P.O.W.s who, like Vonnegut, survived the firebombing of Dresden.

Dear George Strong—

I'm home again, to the extent that anybody's really got a home anymore. Maybe my fundamental home is in Dresden, since that is where my great adventure took place, and where one hundred of us selected at random were bonded by tremendous violence into a brotherhood—and then dispersed to hell and gone. Your seeking me out and greeting me like a brother was a profoundly important event for me. So I thank you for that.

You, it turns out, are our meticulous historian, so I enclose some documents which may be of interest to you. I thought when I published *Slaughterhouse-Five* so long ago that I would hear from everybody who had been there with us. I only heard from three: Bill Burns, who is in broadcasting in Cincinnati, "Frenchy" LeClaire, an admittedly alcoholic house painter in New Hampshire, who died mainly of booze about fifteen years ago, and Dick Coyle, a contented high school English teacher and football coach in Ohio, who has a bad cancer in remission. He still goes to work, and says, "You play the cards they deal you." My closest buddy in I&R, 2nd Bn. Hq., 423rd Inf. Rgt., B.V. O'Hare, I never lost touch with. As I told you, he is a hot shot criminal lawyer, a former D.A., and can be reached at 1431 Easton Road, Hellertown, Pa. 18015. He smokes even worse than I do, and has had a throat operation, but is still in active practice. I'm ashamed to say that I don't have addresses for the rest. This is an intolerably sloppy office I run, with me as the only employee.

In the last chapter of what may be my last book, *Bluebeard,* I describe the valley we came to after we walked away from the schoolhouse at Hellendorf. Six of us appropriated a Wehrmacht horse and wagon, and traveled around for several days unimpeded by anyone. We made it back to the slaughterhouse, I'm not sure why, and were arrested by Russians, who locked us up in the barracks of what used to be a training camp for Army Engineers. That was outside Meissen, I think. Then we were taken in Model A trucks to the Elbe at Halle, and traded one-for-one for subjects of the U.S.S.R. held by the Americans on the other side. Many of these, including Gypsies and Ukrainian turncoats, I heard later, were shot or hanged almost immediately. What fun!

I enclose the original of a letter from Robert G. Allen, 1212 56th Street, Des Moines, Iowa, 50311, since it is hard enough to read without being a Xerox. The names he lists mean nothing to me, but may ring bells with you. Guys I wish I could see again: Bob Lehr, Bob Kelton, Jim Donnini, Richard E. Davis. They are as silent as the tomb. Mike Pallaia (spelling?) and Joe Crone (Billy Pilgrim) died in Dresden, of course. And the nice Italian kid I mentioned, whose name I've forgotten, was accidentally shot by an Italian who had just found a loaded Luger in a ditch. So what are we up to: maybe fifteen per cent now accounted for?

Fraternally yours,

Kurt Vonnegut

April 25, 1989

New York City

To Don Farber

John D. MacDonald (referred to here as "John D.") was a prolific writer of crime and suspense novels, most known for his "Travis McGee" series, set in Florida, where MacDonald lived. He was named a Grand Master of the Mystery Writers of America, and in 1980 his novel The Green Ripper *won the National Book Award for Mystery.*

Don—

John D.'s wife died recently, as you probably know. The son is arranging a memorial service, and asking people like me to submit something to be read aloud there. This is my contribution. KURT

There are lots of good little families which go unnoticed by even parochial little histories. One such had John D. and myself and our dear wives as members, as children, if you will, and with editors and agents in New York City as parental figures. When we came home from the Second World War, and having published nothing, we were determined to prosper by selling stories to the then exceedingly rich and popular magazines. When I say "we," I include the wives and eventually the children we had, since freelance story-telling was and remains very much a family enterprise. Without our mates, we would have sunk like stones.

And again, we still would have sunk like stones if it had not been for strangers in New York City, far away, who knew one hell of a lot more about story-telling than we did in the beginning, although they themselves were not writers, and who volunteered to be our wise elders in a much larger family. They would become in time our most powerful supporters and, along with their wives, our dearest friends. To speak now of wives as natural assistants to working men is archaic, I realize. But the extended family to which John D. and I belonged was a creation of a more aggressively patriarchal society. For good or ill, that is the way things were back then. John D. and Dorothy are now both gone, still beloved and sorely missed. Also gone is our agent, well-known to many of you in Sarasota, Max Wilkinson, and his wife Mary, and his partner, Kenneth Littauer, a Colonel at the age of twenty-three in World War One, incidentally, and his wife Helen. Still alive is Knox Burger, an agent now, who, when fiction editor of *Collier's* Magazine, insisted that John D. and I and many returning veterans like us could become effective writers if we did not give up, if we kept on and on.

So we kept on and on. John D. achieved greatness, and so did Dorothy. They were one flesh, and God love them.

Kurt Vonnegut
      Manhattan

June 4, 1989

New York City

TO SHELDON ZALAZNICK

Sheldon Zalaznick was managing editor of Forbes *magazine.*

Dear Mr. Zalaznick—

The personal tales anyone tells about good or bad manners in this country are sure to depend on what the teller looked like to others at the time, and what the others looked like to him or her—rich or poor, black or white or whatever, sober or high as a kite on god-knows-what, or tall or short or whatever. Ask Tom Wolfe.

Considering the age-old tendency of shorter persons to treat taller ones with more than average politeness: I am reminded of the United States Army's making my friend the gentle and shambling poet George Starbuck a Military Policeman, simply because he was tall. George told me afterwards that he was actually quite a weak guy with no fighting skills, but never met anything but politeness in the exercise of his duties. I myself have an impractical build like his, resembling a home-made stepladder. You would have thought that somebody would have slugged me by now, or at least dared me to fight, but nobody has—because I'm tall.

As luck would have it, I have recently come into social contact with several persons whose names are well known to readers of financial journals, whose most striking dimension is not altitude, who are commonly quite short, in fact, but who are awe-inspiring for being freshly minted billionaires. Old joke: "What do you call a six-hundred-pound gorilla? You call him 'Sir.' "

I asked Joseph Heller if he had any impolite feelings when being regaled by persons who on that very day may have made more money than the total earnings of the great and permanent cultural treasure *Catch-22*. He replied that he had one thing they could never have. The nature of that something I now withhold until the end of this essay, and so make a radical change in subject by asserting that American manners have improved considerably since we have taken to drinking a lot less alcohol when away from home. We drink less because we don't want the police to revoke our puberty by taking our drivers' licenses away.

Speaking only of members of my own profession: male writers don't slug and insult each other the way they used to, since they aren't a bunch of drunks any more. They would be drinking less even if it weren't for the sudden humorlessness of the judiciary with respect to driving while under the influence. Not just male writers, but male artists of every sort, are no longer pressured to prove that they are real men, even though they have artistic sensibilities. As I've said elsewhere, my father was a gun nut like Ernest Hemingway, mainly to prove that he wasn't effeminate, even though he was an architect and a painter. He didn't get drunk and slug people. Shooting animals was enough.

But male American artists don't even have to shoot off guns anymore. They can even be homosexuals, and the hell with it. This is good.

It is also good, which is to say intelligent and humane, that we are much politer to people of other races and sub-races than we used to be, and even to the animals, what's left of them, which my father and Hemingway used to [kill].

Kurt Vonnegut

October 24, 1989
New York City

To Marc Leeds

Marc Leeds is author of The Vonnegut Encyclopedia: An Authorized Compendium, *and editor of* The Vonnegut Chronicles: Interviews and Essays.

Dear Marc—

I'm relieved to hear from you after all this time. I thought maybe something had happened in Iowa which really pissed you

off. I couldn't imagine what that might have been. You have made
me so happy that I give you permission to address me by my first
name. You might recall that you used to be on a first-name basis
with Loree Rackstraw, too, at the University of Northern Iowa, and
Peter Reed, at the University of Minnesota, who thought you were
bright and nice, and might be able to help you get a better job.

Be that as it may:

I regularly lift the names of characters from short stories, not to
show off the breadth of my reading but to make sure they are O.K.
for persons of such and such a nationality. I also use the New York
City phone directory, especially for Hispanics. The "Karass" in
Cat's Cradle I got from a Greek's mailbox on Cape Cod.

I am aware that I enrage a lot of English professors. I haven't
a clue as to why this is so. As I said in a speech about Erich Segal
at Harvard, getting mad at him for writing *Love Story* is like getting mad at somebody for making a banana split. Same thing
goes for my stuff. Since you have chosen to immerse yourself in
trivia about me, why not go all the way and find out what sorts
of people really loathe me, and why. I suspect that I may be part
of the New Right's roster of impossible wrongos. But maybe I'm
flattering myself.

As your friend on a first name basis, I dare to suggest that you
at least consider becoming an editor rather than a teacher. You
would be a good one.

Cheers,

Kurt Vonnegut

November 13, 1989

New York City

To ROBERT WEIDE

Dearest Whyaduck—

Where indeed is your *Slaughterhouse-5*? Have you considered
cutting off an ear and sending it to a prostitute? These things take

time. Remember Herman Melville. Remember F. Scott Fitzgerald, who was completely out-of-print when he died so young. Remember Francois Villon, who made himself immortal with a mere thousand lines of poetry and then, like Ambrose Bierce, simply disappeared. It seems to me that your permanent contributions to civilization have been substantial, although the paymasters, being thugs, may never come to see that. Or care.

The important novelist Richard Yates and I used to deliver a highly unpopular joint lecture each semester at the Writers Workshop in Iowa City on the subject of how to survive in a Free Enterprise Economy by means of hackwork. We had both done a lot of that, without serious damage, seemingly, to our souls or intellects. Not that it felt good.

Speaking of hackwork: I finally heard from the bright and sweet and melancholy Marc Leeds—only a week ago. I thought maybe he had found our Iowa roadshow repellent somehow. Not at all. The trouble was that he had to take a second minimum wage teaching job at an even creepier little college in order to feed his family, so now, like the Flying Dutchman, he is forever commuting between Portsmouth, Ohio, and Johnson City, Tennessee. I hope he knows how to change a tire.

The relief agency CARE sent me to Mozambique a few weeks ago, in an effort to get some publicity in this country about the hell Freedom Fighters have been making of that place since 1976. We flew from refugee center to refugee center in light planes, since the Freedom Fighters made Swiss cheese out of anything that dared venture out of town on a highway. There was a TV crew along, and they got a lot of footage of me looking at people who were slowly starving to death. Want to see it and maybe copy it? It wouldn't cost you anything.

Love as always,

Kurt Vonnegut

THE NINETIES

After going to Mozambique at the end of 1989, Kurt wrote of the experience in *Fates Worse Than Death* that "if you color the people in old photographs of Auschwitz shades of brown and black, you would see what was commonly seen in Mozambique." When he got back and wrote his article about it, "I got a room at the old Royalton Hotel in Manhattan, and I found myself crying so hard I was barking like a dog. I didn't come close to doing that after WWII. The last time I cried (and I did it quietly, and didn't bark like a dog) was when my first wife . . . Jane died."

In 1990, *Hocus Pocus* was published, and the next year *Fates Worse Than Death,* his "autobiographical collage," came out. His next and last novel, *Timequake* (1997), was itself a kind of collage—of autobiography and fiction. He would add to his autobiographical writing at the end of the decade in an introduction to *Bagombo Snuff Box* (1999), a collection of previously uncollected short stories that Peter Reed assembled and persuaded Kurt to publish. That same year he wrote a series of twenty-one segments broadcast for WNYC (New York's public radio station), imagining himself as a "reporter on the afterlife," with interviews of the famous and infamous ranging from Shakespeare to Hitler; they were published as the book *God Bless You, Dr. Kevorkian.*

He had struggled with the writing of *Timequake,* and his long-time professor friend Jerome Klinkowitz helped him devise a category for the second draft that satisfied his editor, calling it "the autobiography of a novel." He complained he was tired of writing during these years, explaining in *Timequake* that he was feeling "like whalers Herman Melville described, who didn't talk anymore. They had said absolutely everything they could ever say."

It turned out Vonnegut would find more to say in other forms than the novel, but he also found a way to spend more time with the artistic endeavors he enjoyed, making silk-screen prints of his drawings. An invitation to speak in Lexington, Kentucky, by an old friend from his days working for General Electric started the ball rolling. Ollie Lyon, who had worked as a fellow publicist with Kurt back in the forties in Schenectady, New York, had become chair of the Midway College (Kentucky) Development Fund and invited his old friend to speak at a fund-raiser. He got Joe Petro III, a local printmaker, to design a poster for the event using Vonnegut's drawing of himself with a tear falling from his eye, which adorned the "About the Author" page of *Breakfast of Champions*. This began a partnership between Petro and the author that Vonnegut described in *Timequake*:

"I myself paint pictures on sheets of acetate with black India ink. An artist half my age, Joe Petro III, who lives and works in Lexington, Kentucky, prints them by means of the silk-screen process. . . . There may be easier, quicker, and cheaper ways to create pictures. They might leave us more time for golf, and for making model airplanes and whacking off. We should look into that. Joe's studio looks like something out of the Middle Ages. . . . I can't thank Joe enough for having me make negatives for his positives after the little radio in my head stopped receiving messages from wherever it is the bright ideas come from. Art is so *absorbing*. It is a *sopper-upper*."

In 1996, Vonnegut's *Mother Night* was made into what Kurt gratefully felt was "a swell movie" by Robert Weide, starring Nick Nolte. First published as a paperback original in 1962 for $3,000, that novel had not been reviewed at the time.

So it goes.

January 3, 1990
New York City

To Jerome Klinkowitz

The "Twayne" book was Slaughterhouse-Five: Reforming the Novel and the World *by Jerome Klinkowitz, published by Twayne's Masterwork Studies. Vonnegut had dedicated* Slaughterhouse-Five *to Mary O'Hare, the wife of Kurt's war buddy Bernard V. O'Hare. Granville Hicks was a literary critic, whose books include* The Great Tradition: An Interpretation of American Literature Since the Civil War.

Dear Jerry—

If Twayne sent me the hardcover, it got lost in the Christmas pandemonium. The softcover will do. I thank you for taking my work so seriously. I have just written a preface to a novel I'm finishing in which I object to the school of criticism which treats authors as idiot savants. But I have to admit, after reading about all I managed to put into *Slaughterhouse-5*, that I really was flying by the seat of my pants and was lucky as hell. The biggest break, I think, was Mary O'Hare. [. . .]

I had forgotten that Granville Hicks had heard me speak. It really makes a difference, I find, if people hear me speak. [. . .]

Happy New Year,

Kurt Vonnegut

March 22, 1990
New York City

To Victor Jose

This letter was to confirm Vonnegut's attendance at the fiftieth reunion of his class at Shortridge High School. He did not attend due to contracting Lyme disease.

Dear Vic—

As far as I know I'll be there on June 16. My own views of the future are famously depressing. I would a lot rather talk about the past, or hear other people talk about it. But what the heck. Whatever you say. Again I am startled by how few of us have died. Whatever happened to the bell-shaped curve?

And I say again that my high school was better than any college I attended, and I attended Cornell, Butler, Chicago, and the University of Tennessee.

Skip and Majie Failey said I could stay with them. I am plumb out of relatives out that way.

Cheers,

Kurt Vonnegut

Undated, Spring, 1990

[New York City]

To BEN HITZ

Dear old Ben—

[. . .] I have always felt honored by your friendship, since you are so intelligent and kind and funny, and extraordinarily well informed. I am an enemy of Popes, and particularly of the present incumbent, but surely not of the Catholic Church, the Family of Man. Trained in agnosticism and the social sciences, I find superficial and obvious explanations for whatever whenever possible. So I celebrate your finally responding to the hideous and low comedy historical glitch represented by the unspeakable Henry the Eighth and all that, stinking of nationalism, and rejoining, again, the Family of Man.

I am now, because of my age and steadfast lack of faith, at least a Bishop in my own religion, German Freethinking, and am, in fact, treated as a peer by the likes of Paul Moore, who has become one of my closest friends. I also get along fine with Jesuits.

It wasn't until I was sixty-four that I came across a statement by
Nietzsche that I could articulate why committed Christians and
Jews sometimes find me respectable: "Only a person of deep faith
can afford the luxury of skepticism."

Cheers, and love to you, too. Our fiftieth reunion approaches!
[. . .]

May 16, 1990

[New York City]

To Robert Weide

Dear Whyaduck—

I spoke at the Air & Space Museum in Washington a few
days ago as one of a series of lecturers on "The Legacy of Strategic Bombing." Tom Jones, a guy I was in prison with, gave
me a snapshot which I had blown up. It shows a group of us
after our guards disappeared. We took charge of a horse and
wagon abandoned by the German Army, painted American stars
and USA on it, and wandered around Sudetenland for maybe
six days before the Russians finally occupied that area. I am in
the wagon on the extreme right. O'Hare, presently dying of cancer and tuberculosis, is right in front of me, his foot up on a
rail.

Cheers—

Kurt Vonnegut

July 25, 1990

[New York City]

To Ben Hitz

Dear B.D. III—

How nice to hear that a friend from childhood has now earned
a busy and happy retirement. Well done. I recall your regret expressed in Baja that you had not become an ornithologist. There is
still time. There is still time for you to become a writer, too. I recall
that you passed the English VI test with flying colors. I would
rather read you than T.S. Eliot on the subject of Anglicanism. (Why
wasn't he laughed off the face of the Earth for transmogrifying
himself into an Englishman? You would never do that.)

Lyme disease may have been a blessing. There would have been
faces (once decoded from old age) at the reunion who would have
reminded me of insulting and demoralizing times. The disease is a
spirochete, so syph is its big brother. Doctors treating it are of necessity practicing medicine as an art, which is to say hoping and
bluffing. The best in the business (Mount Sinai Hospital in New
York) have loaded me up with anti-biotics and drugs which cause
my body to retain them longer than usual. I feel fine. We now wait
to see if the little corkscrews will go after my joints or the lining of
my heart. The Doctors told me, incidentally, that AIDS patients
supposedly cured of syphilis are coming down with it again.

Much love to you, old pal—

K

August 15, 1990

New York City

To Marc Leeds

Dear Marc—

Thanks for your friendly letter. I trust that you have received
Hocus Pocus by now, and that it will duly be fed to your incredi-

ble machinery, to what end I am at a loss to guess. In any case I
am honored by your obsession. [. . .]

In response to your question about the relationship of my
style to jazz and comedians: I don't think about it much, but,
now that you've asked, it seems right to say that my writing
is of a piece with the nightclub exhibitionism you witnessed
in Davenport, lower class, intuitive, moody, and anxious to
hold the attention of a potentially hostile audience, and quick
(like a comic or a jazz musician) to change the subject or
mood. [. . .]

Cheers,

Kurt Vonnegut

January 27, 1991

New York City

To William Rodney Allen

*William Rodney Allen is an author and professor of English at the
Louisiana School for Math, Science, and the Arts. His books include*
Understanding Kurt Vonnegut *and* Conversations with Kurt Vonne-
gut.

Dear William Rodney Allen—

Understanding Kurt Vonnegut arrived here yesterday morning
(Superbowl Eve). It is such a friendly book. I had no idea it was
in the works. I spoke at the University of Pennsylvania a few
months ago, and was startled to be introduced by a member of
the English department. That had never happened before. He
spoke so well of me! I had grown used to being treated by faculty
as though I were a crazy invited by the kids, like Timothy Leary
or G. Gordon Liddy. Faculty stayed away.

I was reminded of the sculptor Louise Nevelson, who told me
that she had to wait until she was seventy before critics would

take her seriously. "It took that long for people to realize that I really *meant* it," she said.

I am forever in your debt.

Cheers,

Kurt Vonnegut

February 15, 1991

[New York City]

To Loree Rackstraw

Kurt Vonnegut's Monkey House *was a series of seven twenty-five-minute episodes based on stories from* Welcome to the Monkey House. *The episodes were aired on Showtime in 1991 and 1992.*

Dear Loree—

I just talked to Bob Weide on the phone, and learned that you and Jerry are his consultants on *Mother Night*. That's going deep. I was most touched.

I'm back from five days solo in Monaco, where the Canadian outfit Atlantis and I were hustling a TV series to European networks. We had three half-hour episodes to show, each one costing six-hundred thousand dollars. We were the class act there, and everybody bought. Everybody else had schlock (e.g. "Mom, P.I."). Showtime will be our outlet here and in Canada. At Monaco we were after enough money to make ten more episodes. I think we got it. I'm waiting to hear. I am so stimulated that several of the episodes will be brand new stuff.

Paul Schrader the producer told me at a party a month ago that Yates was physically sick and broke. So several of us, including Woody Allen, have sent money to his agent for a rescue fund. I don't have his address. He has a lot of worthwhile admirers. I think he knows that, and that must be at least a little valuable to him.

Never mind the war. That's what I've told my daughters:
"Never mind the war."

Love as always—

Kurt

June 12, 1991

[Sagaponack, NY]

To Robert Weide

Dearest Whyaduck—

[. . .] I thank you for your richly supportive letters. I am off to a book festival in Chicago this Friday. [. . .] I will be back here at Box 27, Sagaponack 11962 on the evening of June 20, by which time Jill Krementz and [name deleted] will have been served subpoenas to defend themselves in my divorce action which charges them with adultery. He has been living in Jill's studio next door to our house in Manhattan for several months, without my even suspecting it. And, with me at home, putting Lily to bed or whatever, she would go over there "to finish her book." Such class!

I am ashamed of few things I have done in this life. But I can never forgive myself for giving darling, intelligent, good-hearted Lily such an awful mother. Lily is now eight.

As for marrying anyone else I will be 69 in November, and my father, who abused his heart and lungs with tobacco just as I have done, made it to 72, gasping and coughing for the last two years. So I would never ask any woman to commit herself to seeing me through that fast-approaching mode of departure. I feel fine, but it seems highly improbable that I really am fine.

This humiliating business with Jill has not only stopped my writing, which was going well. I can't even read a newspaper. Gutenberg might as well never have lived as far as I'm concerned.

Your continued friendship is most nourishing.

Kurt

July 17, 1991
Sagaponack, NY

To Billie Lyon

Billie Lyon was the wife of Ollie Lyon, a friend of Kurt's from the time they worked together as publicity writers for General Electric in 1949. They remained friends throughout their lives.

Dearest Billie—

I think you should know that your husband said to me in a letter forwarded from what used to be my Manhattan address that he loved you a lot. If I have calculated properly, you will be back home from the hospital, and so in reasonably good shape to deal with this shocking news.

I am sure you know that back in the days of Lillian Russell and Diamond Jim Brady and so on, fashionable women often carried canes as stylish ornaments. And I say the heck with ornaments. The wonderful thing is that you are going to be without pain for the first time in years. Buddy Hackett had heartburn from his mother's cooking every day of his life until he joined the Army. After his first day in the Army he went on sick call. He told the doctor his fire had gone out.

Ollie says that his church life comes to mean more and more to him. Harvey Cox, the Harvard Theologian, said that one of the most rewarding aspects of Christianity, when compared with other religions, was membership in a stable congregation. When I, an atheist (there's money in it), hear from a man about to get out of prison who has no family waiting for him, who wants to know what to do with freedom, I tell him, "Join a church." The risk in that, of course, is that he might join the wrong one, and wind up back in the cooler for blowing up an abortion clinic.

Cheers,

Kurt Vonnegut

September 19, 1991

Sagaponack, NY

To Sidney Offit

Sidney Offit's book was Memoir of the Bookie's Son.

Dear Sid—

These synchronous things keep happening. I don't know how much longer I can hold out as an atheist. A couple of days ago I got into a conversation about what a roman fleuve was. I wasn't sure, and neither was anybody else. So we looked it up. And then I started reading your new book, and it made your life seem a river, and I was able to exclaim, "Sid has written a roman fleuve!"

It is beautifully written, Sid, and gives me the feeling that it turned out exactly as you hoped it would. Unlike so many of us, you didn't sing sweet and have it come out sour. All credit to your parents, who are perfect children of the Enlightenment, as are you in turn. Truthfulness and a deep appreciation of scale and shapeliness. No social climbing.

I am half way through, and must depart for the West Coast to hustle my own latest book, no roman fleuve, but the sweepings from the floor of a chopshop.

Cheers,

Kurt Vonnegut

October 16, 1991

Sagaponack, NY

To Gerald L. Bepko

Gerald L. Bepko was chancellor of the Indiana University–Purdue University campus in Indianapolis, known as IUPUI. In a talk there, Vonnegut jokingly suggested that the name be changed to "Hoagy Carmichael University," in honor of the Hoosier songwriter who wrote "Stardust." The chancellor wrote him back a letter of thanks with stationery he had made up with the letterhead "Stardust University." That is the "letterhead" Kurt refers to here.

Dear Chancellor Bepko—

I am unsurprised by the grace and wit and letterhead of your letter of five days ago. I lecture at all sorts of colleges and universities, and find torpor in the schools social climbers send their kids to, and all sorts of merriment and hope in urban schools like yours, whose diplomas are not famous for being tickets to establishments of the ruling class. Your students are miles ahead of the Ivy League, since they feel no obligation to pretend that America is something it obviously isn't. I believe as you do that, fifty years from now or less, all over the world people are going to be asking where all these wonderful, realistic, honorable leaders came from, and . . .

Cheers,

Kurt Vonnegut

January 16, 1992

Sagaponack, NY

To MARC LEEDS

Dear Marc—

Rest assured that I think of you often, and that the bell you gave me is on my mantelpiece. I have been slow to answer your good letter of more than a month ago because my domestic life continues to be a shitstorm. My wife demanded a divorce, but then, as her love life failed to take the course she thought it would, she wants me back again. She thought she had another escort and meal ticket, but she was mistaken. Of all the words of mice and men, the saddest are, "It might have been."

[. . .] I should have warned you that Putnam is a bottom line operation, no more interested in art and learning than a department store. I suppose you know that soon after it published *Hocus Pocus* it became one more property of the Japanese.

On occasion, Nature can be surprisingly merciful. It has always been the case with me that when my life is a mess I can find some relief by writing. So I am, after a year of hacking out trash on my IBM Selectric, at last in control of material which can be another novel. I feel good about it. It is called *Timequake*. Like this country, it should be completely finished in another year.

Cheers,

Kurt Vonnegut

March 7, 1992
Sagaponack, NY

To Jerome Klinkowitz

The "interesting book" by Klinkowitz was Structuring the Void.

Dear Jerome—

I am honored yet again to be taken seriously in an interesting book by you. You remind me, superficially to be sure, of the late psychiatrist Edmund Bergler, who specialized in treating writers, but who himself wrote more books than had his patients in combination. It is possible that he also owned a baseball team, but I doubt it. He was said to be very good at stud poker. I never met him.

Marc Leeds has completed his concordance of my works to date, and I have told him that he makes me feel like the soul of an orange whose juice has been extracted, dehydrated, reconstituted, and now awaits a customer in a vast shopping mall. I reminded him, too, of the kidding you and Asa have received for having made a meticulous catalogue of the works of such a minor author. Ah me.

I don't consider myself minor, you'll be happy to hear. I have just been inducted into the upper chamber of the American Acad-

emy and Institute of Arts and Letters, the Academy, barely in time
to vote the Academy out of existence as a separate and nobler en-
tity. From now on, I guess, everybody in the Institute will become
a member of the Academy, and the Institute will disappear. The
first person to try to make this happen, incidentally, was William
James. He was voted down. By whom? By members of the Academy. One nice thing: I got to have my nameplate affixed to the
back of one of the numbered chairs. It used to belong to Robert
Motherwell, and then Georgia O'Keeffe, and then e e cummings
(in l.c. on his nameplate) and Douglas Southall Freeman.

Your latest book suggests to me why so many critics educated
as gentlemen at prep schools and then old, elitist colleges and universities dislike my work. Gentlemen know of the void, but do not
speak of it lest they alarm the lower classes, who might run amok.

Cheers,

Kurt Vonnegut

April 10, 1992
Sagaponack, NY

To ROBERT WEIDE

The principal character in Mother Night *is Howard W. Campbell, Jr.*
That character was played in the movie by Nick Nolte.

Dear Bob—

The news that you were going to try to interest Bill Hurt in
Mother Night was a thrill for me. I actually know him the least
little bit. The two of us went to hear a vocal group he liked a lot
after an off-Broadway performance of his maybe ten years ago.
Time flies!

What excites me when I think of his playing Howard Campbell is his extraordinarily high intelligence, and his athlete's body,
which implies that, if he wants to do so, that he can be ruthless,
as cold as ice, in order to save his own skin.

If you get to talk to him about this project, tell him that the book was inspired not only by my own experience with Germans, but by a conversation I had at a cocktail party on Cape Cod with a man who had been a career man, including pre-war, in American intelligence. He said that whenever we recruited an agent in the enemy camp, he would have to be a schizophrenic, a mentally ill person, if he was going to be any good, and that, in all probability, he would be of more use to the enemy than he was to us, or he couldn't last for long.

   Cheers,

     Kurt Vonnegut

October 16, 1992

Sagaponack, NY

To Robert Maslansky

"Larkin" was the English poet Philip Larkin.

Dear Bob—

   All of a sudden everybody is telling me about Larkin. Years ago, I remember, everybody was telling me to read Blake, Blake, Blake. So I did. Another year it was Céline, Céline.

   In my present condition, though, I find important art (even by persons as wicked as Céline) almost unbearable. Maybe that is because I myself can't produce important art, and can't stand proofs that such art is possible. Things could be worse. I could be in what used to be Leningrad, with nothing to eat and without a clue as to what the fuck to write now.

   Whether I am here or not, the back door of the ell where I write is always unlocked for you and Lee, and the heat is on and there is firewood. So at any time, just like people in the movies, you can take off for this house in the country. There is even a white cat with one blue eye and one yellow one. Such a freak, I am told, is deaf in the ear on the side of the blue eye.

I am off to the city tomorrow, Thursday, and then to the out-
skirts of Chicago, to Harper College, where I will tell my audience
about the pregnant woman who asked me in a letter if it was wrong
to bring an innocent baby into a world as awful as this one. I told
her that what made being alive almost worthwhile for me was all
the saints I met almost anywhere, people who were behaving decently in an indecent society. I will tell the audience that I hope
some among them will become saints for her child to meet. [. . .]

    Cheers,

      Kurt

                            May 7, 1993
                        Sagaponack, NY

To Knox Burger

Dear Knox—

    That's something nice I'd given up hoping for, an easy and
friendly letter from you. The brutality of the choice I was forced
to make between you and Max is now as little remembered,
thank goodness, as Shays' Rebellion or whatever.

    I lectured at Cornell a couple of weeks ago, and the editor of
The Lunatic [a Cornell University humor magazine founded in
1978] had the effrontery to treat me as a colleague and peer. The
man's crime, aside from his being among us, is his failure to go
looking for the witty writers and first rate artists who are surely
part of a student body as large and diverse as Cornell's.

    For the sake of our darling adopted daughter (half Jewish,
half Ukrainian, kind of like you, now that I think about it), Lily,
now ten, Jill and I are not divorced. I am too old, anyway, for all
the paperwork. Divorce has become as obsolescent as marriage.
My son Mark is in the process of getting divorced, and I've said
to him, "Why bother?"

    I dropped out of the *Don Juan in Hell* fiasco because I
thought it was the worst thing my hero Shaw ever wrote. I was in

OK health, but Mailer asked me to say I was sick so as not to blemish the publicity. It was little enough to ask, and it wasn't anything I hadn't done before—in the seventh and eighth grades, for example.

I was awarded a Lifetime Achievement Award by an arts support outfit in East Hampton a couple of years ago, and I said in my acceptance speech, "Does that mean I can go home now?" I wish I knew where home was.

Cheers (As Max used to say)

Kurt Vonnegut

September 2, 1993

Sagaponack, NY

To Peter Reed

Dear Peter—

[. . .] You sound generally OK. Good. I am generally OK, too, I guess, considering that the erotic dimensions of my life are in my head and nowhere else. I have now lived longer than most American writers you ever heard of. [. . .] About five years ago I thought of a promising premise for a novel, everybody's having to endure ten years of the past exactly a second time. It turns out that this is a terrific responsibility, and perhaps too much for me. I do what I can, but it never seems enough.

Fraternally yours,

Kurt Vonnegut

November 22, 1993

New York City

To John Dinsmore

John Dinsmore is a bookseller and art dealer in Lexington, Kentucky, whom Vonnegut met when he spoke at Midway College, Kentucky.

Dear John—

I like what you do for a living, and I enjoyed seeing you and
Carol out that way, and then getting such a nice letter from you
afterwards. Yes, and you and Joe Petro arc now members of a
sweet and very odd little gang which growed like Topsy, previously consisting only of Marc Leeds, Peter Reed, and Asa Pieratt.
Our motto, I think, should be the Mad Hatter's "No room! No
room!"

As for the wonderful art Joe and I made and gave to Midway:
It was obviously a pipe dream that it could be sold easily. Business is business, unfortunately. Ollie wants my publicity person to
get the word out in national news outlets that the pictures are
available and wonderful, but I don't have a publicity person. It's
just me, Lord, standing in the name of prayer. Whatever the college wants to do with the huge remainder is OK with me. Maybe
anybody who donates $250 to Midway could take the tax deduc-
tion and a picture, too. Whatever.

Cheers,

Kurt Vonnegut

January 25, 1994

New York City

To Paul Cody

Paul Cody was associate editor of the Cornell Alumni Magazine, *who
had asked a number of alumni and friends of the university, "At this
stage of your life, knowing what you know now, what advice would
you offer to your graduating-from-college self?"*

Dear Paul Cody—

In reply to your friendly letter of January 3:

What I have become has almost nothing to do with Cornell,
where, on the bad advice of my brother and my father, I was attempting and failing to become a biochemist. It has everything to

do with the absorbing adventure of writing for and editing *The Cornell Daily Sun,* a quite separate corporation.

My colleagues on the *Sun* were almost all liberal arts majors of one sort or another, a few of them still close friends of mine, and they passed on to me in conversations what they themselves had learned about writing and history and literature.

Advice? Somebody should have told me not to join a fraternity, but to hang out with the independents, who were not then numerous. I would have grown up faster that way. Somebody should have told me that getting drunk, while fashionable, was dangerous and stupid. And somebody should have told me to forget about higher education, and to go to work for a newspaper instead. That is what a lot of the most promising and determined young writers used to do back then. Nowadays, of course, you can't get a job on a newspaper if you don't have a college education. Too bad.

My experiences at Cornell were freakish in the extreme, as have been most of those which followed, mostly accidents. So the advice I give myself at the age of 71 is the best advice I could have given myself in 1940, when detraining for the first time at Ithaca, having come all the way from Indianapolis: "Keep your hat on. We may wind up miles from here."

Cheers,

Kurt Vonnegut

Undated, 1995

[New York City]

To Robert Weide

This letter was sent during Robert Weide's preparation for filming Mother Night.

TO BOB WEIDE

FROM KURT VONNEGUT

Put Eichmann and Campbell in any sort of jail which suits the show.

They should be segregated from other prisoners, since somebody might want to kill or rescue them. It might be visually interesting to have just the two of them shower in a room with hundreds of showerheads and drains, reminding us of the "shower baths" at Auschwitz. [. . .]

Campbell is modeled after "Lord Haw Haw," a British subject who was hanged after the war for doing what Campbell did.

Lord Haw Haw was objectively a war criminal, giving great encouragement to the Nazis. War crimes cannot be forgiven if it is argued that the accused did good things, too.

Campbell was not a just pretend monster. He was a real monster. So there was no way to say convincingly to holocaust survivors and so on after the war that he was really a good guy. He wasn't. If he had been a good guy, the Nazis would have caught on and hanged him from a meat hook.

I wrote the book as a paperback for a quick three grand, and can't remember what I was thinking when I mentioned a major Donovan. General "Wild Bill" Donovan was head of OSS, and would have been Wirtanen's boss when we got into the war. He was a pal of Roosevelt. I say now that General Donovan and Wirtanen did an Ollie North in keeping Campbell's activities strictly to themselves, since their best agent, in order to stay alive, was doing all of the things which were bad news for Jews and Allied troops in order to stay alive.

Is this any help?

January 8, 1995
New York City

To Stig Claesson

Stig Claesson was a Swedish writer, visual artist, and illustrator.

Dear Stig—

Always good to hear from you, as though from a friend I've seen a lot of. Whenever I meet a Swede, I ask how you are. They all know who you are and think well of you.

That's pleasant news that you think I'm a good writer, but I'm pretty much out of steam now, having turned 72. Most American male writers have done their best work by the time they're 55, for whatever reason. I was delighted to hear recently that Brahms was sick of composing by the time he was 54, and wrote just one short piece for a remarkable clarinetist after that. My architect father was sick of architecture by the time he was 55, and that seemed reasonable and honorable to me. He died 19 [*sic*] years later, at 72, having turned to making pottery.

I myself have taken to making silk screen prints, painting on acetate with india ink or pens loaded with opaque silver paint. It's a way to cover a lot of space in a hurry. Using language, I'm lucky if I can cover a page in a day.

Actually, I do work some every day on a book promised long ago, with the working title "Timequake." It has such a wonderful premise, though, that I haven't been intelligent enough to do it justice, so far. I don't want my final book to be a piece of crap. At the end of his life, Mark Twain was writing mostly crap.

Cheers,

Kurt Vonnegut

January 14, 1995
New York City

To David Markson

Wilfrid Sheed was a novelist, biographer, and reviewer of books and movies for journals including The New York Review of Books *and* Esquire. *He was author of* In Love with Daylight: A Memoir of Recovery.

Wittgenstein's Mistress *was a novel of Markson's that was greatly admired by Kurt.*

Dear David—

[. . .] You must know that Knox has also been playing games with cancer, and also Bill Sheed, who is about to publish a book on the subject, and about depression and addiction in the bargain. It's entitled *In Love with Daylight.*

As for myself, I surely deserve a serious illness, but who says life has to be fair? The past four years have gone down the toilet because I thought up a premise I'm too fogbound to exploit properly. The older my father got, the dumber he got, and the same thing turns out to be true of me. I used to play a reasonably good game of chess, but always hated end game with so little material still on the board. I keep thinking, "Oh my God, is it really my turn to move again."

I am not surprised that *Wittgenstein's Mistress* has attracted the interest of alert and cultivated academics. Congratulations.

Cheers,
Kurt Vonnegut

February 17, 1995
New York City

To Marc Leeds

Dear Marco Polo—

I should have thanked you for the ass-backwards clock long before now. If only it could make real time run backwards as well. It was such a trivial gift, however, when compared with your enormous and witty encyclopedia. Walt Whitman bought himself a fancy mausoleum before he died. I don't have to do that. Critics who have spoken ill of my work must be flummoxed by such an imposing monument. When Klinkowitz and Pieratt brought out their list of my published works, one such commented that it appeared to be a nice job, but why on earth would someone spend so much time on an author so inconsequential.

The 50th anniversary of the Dresden firestorm came and went without my saying anything in public about it, in spite of many invitations, one from Dresden itself. I am annoyed that the Frauenkirche, whose spire topped by Virgin Mary survived the calamity, is to be rebuilt. I thought it was a perfect monument when a ruin to Western Civilization's efforts to commit suicide in two world wars.

I am sorry your job is so tedious. So is mine. Mine is like the end of a chess game, with very few opportunities or pieces left on the board.

Thanks again.

Kurt

April 7, 1995

[New York City]

To Peter Reed

Dear Peter—

[. . .] I was invited to make all sorts of appearances on the 50th anniversary of the firebombing of Dresden, but it was easy for me to stay home and quiet. I had indeed achieved catharsis with *Slaughterhouse-5*. I don't think or dream about the event at all. I did give a couple of reporters a simple statement to the effect that the ruined Frauenkirche should not be restored, since it was a perfect monument to Western Civilization's efforts to commit suicide in two world wars. A few years back I spoke to your Landsman Freeman Dyson about the atrocity, since he had been an RAF bureaucrat. He said it was purely bureaucratic momentum which caused the raid. Now the same sort of dumb juggernaut will cause the Frauenkirche to be rebuilt. What shall we do today?

My lawyer and agent Donald Farber has been accumulating what is now a huge archive of my career and stumbles, many cubic feet going back at least 30 years. We are now putting it on the market. Indiana University is interested, as well they might be. I have always been proud to be a Hoosier, a son of the state which gave us Cole Porter and Eugene Debs.

I told Asa recently that I never expected to be putting my own generation to bed. But here I am, saying "Sleep tight" to damn near everyone I ever cared about.

Am I writing anything any good these days? Nope.

Cheers,

    Kurt Vonnegut

July 31, 1995

Sagaponack, NY

To William Detweiler

Dear William Detweiler—

I am honored by your invitation to speak at the Legion's 77th National Convention in what happens to be my own home town. I regret that I can't accept. I have a long-standing commitment to speak elsewhere at that time.

If I could be there, my speech would be a short one. The older my father became, the dumber he became, and the same thing is happening to me. I am not talking about Alzheimer's. I'm talking about plain old age.

I would probably have said to Legionnaires that veterans my age would all have gone to Vietnam, if that had been our war, even though, as Robert McNamara has now made clear, that war was loony-tunes. We were raised to believe that when our country went to war, no matter what the reason, healthy young men of every social class and degree of education should beg to serve. Not many people are raised that way any more, and most of the famous fire-eating patriots of today found ways to stay out of uniform when their country said it needed them. I don't like them.

My generation was extraordinarily lucky to have fought in that greatest of rarities, an unambiguously just war. I include Korea. And anyone who was actually in battles in those wars and survived found himself, as do I, a member of a great fraternity composed of all who have ever been in battle—in any military service of any country, friend or foe. I can't tell you how much this fraternity has meant to me wherever in the whole wide world I go.

Cheers,

Kurt Vonnegut

12102964

VOLUNTEER

October 11, 1995

[New York City]

To Bernard Vonnegut

Kurt's brother, Bernard, wanted to know why paintings couldn't be judged as art by their quality or lack of it without knowing anything about the artist.

Dear Brother—

This is almost like telling you about the birds and the bees.

There are many good people who are beneficially stimulated by some but not all man-made arrangements of colors and shapes on flat surfaces, essentially nonsense. You are gratified by some music, arrangements of noises, again essentially nonsense.

If I were to kick a bucket down the cellar stairs and then say to you that the racket I'd made was philosophically on a par with *The Magic Flute*, this would not be the beginning of a long and pooping debate. An utterly satisfactory and complete response on your part would be, "I like what Mozart did and I hate what the bucket did." Contemplating a purported work of art is a social activity. Either you have a good time or you don't. You don't have to say why afterwards. You don't have to say anything.

You are a justly revered experimentalist. If you really want to know whether your pictures are, as you say, "art" or not, you must display them in a public place somewhere, and then try to judge whether or not strangers liked to look at them, were glad that you had made them. That is the way the game is played. Let me know what happens.

People capable of loving some paintings or etchings or whatever can rarely do this without knowing something about the artist. Again, the situation is social rather than scientific. Any work of art is one half of a conversation between two human beings, and it helps a lot to know who is talking at you. Does he or she have a reputation for seriousness, for sincerity? There are virtually no beloved or respected paintings made by persons of whom we know nothing. We can even surmise a lot about the lives of whoever did the paintings in the caves underneath Lascaux, France.

So I dare to suggest that no picture can attract serious attention without a human being attached to it in the viewer's mind. If you are unwilling to attach your name to your pictures, and to say why you hope others might find them rewarding to look at, there goes the ballgame right there. Pictures are famous for their human-ness and not their picture-ness.

There is also the matter of craftsmanship. Real picture lovers like to "play along," so to speak, to look closely at the surface to see how the illusion was created by nothing but an unusual human being, with hands and eyes. If you are unwilling to say how you made your pictures, there goes the ballgame a second time.

Good luck, and love as always—

    K

October 17, 1995

New York City

To Jerome Klinkowitz

Dear Jerry—

[. . .] I of course continue to be flattered by your interest in my work, which now consists mainly of public speaking, six engagements in the springtime, six more at harvest time. I have held many shit jobs in the process of survival as a family man, and so sympathize with any book salesman unable to enthuse about a book on the subject of me as a public speaker. I do continue to fill all available audience space, and to be applauded when I am done. Weide has some tapes of my performances, and those are more convincing reports, for good or ill, than words on paper could ever be. As you surely know, my exclusive lecture agent Janet Cosby maintains an archive of write-ups in local papers. The Koran, of course, is a collection of jottings by scribes of sayings by Muhammad, who could not read or write. Could we found a new religion? A new thing I do now as a finale is to ask all in the audience to hold up their hands who had a teacher who made them more enthusiastic about life and themselves. Then I tell those who held up their hands to say the name of that teacher to someone sitting next to them.

[. . .] You will probably receive this on Friday, October 20th, at which time I will be departing to lecture in Boston and then teach the next day. I intend to call for a Constitutional Convention, in order to add four amendments to the Bill of Rights, guaranteeing that every newborn will be sincerely welcomed, that every young person upon reaching puberty will be declared an adult, that every citizen will be given worthwhile work to do, and that every citizen will be made to feel that he or she will be sincerely missed when he or she is dead.

Cheers,

Kurt Vonnegut

November 5, 1995
Sagaponack, NY

To Marc Leeds

Wolcott Gibbs was an editor and theater critic as well as a writer of parodies and short stories for The New Yorker. *He worked for the magazine from 1927 until his death in 1958.*

Dear Young Man—

I thank you for the existence of the encyclopedia of me, a work of love. You must already know that I like you a lot.

You might have a look at Bellow's *Augie March,* which was somehow of spiritual use to me when my situation was superficially similar to yours. It may read like a piece of junk now. Businesses and institutions were commonly like families then, paternalism's or maternalism's being a widespread technique of management. I used to think that was a swindle, making relatives of employees in order to keep wages low. So when we went looking for work, we were shopping for a family. When I got a job with General Electric, that was really something, because nothing could hurt GE in the next 100 years at least, seemingly, and my job was for life. The same seemed true about the luggage store on Main Street, and the stationery store next door to it. "Good! Then you'll come to work tomorrow! We open at eight, so you should be here no later than seven-thirty."

The excellent writer Wolcott Gibbs when a young man was interviewed by Harold Ross, founder of the *New Yorker.* The interview went very well. Gibbs got a job. But as he was leaving, and Ross believed him to be out of earshot, Ross cried out, "God damn it, I'd hire anybody!" Until very recently, jobs at the *New Yorker* were also for life, but the pay was low. The pay is very high now, but goes to jittery, hand-to-mouth independent contractors, in effect. Like actors, they are in for lifetimes of seeking work, hat in hand.

New technologies are doing this to everybody, and for that reason I am a Luddite. Video stores and TV cable systems are already

obsolescent. My wife is a superb portraitist in black and white photography, which reveals so much about the topography of human
faces. But everybody wants color now. In all of New York City, she
can't find a lab to print meticulously black and white for her. As we
used to say back when I was part of the GE family, and my wife
and kids were included: "Progress is our most important product."

The mood of my generation? Wry disappointment with what
the world has actually become, so inhospitable and snide. Once
the Great Depression and the Second World War were over, we
planned to build a Garden of Eden here. But you'll be OK. It's
other people, surely including my own kids, I worry a lot about.

Yours truly,

Kurt Vonnegut

(The man who broke the bank at Monte Carlo)

January 6, 1996

New York City

To Peter Reed

Dear Peter—

When I teach creative writing, I make Vincent van Gogh the
class hero, since he responded to life rather than to the market-
place, and the class motto is: "Whatever works works."

[. . .] The filming of *Mother Night* in Montreal ended, with
everybody pleased, on November 10th. It has now been cut by a
third. Unbelievably, it was made for five and a half million dollars! Nolte himself usually gets paid much more than that. When
he saw Weide's script, he said it reminded him of why he became
an actor. I have bought back *The Sirens of Titan* from Jerry Garcia's estate for what he paid me for it decades ago. Weide would
like to do a script for that next. With no studio involvement, he
and I can make it, as we did with *Mother Night,* exactly what we
feel it should be. And then we captivate another important actor.
That's when we go to a studio for money only and no advice.

As for still pictures: I am trying to recover the cost of frames, and Joe must have spent a small fortune on what he does. People have trouble understanding that they are rarities, made with great pains one at a time. They think we are putting high prices on posters run off in unlimited quantities by a printing press. Joe now has about ten more acetates I've done, but which have yet to be printed. I have stopped making more until we can somehow start feeling like we are a business. A number of our prints will be hung in the cafe of a Barnes and Noble superstore in the Citicorp Building in February. Barnes and Noble will not be selling them, or trying to, since they don't handle items that expensive. Interested collectors, if any, will be referred to the Margo Feiden Gallery, where I had a one man show years and years ago. [. . .]

Cheers,

Kurt Vonnegut

January 12, 1996

[New York City]

To Susan Abbadusky

Susan Abbadusky was a high school teacher in Monmouth, Illinois, when a student and her parents charged her with having the student read a "pornographic book," Vonnegut's Breakfast of Champions. *The issue became a local controversy, leading to some parents wanting to remove not only that book but other books they considered unsavory from the local library. Cooler heads prevailed, and Ms. Abbadusky later retired from the high school and now teaches communications at Monmouth College. Now using her former name, Susan Van Kirk, she has written a book about her experiences, called* The Education of a Teacher: Including Dirty Books and Pointed Looks.

Dearest (to be mildly pornographic) Susan Abbadusky—

My goodness! I would certainly have replied to your excellent letter (and accompanying materials) of December 12, 1995, long before now, if only my publisher hadn't kept it in dead storage so long. I got it today at noon!

During the past thirty years or so, I have received many letters from teachers and librarians about books by me which have caused teapot tempests or worse in their communities. You win the prize for the best one. The teacher in Drake, North Dakota, who was fired for teaching *Slaughterhouse-Five,* also had his windows broken and his dog was shot. The ACLU showed up, and sued members of the School Committee personally on his behalf, and he left town with $30,000, and a glowing letter of recommendation addressed to whom it may concern. Ain't that sweet?

The censorship stories are all so *regional.* The Mason–Dixon Line still matters a lot. In small towns in Dixie, the general population is almost always solidly behind the censors and, of course, the football team. You and your students are lucky to be in Norman Rockwell America, where Jeffersonian debates are possible and usually entertaining. One community banned *Slaughterhouse-Five,* and a reporter called me to find out what I had to say about it, and I said the head of the School Committee was a piss-ant, and he dropped dead the next day.

The first story of mine to arouse censors was about time-travelers who go back to the Holy Land at the time of the Crucifixion. It turns out that the Bible had it right, the three crosses, the crown of thorns and so on. As long as they're back there, they decide to measure Jesus. He is five feet and three inches tall, the same height, incidentally, as Richard the Lion Hearted. Outrage! Pandemonium!

Love you madly,

Kurt Vonnegut

April 18, 1996
New York City

To Stig Claesson

Dear Stig—

My adopted thirteen-year-old daughter goes to school with
the daughter of the Swedish Counsel here, and his office is close
to where I live. I see him often, and never miss an opportunity to
ask him why I haven't received a Nobel Prize, particularly in view
of the fact that I was the second or third SAAB dealer in the USA,
and the car had suicide doors and a two-stroke engine that would
lay down a smoke screen if you let it sit too long.

As for the silk screens: I simply paint the positives on acetate,
and a friend in Lexington, Kentucky, prints them and breathes the
fumes. If he dies, I can always find another printer. How's that for
taking really good care of myself!

I never thought I'd be the one to put the rest of my American
literary generation to bed, but it's happening, a funeral every
month and a half or so. Terry Southern of *Dr. Strangelove* and
Easy Rider fame is the biggest reputation to depart this year so
far. Crazy as hell.

God love you—

Kurt Vonnegut

May 18, 1996
New York City

To Alex Maslansky

Alex Maslansky is a nephew of Dr. Robert Maslansky.

Dear Alex—

Your Uncle Bob says you want to become a writer.

I have never regretted helping people to write better, even
though they weren't going to make livings with that particular

skill, since they were learning how to be more graceful. My father and mother and grandparents wrote expressively and beguilingly simply because they were civilized.

If you want to write fiction, then you must be patient, for you need experiences, and those take time to accumulate. Unfortunately, television offers the illusion of experiences writers used to come by the hard way, in courtrooms, on ships, in hospitals, whatever. Please don't rely on those, unless you want to be popular.

I say go for truths, very personal ones, not likely to be learned from TV sets. We need to know what those are. Or I do.

The secret of universality is provincialism. Don't open a window and make love to the world. Literary masterpieces since the birth of the novel and short story have all been obsessed with narrow societies, Emma Bovary's, Leopold Bloom's, about which most readers cannot be expected to know much. They'll learn, those readers will. A writer is first and foremost a teacher.

When I teach creative writing, my lessons are mainly about sociability. Please, please, please, make sure the reader is having an interesting time, and the hell with you. Young people find this dictum very inconvenient, an exasperating barrier between themselves and where they want to get as soon as possible.

Cheers,

Kurt Vonnegut

June 18, 1996
Sagaponack, NY

To Ollie Lyon

The reference to "my former son-in-law Jerry Rivers" was to Geraldo Rivera, the first husband of Kurt's daughter Edie. After the divorce, Rivera was not a favorite of the Vonnegut clan.

Dear O.M.—

Joe's print business has to be a cover for drug traffic or kiddie porn. How else could he afford a telephone? I haven't sold enough of our pictures during the past three years to cover the cost of frames for shows. We are not popular. My interest wanes.

A German has turned *Slaughterhouse-5* into an opera, which premieres in Munich on June 28. I have heard nothing from the composer. He apparently assumes I'm dead. I was invited over, but said I had a previous engagement. Years ago, he asked my agent for permission, which was given, and that was the end of the correspondence. But the whole idea upsets me somehow. It would be a nightmare for me to be trapped in a theater, having to hear that language I barely understand, and which for me has unpleasant associations.

How's the writing? I bore the shit out of myself. I'm like Melville's whalers, who didn't talk any more because they'd said all they had to say. I sleep a lot.

Politics? I will vote Democratic because that is the most humane of the two parties, but not by much. The Clintons are shallow, opportunist Yuppies, but they are the only game in town. Doesn't Dole make you ashamed to be a World War Two vet? What a crabby old poop!

As my former son-in-law Jerry Rivers used to write and may still write when giving an autograph:

Love you madly,
Kurt

November 13, 1996

New York City

To Emily Glossbrenner

Dearest Cousin Emily—

[. . .] My *Mother Night,* a paperback original which was never reviewed, has been made into a really swell movie. The movie is not for everybody, since it is actually *about something,* no chases, no explosions, no nudity. I would be proud to have you see it. I've been luckier than most novelists with Hollywood, with two movies at least as good as my books, the other one being *Slaughterhouse-5.* Both are works of love, with everybody working for next to nothing. *Mother Night* was shot entirely in Montreal, which served as Berlin and then Greenwich Village.

I was in Indianapolis a month ago, to speak at an anniversary celebration for my Grandfather Bernard Vonnegut's landmark building the Athenaeum.

Your sister Mary was there, as beautiful as ever. I hadn't seen her for maybe thirty years. She was again the belle of the ball. Everybody wanted to talk to her instead of me. What could be more understandable?

Your sister Catey of course has had a lot to do with the restoration of the Athenaeum. [. . .]

Love as always—

K

January 18, 1997

New York City

To Alexander and Jackson Adams

Alexander and Jackson are the sons of Kurt ("Tiger") Adams, the third son of Kurt's sister, Alice, and her husband, Jim.

Dear Alexander and Jackson—

What sweet people you two are, and I am not surprised, since
your mother and father are so decent and good-hearted. I will not
name names, but not all my grandchildren respond as warmly as
you, or in fact respond at all. Zilch! Zero! Zip!

Jackson, that is a really swell piece of writing about your
brush with death, and I hope your teacher told you so. Writing
well is more than a way to make money. My father Kurt senior
wrote like an angel, simply in order to be civilized, to make the
lives of those around him more amusing and interesting.

I try to think now about who else in our family has had a serious life-threatening experience when young. I believe your dad is
the only one.

Next Christmas, I am going to give you two a one percent
bonus! What do you think of that?

Love as always—
    Grampy K

January 19, 1997
New York City

To JEROME KLINKOWITZ

Dear Jerry—

I look at the index of *The Crab Orchard Review,* or of *Breeze,*
published in Bloomington, Indiana, and then the contents, and
am impressed yet again by how many wonderful writers there are
for such small audiences. That's good, not bad. That is art on a
human scale. Your excellent piece is about sports on a human
scale. Human is beautiful. All else is business.

Mother Night was a movie on a human scale, not business,
and so has gone the way of Waterloo Professional Baseball. It was
about something.

I have finished up *Timequake* yet again. It is short and

dense. The keeper of my archives Glenn Horowitz has at least a thousand pages of scrapped material. Peter Reed has the penultimate manuscript. This one will be published next autumn, no matter what. It's beyond post-modern. It's positively posthumous.

Joe's and my print business is picking up. We're very big in Denver.

Slaughterhouse-Five was a movie in 1972. It was a musical in the Red Army Theater in Moscow in 1980. It was an opera in Munich last July. It was a straight play in Chicago last fall. It is also a book.

    Cheers,

      Kurt

January 26, 1997

[New York City]

To the Junior League of Indianapolis

It has been brought to my attention that the Junior League of Indianapolis, of which my mother and sister were members, is about to vandalize its headquarters there, and Indianapolis history as well, by naming it what it is not, *Victorian Mansion*.

It is not of the Victorian era, nor was it inspired in the least by architecture of that time. To call it *Victorian,* then, would be to proclaim that the Junior League is indifferent to the truth, and moreover insensitive to important distinctions in the fine arts, which include architecture. So what else is new?

On November 17th of last year, I, of Shortridge High School, and the world-renowned architect Michael Graves, of Broad Ripple High School, held an informal but public discussion about architecture and a sense of place. A person in the audience asked us, apropos of nothing he or I had said, why Indianapolis had an inferiority complex. Your organization gives me an answer I wish I'd had back then: It knows nothing of its past, which is in fact neither shameful nor boring, and so destroys even the most beautiful and imposing proofs that it ever had one.

For your information, and you surely know this already: 3050 North Meridian Street was a brilliantly conceived machine for genteel living, designed by my grandfather Bernard Vonnegut, an Indianapolis native educated in Europe and at MIT, the first licensed architect in the State of Indiana. The Athenaeum, a National Landmark, was designed by him.

The former Confederate States are proud of grand houses where the owners held really swell parties and family reunions and weddings and so on, and have made them tourist attractions.

Terrific celebrations were held, and in my time, too, in the Schnull–Rauch house. Indianapolis is going to deny, with the help of the Junior League, that people whose names were known lived happier and more gracious and productive lives on North Meridian than Scarlett O'Hara lived at Tara?

We haven't been in a movie? Is that the problem?

Giving a piece of property a supposedly cute or quaint name, in the hopes of increasing its market value, is an act typical of a very average real estate broker anywhere in the world. Perhaps Indianapolis deserves its inferiority complex after all, since it is rapidly becoming nothing but a real estate development and a so-so football team stolen from Baltimore.

Very truly yours—

Kurt Vonnegut (Jr.)

March 8, 1997

[New York City]

To FAITH SALE

Faith Sale was Vonnegut's editor at Putnam.

Dear Faith—

I hope the editing isn't too tedious.

About the cover, in which I guess Putnam has already invested a lot of money and thought: Your people certainly know a lot more than I do about tempting browsers to buy a book. The fractured clock might indeed be an eye-catcher.

But I ask your marketing people to consider the possibility that my name and the title and the provocative subtitle alone, on a plain background, and with the picture of Trout on the back, might inspire curiosity about the contents even quicker.

The message would be so simple, so direct, for good or ill. I am a brand name, with equal numbers of friends and loathers. Your brother-in-law, of course, is among the latter.

KV

March 27, 1997

New York City

To Robert Maslansky

The letter was in response to the medical journal Lancet *rejecting an article Dr. Maslansky had written.*

Dear Bob—

In my trade, a new idea, if clearly and simply stated, is dismissed as something educated people knew all along.

In your trade, and my brother's too, a new idea is noise, a jackhammer next door. Will it never stop? Specialists whose paradigms are threatened by a new idea behave unscientifically, taking each other's word that the idea is noise, assuming that one of them may actually have looked into it.

You are, of course, an obvious nut case, writer of crank letters about methadone and heart disease. The unread last paragraphs no doubt deal with the electrification of thunderstorms and flying saucers. The writer is surely a patient and not a physician at Bellevue.

You remind me of the nut who thought childbed fever in hospitals could be reduced if physicians and nurses would wash their hands before visiting the maternity ward.

Cheers—

Kurt Vonnegut

May 5, 1997
New York City

TO HARRY JAMES CARGAS

Dear old friend Harry—

I thank you for your condolence note about my brother. He didn't call for a priest at the end, but he had the good sense to spend the last ten days in a Catholic hospice, St. Peter's in Albany. One person there described his manners while dying as "courtly" and "elegant." I myself said at the memorial service last Thursday, in the non-denominational chapel of SUNY Albany, "I don't have anybody to show off for anymore." [. . .]

Cheers—

Kurt Vonnegut

May 30, 1997
Via Fax to Robert Weide

LETTER TO BE READ AT A LOS ANGELES TRIBUTE
TO ALLEN GINSBERG ON JUNE 1, 1997

Allen Ginsberg and I were inducted into the American Institute of Arts and Letters in 1973. A reporter from *Newsweek* telephoned me at that time, and asked me what I thought about two such outsiders being absorbed by the establishment. I replied, "If we aren't the establishment, I don't know who is."

Allen was inducted nominally as a poet, but had in fact become world famous for the radiant love and innocence of his person, from head to toe.

Let us be frank, and admit that the greatest poetry satiates few deep appetites in modern times. But the appearance in our industrialized midst of a man without guile or political goals or congregation, who was doing his utmost to become wise and holy, was for many of us a surprising, anachronistic feast for our souls.

Allen and I met at a dinner given in Cambridge by the Harvard Lampoon in the late 1960's. We would hold hands during the ensuing entertainment.

I had returned from witnessing the end of a civil war in southern Nigeria. The losing side, the rebellious Ibos, had been blockaded. There had been widespread starvation. I was there with my fellow novelist Vance Bourjaily. We arrived on a blockade-running Catholic relief DC-3. We were surrounded at once by starving children begging for mercy. They had distended bellies, everted rectums, hair turned yellow, running sores, that sort of thing. They were also dirty.

We were afraid to touch them, lest we get an infection to take back home. But Vance was ashamed of his squeamishness. He said that if Allen Ginsberg had been with us, Allen would have hugged the children, and gone down on his knees and played with them.

I told this story at the Lampoon dinner, and then said directly to Allen: "We have not met before, sir, but such is your reputation."

—Kurt Vonnegut

November 22, 1997
New York City

To Ben Hitz

Dear Ben—

Yeah—I spoke at the Athenaeum pro bono publico, in honor of a grandfather I and my siblings never met, and about whom, inexplicably, our father, his partner, told us almost nothing. Father may have been silenced by the fact that his own father was a much more gifted draughtsman than himself. I sometimes wonder if Father wouldn't have preferred to be something other than an architect, if he'd been allowed to choose. [. . .]

I was back in Naptown last week, this time speaking at Butler in company with Dan Wakefield and John Updike. We blathered about spirituality on the stage of Clowes Hall. I think we were funny, but a tape might not confirm that. [. . .]

Love as always, old pal—

K

December 22, 1997
New York City

To GALWAY KINNELL

Galway Kinnell won both the Pulitzer Prize and the National Book Award for his Selected Poems *in 1980, and his* A New Selected Poems *was a finalist for the National Book Award in 2000.*

Dear Galway Kinnell—

At the age of 75, I had come to doubt that any words written in the present could make me like being alive a lot. I was mistaken. Your great poem *Why Regret?* restored my soul. Jesus! What a language! What a poet! What a world!

Cheers—

Kurt Vonnegut

December 29, 1997
New York City

To MILLER HARRIS

Dear Miller—

I was honored by your out-of-the-blue phone call a while ago. You were my mentor, although only one year my senior, at Cornell. The relationship remains prominent in my memory, and should. You helped me. You wished me well. I now wish that you would become the essayist you started out to be, possibly trying some op-ed pieces or letters to the editor of *The New York Times*. You are entitled to write wisely, as a very bright, wryly witty, fair-minded, tough-minded elder, who has experienced one hell of a lot by now.

About the year 2000; the best information we have is that Jesus was born in five B.C., five years before Himself. Chalk that up as another miracle. So the two-thousandth year of the Christian era was 1995, and the long-awaited apocalypse was the O.J. Simpson case.

Cheers—

Kurt

February 23, 1998
New York City

To Miller Harris

Dear Miller—

[. . .] Ancestors of the Jews I grew up with in Indianapolis came over the same time yours and mine did, and so missed the harrowing romance of Ellis Island and the sweatshops and all that. They were just more Germans who didn't want to be Europeans any more, who wanted to be defined by the Declaration of Independence, and also get rich. The first Vonnegut to hit Indianapolis was wearing silk and selling silk, so he might as well have been Jewish.

In the over-achievers' high school I attended, we Gentiles considered the Jews, children of established professionals and businessmen, to be on the lunatic fringe of Christianity, trying to get through life with only half a Bible. One of them was Madelyn Pugh, who became head writer on *The I Love Lucy Show*. Many of their ancestors, again like my own, had been Freethinkers, for whom *Origin of the Species* was holy writ.

The Unitarian minister who buried my father (because he was dead) was Jack Mendelsohn, who later had a church in Boston. It offered sanctuary to draft resisters during the Vietnam War and lost its fire insurance.

Kurt

May 28, 1998
Sagaponack, NY

To Linda and Robert Weide

Dear Linda and Bob—

I've just FedExed your wedding present to your Whyaduck address. It is a pair of Victorian candlesticks—not cheap, but not unbelievably expensive either. They are identical with a pair I inherited from my father. I have since given their like to each of my children, and also to the Adamses. They have become our family totem. At every family gathering, all the candlesticks are put in the middle of a table for the feast. Bring yours, too, if you're lucky enough to be invited.

I can't come to the wedding. I have to deliver Lily (who got her own candlesticks when a neonate) to summer school in Massachusetts.

Be Happy!

Kurt

June 3, 1998
Sagaponack, NY

To David Miller

In 1993 the New York Philharmonic commissioned Vonnegut to write a new libretto for Stravinsky's L'Histoire du Soldat. He set his work in World War II around the episode made famous in William Bradford Huie's The Execution of Private Slovik. It has been performed many times since, and this seems to be Kurt's favorite production, put on by David Miller and his Orchestra X at the Steppenwolf Theatre in Chicago. Miller persuaded Vonnegut to come and be interviewed on the stage about his experience as a U.S. infantry private who was a P.O.W. during the firebombing of Dresden—the subject of Slaughterhouse-Five.

Dear David Miller—

I love you for what you did for me and Igor Stravinsky, and the audience that night. Perfection was achieved. Epiphany!

I pray that Robert Johnson, whose property my libretto is, will allow you to repeat your musical and theatrical triumph again and again. He himself masterminded five previous performances, including one at Lincoln Center, with Eli Wallach and Ann Reinking, so his deep feelings of proprietorship are understandable, God knows.

With his permission, you blindsided him with an overwhelming demonstration of how to make *Histoire* impress as a masterpiece. His emotions can only be mixed. I myself have to stay out of this unhappy situation. Time heals all wounds, or so they say.

In any case, I consider you the cat's pajamas.

Kurt Vonnegut

July 27, 1998
Sagaponack, NY

TO ELLIE AND BEN HITZ

The humorist Will Cuppy was from Auburn, Indiana, and after college at the University of Chicago moved to New York City, where his articles for The New Yorker *magazine were collected in books such as* How to Tell Your Friends from the Apes.

Dear Ellie and Ben—

God bless you, Ellie, for saving that friendly summarization of my career, which needs no update, although written 27 years ago.

My feeling then, and correctly, too, was, "Please, can I go home now?" The *Saturday Review* piece will depart for the Lilly Library in Bloomington in the same mail with this, to be entombed in the state of my enchanting boyhood, the home I long to go back to, if only I could. "Where's my good old gang done gone?" I heard a sad man say. I whispered in that sad man's ear, "Your gang's done gone away."

So the wisp of that vanished past which you two represent by summering in Leland [Indiana], where so many Hoosiers used to be in the hot months, is permission for me to wallow happily in nostalgia. The humorist Will Cuppy years ago entitled a book, "The Night the Old Nostalgia Burned Down."

As for the Modern Library's list of good novels—I myself would throw out *Lolita,* and confess to be unable to read Henry James. But I am a beneficiary of previous lists, however arbitrary, including the Modern Library's first batch, and the Harvard Classics, and the first four years of Chicago's Great Books. They were my teachers. Some faculty!

Cheers—

KAY

March 6, 1999
New York City

To Stephen Jay Gould

Dear Stephen—

What a stroke of luck, running in to you last night! I am always happy to see you, or even think about you, but I have been ruminating extra-hard about natural selection recently—almost, one might say, like Einstein on an elevator, pondering, every time the thing started or stopped, what the fuck was really going on.

I myself wonder about rattlesnakes and lightning bugs. Only a completely humorless person could believe that such preposterously elaborate Dr. Seuss creatures could be the result of judicious shopping in the marriage market, so to speak. I have the same problem with the Big Bang Theory. Anybody with a sense of humor has to laugh.

Anyway, as the poor man's Einstein, I have factored into the Darwinian persuasion the fact that, only a few blocks north of here, at Rockefeller University, nerds and dweebs are playing and winning ever fancier games with genetic materials. That such games have been played elsewhere in the Universe, even in our own Milky Way, is statistically a sure thing, wouldn't you say? We can't be the only biologically CREATIVE animals. Give me a break! So: Eons ago, and I expect the fossil record to confirm it (You read it here first!), CREATORS like us in space ships or the fifth dimension or whatever played some games with animals which had already EVOLVED here. Like Dr. Seuss, they had some FUN, introducing lizards, like the Wright Brothers, to the joys and heartbreaks of aviation, and making snakes with hypodermic syringes in their mouths and doorbells on their tails, and so on. And lightning bugs. [. . .]

In Christ—

Kurt Vonnegut

May 4, 1999

New York City

To MILLER HARRIS

Dear Miller—

How tender and generous of you to cut and paste as you did in your letter of a couple of days ago. Typical. I wonder now how on Earth I could have done what they say I've done, and am reminded of Tony Costa, a murderer of perhaps twenty women, about whom I did a story for *Life* magazine so long ago. We corresponded some after he was put away with the Bos-

ton Strangler in Bridgewater State Prison in Massachusetts. He
said a person like him couldn't possibly have done what people
said he'd done.

I am reminded, too, of what Samuel Johnson said about
Gulliver's Travels: "Once you'd thought of the little people, the
rest was obvious." Once I survived the firebombing of the
Florence of the Elbe as a captured PFC, maybe the rest was
obvious.

And, on my Word of Honor, you were my mentor when we
were very young. I've said that before, but maybe you didn't hear
me. And I'm so happy that you're still O.K. Me, too. Damned if
we didn't survive the Second Battle of the Somme.

Cheers and love as always—

Kurt

August 7, 1999

Sagaponack, NY

To Don Farber

Dear Don—

Let me say again, if I die, that I should not be given a fancy
casket, nor should there be a viewing of my remains even by
closest friends and family. I should be cremated as quickly
and cheaply as possible, and my ashes should be scattered by
family in Barnstable Harbor, not far from the foot of Scudder's
Lane.

I am not, nor have I ever been a Christian, so I should not be
given a funeral or memorial service under any sort of Christian
supervision or in any Christian space, and surely not in any funeral home, and not in New York City.

Any memorial service should be small, modest, on Cape Cod,
and managed by my son Mark.

Kurt Vonnegut

October 3, 1999
New York City

To Miller Harris

Dear S. Miller—

The *Sun* for so many of us has been almost the only big reason we are glad to have gone to Cornell and not someplace else. My Putnam editor Faith Sale, by the way, is a *Sun* alumna, and was voted the best book editor in town by P.E.N. a couple of years ago.

As you know, I live directly across the street from 229 East 48th, the yellow Turtle Bay townhouse inhabited by E.B. White for so many years. Jill and I bought this house from the Knopf editor Bob Gottlieb in 1975, about a decade after White took off for Maine. Jill became a good friend of his in her line of business, visiting him in Maine several times. I met him once, thanks to Jill, in our living room. I'm sure I've already told you the memorable thing he said on that occasion: "I never knew a male writer worth a damn who wasn't a heavy boozer." Or words to that effect.

That such tragically romantic, self-destructive balderdash could be spoken so emphatically by a famously wise member of a generation before ours puts me in mind of other radical changes in our culture since World War Two. Booze is no longer a respectable adventure for full-grown men. And brothers in Cornell Delta Upsilon no longer sing, as I once did, and perhaps E.B. White did, too:

> The coed leads a dirty life,
> > dirty life:
> She eats potatoes with her knife,
> > with her knife.
> And once a year she takes a scrub,
> And leaves a ring around the tub!
> > The dirty thing!

And I recall, late in 1942, maybe, when Sam Pierce, much later to be innocently involved in an H.U.D. scandal, was the only black Cornell student I knew or even noticed. And the *Sun* published a letter from a white southern football player who said Yankees should be more sympathetic with Dixie's customs with respect to race. Foreshadowing Rosa Parks, Sam paid him a call.

Und so weiter.

During my training as a cultural anthropologist at the University of Chicago after the war, dear S. Miller, I was taught that messing with somebody's culture was like messing with his or her liver or pancreas. It is not so. Good news!

Cheers and love—

Kurt

October 4, 1999
New York City

To ROBERT MASLANSKY

Kurt was not a "patient" of Dr. Maslansky; the doctor was a friend who sometimes offered advice.

Dear Dr. Bob—

I thank you for yet another poem which is nourishing. I am dipping from time to time these days into Boswell's life of Johnson. Poetry used to matter tremendously to people of that class. They could argue about poems every night until bedtime. I note, too, that Johnson, so critical of illogical thinking, nonetheless swallowed the jerry-built tenets of his religion hook, line, and sinker.

I continue to agonize over my loss of faith in both natural selection and the big bang theory. Both seem to me to be absurd—testimony only as to how we are presently doomed to reason, with great big things necessarily having to come from teeny seeds as time creeps by. No other story of how things have come to be as they are is for our brains acceptable.

The Arab's gift of zero allows us to give serious thought to NOTHING, which in equations can have such a vivid personality. I now yearn for a symbol representing something else supposedly not worth thinking about, which is ALWAYS.

Your patient, going nuts like all the rest of them—

Kurt

October 8, 1999
[New York City]

To Nanny Vonnegut

Darling daughter Nanny—

In my sunset years, I missed the precise moment of your forty-fifth birthday. These things happen. And you have been most forgiving and modest about this lapse. But scarcely a waking hour passes, any day, any month, in which I am not serene about how beautiful my daughter Nanny is in every way.

Physically? A stately knockout!

Intellectually? Cultivated! A first-rate mind in love with pictures and music and justice and language—humorous, humanely wise.

Creatively? A clarinet solo. A brook. A tree. A house. A burp. A hiccup. A lake. A cigarette. People. Lightning bugs, a dripping faucet, food and children—and God and Jane and shooting stars.

DAD

October 30, 1999
New York City

To Robert Maslansky

Steven LaForge was a scientist who wrote on the psychopharmacology of addiction. The poem at the beginning of the letter is from Cat's Cradle.

Dear Bob—

> Tiger got to hunt, bird got to fly,
> Man got to sit and wonder, "Why, why, why?"
> Tiger got to sleep, bird got to land,
> Man got to tell himself he understand.

Yes, and Steven LaForge writes better ("lioness's share of oxygen") and thinks better than I do, but can he dance?

In any case, he has provoked me into coming up with this, although I flunked thermodynamics at Carnegie Tech and then the University of Tennessee, courtesy of the United States Army:

Stephen Hawking wonders why we can't remember the future, but that doesn't mean, for him or for me, that it isn't there. This amnesia is simply a human failing. And I see no reason why the future can't be as influential in our present as Darwin found our past to be.

Ergo, it is the future, and not Jerry Falwell or flying-saucer biotechnicians, which somehow gave us the rattlesnake and the lightning bug.

Q.E.D.

Kurt

November 7, 1999

New York City

To Ms. Noel Sturgeon

Noel Sturgeon was the third child and second daughter of Theodore and Marion Sturgeon and the trustee of Theodore's literary estate. She had written Vonnegut to ask if he would write an introduction to a new edition of her father's short stories. She said that many readers were curious about the relationship between Vonnegut's character Kilgore Trout, the science-fiction writer, and her father, a well-known and highly regarded science-fiction writer.

Dear Ms. Sturgeon—

I created a character Kilgore Trout, an impoverished, uncele-
brated science-fiction writer, who made his debut in 1965, in my
novel *God Bless You, Mr. Rosewater*. Trout would subsequently
make cameo appearances in several more of my books, and in
1973 would star in *Breakfast of Champions*.

Persons alert for word-play noticed that Trout and Theodore
Sturgeon were both named for fish, and that their first names
ended with "ore." They asked me if my friend Ted had been my
model for Kilgore.

Answer: Very briefly, and in a way. Kilgore, like Ted when we
first met in 1958, was a victim of a hate crime then commonly
practiced by the American literary establishment. It wasn't racism
or sexism or ageism. It was "genreism." Definition: "The unex-
amined conviction that anyone who wrote science-fiction wasn't
really a writer, but rather a geek of some sort." A genuine geek,
of course, is a carnival employee who is displayed in a filthy cage
and billed as "The Wild Man from Borneo."

Genreism was still rampant in late autumn, 1958, when I was
living in Barnstable, on Cape Cod, and Ted and his wife Marion
had just rented a house near the water in Truro—no place to be
when winter came. We knew each other's work, but had never
met. Bingo! There we were face-to-face at last, at suppertime in
my living room.

Ted had been writing non-stop for days or maybe weeks. He
was skinny and haggard, underpaid and unappreciated outside
the ghetto science-fiction was then. He announced that he was
going to do a standing back flip, which he did. He landed on his
knees with a crash which shook the whole house. When he got
back on his feet, humiliated and laughing in agony, one of the
best writers in America was indeed, but only for a moment, my
model for Kilgore Trout.

Respectfully yours—
    Kurt Vonnegut

December 3, 1999
[New York City]

To Nanny Vonnegut

Dearest Nanny—

To bring you and the rest of the family up to date: It really was a fancy spill I took up that way, most of all reminding me of how old I was. The black eye is vanishing, and the stitches will come out next Monday. And now it's cold out, but I have a bed here, and a kitchen downstairs.

Most of all, I have done all I could to keep Lily out of a lockdown, punishing school, where she can be put away, pretty much out of sight, until she's eighteen. And I got lucky, since Jill, providing an alternative scheme to Northampton as quickly as possible, discovered a great little private school in a townhouse only two blocks north of here—The Beekman School. It is for good kids like Lily who have gotten into some sort of not-so-terrible teen-age trouble. There is heavy one-on-one tutoring. Ninety per cent of the graduates go on to college. There is now only one other kid in Lily's English class! And it isn't all that expensive, much cheaper than Cushing Academy. I had no idea such a sweet institution existed so close to home. Lily likes it a lot, and it likes Lily.

I am living one day at a time, and have to, Jill is so volatile. A Christmas and New Year's vacation in a beachfront cottage on St. Barts was planned and paid for (no refunds) almost a year ago. There are three airplane tickets, and it is now understood that I will not use one of them, but that Lily can bring along a friend in my place. I pray this really happens. Jill, as punishment for some very slight offense, could easily cancel so as to sicken me and make Lily cry. Departure date is December 22.

Love—
DAD

December 10, 1999

[New York City]

To Mary Jane "Majie" Failey

Dear Majie—

Mary Batch asked me what I wanted for my birthday, and I said, "A photo of when you were sixteen," which she sent me. This old geezer looks at that unearthly beauty and damn near swoons.

I love you, too, and am so relieved that you are getting rid of one more damn house to worry about. I wish I could do the same with our poor old sick and empty relic in the Hamptons, but, alas, my co-owner, who doesn't like it, says it "isn't her taste," will not let that happen.

As you may know, I took a bad spill while crossing a blacked-out parking lot in Northampton November 22nd, messed up my left side and strained my ribcage, and so am com-pelled at last to admit how awfully old I am. So now I stay in my room here, and, like other old folks, watch TV and pretty much hibernate.

K

December 14, 1999

New York City

To Nanny Vonnegut

Dearest Nanny—

I reply to your good letter about what I've done to your heart—not once but several times:

One of my dear brother's favorite stories, which he got from a newspaper, I think, was about a woman whose car went out of control in a suburb. The car went through front yards, knocking down mailboxes and picket fences and post lanterns and shrub-bery and so on. But then it made a u-turn at the end of the block, and went through the back yards of the same houses, wrecking barbecues and wading pools and teeter-totters and slides and so on. It finally stopped up against a big tree. The woman, miraculously, was still OK. When asked why she hadn't turned off the ignition, she said, "I was too busy steering."

So whenever I've broken your large and blameless heart, it was because I was too busy steering. Like the woman in the car, I have almost always been without a female pal—a come-hell-or-high-water sidekick in the passenger seat. I have tried to do what was best for my children, which, among other things, required that I somehow make money any way I could—selling cars, writing ads in Boston, teaching writing at a university a thousand miles away from my family. For a very brief but unforgettable time, I really did have a female sidekick in Iowa City, who really enjoyed what I believed and wrote. Guess who.

When my car went out of control most recently, and I actually wound up in an ER, I was hoping to rescue normal Lily from incarceration in a maximum security lockdown for teen-age criminals. You made a plan which would allow me to do this, and, until I took a tumble in the dark, I was all set to do it—even though I would be without a female sidekick under the same roof when the sun went down in the wintertime in Northampton. I had done as much for Edie, getting her out of brain-dead Barnstable High so many years ago.

When I got back to this city all bunged up, and realizing that I was 77, for God's sake, and having been told that Jill would do all within her power to prevent Lily's going to Northampton High, and that Jill had found what is really a good school for Lily, which we didn't know existed, only two blocks away, I went to bed in a bed which had been mine for years, in a room where all my things were. I was exhausted and actually injured, and so gave myself what was unavailable from anyone else, which was TLC.

Jill and I are not speaking, thank goodness, and I am on the mend and Lily has begun to recapture the lost half of her junior year, and has made a lot of new friends. She is now the fourth member of our family to swear off liquor for the rest of her life, proudly counting the days since she has done so—although she, unlike the other three, is not a genetic alcoholic.

And I am not about to turn off the ignition. I could never do that to the rest of you.

Love as always—
DAD

THE TWO THOUSANDS

In the first month of the new millennium, Vonnegut was on his bed watching the Super Bowl and smoking his customary Pall Malls, when an ashtray overturned and started a fire. He tried to put it out himself with a blanket, causing the flames to spread to the whole top floor of his townhouse. Kurt was rushed to the hospital, suffering from smoke inhalation, and was listed as critical, but he recovered to be released five days later. He had often complained that the Pall Malls he smoked had failed to live up to their promise on the package to kill him, and now—although not in the manner promised—they almost did.

When he was released from the hospital, Kurt repaired to an apartment in Northampton, Massachusetts, where his daughter Nanny and the three Adams brothers were nearby to look after him and drive him on errands. His son, Mark, in Boston and his daughter Edie on Cape Cod came to check up on him, so all six of his children were within comfortable driving distance. During this difficult period, which he compared to "The Battle of the Bulge," he enjoyed the support of the kind of extended family he had spent a lifetime extolling.

Kurt signed on to teach at Smith College that fall and had a show of his silk-screen paintings at a local gallery in October. He stayed on to teach in the spring semester and began a new novel about a stand-up comedian, titled *If God Were Alive Today,* based on the joke that "If God were alive today he would be an atheist." He returned to New York just before Memorial Day of 2001.

The novel didn't seduce him into completing it, and he spoke little about it but continued with his drawing and silk screens. The artwork gave Kurt an important creative outlet in the times when he felt like one of Melville's whalers who "had said absolutely everything they could ever say."

An exhibition of the silk screens of Kurt and his collaborator, Joe Petro III, was held in July of 2004 at the Indianapolis Art Center, along with paintings by Vonnegut's architect and painter grandfather, his architect and painter father, his painter daughter Edith, and his son, Mark, the doctor–writer–painter. In an author's note at the end of *A Man Without a Country,* Vonnegut said that the English artist Ralph Steadman sent him a note of congratulations when he heard about this "family show" from Joe Petro III. Kurt wrote in reply that Petro had "staged a reunion of four generations of my family in Indianapolis, and he has made you and me feel like first cousins." In that same Author's Note, Vonnegut wrote that "one of the best things that ever happened to me, a one-in-a-billion opportunity to enjoy myself in perfect innocence, was my meeting Joe . . . it seems quite possible in retrospect that Joe Petro III saved my life. I will not explain. I will let it go at that."

It turned out that Vonnegut, unlike Melville's whalers, had more to say after all—if not in the novel he thought he had been seduced by in 2000 then in op-ed pieces, speeches, political commentaries, and poems. W. H. Auden wrote of William Butler Yeats that "mad Ireland hurt him into poetry." In the same sense, one could say that the America of the Bush administration during those years—the war in Iraq, the "Wall Street crapshoot," the country's blithe refusal to deal with the urgent ecological threats—drove Kurt back into writing.

At the urging of Joel Bleifuss, the editor of *In These Times,* a Chicago biweekly, Vonnegut wrote a series of luminous essays that Dan Simon, the publisher of the small Seven Stories Press, had the good sense and foresight to publish as a book. *A Man Without a Country* became an overnight bestseller. It was Vonnegut's "last hurrah" and it was not only comprised of scathing commentaries on war, greed, and the destruction of the planet but also hard-earned wisdom, humor, insight, and instruction on writing and on life, which might be summed up in the advice he gave a young fan: "There's only one rule that I know of [. . .] God damn it, you've got to be kind." He first delivered that message in his 1965 novel *God Bless You, Mr. Rosewater.* It was implicit in all his work, what Henry James called "the figure in the carpet"—the thread that was woven through the story, including the story of his life.

Throughout all the public and personal pressures and challenges, Vonnegut produced new work in both writing and art, and continued major speaking engagements in his eighties. He finished writing a speech he was to give in his hometown of Indianapolis (published in *Armageddon in Retrospect*), where at last he was fittingly honored with what had been officially decreed as "The Year of Vonnegut." Only weeks before he was scheduled to give the talk, he fell from the steps of his brownstone in Manhattan and, in the words of his doctor son, Mark, "irreversibly scrambled his precious egg" and died in the hospital on April 11, 2007.

From all indications, there will be many more "years of Vonnegut," not only in Indianapolis, where a Vonnegut Museum and Library has been established. Just as his novels of the 1960s had a special appeal for the youth of the time, he was rediscovered by another young generation with the publication in 2005 of *A Man Without a Country.* He appeared on *The Daily Show with Jon Stewart* to an appreciative audience and applause. All his books are still in print, and his books are taught in college and high school literature courses throughout the country. My friend Shaun O'Connell, professor of English at the University of Massachusetts at Boston, told me recently he couldn't get his students interested in Updike or Bellow anymore, "but they still love reading Vonnegut."

Last fall I was having a Coke after school with my goddaughter, Karina Corrales, who's a sophomore at Miami Senior High School, when she told me her class in literary arts had just read a really cool story. The only reading she had found to be really cool in the past several years centered around vampires, and I was curious to know if high school teachers had resorted to using tales from the crypt. Karina couldn't remember the name of the story or the name of the author, but she said it was about this time when everyone had to wear weights so everyone could be equal, but there was this one guy who didn't like it, and he threw off his weights and told everyone else to do the same.

"Was the guy who didn't want to wear the weights named Harrison Bergeron?" I asked her.

"Yeah!" she said. "How did you know?"

"The guy who wrote it went to my high school," I said. "A guy named Vonnegut."

January 1, 2000
[Northampton, MA]

To Edie Vonnegut

Dearest Edie—

What a good-looking and honorable family we continue to be. I am so heartened by that supremely dignified photograph of Will. I only wish his name was Vonnegut.

In the same mail with that picture I received from a stranger a photograph of my father when he was Will's age—in 1902. Born in Indianapolis, as was his father Bernard, he nonetheless went to a high school for Americans in Strasbourg, France, for I think one year. That is where the picture was taken. I don't have to tell you Kurt Senior is the one on the picture's right. These faces live on and on. Father, like you, was a good citizen, a founder, among other virtuous activities, of the Children's Museum of Indianapolis, one of the best in the world, and designer of a landmark clock at the corner of Washington and Meridian Streets, in the precise center of town, which intersection was and may still be called "The Crossroads of America." I was in Indianapolis last June,

and I walked under that clock, and I looked up at it, and I said
out loud, "Hi, Dad."
  Love as always—
    DAD

March 25, 2000
[Northampton, MA]

To Knox Burger

Dear Knox—
  How sweet it is to hear from you, old friend, and to know that
bygones are really bygones. I worry about your health. Your warm
letter finds me writing a tribute to Joe Heller, to be read at the
academy on April 4th. That will be my first return to Manhattan
since a fire in our brownstone ruined only one room on Superbowl
Sunday. But in that room, lost to me now, were my papers, books,
bed and clothing, including my tuxedo. Jill's and Lily's quarters
and the rest of the house, save for minor water and smoke damage,
are still O.K., but Jill doesn't want me back until repairs are made.
The property is generously insured, but Jill has yet to let in workmen. And yes, good old Knox, I am a neighbor of relatives, my
daughter Nanny and the three Adams brothers, who drive me on
errands and otherwise take good care of me. [. . .]
  Cheers—
    Kurt Vonnegut

April 28, 2000
Northampton, MA

To Miller and Mary Louise Harris

Dear Miller and Mary Louise—
  Find above my new address, as of May 1, where my telephone

number remains the same. I am always happy and encouraged when I hear from you. You have been so supportive as I muddle through this new adventure. Battle of the Bulge indeed. But not really, except that the weather has been terrible. I now have four of my six middle-aged children within a radius of only twenty miles, and the other two, one in Boston and the other on Cape Cod, are coming to check up on me this weekend. I am getting divorced, and have a one-year lease on the above property, and expect to do some teaching at Smith, and maybe Amherst, too, when the leaves turn to gold. I read the obituaries in the *New York Times,* and all those making their departures are in their eighties and nineties now. Merde!

Strictly entre nous: I understand better than ever why the Muses are women, not children or men. Women have the power to renew the ambition and wit of men adrift, and have done that twice for me so far, once in Iowa City in 1965, and then in Saga-ponack, to which place I had been exiled in 1991. Both times, after sleeping with these angels, I started writing and making pictures again. Not a word of this to anyone! Bellow and Mailer have renewed themselves in this fashion again and again, as though buying new cars—but, my God, just think of the paperwork!

There will be a show of about forty of my silk-screen pictures in a gallery here next October or so. The foliage itself is worth a trip that time of year.

Love—

Kurt

May 11, 2000

[Northampton, MA]

To Norris and Norman Mailer

Norris Church (born Barbara Jean Davis in Russellville, Arkansas) was married to Norman Mailer in 1980. A novelist herself, she died in 2010.

Dear Norris and Norman—

Here's a dirty postcard I picked up on my recent trip to Gay Paree. That's sweet news that your treatments are going well, Norris. I'm better, too, thank you, but don't think I'll live in New York City any more. I've been offered a job by Smith College, and I sure need something to do. My writing grows clumsier with each passing day, my blurb for your fine book, Norris, a case in point.

Günter Grass asked me one time when you and I were born, Norman, and I said "1923" and "1922," and he said, "Do you know there is no male your age in Europe for you to talk to?"

Cheers and Love—

Kurt Vonnegut

June 4, 2000

Northampton, MA

To MILLER AND MARY LOUISE HARRIS

Dearest of Old Friends—

Your unexpected and typically unstinting gift to me of finest raiment put me in mind of Napoleon in exile on Elba. I am taller than he was, but I know as did he what it was like to be a Corporal, and then to be ousted from scenes of triumphs in later years. My own Corporalcy was a brevet rank, awarded shortly before my discharge. I don't know about his. His quarters on Elba were reasonably comfortable, as are mine in Northampton—and he too must have received well made and tasteful gifts like yours from those who still thought well of him. Smoke and flames in my face from a fire possibly but not certainly caused by my own careless disposal of smoking materials were my own Waterloo. In any case, Napoleon was humbled, and so am I. Come see me! I have a guestroom with its own sanitary facilities indoors. Do you suppose Napoleon had to use a privy out back?

Smith College is only two thousand yards from here, and I expect to teach "creative writing" there next fall. Can do! I will not do there what I did when in exile in Iowa City in 1965, which was to interfere with a student's clothing.

I have been asked by New American Library to write a preface for their popular volume containing *The Scarlet Letter, The Red Badge of Courage, Billy Budd,* and *Huckleberry Finn.* Before setting to work, I intend to read all four of those. What I have already read is Oscar Wilde's *De Profundis,* which knocked my effing block off.

Thank you so much, dearest of old friends.

Kurt

August 6, 2000
Sagaponack, NY

To Robert Maslansky

Dear Bob—

Do you Darwinists ever consider the possibility that somebody might do something for the sheer hell of it, and the heck with survival?

I will play your game about religion for the sheer hell of it, and call your attention to this conclusion by the late Harvard theologian Harvey Cox: What made Christianity comforting to so many was the congregation. Surprise, surprise, an extended family, as essential to human health as food.

If you want to fatten your essay some, why not write about the fantastic growth of Christianity in a Roman Empire which was so cruelly opposed to it. The state religion formed crowds of strangers to propitiate gods in enormous buildings or plazas. Christians prayed with cozy little bunches of friends who met regularly in cozy little places, which felt much better. The mottos of both Christian and Jewish congregations in those days might have been this: "Religion on a Human Scale." And never mind fighting or reproducing.

Cheers—
Kurt

March 6, 2001

[Northampton, MA]

To Knox Burger

President Clinton granted most of his 140 presidential pardons on his last day in office.

Dear Knox—

I remember you. Didn't I dedicate a book to you one time? [. . .]

I myself am all alone and as celibate as any heterosexual Roman Catholic priest, in a spiffy apartment in Northampton, the dyke capital of the world, where the only African-American resident is my boss Ruth Simmons, the president of Smith. Maybe you heard she's going to be president of Brown next year. A twofer! Her PhD is in French literature. When I was at Iowa a thousand years ago, we invited Ralph Ellison to lecture. His subject turned out to be guess what? French literature. He used to work in a slaughterhouse, and he said the best cut of beef is the strip which wraps the filet mignon. I don't eat steak anymore. A steak now looks like a great big plate of fudge. Too much! My two African-Americans at Iowa hated *Invisible Man*. Generation gap! Ellison collected pre-Columbian pottery. A guy is now writing a biography of Dick Yates, and he called me. I told him about the time Yates set his bed on fire, and I visited him in the burn ward at Bellevue, and he asked me for a cigarette. I asked the biographer if he had read *Winnie the Pooh*. He had, and I told him Dick Yates was Eeyore. Just for fun I told him what Nelson Algren said to the Chilean novelist Jose Donoso out there in Iowa: "It must be nice to come from a country that long and narrow."

I still smoke like a house afire, having at last actually set my house afire. That's why I came up here, to be near my daughter Nanny and my three adopted nephews, while recovering from smoke inhalation. I am suing Brown & Williamson. They promised to kill me on every pack of Pall Malls, but here I am, having accepted an enormous advance from Putnam for a book I can't write.

My efforts reek of ennui. Clinton's pardons cut my nuts off. It would be a tremendous relief to have supper with you and Kitty and the Harrises during Smith's spring break, which begins on the fifteenth of this month. I will be in New York and will give you a ring.

Cheers—

Kurt Vonnegut

October 11, 2001

[Northampton, MA]

TO ROBERT AND LINDA WEIDE

Bob & Linda—

If you haven't yet screened *Mother Night,* explain that Campbell is a stand-in for the Germans who participated in the Holocaust, who said afterwards, "Anybody who knows me knows that really wasn't the real me."

You might say, too, that the film has never been shown in Germany and Israel because what was *said* by Nazis about Jews is unbearable. What was done to Jews has become an acceptable staple in films.

About *Happy Birthday* [*Wanda June*]: Hemingway was never a soldier, and never killed a human being.

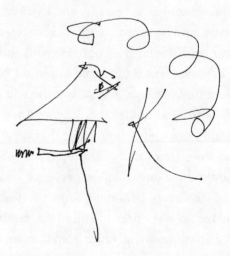

10 AM EST
OCT. 11, 2001

October 17, 2001
[New York City]

To Robert and Linda Weide

Dear Bob and Linda—

[. . .] My mistake in *Player Piano* was my failure as a futurist. I did not foresee transistors, and so imagined that super computers would have to be huge, with bulky vacuum tubes taking up a lot of space.

As for *Happy Birthday*:

I once led a Great Books Study Group on Cape Cod, and we read and discussed Homer's *Odyssey*. I found the behavior of Odysseus after arriving home unexpectedly from the Trojan War hilariously pig-headed and somehow Hemingway-esque. And then I remembered the blowhard father of a girl I dated in high school, who had heard of huge rubies to be found in the Amazon Rain Forest, and wanted to quit his job and go look for them. The rest is history. We would be running still at the Lucille Lortel Theatre down in the village, if Equity hadn't called an off-Broadway strike which went on for months. We had had full houses every night. We were already paying more than what the union was striking for, but the theater owner, in sympathy with other theater owners, closed us down. Our cast, Kevin McCarthy and Marsha Mason and Bill Hickey and on and on, had become as adept and merry an ensemble as the Harlem Globetrotters. A movie was based on my masterpiece, but without our cast it was a stinker.

I can't attend the opening, but break both legs.

Kurt

January 11, 2002
New York City

To Jerome Klinkowitz

Klinkowitz had asked Kurt for background information for one of the books he was writing.

Dear Jerome—

The ASTP was a scheme for stockpiling college kids, with no hope of promotion or getting into OCS, until they were needed as riflemen. There was already a glut of officers and noncoms. I studied calculus and mechanics and thermodynamics and so on, for which the Army had no use, God knows, at Carnegie Tech and then the University of Tennessee. I was then assigned to the 106th Division, from which all Privates and PFC's had been stripped as overseas replacements. It still had its original officers and noncoms. I was made an Intelligence and Reconnaissance Scout, Second Battalion, 423rd Infantry, although my only basic training was on the care and feeding of a 240 mm howitzer. Fortunately, my father had been a gun nut. So practically all my fellow prisoners in the Schlachthof were college kids stockpiled in ASTP. Our own suspicion afterwards, since we had so little ammunition and were still awaiting winter equipment, and never saw an American plane or tank, and were not warned that the Germans were massing large numbers of tanks for one last major attack, is that the 106th was bait in a trap. In chess this is called a gambit. Take the exposed pawn and you've lost the game.

My sister Alice early in the war married a girlhood sweetheart James C. Adams, one of the first draftees and a Second Lieutenant. He would eventually wind up a Captain in Army Public Relations in London and then Paris, although the Army had taught him to fly a spotter plane for the Field Artillery. He got home before I did, and met his son, whom I had already met. In Army PR, as you might imagine, he had met a lot of East Coast people who had been successes in civilian life in publishing of every sort, in sales promotion, as show business press agents, and on and on. So only the East Coast would do. So yes, he and his wife and kid moved to New Jersey at once, alert for opportunities for an all-purpose go-getter like himself. Indianapolis could not hold him.

He would become a passenger on, as far as I am able to determine, the only railroad train to go full bore off an open drawbridge. This being America, one would have thought that must have happened a hundred times.

Cheers—

KV

September 12, 2002

New York City

To THE EDITORS OF *The New York Times*

Dear Editors:

It may give us some comfort in these worrisome times to know that in all of history only one country has actually been crazy enough to detonate atomic weapons in the midst of civilian populations, turning unarmed men, women and children into radioactive soot and bonemeal. And that was a long, long time ago now.

Yours truly,

Kurt Vonnegut

November 30, 2002

New York City

To STIG CLAESSON

Dear Stig—

[. . .] Not only have all my contemporaries, like yours, gone to paradise, but the country I used to write for is no longer anywhere to be found, hard as I may look for it. What made it disappear is TV, which turns out to be life enough for almost everybody, including my twenty-year-old daughter, and in large measure my sixty-year-old wife, too, these days. Quite a success for technology! The H-bomb and antibiotics pale by comparison.

The late humorist James Thurber wrote a fable set in a medieval court, and he has the Royal Astronomer report that all the stars are going out! It turns out that he is simply going blind. I am probably making the same mistake.

Cheers—

Kurt Vonnegut

June 6, 2004
New York City

To Jerome Klinkowitz

This is one of the postcards Vonnegut began sending out to friends, which reflected his feelings about the state of the world in this era.

Dear Jerry—

I consider the sentiment on this card to be my own $E=MC^2$. What do you think?

K

Life is no way to treat an animal.
Kilgore Trout

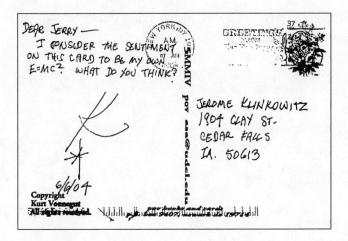

DEAR JERRY —
I CONSIDER THE SENTIMENT
ON THIS CARD TO BE MY OWN
E=MC². WHAT DO YOU THINK?

GREETINGS
FROM

JEROME KLINKOWITZ
1904 CLAY ST.
CEDAR FALLS
IA. 50613

6/6/04

Copyright
Kurt Vonnegut
All rights reserved.

July 6, 2004
[New York City]

To Robert Weide

Dear Bob—

That's nice to hear that you will be writing in Barnstable.

Have Edie show you the underpass on Rte. 6A, where she
has painted angels, and the stone garage in West Barnstable,
where I sold SAABs and wrote "Rosewater," and the Barnstable
Comedy Club, of which I was once President and which inspired "Who Am I This Time," and the Madonna in St. Mary's
Church, which used to be in our atheistic homes in Indianapolis,
and which I gave to the church in memory of my sister after our
father died.

As for "Cold Turkey:" I sent you a video of my performing it
in full in Spokane.

I now hate travel, and on Thursday will make what I hope
will be my last trip. It will be to Indianapolis, where the Indianapolis Art Center is hanging a show of paintings by my paternal
grandfather, my father, myself, my son the doctor Mark, and
Edie. I'll be back home in the city on Saturday. I never want to
see the Hamptons again, but will almost certainly be forced to do

so. I have scarcely had a day worth living since the fire, am bored
absolutely shitless by myself.

    Cheers—

      Kurt

November 21, 2004

New York City

To STEVE ADAMS

Dear Steve—

    This book is bound to be fun for those of us who know and
love you, but not for total strangers. For you to make any money
from it you have to give strangers a reason to spend money on it:
because you are famous, or highly trained and experienced in
helping others deal with life, or you converse regularly with
God, or whatever. From the very first, you yourself declare yourself ignorant and undistinguished amd uninvolved in helping
others, a sort of charming thing to do, I guess, but surely no in-
ducement for a browsing stranger, troubled or not, to buy a
book.

    What shows is your longtime involvement with standup co-
medians. This is their kind of material, their kind of delivery.
They do have authority, by God, since they have wound up in
front of an audience, are in person, not ink on paper, and are
known to entertain with highly idiosyncratic, off-the-wall ideas
and a twanging stage presence. I have often thought that you
might become a first rate standup. And now I imagine your
doing the bit about which of two things I would hit with a
shovel. Perfect. And about the cardboard sex symbol in the record store, with your two boys looking at a lava lamp, and on
and on.

    But you have to be alive and desperate in front of a mike in a
club, or you can't get away with it. Or such is my opinion, and I
agree with what you say about opinions, that they are "not

stuff," and thus famously insubstantial and subject to change. So it is quite possible that a publisher will see in this a goldmine. So by all means show it around, or find an agent willing to do that.

Love and respect as always—

K

December 6, 2004
New York City

To Mary Lyon Robinson

Mary Lyon Robinson was the daughter of Ollie Lyon, who was a friend of Kurt's when they both worked at General Electric in 1949 and remained a friend throughout his life.

Dearest Mary—

What a pleasant surprise to hear from you, and so glad you're O.K. The signed book is on its way. I telephone your dear dad from time to time. He has good reason to be as sad as he is, and neither one of us can do one heck of a lot to cheer him, but it's good we try. Merry Christmas and love—

Kurt Vonnegut

January 31, 2005
New York City

To Peter Reed

How typically smart and kind of you to know what a loss the death of Ollie Lyon was for me. As I wrote for his memorial service: "We had both been infantry privates in combat in Europe during World War Two. When we met, coming to work at General Electric soon afterwards, bingo! Love at first sight!"

My love to you and Maggie as well—

KV

April 19, 2005
[New York City]

To Robert Maslansky

Dear Dr. Maslansky:

Find enclosed your short story "Incident on a Hill," of which I have read every word.

Listen: Story-telling is a game for two, and a mature story-teller, which you are not, is *sociable,* a good date on a blind date with a total stranger, so to speak. In this story, you are obviously unconcerned as to whether the reader is having a good time or not, or even whether he or she has a clue as to what in hell or where in hell you're talking about. If this is Korea fifty years ago, why couldn't you say so? Talk about being anal-retentive!

Nowadays, moreover, practically nobody knows anything or has even heard about that war. You might as well have expected people to respond emotionally to an incident from the Franco–Prussian War.

As for Karl Marx? Was he the one who played the harp or the one who played the piano? Who cares? Not one American in a thousand today has even heard of the Marx Brothers.

And, since you are a doctor, couldn't you *please* tell us what's wrong with this nut?

And who's Yeats?

"Sassoon?" Please!

Don't give up your day job, Doc!

Kurt Vonnegut

October 19, 2006
New York City

To Peter Adams

Peter Adams was the youngest of the four sons of Kurt's sister, Alice, and her husband, Jim.

Dear Peter Boo:

Find enclosed a gift from your mother, my dear sister Allie, a sweet, artistically gifted, knockout blonde almost six feet tall, which she made for you fifty-four years ago.

I do not doubt for a moment that Allie meant for you to have it now. Otherwise, why would a distant cousin, who somehow came into possession of it, have just sent it to me? And why should I feel such urgency about getting it to you as soon as possible?

Allie was "Moptop," living then in New Jersey, and "Doc" was our father, the widower Kurt Vonnegut, Sr., in Indianapolis.

The mother of the distant cousin, whose name need not concern you, was a relative of Kurt, Sr. She must have gotten this treasure from him. The distant cousin explains that she found it among her late mother's effects, which had been in a fire. So this gift to you from your mother has been licked by flames, and also broken in two and mended. So it is alive with a story all its own, which it now tells to you. And you can tell it yours. And you two are together at last, as your mother, I am sure, wished and wished so long ago.

Cheers!

UNKY K

February 6, 2007

New York City

To Professor Alice Fulton

Alice Fulton is an American poet and a member of the faculty at Cornell.

Dear Professor Fulton:

I am of course honored by your invitation and praise of my work, and especially since your department at Cornell is said to be a strong one, as it was in my time there, Class of 1944. Unfortunately back then I was majoring in chemistry, at the insistence of my father: "Learn a trade!"

In any case, I cannot be of any use to you and your students nowadays, alas, since, at 84, I resemble nothing so much as an iguana, hate travel, and have nothing to say. I might as well send a spent Roman candle in my stead.

So no gig there, for want of a performer.

I scarcely write anything anymore, save for letters like this one. I am making pictures, though, which my partner turns into silk screens, [. . .] If you are curious about their nature, you can find some of them at www.Vonnegut.com. I myself can't find them that way, since I don't have a computer, nor a cell phone, nor even an answering machine.

But God bless you for being a teacher.

Cheers, dear Alice, also my sister's name.

* * *

THESE WERE THE last words of advice Vonnegut wrote to be delivered to an audience:

"And how should we behave during this Apocalypse? We should be unusually kind to one another, certainly. But we should also stop being so serious. Jokes help a lot. And get a dog, if you don't already have one. . . . I'm out of here."

EDITOR'S NOTE AND ACKNOWLEDGMENTS

Kurt's letters, which he wrote on the typewriter (he was proud of being a Luddite who never switched to computers) sometimes contained spelling errors that he didn't bother to correct, and I have silently made those corrections for smoother reading. I have also silently corrected punctuation errors. A few of Kurt's later letters were written all in caps, though the content didn't indicate any need for such an emphasis, and I have put them in upper/lower case. (As an old typewriter user, my guess is that the key was already locked on caps and he didn't bother to change it.) I have also removed underlinings, which were often added by hand in the earlier years. In some instances I have removed passages of certain letters—most often to avoid repetition, or to leave out commonplace details such as telephone numbers or lines that the passage of time has made irrelevant or obscure. These deletions are marked with an ellipsis between brackets. In most instances I have removed addresses, except when it seemed the address would be of interest. I have sometimes had to infer the place Kurt was writing from when the letter didn't make it clear and he did not include a return address. In such cases the presumed location is marked within brackets.

Thanks first of all to my longtime friend Mark Vonnegut and my newfound friend Don Farber for making this book possible. Thanks to Don, Mark, and Kurt's daughters Edith and Nanette Vonnegut for generously providing letters for this book.

My thanks to the many friends of Kurt who shared not only

letters but also valuable information based on their friendship with him. These gracious and generous friends include Mary Jane "Majie" Failey, who was a friend of his from childhood throughout his life; Victor Jose, another lifelong friend, from the time they were members of the Owls Club at Shortridge High School to the Chicago News Bureau as fellow journalists after returning home from the Army after World War II and on many of Kurt's trips home to Indianapolis; and Sidney Offit and Dr. Robert Maslansky, Kurt's good friends in New York. S. Miller Harris, his valued friend and mentor from their days on *The Cornell Sun* and throughout his life, has been a great mine of information for me and generous in providing it. At ninety, he is my role model and hero, still working and loving what he does. I found him on Facebook.

The first and perhaps most perceptive critic of Vonnegut's work was Robert Scholes, whose book *The Fabulators* gave the earliest appraisal of Vonnegut's writing. A research professor at Brown University in the department of modern culture and media, his many articles and books include, recently, *The Rise and Fall of English*. He became a friend of Vonnegut's and gave me important letters and information.

Professor Jerome Klinkowitz of the University of Northern Iowa was one of the early academic advocates of Vonnegut's work and an important friend, whom I met because of Kurt's introduction in 1972. He has been an invaluable resource in my work on this book and through his critical books on Vonnegut, most recently *Kurt Vonnegut's America*. Jerry and Julie Klinkowitz supplied invaluable research and support throughout this project.

Thanks to Charles Shields for generously sharing letters and background information.

Thanks to Noah Eaker for his patience and editorial skill.

This work could not have been done without the initial help of my former student at Florida International University, Michele Frau. The final and most arduous, painstaking help was supplied by Kacee Belcher, a graduate student at FIU, who attended to detail, printing, organization, research, technology, and fact checking and editorial assistance of every kind with diligence, intelligence, and expertise. All this was done with the patience of Job and the good humor of Mother Teresa.

Thanks for the support of Les Standiford, chairman of the writing program at Florida International University, and my colleagues there as well as my ally in the English department, Meri-Jane Rochelson; Rick Mulkey, director of the M.F.A. in writing program at Converse College in Spartanburg, S.C., and my colleagues there, including Leslie Pietrzyk, Susan Tekulve, and Denise Duhamel, my former student at Emerson College and later a colleague at FIU and Converse. I am grateful for my gracious and talented students throughout the years from Boston, Iowa, Illinois, Miami, and Spartanburg.

Thanks to Breon Mitchell and Cherry Williams of the Lilly Library, Indiana University, for special assistance and consideration.

Thanks to the following libraries that house the letters of the following correspondents: Princeton University, the letters of José Donoso; University of South Carolina, William Price Fox; University of Delaware, Leslie Fiedler, Seymour Lawrence, Osborne Elliott, Helen Meyer; Boston University, Anatole Broyard; University of North Carolina at Chapel Hill, Gail Godwin; University of Mississippi, Seymour Lawrence; University of Northern Iowa, Jerome Klinkowitz; Bowdoin College, Vance Bourjaily; Coe College, Paul Engle; Stanford University, Allen Ginsberg, Jerry Lefcourt; University of Iowa, Paul Engle, Seymour Krim; University of Connecticut, William Meredith; the Lilly Library of Indiana University, Kurt Vonnegut, S. Miller Harris, Donald Farber, Donald Fiene.

I am appreciative of the sustaining friendships I am fortunate to have across the country, from New York and Boston to San Francisco, and Rancho La Puerta in Tecate, Mexico. Closest to home in Miami and thus subjected to regular entreaties and needed support: Maureen Langer; Marian and Frank delVecchio; Jennifer Hearn; Michele Fievre; Cecelia Fernandez; Jennifer Ammons; Lana Callen and the memory and spirit of her late husband and my great friend, Anthony Gagliano; and Lisette Lezama, the excellent math tutor of my goddaughter and a valued new friend. I must also acknowledge the lifesaving care of Dr. Jane Cohen, Elizabeth Retivov, Judith Hirsch, and May Wong. I ask forgiveness in advance for those I have unintentionally left out and will curse myself later for omitting. Finally, I am blessed with the inspiration of my recent years, my goddaughter, Karina Corrales.

INDEX

Page numbers in *italics* indicate
correspondence with individuals.

Abbadusky, Susan (Susan Van Kirk),
      365–66
abstract expressionists, 310, 315
Academy Awards, 216, 237, 268
"Account of the Ancestry of Kurt
      Vonnegut, Jr., by an Ancient Friend of
      His Family," (Rauch), 4, 166
      see also movies; movie stars
Adams, Alexander, *370–71*
Adams, Alice Vonnegut "Allie" (KV's
      sister), xiv, 9–11, 62, 201, 256, 270,
      370, 372, 405, 410
      death of, 30
      marriage of, 404
      Peter's gift from, 411
Adams, Cindy, *236*
Adams, India, 264
Adams, Jackson, *370–71*
Adams, James, Jr., 30, 96, 109, 110, 176,
      196, 201, 224–25, 312, 323, 379, 393,
      397, 398, 401, 404, 405
      as farmer, 165, 195, 208, 211
Adams, James, Sr., 30, 201, 370, 404–5,
      410
Adams, Kurt "Tiger," 30, 96, 109, 110,
      196, 201, 208, 211, 224–25, 312, 323,
      370, 371, 379, 393, 397, 398, 401
Adams, Louise, 10, 12
Adams, Peter, *410–11*
Adams, Steve, 30, 96, 105, 109, 110, 126,
      137, 152, 196, 201, 208, 224–25, 312,
      323, 379, 393, 397, 398, 401
      KV's concerns about, 194–95, 211
      writing of, *408–9*
Adler, Renata, 229

adoption, 30, 196, 272, 292, 312, 323
advances, 129, 182–83, 238, 254, 401
Advertisements for Myself (Mailer),
      70, 93
advertising, 45, 47–48, 82, 116
      KV's work in, 29, 30
afterlife, xvi, 336
Ah, Wilderness! (O'Neill), 92
"Ain't God Good to Indiana"
      (Herschell), 57
Albee, Edward, 273
Alcoholics Anonymous, 153
Algren, Nelson, xxi, 111, *122,* 153, 282,
      314, 401
      death of, 272
      at Iowa Workshop, 73, 101, 102, 106,
      108, 114, 115, 117, 122, 123
      picture of, 115
      wife of, 106, 111, 115
Allen, Robert G., 329–30
Allen, William Rodney, *342–43*
Allen, Woody, 343
Allende, Salvador, 205
"All the King's Horses" (Vonnegut), 35,
      37–38
Alplaus, N.Y., 22–23, 40
Amalrik, Andrei, 225
Ambrosia (band), *231*
Ambrosia (album), 231
American Academy and Institute of Arts
      and Letters, 348–49
American Civil Liberties Union (ACLU),
      279–81, 366
American Humanist Society, xxiv, xxvi
American Institute of Arts and Letters, 259,
      262, 375
Amos, William, *307*
Angels Without Wings (Vonnegut
      Yarmolinsky), 30

Anglo-Saxons, 295, 300
animation, 172
anthologies, 212
Anthony, Mr., 37, 42, 43
anthropology, 316
  cultural, 74
  see also Chicago, University of,
    anthropology department of
anticommunism, 37, 54–55
anti-Semitism, 203, 275–76, 307, 402
antiwar movement, 75, 111
Any God Will Do (Condon), 160–61
Architectural Digest, 271
architecture, xiii–xiv, xv, xviii, 126, 137,
    138, 180, 243, 246, 260, 270, 271,
    333, 356, 370, 372–73, 377
Archy and Mehitabel, 92
Arena (TV show), 292
Arkin, Alan, 162
Armageddon in Retrospect (Vonnegut),
    272, 395
"Arme Dolmetscher, Der" (Vonnegut), 35
Armstrong, Louis, 306
Army, U.S., 3, 4, 7, 9–10, 12–13, 17, 32,
    181, 223, 252, 298, 332, 345, 387,
    404
Army-McCarthy hearings, 54–55, 56
arts, 40, 52, 117–18, 174–75
  see also specific arts
Asimov, Isaac, xxvi
Association of Japanese Graphic Artists,
    271, 303
ASTP (Army Specialized Training
    Program), 3, 4, 32, 404
Atheneum, xiii, xiv, xviii, 246, 370, 373,
    376
Atlantic, 35–36, 39, 137
Atlantic/Little Brown, 127
Atlantic Monthly Press, 74, 126–27
atomic weapons, 405
Auden, W. H., 324, 394
Aurthur, Robert Alan, 61, 62
Auschwitz, 216, 336
Austria, 175, 176–77
Authors Guild, 235, 250, 251
autobiographies, problem with, 314
Autobiography of a Spy (Bancroft), 181
autographs, 100, 148–49, 286, 369
Axel's Castle (Wilson), 85

Bachelor, Roger, 219
Bagombo Snuff Box (Vonnegut), xvii, 29,
    336
Ballad of Dingus Magee, The (Markson),
    122
Bancroft, Mary, 181–82

Barnes and Noble, 365
Baron, Carole, 310
Barth, John, 95, 133, 134
Barthelme, Donald, 311
Baruch, Bernard, 59
Batch, Mary, 390
Baxendale, R. A., 322
BBC, 292–93, 299, 305
Beatles, 75, 76, 141
Beauvoir, Simone de, xxi
Beekman School, 389, 391
Bell, Marvin, 298
Bellevue Hospital, 297, 401
Bellow, Saul, 135, 363, 395, 398
Bepko, Gerald L., 346–47
Bergler, Edmund, 348
Better Homes and Gardens, 77–78
Between the Lines (Wakefield), xvi
Between Time and Timbuktu (TV show),
    172, 173, 174
Bierce, Ambrose, 316, 318, 335
Big Bang Theory, 382, 385
birthday gifts, 115, 148, 173, 221, 292,
    390
Blake, William, 241, 298, 350
Blakemore, Carolyn, 127–28
Bleifuss, Joel, 394
Bloodline (Sheldon), 280
Bluebeard (Vonnegut), 271, 315, 329
board games, 29, 63–64
boats and sailing, 66–67, 83, 84, 91, 99,
    146, 257, 260, 299
  of Mark Vonnegut, 183, 214
Bob and Ray Show (radio show), xxv,
    325
Bobbs-Merrill, 5, 20, 21
Bogart, Humphrey, 149
Boles, Bob, 148
Böll, Heinrich, 305–6, 319
book burning, xxi–xxii, 154, 279
book reviews, 69, 252, 253
  by KV, xx, 74, 81, 103, 156,
    160–61
  of KV's work, xxiii–xxiv, 66, 94, 97,
    272, 284–85
bookstores, xi, 148–49, 365
Boorstin, Daniel, 116, 118
Booth, Wayne, 116–17
Borges, Jorge Luis, 291
Boris (chess robot), 261–62
Boston, Mass., xx, xxiv, 69, 173, 207, 379,
    393, 395, 398
  advertising in, 29, 30, 82
  publishing in, 74, 75, 126, 127
Bourjaily, Tina, 111, 115–16, 206–7,
    213

Bourjaily, Vance, 111, *186, 206–7, 212–13, 244–45, 252,* 376
  at Iowa Workshop, 73, 101, 102, 105, 106, 109, 114–17, 128, 132, 139
  plays of, 179, 186, 213
Bradbury, Ray, 67, 68
Brague, Harry, *49–51, 52–54, 59–60, 64–65*
Brague, Lewis Benjamin, 52
Brandt, Carl, 130
"Brassard, Mourning, Official" (Harris), 32, 34
Bread Loaf Writers' Conference, 136, 137
Breakfast of Champions (Vonnegut), 151, 154, 168, 184, 189, 222, 365, 388
  drawings for, 222, 270, 337
  movie script for, 321–22
Breeze, 371
British Columbia, 165, 170
Brothers Karamazov, The (Dostoevsky), 5, 223
Broyard, Anatole, 253–54, *284–85*
Bruccoli, Matthew J., 142–43
Bruce, Lenny, 90, 321
Buckman, Gertrude, 105
Buffalo, N.Y., 271, 319–20, 321
bureaucracy, 44, 358–59
Burford, Byron, 132
Burger, Knox, 31–32, 37–49, *41–49, 54–50, 60–63, 65–70, 76–78, 79–91, 93, 94, 96–97, 99–100, 115–16, 121, 122–23, 124–26, 136–37, 145–46, 150–51, 152, 158–59, 161–62,* 167, 193–94, 272, *288–89,* 313, *351–52, 397, 401–2*
  at *Collier's,* 6, *25–26,* 28, *37–38,* 42–44
  at Dell, 28, 44, *66–67,* 68
  at Gold Medal Books, *68–70*
  KV discovered and guided by, 6, 25–26, 28, 227, 331
  KV's professional break with, 155, 162, 227–28, 351
  literary agency of, 150, 155, *156, 158–59, 158, 159, 162, 172*
  marital separation of, 121
  Mark Vonnegut and, 172
Burger, Mary Otis, 44, 69, 77, 101, 121
Burns, Bill, 329
Burns, George, 26, 47
Bush, George W., 394
Butler University, xxv, 339, 377

Caine Mutiny, The (movie), 149
Caine Mutiny, The (Wouk), 149
California, 43, 67, 68, 147
Cambodia, 75

Cambridge, Mass., xvi, 376
Camp Atterbury, 3, 9–10, 223
Campbell, Bruce, 322
Canada, 156, 343, 370
Canary in a Cat House (Vonnegut), 35, 84, 85, 87, 93
Cape Cod, xi, xx, 28–30, 51, 73, 74, 167, 196, 205, 210, 211, 224, 308, 334, 350, 383, 388, 398
  KV's revulsion to, 121, 152
  KV's visitors on, 76, 78–79, 126, 127, 150
  SAAB on, 29, 85, 150
  theater on, 29, 41, 70, 100, 152, 159
Cape Cod Community College, 29
Capote, Truman, 49, 153, 272, 286, 311, 314
"Captured" (Vonnegut), 130
CARE, 335
Cargas, Harry James, *275–76, 319–20, 375*
Carnegie Tech, 3, 17, 387, 404
cars, *55–56,* 103, 111, 179, 194, 214, 227, 303, 322, 390–91
  SAAB, 29, 85, 150, 367, 407
  theft from, 194
Casey, John, 177, 178
Catch-22 (Heller), 332
Catcher in the Rye (Salinger), 286
Catholics, Catholicism, 261, 302, 317, 319, 339, 375, 376
Cat's Cradle (Vonnegut), xix, 30, 50–53, 65, 74, 80, 87, 88, 95, 154, 316, 334
  movie option for, 89, 150–51, 161–62, 293
  music and, 231
  poetry in, 386–87
  reviews of, 97
Cedar Falls, Iowa, 315, 327
Cedar Rapids, Iowa, 105, 114, 132, 138
Celeste (Vonnegut), 54
Céline, Louis-Ferdinand, 203, 241, 299, 350
censorship, xi, xxi–xxii, 49, 78, 154, 207–10, 222, 300, 365–66
  ACLU and, 279–81, 366
  Welcome to the Monkey House and, 322–23
Cerf, Bennett, 49, 50
Chaplin, Charlie, 41, 293
"Charles Atlas Bodybuilding Course," xvi–xvii
Charles Scribner's Sons, 44–45, 49, 50, 56, 64–65, *65*
Chayefsky, Paddy, 61, 268, 269
Cheever, John, 311
Chekhov, Anton, 177

Chermayeff, Ivan, 270, 274, 276–77
chess, 4, 48, 261–62, 357, 358
Chicago, Ill., 5, 19–20, 32, 105, 108, 123,
      204, 297, 344, 351, 380
Chicago, University of, 5, 31, 117, 118,
      339
   anthropology department of, xi, 5,
      16–17, 20, 23, 32, 38, 74, 116,
      248–49, 276, 385
Chicago News Bureau, xvii, 5, 6, 20
children's books, 270, 274–77, 401
Chile, 200, 205–6, 281, 401
Christians, Christianity, xii, xxiv, 192, 266,
      300, 319, 324, 340, 345, 378, 383,
      400
Church Latin, 271, 319, 321
Ciardi, John, 136, 137
City University of New York (CCNY), 206,
      207, 209, 230
Claesson, Stig, 356, 367, 405–6
Clinton, Bill, 369, 396, 401
Clinton, Hillary, 369
Cody, Paul, 353–54
Cohan, George M., 91
Cohn, Sam, 269
Colette Collage (musical), 161
Collier's, 5, 25–28, 35–38, 40, 42–44, 242,
      331
   fiction folio of, 45–46
   KV's first story in, xii, 6, 25, 28
Collins, John F., 319
Columbia University, 301
Columbus, Christopher, 239
comedians, 320–21, 325, 342, 393, 408
commercial art, 172–73
communes, xx–xxi, 76, 156
Communists, 37
Condon, Richard Thomas, 160–61
Connecticut College, 239
Connection, The (movie), 89
Conrad, Joseph, 177
conscientious objectors, 140–41, 148
Constitution, U.S., 300, 362
   see also First Amendment
Cook County Hospital, 297
Cool World, The (movie), 89
Coover, Robert, 163
copyrights, 179, 220, 221
Cordell, Mr., 91–92
Cornell Alumni Magazine, 353–54
Cornell Alumni News, 97
Cornell Club bar, 47
Cornell Daily Sun, 3, 6, 17, 26, 31, 354,
      384, 385
Cornell University, 3, 6, 17, 55, 56, 291,
      339, 351, 353–54, 377–78, 384–85

Corrales, Karina, 395–96
Cosby, Janet, 362
Costa, Tony, 382–83
Cox, Harve (Jane's father), 96–97, 102
Cox, Harvey (Harvard theologian), 345,
      400
Cox, Jane, see Vonnegut, Jane Marie Cox
Cox, Riah, 71, 81, 97, 102, 115, 117
Coyle, Dick, 329
Crab Orchard Review, 371
creative writing courses, 72–73, 107–8,
      115, 157–58, 354, 368, 399–400
Crone, Joe, 330
Cruger, Frank M., 245–46
Crumb, Robert Dennis (known as R.
      Crumb), 276–77
Cuppy, Will, 380, 381

Dartmouth College, 96, 126, 137
Darwin, Charles, 387
Darwinism, 194, 299, 303, 382, 400
Davis, Richard E., 330
Dayton Daily News, 20
Deadeye Dick (Vonnegut), 271, 292,
      293–94
Dead Souls (Gogol), 255
death, 192, 272–73, 312–14, 339, 398
   see also funerals and memorial services;
      suicide
Death on the Installment Plan (Céline), 203
Debs, Eugene V., xix
DeLa, Chuck, 246
Delacorte, George T., 232, 233
Delacorte/Dell, 129, 310
Delacorte Press, xx, 126, 211, 232–33
Delacorte/Seymour Lawrence, 85, 126
Dell, 28, 44, 51, 65–68, 88, 126, 144, 183,
      184, 232–33
   Doubleday's merger with, 232–35,
      310–11
   Palm Sunday and, 275, 277
Democratic National Convention (1968),
      204
Democrats, xviii, 37, 145, 369
De Profundis (Wilde), 400
detective novels, 81
Detweiler, William, 359–60
Dickens, Charles, 151
Dickey, James, 310
Dien Bien Phu, fall of, 55, 56
Dinsmore, John, 352–53
Dissent, 93
divorce, 247, 344, 347, 351, 368, 388
Dobrynin, Anatoly, 309
Doctorow, E. L., 229
Dole, Robert, 369

Don Juan in Hell (Shaw), 351–52
Donnini, Jim, 330
Donoso, José, 73, 114, 130, 137, *141–42,*
   164–65, 168, 170, 173–74, 191,
   199–200, 205–6, 253–54, 281–82,
   290–91, 305–6, 308, 316–17, 401
Donoso, Maria Pilar, *191,* 205, 206,
   290–91, 305–6, 308, 314, *316–17*
Donovan, Arlene, 269
Donovan, "Wild Bill," 355
Doubleday, 31, 34, 232–35, 310–11
Doubleday Fiction Book Club, 28
Douglas, Kirk, 125
Draft Board #1, *140–41,* 148
Drake, N.Dak., xxi–xxii, 154, 207–10, 366
Drake School Board, 207–10
drawing, 137, 190, 191, 260, 270, 278
   silk-screen prints of, 337, 356, 367, 369,
      372, 393, 394
Dreiser, Theodore, 314
Dresden, 17, 123, 307
   bombing of, 4, 6, 8, 10–11, 75, 95, 136,
      146, 272, 275, 328–30, 358, 380, 383
   KV's return to, 74, 134–38
Driven (Gehman), 80, 81
drugs, 4, 76, 204, 243, 272, 341
Dubin's Lives (Malamud), 262–63
Durrell, Lawrence, 72, 133
Dürrenmatt, Friedrich, *96,* 97
Dysen, Freeman, 358–59

Eagle Shirtmaker, 31, 33, 292
Eden Express, The (Mark Vonnegut), 170
elections, U.S., 145, 184, 204
Eliot, T. S., 85, 298, 341
Elkins, Hilly, 128, 129, 150, 161–62, 293
Elliott, Bob, xxv, 325
Elliott, Osborn, *230*
Ellison, Ralph, 401
End of My Life, The (Bourjaily), 101
England, KV in, 81–82, 90, 172, 187, 190,
   292–93, 295
Engle, Paul, 73, 100, 109, *116–18, 120,*
   122, *197–98, 314*
   KV's relationship with, 103, 105, 106,
      112
   KV's views on, 132
   Rait and, 197–98, 201
"EPICAC" (Vonnegut), 138
Episcopalians, 312, 327
Esquire, 6, 76, 108, 141, 296, 357
"Euphio Question, The" (Vonnegut), 93
Europe, Europeans, 175, 176–77, 226,
   252, 258, 275–76, 278, 300, 343, 378
Ever Since Darwin (Gould), 315
Ewick, Charles Ray, *293–94*

Execution of Private Slovik, The (Huie),
   379

Fabulators, The (Scholes), xxii, 72, 133–34,
   135
Failey, Mary Jane "Majie," *287, 390*
Failey, William "Skip," 287
fall-out shelters, 86–87
families, extended, 152–53, 299, 311, 331,
   393, 400
Family of Man, The (Steichen), 115
Fan Man, The (Kotzwinkle), 193
Farber, Annie, 155, 159, *255, 261–62*
Farber, Donald C., 155, *159,* 161, *179,*
   184, *234–35,* 249, 250, *255, 261–62,*
   268–69, 274–75, 359, 383
   KV's divorce and, 247
   KV's MacDonald memorial contribution
      and, *330–31*
farms, farmers, 111, 165, 195, 208
Farrar, Straus & Giroux, 238
Farrell, James T., 265
Farrow, Mia, 141
Fates Worse Than Death (Vonnegut), 5, 27,
   270–71, 297, 319, 356
Faulkner, William, 5, 49, 50, 219, 240, 245
Fawcett/Gold Medal Books, 81
Feuer, Jed, *304–5*
Fiedler, Leslie, *211–12*
Fiene, Donald M., *222–23, 239–42,*
   276–78, 309–11, 315–16
   Klinkowitz's letter to, 235
   Rait and, *200–201, 220–21,* 222,
      225–26, 240, *254–55, 273–74,* 278,
      301
Film Sense, 161
Finch, Nigel, 292–93
Finholt, Bob, 23
First Amendment, xxii, 154, 279, 280
fish, fishing, 66–67, 83–84, 91, 99, 140,
   299
Fitzgerald, F. Scott, 5, 58, 142, 335
Fixer, The (Malamud), 160, 280
Fonda, Peter, 162
football games, 100, 125, 126, 132, 137
Foote, Horton, 61
Forbes, Gordon, 83, 84
Forster, E. M., xxv
Foss, Lukas, *324–25*
Fox, Sarah, 124, 125
Fox, William Price, *124,* 125, 127, *128–29*
France, 55, 135, 396
   in World War II, 8–9, 10, 12
Frankfurt Book Fair (1977), 252, 254
Freedman, Gerry, 161
freedom, 186, 204, 206

French language, 173–74, 177, 226
Freud, Sigmund, 62
Friedman, Martha, 180–81, 195
friendship, friends, 40, 73, 96, 105, 196, 212, 255, 257
Fuentes, Carlos, 130
Fulton, Alice, 411–12
funerals and memorial services, 252, 265, 312, 330–31, 367, 375, 383, 409

Galápagos (Vonnegut), 271, 300, 303, 306, 308, 309, 310
    Gould's opinion of, 315, 316
García Márquez, Gabriel, 291
Gehman, Richard "Dick," 80–81, 131–32, 143, 298
General Electric, xxii, 20–25, 32, 38, 40, 45, 337, 345, 363, 409
    Bernard Vonnegut's work for, 5, 24, 25
    pay at, 5, 27, 28
General Electric Monogram, 46
General Motors, 16–17
Gerber, John C., 98–99, 112
German language, xiv, 8, 177, 181, 369
Germany, Germans, xiv–xv, 37, 173–74, 255, 378
    in World War II, 3–4, 6–12, 32, 136, 140, 181–82, 243, 275–77, 307, 329, 340, 402, 404
Gertrude (typist), 105, 106
Gibbs, Wolcott, 363
Gilpatric, Guy, 172
Ginsberg, Allen, 76, 170, 375–76
Glaser, Milton, 172–73
Glass Menagerie, The (Williams), 328
Glass People (Godwin), 185–86
Glencannon stories, 172
Glossbrenner, Catey, 370
Glossbrenner, Daniel, 198, 201, 257–58
Glossbrenner, Edna, 198, 201
Glossbrenner, Emily, 201–2, 257–58, 370
Glossbrenner, Mary, 219, 370
God Bless You, Dr. Kevorkian (Vonnegut), 336
God Bless You, Mr. Rosewater (Vonnegut), 30, 94, 95, 104, 267, 388, 395, 407
    movie option for, 128, 129
Goddard, Harold, 241–42
Godfrey, Arthur, 57, 58
Godwin, Gail, 73, 139–40, 163, 177–78, 185–86, 199, 267, 308
    in New York, 196–97, 213, 267
Goethe, Johann Wolfgang von, 39, 242, 252
Gogol, Nikolai, 241
Going All the Way (Wakefield), xx

Gold Medal Books, 68, 79–80, 82, 85
Goldsmith, Les, 161
Gone with the Wind (movie), 153
Goodbye Columbus (Roth), 280
Goode, Jim, 156–57
Good School, A (Yates), 259
Gorey, Edward, 228
Gorky, Maxim, 62–63
Gottlieb, Robert, 199, 213, 384
Gould, Lois, 259
Gould, Stephen Jay, 315, 316, 381–82
Goulding, Ray, xxv, 325
Grana, Edgar, 319, 321
Grass, Günter, 399
Graves, Michael, 372
Great Books course, 29, 48–49, 241, 381, 403
Great Britain, 7, 8, 12, 317
    see also England
Great Depression, xv, xviii, 3, 98, 243, 245, 271, 364
Greece, 150, 225–26, 260
Greene, Graham, 97
Grijalbo, Senor, 173–74
Grivnina, Irina, 263–64, 278, 309
Grossman, Gary, 285–86
Guggenheim Foundation and Fellowships, 126, 127, 142
    KV's receipt of, 74, 135–36, 230
    KV's rejection by, xi, 29, 68
guns, 318, 328, 333, 404

Hackett, Buddy, 345
Halberstam, David, 210, 213
Hamalian, Leo, 207
Hammarskjöld, Dag, 191–92
Handy, Mike, 63–64
Happy Birthday, Wanda June (Vonnegut), 152–53, 161–65, 167, 173, 278, 402
Harper & Row, 117, 122, 135, 163, 275
Harper College, 351
Harper's, xviii, 39, 110, 117, 184
    Miller Harris's work in, 31, 32, 34
Harrington, Alan, 95
Harris, Josephine, 157–58
Harris, Mary Louise, 291–92, 295, 397–98, 399–400
Harris, S. Miller, 31–36, 38–41, 51–52, 97–98, 291–92, 295, 377–79, 382–83, 384–85, 397–98, 399–400
Harvard Lampoon, 376
Harvard University, 51–52, 170, 197, 219, 315, 334
    KV's teaching at, 160, 165, 166, 208, 230
Harvard University Press, 277

Hawkes, John, 133
Hawking, Stephen, 387
Hayman, David, 133, 134, 143, 222
Hearst, William Randolph, 78
Heatter, Gabriel, 54, 56
Heller, Joseph, 207, 213, 321, 332, 397
Help!, 86–87
Hemingway, Ernest, 6, 39, 50, 142, 186, 333, 402, 403
Herschell, William, 57
Hickey, Bill, 173, 403
Hicks, Granville, xxiv, 144, 338
Hill, George Roy, 61, 153
Hills, Rust, 95, 108–9, 212, 296–97
"Hip" (Mailer), 93
hippies, xx–xxi, 75–76, 193, 202
Histoire du Soldat, L' (Stravinsky), 379–80
Hitler, Adolf, 7, 89, 275–76
Hitz, Ben, xvii, 90, 302, 339–40, 341, 376–77, 380–81
Hitz, Ellie, 380–81
Hocus Pocus (Vonnegut), xix, 270, 271, 336, 341–42, 348
Hoffman, Abbie, 76, 204–5
Hollywood, Calif., 43, 117, 124, 237, 370
Holocaust, 275–76, 402
Holt, Rinehart and Winston, 50–51, 65, 66, 94, 95, 126, 127
Homer, 403
Horgan, Paul, 125
Horizon, 278
Horovitz, Israel, 207
Horowitz, Glenn, 372
horses, 29, 84, 111, 116, 151, 340
Houghton Mifflin, 80
Housman, A. E., 324
"HQ" (board game), 63–64
Hudnut, William H., 326, 327
Hughes, Howard, 282
Huie, William Bradford, 379
Humanists, xxiv, xxv–xxvi
Hume, Kathryn, 294–95
humor, xvi, xxv, 74, 108, 217, 316, 318, 351
  see also comedians; jokes
hunting, 111, 140, 148, 333
Hurt, Bill, 349–50

Iceman Cometh, The (O'Neill), 77
If God Were Alive Today (Vonnegut; incomplete novel), 393–94
Image, The (Boorstin), 116
"In a Manner That Must Shame God Himself" (Vonnegut), 184
"Incident on a Hill" (Maslansky), 410

Indianapolis, Ind., xii–xviii, xx, xxv, 3–6, 23, 53, 81, 102, 202, 326, 327, 372–73, 396–97, 407
  Alcoholics Anonymous in, 153
  Athenaeum in, xiii, xiv, xviii, 246, 370, 373, 376
  Bobbs-Merrill in, 5, 20, 21
  jazz music in, 295
  Jews in, 378
  KV's cool reception in, 149
  reunions in, 21, 338–39, 394
  Vonnegut Hardware Company in, xii–xiii, xv, 245–46
  Vonnegut Week in, 287
  "The Year of Vonnegut" in, 149, 395
Indianapolis Art Center, 394, 407
Indianapolis *Turngemeinde* (later Athenaeum Turners), xiii
Indiana State Library, 293–94
Indiana University, 359
Indiana University–Purdue University (IUPUI), 346–47
Ingres, Jean-Auguste-Dominique, 309
inheritance, 214, 266, 379
  financial, 30, 183, 195
  genetic, 190, 241
In Love with Daylight (Sheed), 357
International Copyright Agreement, 220, 221
In These Times, 394
Invisible Man (Ellison), 401
Iowa, University of, 100, 109, 131–32, 219
  KV's course assignments at, 118–20
  KV's program improvement advice for, 117–18
  Writers' Workshop at, 72–74, 98–125, 128–29, 131–32, 139, 177, 178, 185, 203, 208, 230, 247, 335, 401
Iowa City, Iowa, 198, 245, 391, 398, 400
  description of, 104, 105–6, 110, 131–32
  Jane Vonnegut's visits to, 105, 113, 114
  KV's apartments in, 101, 103–4, 106, 111–12, 113
  time in, 102
  University High School in, 112, 113, 117, 120
Iran, 225–26
Iraq, xxv, 394
Ireland, 256
Irving, Clifford, 282
Irving, John, 73, 185, 282, 308

Jailbird (Vonnegut), 155, 260–61, 262, 267, 269, 275, 284, 293
  Slaughterhouse-Five compared with, 155
Jamaica, 165, 184, 194, 195, 201, 210

James, Henry, 381, 395
James, William, 349
Japan, Japanese, 278, 302, 303, 348
Jefferson, Thomas, 186
Jefferson Davis High School, 279
Jesus Christ, xii, xxiv, 270, 274, 324–25,
    366, 378
Jews, 203, 221, 273, 275–76, 321, 340,
    355, 378, 400
    see also anti-Semitism
Johnson, Lyndon, 145
Johnson, Robert, 380
Johnson, Samuel, 383, 385
jokes, 261, 282, 318, 332, 393, 413
Jones, Angela, 103
Jones, James, 153, 183, 248, 252, 272, 314
Jones, Mrs. James, 248
Jones, Tom, 161, 340
Jose, Victor, xvii, 6, 20, 338–39
Journey to the end of the Night (Céline),
    203
Joyce, James, 49, 62, 85, 133
Joyce, Jeremiah, 280
Junior League, Indianapolis, 372–73
Justice, Donald, 117
Just Like Someone Without Mental Illness
    Only More So (Mark Vonnegut), xii,
    29, 152, 170

Kahn, Madeline, 283, 290
Kandy-Kolored Tangerine-Flake Streamline
    Baby, The (Wolfe), 96, 97
karass, concept of, xix
Katmandu (working title; Vonnegut), 277
Kaul, Donald, 125
Keaton, Buster, 320
Kellems, Vivien, 47
Kelton, Bob, 330
Kennedy, Caroline, 100
Kennedy, John F., 93, 320
Kennedy, William G., 322–23
Keough, William, 316
Kinnell, Galway, 377
Klein, Roger, 117
Klinkowitz, Jerome "Jerry," 315–17,
    317–19, 346–47, 348–49, 369–70,
    371–72, 404–7, 406–7
  KV's "biographical" letters to, 3, 4, 24,
    242–44, 248–49, 404–5
  KV's work and, xxiii, xxiv, 154, 188–89,
    242–43, 327, 336, 338, 343, 358, 362
  SUNY Albany professorship and, 235–36
Knopf, 127, 130, 199, 213, 308
Koning, Hans, 239
Korea, 225–26
Korean War, 37, 360

Kotzwinkle, William "Bill," 193–94
Krementz, Jill, see Vonnegut, Jill Krementz
Krieger, Murray, 116, 118
Kunitz, Stanley, 242
Kurt Vonnegut's Monkey House (TV
    series), 343
Kurtzman, Harvey, 86–87

LaForge, Steven, 386, 387
Laos, 75
Lardner, Ring, 173, 316, 318
Larkin, Philip, 350
Laurel and Hardy, xxv, 320
Lawrence, D. H., 263
Lawrence, Seymour "Sam," 74, 126–27,
    129–30, 135–36, 137–39, 144, 147,
    149–50, 151, 156, 168, 184, 188, 193,
    218, 226–27, 229, 234, 259–60, 262,
    274–75
  author's first novel and, xix–xx
  end of his association with Dell, 233
  in Europe, 253, 254, 255
  KV's three-book contract from, 72, 75,
    129
  KV's views on, xix, xxvi
  Mark Vonnegut's writing and, 183
  Slaughterhouse-Five and, xix, 75
  Stafford and, 238–39
LeClaire, "Frenchy," 329
Lee, Harper, 128
Leeds, Marc, xxiii, 333–34, 335, 341–42,
    347–48, 353, 357–58, 363–64
Leen, Dexter, 93
Leen, Percy, 93, 94
Lefcourt, Jerry, 204–5
"Legacy of Strategic Bombing, The" series,
    340
Le Havre, 8–9, 10
Lehr, Bob, 330
Leningrad, 254–55, 263–64, 350
Leonard, John, 196, 197
Lewis, Jerry, 278, 283, 289–90, 300
Lewis, Sinclair, 240
Lexington, Ken., 246, 337, 352–53, 367
libraries, librarians, 293–94, 326–27, 381,
    395
  censorship and, xxii, 154, 279–80, 365,
    366
Library of America, 286
Library of Congress, 327
Liebling, A. J., 238–39
Life, xx, 45, 156, 382
Lindsay, Vachel, 314
Lippincott, 127
literary criticism, 338, 349
Literary Guild Selection, 147

Littauer, Helen, 331
Littauer, Kenneth, 26, 39, 44, 194, 227–28, 313, 331
  KV's plays and, 53–54
  KV's short stories and, 42, 43
Littauer and Wilkinson agency, 27, 39, 46, 66, 95, 127
Little Red Riding Hood, musical version of, 304–5
London, 81, 172, 305
Long Island, 155, 248, 252, 272, 282, 352, 398, 407–8
  KV's house on, 153, 259, 308, 390
"Long Walk to Forever" (Vonnegut), 4
"Lord Haw Haw" (William Joyce), 307, 355
Los Angeles Times, 284
love, 103, 170, 174, 175, 187, 202, 273, 320–21
love affairs, xxi, 73, 178
  stories about, 139, 140
Love As Always, Kurt (Rackstraw), 73
Love Story (Segal), 334
Lowell, Robert, 73
Lumet, Sidney, 61
"Lumumba Lives" (Matthiessen), 328
Lunatic, 351
Lyme disease, xviii, 338, 341
Lyon, Billie, 345
Lyon, Ollie, 337, 345, 353, 368–69, 409

Macauley, Robie, 130–31
McCarthy, Charles, 207–10
McCarthy, Eugene J., 145, 146
McCarthy, Joseph, 37, 54–55
McCarthy, Kevin, 403
McConnell, Suzanne, 118
McDonald, Dorothy, 313–14, 330–31
MacDonald, John D., 272, 313–14, 330, 331
McGuane, Tom, 129
MacMillan, Ian, 117, 118, 128
McNamara, Robert, 359
Madame Bovary (Flaubert), 185
magazines, 139, 154, 310
  golden age of, 5–6, 272, 313
Magnificent Ambersons, The (Tarkington), 53
Maharishi Mahesh Yogi, 75–76, 141, 142
Mailer, Norman, 70–71, 78–79, 93, 193, 311, 352, 398–99
Mailer, Norris, 398–99
Malamud, Bernard, 160, 262–63, 280
Manchurian Candidate, The (Condon), 160
Manchurian Candidate, The (movie), 160
Mantell, Harold, 289

Man Without a Country, A (Vonnegut), xxi, 76, 395
  Author's Note in, 394
  drawings for, 270
Man with the Golden Arm, The (Algren), 101
Margo Feiden Gallery, 270, 278, 365
Markings (Hammarskjöld), 191–92
Markson, David, 122, 123, 357
Marquis, Don, 92
Martian Chronicles, The (Bradbury), 67
Marty (Chayefsky), 268
Marx Brothers, 289, 410
Marxists, 79, 206
"Mary Kathleen O'Looney," see Jailbird
Maschler, Tom, 138
Maslansky, Alex, 367–68
Maslansky, Robert, 297–99, 350–51, 367, 374–75, 385–87, 400, 410
Mason, Jackie, 321
Mason, Marsha, 403
Masters, Edgar Lee, 314
Matchan, Don, 17–19
Matthiessen, Peter, 327–28
May, Ruth, 48
Mayo, Charley, 66–67, 84
Meade, Margaret, 169
Melville, Herman, 335, 337, 369, 394
Memoir of the Bookie's Son (Offit), 346
Mendelsohn, Jack, 379
Mendelson, Jack, 327
Meredith, William "Bill," 231–32, 239, 298
Metropole, 274
Meyer, Helen, 232–34
Miami Senior High School, 94, 395
Midway College, 352–53
Miller, Arthur, 273, 311
Miller, David, 379–80
Miller, Jacob, 31
Miller, Walter James, 256–57, 272, 301–2
Miller, Warren, 89, 90, 103
Mills, C. Wright, 44
Mills, Margaret, 236–37
Mineo, Sal, 232
Mirsky, Mark, 207
Miss MacIntosh, My Darling (Young), 105
Miss USA Beauty Pageant (1976), 236
Mobile, Ala., 156–57
Modern Library, 241, 381
Modern Times (movie), 293
Monthly Review Press, 239
Moore, Paul, 288, 327, 339

Moscow, 216–17, 219, 220–21, 240, 242, 244, 274, 309
  Slaughterhouse-Five in, 222, 225, 372
Mother Night (movie), 289, 337, 343, 349–50, 354–55, 364, 370, 371, 402
Mother Night (Vonnegut), 30, 77–80, 85, 87, 88, 90, 310, 337, 355, 370
  inspiration for "Howard Campbell" in, 307, 355
  movie option for, 161, 293
  reprint of, 117, 122
movies, 53, 101, 107, 122, 128, 149, 160, 178, 216, 268, 269
  in Iowa City, 107, 116, 132
  KV's work and, 61, 70, 89, 125, 127, 128, 129, 150–51, 153, 161–62, 164, 180, 269, 289–90, 293, 300, 337, 343, 349–50, 354–55, 364, 403
movie stars, 75, 141, 149, 160, 216
Mozambique, 222, 335
Müller, Gerhard, 146
Mungo, Ray, xx–xxi, 76, 156, 157
Murdoch, Iris, 72, 133
music, 76, 94, 106, 187, 194, 231, 252, 356, 379–80
  jazz, 295, 342
  Requiem Masses, 270–71, 317, 319–20, 321
musicals, 267, 304–5, 372
My Lai Massacre, 75, 181–82

Naked and the Dead, The (Mailer), 70
Nation, 103, 284
National Book Awards, 230, 232, 236–37, 327, 377
National Educational Television, 172, 173, 174
National Institute of Arts and Letters, 153, 230, 236–37, 273, 301
"Nation of Two" (Vonnegut), *see Mother Night*
Natural, The (Malamud), 160
natural selection, 381–82, 385
Nazi Germany, Nazis, xv, 3–4, 6–12, 32, 37, 77, 78, 181–82, 275–76, 402
  radio propaganda for, 307
NBC Hollywood, 93
Netherlands, 309
Nevelson, Louise, 342–43
New American Library, 400
New Republic, 164
Newsweek, 147, 154, 164, 230
New York, N.Y., 58, 120, 167–75, 180, 186, 198, 281, 297, 336, 383, 393
  churches in, xix, xxv, xxvi, 288
  Godwin in, 196–97

hospitals in, 272, 297, 301, 341, 393
International PEN Congress in, 306, 308
KV's apartment in (East 51st Street), 167, 168, 174, 179, 180, 187
KV's art show in, 270, 278
KV's townhouse in (East 48th Street), 153, 207, 210–11, 213, 214, 301, 344, 384, 391, 393, 395, 397
KV's move to, xvi, 60, 152–53, 167, 196, 214, 243, 247
KV's studio in, 302, 303
KV's views on, 212–13
KV's visits to, 23, 26, 40, 43, 50, 51, 58, 63, 88, 95
KV's wedding in, 266
photo labs in, 364
Rivera in, 177, 178
theater in, 161, 164, 167, 267, 403
New Yorker, 39, 40, 43, 45, 147, 161, 238, 286, 309, 363, 380
  as extended family, 311
New York Philharmonic, 379
New York Post, 236
New York Public Library, 326–27
New York Review of Books, 154, 241, 357
New York Times, xxiii, 86, 97, 125, 154, 196, 210, 216, 253, 288, 378, 398
  KV's letter in, *405*
  KV's op-ed piece in, 154
  Moscow bureau of, 220
New York Times Book Review, xxii, 45, 134, 147–48, 160, 252
  KV's dictionary piece for, 74, 127, 138
New York Times Magazine, 136, 148
New-York Tribune (renamed the *New York Herald Tribune*), 92
New York University, 181
Nhu, Madame, 122, 123
Nicholson, Jack, *321–22*
Nieh, Leslie, 132
Nietzsche, Friedrich, 340
Nigeria, 376
Nobel Peace Prize, 125, 191
Nobel Prize for Literature, 291, 305, 367
Nolte, Nick, 289, 337, 349, 364
Nora's Tale (Edith Vonnegut), 227, 228
Northampton, Mass., 390, 393, 397–98, 399, 401
Northampton High, 389, 391
Northern Iowa, University of, 235–36, 327, 334
North Vietnam, 123
novels, 5, 310, 326
  of Broyard, 253–54
  detective, 81
  see also specific novels

O'Brien, Tim, 129
O'Connell, Ralph, 301
O'Connell, Shaun, 395
O'Connor, Frank, 129
Odyssey, The (Homer), 29, 403
Office of Strategic Services, U.S. (O.S.S.),
    181, 355
Offit, Sidney, *286–87*, 301, *346*
O'Hara, John, 142, 199, 311
O'Hare, Bernard V., 136, *146*, 180, 257,
    329, 338, 340
O'Hare, Mary, 146, 338
106th Infantry Division, 3, 4, 7, 10, 223,
    404
O'Neill, Eugene, 49, 54, 92
On the River Styx (Matthiessen),
    327–28
opera, 369, 372
Oppenheimer, Joel, 207
Orchard School, xv, 287
Origins of the Second World War, The
    (Taylor), 89
Orleans Arena Theatre, 29, 41, 159
Osterville, Mass., 28, 48–49, 53, 57–58
Oswald, Lee Harvey, 93, 320
Our Time Is Now (Vonnegut), xviii
Oxford, Miss., 219, 245
Oxford University, 295
Oxford University Press, 135

Paine, Thomas, 204
painting, 132, 165, 169, 360–61, 394
    by Edith Vonnegut, 145, 165, 227, 228,
        267, 394, 407
    by KV, 94, 187, 407
    KV's work and, 294–95, 310, 315
    by Mark Vonnegut, 94, 145, 148, 394,
        407
    by Prior, 290
Pakula, Alan, 128, 129
Pallaia, Mike, 330
Palm Sunday (Vonnegut), 271, 274,
    277
    autobiography in, xiii, xiv, xv, 4, 74,
        164, 166
    reviews of, 284–85
paperbacks, money from, 183
Paris, 40, 219, 220, 260, 399
Paris Review, KV's interview with, xxiii,
    25–26, 28, 154, 289
Parsons, Estelle, 298
Pasteur, Louis, 58
Paul, Steven, 278, *283–84*, 290, 300
PEN, 153, 221, 225–26, 271, 302, 320,
    384
    New York Congress of, 306, 308

Penelope (Vonnegut), 29, 41, 152, 159,
    161
Pennsylvania, University of, 342
Penrod and Sam (Tarkington), 53
Perelman, S. J., 311
Petrakis, Harry Mark, 125, 126
Petro, Joe, III, 337, 353, 365, 394
Phillips, Jayne Ann, 129
photography, 115, 153, 318, 364, 396
Physicists, The (Dürrenmatt), 96, 97
Piaf, Edith, 291
Piece of Cake (Taylor), 317–18
Pieratt, Asa, xxiii, 353, 358
Pierce, Sam, 385
Pinochet, Augusto, 205
Pius V, Pope, 270
Plato, 49, 212
Platt, Frank, 286
Playboy, 130–31, 136–38, 156
Playboy Press, 277
Player Piano (Vonnegut), xxii, 28, 43,
    44–45, 49, 60, 80, 293, 403
Playhouse 90 (TV show), 61
plays, 58, 70, 96, 97, 162, 163, 178
    of Bourjaily, 179, 186, 213
    KV's writing of, 29, 41, 53–54, 59, 60,
        62, 85–86, 88, 152–53, 159, 161–65,
        308
Plimpton, George, 168, 169
Poetics (Aristotle), 58
poetry, 57, 92, 192, 231, 232
    of KV, 82–83, 173, 386–87
    KV's views on, 298, 375–76, 377, 385
Polanski, Roman, 261
police, 194, 204, 333
police reporting, 20, 32
Porter, Katherine Anne, 127
Potter, Stephen, 76, 77
pottery, 270, 271, 302, 303, 356, 401
Potts, Marjorie, 91–92
Pound, Ezra, 307
Prather, Richard S., 81
Prescott, Peter S., 230
Pricksongs & Descants (Coover), 163
Princeton University, 53
Prior, Scott, 290
prisoners of war (POWs), 146, 305, 307,
    317–18, 328–30
    see also Vonnegut, Kurt, as POW
Producers' Showcase (TV show), 61
"Professionals, the," 272, 314
Professor of Desire, The (Roth), 252
promotional tours, 144, 148–49
Proust, Marcel, 85
Provincetown, Mass., 66–67, 71, 78, 84
psychiatry, 180–81, 195, 197, 224

Pugh, Madelyn, 378
Putnam, 347–48, 373–74, 401

Quakers, 5, 117, 273

Rackstraw, Loree Wilson, 73, 334, *343–44*
Rackstraw, Louis, 343–44
radio, xxv, 54–57, 83, 85, 231, 325, 336
   KV on, 149, 256
   Nazi propaganda and, 307
Rait, Rita, 216, 219–22, 254–55, 263, 264,
   273–74, 286
   mail problems of, 200–201
   planned U.S. visit of, 153, 197–98,
     200–201, 240, 242, 244–45, 272, 278,
     301
Rand, Ayn, 49
Random House, 49
   dictionary of, 74, 127, 138
Rauch, Gertrude Schnull, 166, 167
Rauch, John, 4, *166–67*
Redford, Robert, 61, 160
Reed, Peter, xxiii, *188, 300, 302–3, 315,*
   333, 352, 353, 358–59, 364–65, 372,
   409
   Bagombo Snuff Box and, 336
Reinking, Ann, 380
religion:
   censorship and, 280
   KV's views on, 140–41, 153, 266, 299,
     300, 302, 339–40, 345, 362, 378–79,
     385, 400
"Report on the Barnhouse Effect"
   (Vonnegut), 27, 31, 34
Republican Convention (1972), xviii, 184
Requiem Mass (1570), 270–71, 319
Requiem Mass (Vonnegut version; 1985),
   271, 317, 319–20, 321
Requiem Mass (Webber version; 1985),
   270–71
Rhetoric of Fiction, The (Booth), 117
Riley, James Whitcomb, 57
Rivera, Geraldo, 173, 177, 178, 205–6,
   368, 369
Rivers, Larry, 169
Robbe-Grillet, Alain, 135
Robinson, Mary Lyon, *409*
robots, 261–62
Rockefeller University, 382
Rogers, Charles A., 48
Rolling Stone, 154, 277
Roman Empire, 192, 400
Rome, 220, 261
Rosenau, Fred Simon, 31, 45, 46
Ross, Harold, 363
Roth, Philip, 252, 280

Rowley, Ted, 176
Royal Air Force, 7, 8
royalties, 182, 183
Rupel, Mr., 226–27
Russia, Russians, 37, 216–22, 225,
   273–74, 309
   KV's alleged hatred of, 217–18
   KV's visits to, 216–17, 219, 220–21,
     254–55, 263–64
   translation and, 153, 197–98, 200–201,
     216, 219–22, 240, 242, 244–45,
     254–55, 272
   in World War II, 8, 11–12, 307, 329, 340

SAAB Cape Cod, 29, 85, 150, 367, 407
Saalfield, Henry, *63–64*
Sagaponack, Long Island, 153, 259, 344,
   398
Sahl, Mort, 320, 321
St. John the Divine, 288
St. Martin's Press, 310
St. Mary's Church, 407
St. Peter's hospice, 375
Saint Vincent's Hospital, 272, 301
Sale, Faith, *373–74, 384*
Salinger, J. D., 200, 219, 222, 240, 286–87,
   311
Salisbury, Leah, 55, 56
Saturday Evening Post, xvii, 5, 51, 95,
   108–9, 172
Saturday Review, 45, 90, 136, 137, 381
Schenectady, N.Y., 5, 20, 23, 24, 337
Schenectady *Gazette,* 24, 25
Schiller, Friedrich, 264
schizophrenia, 170, 176, 350
Schmidt, Harvey, 161
Scholes, Robert, xxii, xxiii, 72–73, *133–34,*
   135, *142–43, 147–48*
schools, censorship in, xxi–xxii, 154,
   207–10, 279–80, 322–23, 365–66
Schrader, Paul, 343
science, 52, 309, 315, 316, 318
science fiction, xxii–xxiii, 45, 66, 67, 230,
   387–88
"Science Fiction" (Vonnegut), xxii–xxiii
Scribner's, *see* Charles Scribner's Sons
sculpture, 69
Sea Pines, 173, 177
Sebastian, Saint, 192
Segal, Erich, 334
Seldes, Tim, 238
Semmelweis, Ignaz Philipp, 203, 297, 299
Senate, U.S., 55
Serling, Rod, 93
Sermon on the Mount, xix
Seven Stories Press, 394

Sexton, Anne, *164*, 256
shaman, writer as, 135
Shaw, George Bernard, 351–52
Shaw, Irwin, 153, 272, 314
Shawn, Dick, 320, 321
Shawn, William, 311
Sheed, Wilfrid, 357
Sheldon, Sidney, 280
"Shell Scott," 81
Shelter Island, 56, 58, 265
Ship of Fools (Porter), 127
Shortridge Daily Echo, xii, xvii, 157
Shortridge High School, xii, xiv, xvi–xviii,
    3, 4, 6, 53, 149, 287, 302, 372, 378,
    396
  fiftieth reunion at, 338–39
  Mafia of, 156–57
short stories, 4, 28, 31, 41, 42, 43, 51, 52,
    74, 76, 95, 97, 253
  of Chekhov, 177
  in golden age of magazines, 5–6
  of Gorky, 62–63
  of Matthiessen, 327–28
  names of characters in, 334
  of Salinger, 286
Showtime, 343
silk-screen prints, 337, 356, 367, 369, 372,
    393, 394
Simmons, Ruth, 401
Simon, Dan, 394
Sinatra, Frank, 101, 122, 160, 300
Singer, Isaac Bashevis, *202–3*
Sirens of Titan, The (Vonnegut), 30, 64–65,
    80, 82, 147, 269
  dedication of, xi, 202
  movie option for, 293, 364
  paperback edition of, 28, 68, 79–80
  preface to, 135
Sissman, L. E., 298
Slapstick (movie), 278, 283, 289–90, 300
Slapstick (Vonnegut), xxiii–xxiv, 154–55,
    229
Slaughterhouse-Five (movie), 61, 125, 153,
    180, 187, 190, 289, 370, 372
Slaughterhouse-Five (Vonnegut), xix, 30,
    125, 130, 145, 160, 176, 226, 270,
    317, 329, 358, 372
  autobiographical opening of, 73
  as bestseller, 6, 75, 148–49
  censorship of, xxi, 154, 280, 366
  death of Billy Pilgrim in, 231–32
  dedication of, 146, 227, 338
  Dresden and, 74, 123, 135–36, 138, 380
  fame after, xxiii, 6, 66, 76
  Jailbird compared with, 155
  opera of, 369, 372

promotional tour for, 144, 148–49
reviews of, xxiv, 147–48
stage production of, 222, 225, 372
*Slaughterhouse-Five: Reforming the Novel
    and the World* (Klinkowitz), 338
"Sleeping Beauty" (Vonnegut), 271
Slotkin, Sydney, 38–39, 40, 248–49
Smith College, 393, 398–402
SmokeEnders, 285
smoking, 14–15, 76, 116, 146, 151, 254,
    255, 285–86, 329, 344, 393, 401
Socialist Labor Party, 79
"Sokolsky, George," 37, 38
Solzhenitsyn, Alexander, 200, 221
Somer, John, xxiii, 154, 188–89
Sophie's Choice (movie), 216, 269
Sophie's Choice (Styron), 216
Sosnowski, Anthony, 20
Sosnowski, Mrs., 20
Sourdough, Limited, 163
Southern, Terry, 367
South Vietnam, 122
Soviet Union, *see* Russia, Russians
space travel, 173, 174
Spengler, Oswald, 52
Spiegel, Aaron, *217–18*
"Spirit of Helsinki, The," 226
Sports Illustrated, 28–29
Sprague, Kitty, 136, 137, 146, 167, 402
Squibb, John, 177, 308
Squibb, Will, 396
Stafford, Jean, 238–39
Starbuck, George, 114, 117, 132, 185, 207,
    298, 332
Steadman, Ralph, 384
Steal This Book (Hoffman), 204
Steichen, Edward, 115
Steiger, Rod, 164
Stein, Gertrude, 85
Steinbeck, John, 5–6
Steinberg, Saul, 309
Stern, Bill, 83, 84
Steven Paul Productions, 290
Stewart, Ella Vonnegut, xi, 9–13
Stewart, Sam, 65
Stowe, Harriet Beecher, 239
Stratton, Monica Dickens, 151
Stratton, Mr., 151
Stravinsky, Igor, 379–80
Streep, Meryl, 216
Streetcar Named Desire, A (Williams), 328
Strong, George, *328–30*
Structuring the Void (Klinkowitz), 348, 349
Studio One (TV show), 61
Sturgeon, Marion, 387, 388
Sturgeon, Noel, *387–88*

Sturgeon, Theodore, 387–88
Sturgis, Bob, 194–95
Styron, Rose, 216, 217
Styron, William, 216–17, 273
suicide, 3–4, 191, 243, 244, 249
Sun Moon Star (Vonnegut), 270, 274–77
Supreme Court, U.S., 279, 280
Swarthmore College, 4, 5, 31, 223,
    241–42, 273
  Mark Vonnegut at, 96, 98, 105, 117,
    121, 126
swimming, 84, 103, 106, 107, 110, 114,
    116

Tarkington, Booth, 53, 54, 92
Tate, James, 298
Taylor, A. J. P., 89
Taylor, Geoff, 317–18
"Teaching the Unteachable" (Vonnegut),
    136
Teagarden, Jack, 94
teenagers, 230, 389, 391
television, 49, 55, 57–58, 177, 178, 335,
    343, 368, 405–6
  golden age of, 61, 268
  KV documentary for, 292–93, 299
  KV on, 149, 256, 395
  KV's rights and, 269
  KV's writing for, 156, 159, 172, 173,
    174
Tennessee, University of, 3, 17, 235, 240,
    298, 339, 387, 404
Terence, 252
Tet Offensive (1968), 75
textbooks, censorship and, 279, 280
"Thanasphere" (Vonnegut), 36
theater, 81, 91–92, 186, 255, 372
  in Cape Cod, 29, 41, 70, 100, 152, 159
  in New York City, 161, 164, 167, 267,
    304–5, 403
Theatre de Lys, 161, 164, 167
The Chantey (boat), 66–67
Themak, Edward, 25
This Sunday (Donoso), 130
Thoreau, Henry David, 39, 263
Thornton Wilder Prize, 301
Thurber, James, 406
Time, 154
Time Inc., 28–29, 56
Timequake (Vonnegut), xix, xxv–xxvi, 272,
    336–37, 348, 356, 371–72
  autobiographical section of, 273, 336
To Kill a Mockingbird (Lee), 128
To Kill a Mockingbird (movie), 128
Tolstoy, Leo, 186
Tom Sawyer (Twain), 53

Total Loss Farm (Mungo), xxi, 156
Tragic Vision, The (Krieger), 116, 134
Transformations (Sexton), 164
translation, 226
  Russian, 153, 197–98, 200–201, 216,
    219–22, 240, 242, 244–45, 254–55,
    272, 286, 301
"Travelin Man" (Matthiessen), 327
"Trout, Kilgore," 387–88
Twain, Mark, xxiv, 53, 295, 316, 318, 324,
    356
Twayne's Masterwork Studies, 338
typing, typists, 13, 66, 81, 105, 106, 114,
    151, 184

Ulysses (Joyce), 49, 62
Umbrellas of Cherbourg, The (movie), 107
Understanding Kurt Vonnegut (Allen), 342
Unitarians, 104, 134, 266, 271, 319–20,
    321, 379
Unitarian Universalist General Assembly,
    xxiv–xxv
United Nations, 191
United States v. One Book Called Ulysses,
    49
University High School, 112, 113, 117,
    120
"Untitled Poem" (Vonnegut), 82–83
Updike, John, 193, 273, 286–87, 310, 311,
    377, 395
Utopia 14 (Vonnegut), 28

Van Gogh, Vincent, 364
Vermont, xx–xxi, 280
Vestal, Allan, 107–8
Victorians, 309, 372
Vidal, Gore, 61
Vienna, 225, 226
Vietnam War, 55, 56, 75, 111, 122, 123,
    210, 288, 318, 359–60, 379
  conscientious objectors in, 140–41, 148
  My Lai Massacre and, 75, 181–82
Village Voice, 154, 222
Villon, François, 335
violence, 319, 323, 328–29, 333
  in American humor, 316, 318
Visit, The (Dürrenmatt), 96
VISTA (Volunteers in Service to America),
    145
vitamins, 170, 227–28
Vonnegut, Alex (KV's uncle), 9–13, 24–25,
    49, 167, 201, 257
  Alcoholics Anonymous and, 153
  book dedicated to, xi, 202
Vonnegut, Alice, see Adams, Alice
    Vonnegut

Vonnegut, Bernard (KV's brother), xiv, 3,
    21, 23, 198, *252–53,* 266, 299, 312,
    353, *360–61,* 374
  car story of, 390–91
  death of, 375
  at General Electric, 5, 24, 25
  SUNY Albany and, 235
  tornado theory of, 58
Vonnegut, Bernard (KV's grandfather), xiii–
    xiv, xv, 246, 260, 270, 272–73, 368,
    370, 373, 396, 407
  paintings of, 394, 407
Vonnegut, Christopher Robin "Kit,"
    19–22
Vonnegut, Clemens, xiii, 19, 245
Vonnegut, Edith (KV's daughter), 32, 43,
    54, 60, 67, 96, 100, 101, 109, 110,
    112–13, 143, 152, 166, 208, 211,
    227–28, 248, 265, 312, 323, 379,
    396–97
  artwork of, 137, 145, 165, 172–73, 227,
    228, 256, 267, 270, 282, 303, 308,
    394, 407
  divorce of, 368
  education of, 82, 391
  European travels of, 137
  father in Northampton and, 393, 398
  inheritance of, 214, 266
  Iowa City visit of, 110, 112–13, 114,
    117
  in Jamaica, 165, 193
  marriages of, 177, 178, 187, 308
  in New York, 169, 171, 172–73, 201
  writing of, 227, 228
Vonnegut, Edith Leiber (KV's mother), xv,
    3–4, 244, 368, 372
  suicide of, 3–4, 191, 243, 244
Vonnegut, Franklin, xiii, 245
Vonnegut, Helen, *19–22, 312*
Vonnegut, Irma, 201, 202
Vonnegut, Jane Marie Cox, xii, xx, xxvi,
    13–16, 20–22, 29–32, *51–52,* 60, 81,
    89, 93, 96–97, 99, *100–108,* 109–10,
    111–12, 114–15, 127, 142, *169,* 175,
    189, 191–92, 210–11, 221–22, 260
  Adams children and, 30, 96, 109, 195,
    272, 312
  death of, 272–73, 312, 313, 314, 317,
    336
  education of, 5, 221, 223, 241–42, 273
  European travels of, 134, 137, 150
  Great Books course and, 29, 48–49
  health problems of, 273, 290, 306
  Iowa City visits of, 105, 113, 114, 115,
    117, 120, 121, 122
  KV's finances and, 43, 61, 110, 179, 247

  KV's relationship with, 4, 103, 106, 121,
    152, 169, 170–71, 174, 175, 189, 191,
    201, 206, 215, 216, 247–48, 272–73,
    314
  KV's work and, 13, 61, 66
  Mark and, 143, 148, 170, 221, 290, 312
  marriages of, 5, 30, 174, 247, 272–73,
    302, 314
  photography of, 115
  pregnancies and childbirths of, 5, 54, *59*
  separation and divorce of, 152, 169,
    170–71, 174, 175, 189, 207, 214, 215,
    243, 247
  writing of, 30, 112, 221, 282, 312
  Yarmolinsky's relationship with, 205,
    206
Vonnegut, Jill Krementz, 203, 252, 253,
    254, 260, 264, 270, 291, 344, 347,
    384, 406
  ballet book of, 242
  finances of, 265–66
  forty-fifth birthday of, 305
  KV's relationship with, 153, 171, 197,
    214–15, 224, 247–48, 265, 282, 344,
    347, 351, 389, 391
  Long Island house and, 153, 259, 390
  marriage of, 153, 264–66, 273
  miscarriage of, 282
  as mother, 272, 292, 344, 389
  office of, 211, 213, 214
  as photographer, 153, 318, 364
  townhouse fire and, 397
Vonnegut, Kurt:
  agents of, *see* Farber, Donald C.; Littauer,
    Kenneth; Wilkinson, Max
  appearance of, xvi–xvii, 10, 71, 208, *255*
  artistic endeavors of, 94, 187, 191, 222,
    270, 278, 337, 353, 356, 365, 367,
    369, 372, 393, 394, 407
  book reviewing of, xx, 74, 81, 103, 156
  chess playing of, 48, 261–62, 357
  death of, 149, 183, 187, 214, 232, 383,
    395
  depression of, 190, 191, 272
  documentaries on, 289, 292–93, 299
  drinking of, xvi, 107, 152, 176, 223,
    255, 267, 272, 291, 354
  drug use of, 76, 272
  education of, xi, xii, xv–xviii, 3, 5, 6,
    16–17, 20, 23, 31, 32, 38, 55, 74, 114,
    116, 177, 185, 223, 241, 248–49, 258,
    276, 287, 339, 353–54, 385, 387, 411
  extended families of, 152–53, 299, 331,
    393
  fame of, xii, xvi, xviii, xxiii, 6, 66, 74,
    76, 152–54, 166, 202, 212, 246

Vonnegut, Kurt (*cont'd*):
family background of, xii–xiv, 3–4, 141, 166, 396
finances of, *see* Vonnegut, Kurt, finances of
as grandfather, 201, 264, 370–71, 395
health problems of, xviii, 3, 122, 272, 301, 338, 341, 352, 357, 389, 390, 391, 393, 395
homesickness and loneliness of, 103, 110, 203, 215
houses purchased by, 22–23, 59, 60–61, 153, 179, 184, 207, 210–11, 213, 214, 259, 384
humor of, xvi, xxv, 74, 108, 217, 316, 318
marriages of, *see* Vonnegut, Jane Marie Cox; Vonnegut, Jill Krementz
1950s jobs of, 28–29
1970s crises and changes in life of, 152–55
PEN and, 153, 221, 225–26, 271, 302, 303, 308, 320
playwriting of, 29, 41, 53–54, 59, 60, 62, 85–86, 88, 152–53, 159, 161–65, 308
poetry of, 82–83, 173, 386–87
political views of, xviii, 17–19, 37, 184, 202, 205–6, 369
popularity of, xvii, 154, 247
as POW, 4, 7–8, 10–12, 17, 32, 136, 140, 146, 298, 305, 307, 317–18, 340, 380, 383
public speaking of, xiv, xviii, xix, xxiv–xxv, 118, 142, 144, 147, 170, 174, 178, 207, 209, 265, 271, 274, 288, 295, 297, 313, 315, 316, 319, 334, 337, 338, 340, 342, 346–47, 351, 352, 359, 362, 370, 375, 376, 377, 395, 413
reading of, 5, 185, 192, 223, 241, 381, 400, 403
rejections received by, xi–xii, 5, 26, 40, 74, 248
reviews of work of, xxiii–xxiv, 66, 94, 97, 147–48, 154–55, 164, 272, 284–85
sexuality of, 121, 212, 215, 352
sixtieth birthday of, 288–89, 291–92
smoking of, 14–15, 76, 116, 146, 151, 255, 264, 285–86, 329, 344, 393, 401
teaching of, 29, 72–74, 83, 84, 88, 98–125, 128–29, 160, 165, 166, 177, 178, 180, 185, 203, 206–9, 213, 230, 335, 393, 398, 399–400
therapy of, 180, 195, 197, 302

TV writing of, 156, 159, 172, 173, 174
in World War II, xvii, 3–12, 16–17, 32, 42, 55, 74, 95, 136, 140, 146, 208, 223, 257, 258, 298, 305, 307, 317–18, 328–30, 340, 380, 383, 404, 409
writer's block of, 46, 47, 51, 122, 123, 174
writers supported by, xx, xxvi, 193, 197, 367–68, 378
writing start of, xii, 6, 25, 27, 31
writing style of, xxii, 6–7, 72, 74, 342
Vonnegut, Kurt, finances of, 5, 20, 27–30, 34, 43, 53, 63, 72–75, 80, 94, 96, 110, 139, 143, 183–84, 193, 194, 196, 211, 212, 215, 220, 247, 249–51, 268, 278, 391
advances and, 129, 401
Esquire anniversary issue and, 296–97
Great Depression and, xv, 3
houses and, 23, 61, 214
short stories and, 27, 36, 51, 52, 310
taxes and, 169, 179, 183
teaching and, 73, 74, 112, 123, 125
Vonnegut, Kurt, Sr. (KV's father), xiii–xiv, 6–9, 22–24, 27, 30, 32, 59, 148, 173, 201, 242, 256, 344, 353, 359, 376–77, 396, 411
as architect, xiv, xviii, 243, 246, 260, 270, 271, 333, 356, 377
death of, 379
Great Depression and, xv, xviii, 3, 243, 271
pottery of, 270, 271, 302, 356
writing of, 368, 370
Vonnegut, Lily (KV's daughter), 295, 301, 344, 351, 367, 379, 389–92, 397, 406
adoption of, 272, 292, 323
education of, 389, 391
Vonnegut, Mark (KV's son), 60, 67, 93–94, 105, 115, *143, 148,* 165, 166, 169, *180–81, 182–84,* 187, 208, 211, 214, 215, 221, 228, 261, 265, 323, 379
birth and childhood of, 5, 21–22, 30, 32, 43, 54, 67
Burger's sale of work of, 172
as conscientious objector, 140–41, 148
divorce of, 351
as doctor, 270, 290, 298–99
father's death and, 383, 395
father's relationship with, 180
inheritance of, 214, 266
memoirs of, xii, 29, 152, 170, 272
mother's funeral and, 312
painting of, 94, 145, 148, 270, 394, 407
on parental forms of address, 109–10

schizophrenia of, 170, 176
at Swarthmore, 96, 98, 105, 117, 121, 126
Vonnegut, Nanette "Nanny" (KV's daughter), 60, 67, 102, *109–11*, 152, 165, 166, *170–71, 172–73, 175–77, 187–88, 190, 194–96*, 208, 211, *213–16*, 221, *223–25, 247–48, 256, 258–59, 260–61, 264–66*, 308, 323, 379, *386, 389, 390–92*
artwork of, 190, 260, 270
birth of, *5, 59*
education of, 175, 176–77, 184
father's relationship with, 172, 175, 177, 180, 187–88, 195–96, 213–14, 216, 223–25, 266, 390–91, 393, 397
inheritance of, 214, 266
mother's funeral and, 312
wedding of, 290
writing of, 173
Vonnegut, Peter, 252
Vonnegut, Raye, 201, 202
Vonnegut, Richard, *326–27*
Vonnegut, Scott, 252
Vonnegut, Terry, 252, 299
Vonnegut, Walter, Sr., 91–92
Vonnegut, Walter A., Jr. "Colonel," *19–22, 92, 312*
Vonnegut, Zack, 299
Vonnegut (Offit, ed.), 286
Vonnegut Hardware Company, xii–xiii, xv, 245–46
Vonnegut Museum and Library, 395
Vonnegut Statement, The (Klinkowitz and Somer), xiii, 154, 243
Voznesenski, Andrej, 254

Wakefield, Dan, *148–49, 156–57*, 377
Wallach, Eli, 380
Wallant, Edward Lewis, 241
Walton, Linda, 293–94
Wampeters, Foma & Granfalloons (Vonnegut), xxii, xxiii, 76, 136, 141, 154, 184, 189, 218, 274
War and Peace (Tolstoy), 62
Warren, Robert Penn, 298
Warren Commission Report, 320
Watergate, 155, 199
Webber, Andrew Lloyd, 270–71
Weide, Linda, *379, 402–3*
Weide, Robert, *289–90, 292–93, 299–300, 320–21, 325, 334–35, 340*, 362, 379, *407–8*
KV's marital problems and, *344*
Mother Night (movie) and, 289, 337, 343, *349–50, 354–55*, 364, *402–3*

Welcome to the Monkey House (Vonnegut), 4, 26, 30, 35, 75, 84–85, 130, 135, 136, 138, 145, 343
attempted censorship of, 322–23
"Welcome to the Monkey House" (Vonnegut), 279
Welles, Orson, 53
West Barnstable, Mass., 29, 47–48, 388, 407
KV's house in, 59, 60–61, 152, 167, 177, 247
West-Central Writers' Conference, 136
Wheeler, Jack P., *288*
Whistle (Jones), 252
White, E. B., 210, 213, 384
White Collar (Mills), 44
Whitman, Walt, 358
"Who Am I This Time" (Vonnegut), 407
Why Regret? (Kinnell), 377
Wilbers, Steve, 73
Wilde, Oscar, 400
Wilkinson, Mary, 331
Wilkinson, Max, 26, 39, 44, 45, 56, 110, 111, 131, 138, 144, 159, 162, 229, *249–51*, 272, 313
death of, 331
KV's relationship with, 125, 155, 158, 159, 162, 227–28, 249–51, 268, 313, 351
see also Littauer and Wilkinson agency
Williams, Tennessee, 40, 328
Willingham, Calder, 147
Will the Soviet Union Survive Until 1984? (Amalrik), 225
Wilson, Angus, 273
Wilson, Edmund, 85
Wiseman, Frederick, 89
Wittgenstein's Mistress (Markson), 122, 357
Wolfe, Thomas, 59, 96, 97, 142, 255, 332
Women's Home Companion, 6
women's liberation, 13
women's magazines, 139
Woollen, Evans, Jr., 243
World War I, xiv, 97, 198
World War II, xiv–xv, xviii, 31, 70, 89, 150, 243, 271, 336, 350, 355, 358–60, 364, 379, 402
KV in, xvii, 3–12, 16–17, 32, 42, 55, 74, 95, 136, 140, 146, 208, 223, 244, 257, 258, 298, 305, 317–18, 328–30, 340, 380, 383, 404, 409
33rd anniversary of, 257–58
Wouk, Herman, 149, 150
WPA Theater Company, 267
writers' conferences, 136, 137

Writers for the 70s (Reed), 188
Writer's Union, Soviet, 225

Yale University, 277
Yarmolinsky, Adam, 205, 206, 273, 312
Yarmolinsky, Jane Cox Vonnegut, *see*
    Vonnegut, Jane Marie Cox
Yates, Richard "Dick," xxi, 73, 124, 128,
    129, 259, 335, 343, 401
"The Year of Vonnegut" (2007), 149
Yeats, William Butler, 85, 394
"Yes We Have No Nirvanas" (Vonnegut),
    75–76, 141

You Can't Go Home Again (Wolfe), 59
Young, Marguerite, 105, 106
Youngstein, Max, 322
"Youth" (Conrad), 177
youth culture, 72, 75–76,
    395–96
Yugoslavia, 225–27

Zalaznick, Sheldon, *332–33*
Zarris, Rev. George, 280
Zeckendorf, William, Sr., 80
Ziegler, Evarts, 124, 125, 162
Zinnemann, Fred, 161

About the Editor

DAN WAKEFIELD was a friend of Kurt Vonnegut's from the time they met in 1963 until the author's death in 2007. Wakefield is a novelist, journalist, and screenwriter, whose books include the bestselling novel *Going All the Way;* the novel was made as a film for which he wrote the screenplay. His other novels include *Starting Over,* which was also made as a movie, and *Under the Apple Tree.* His memoirs include *New York in the 50s,* which was the basis of a documentary film of the same name that was aired on the Sundance Channel, and *Returning: A Spiritual Journey.*

Wakefield is the recipient of a Nieman Fellowship in Journalism at Harvard University, a grant in writing from the Rockefeller Foundation, an award from the National Endowment for the Humanities, and a Woodrow Wilson Visiting Fellowship. He has taught at Emerson College in Boston, the University of Massachusetts in Boston, the Iowa Writers' Workshop, and won the Faculty Mentorship Award at Florida International University, where he was writer in residence from 1994 through 2010. He is presently on the faculty of the low-residency M.F.A. in writing program at Converse College in Spartanburg, S.C.

816 V947

Vonnegut, Kurt.
Kurt Vonnegut : letters
Central Nonfiction CIRC -
2nd & 3rd fls
11/12